IBN TULUN

IBN TULUN

His Lost City and Great Mosque

Tarek Swelim

With photographs by Matjaž Kačičnik
and
3D renderings, hand drawings, plans, and maps
by ARCHiNOS Architecture, Cairo

The American University in Cairo Press
Cairo New York

1 [PAGE II] – The windows of the *qibla* wall, diagonally centered through the arches of the *qibla riwaq*.
2 [PAGE vi] – The view from the top of the minaret.
3 [PAGE viii] – Shadows of the crenellations on the wall of the mosque.

First published in 2015 by
The American University in Cairo Press
113 Sharia Kasr el Aini, Cairo, Egypt
420 Fifth Avenue, New York, NY 10018
www.aucpress.com

Exclusive distribution outside Egypt and North America by I.B. Tauris & Co Ltd., 6 Salem Road, London, W4 2BU

Dar el Kutub No. 13773/14
ISBN 978 977 416 691 4

Dar el Kutub Cataloging-in-Publication Data

Swelim, Tarek
Ibn Tulun: His Lost City and Great Mosque / Tarek Swelim.—Cairo: The American University in Cairo Press, 2015.
p. cm.
ISBN 978 977 416 691 4
1. Ibn Tulun, Ahmed, 835–884
2. Mosques—History
726.2

1 2 3 4 5 19 18 17 16 15

Designed by Fatiha Bouzidi
Printed in China

To my beloved wife Hend

And my son Karim and daughter Farida

شرع أحمد بن طولون في بناء جامعه، وقال
أريد أن يبنى بناء إن احترقت مصر بقى وإن غرقت بقى

Ahmad Ibn Tulun started to build his mosque;
he said that he wished to build a structure that if Misr was burned down
it would survive, and if it were inundated it would survive.

Ibn Duqmaq,
Kitab al-intisar li-wasitat 'aqd al-amsar

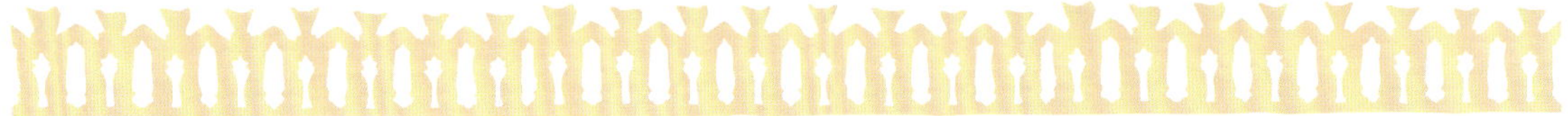

CONTENTS

Illustrations

Acknowledgments

This book was never going to see the light without the help and advice of many people. The idea of the book was first triggered by the late Professor Oleg Grabar, while I was his student at Harvard (1987–1994). Prof. Grabar was an iconic figure to whom I have always had great admiration.

The late Laila Ali Ibrahim had enlightening discussions with me about the mosque of Ibn Tulun, many years ago, and I am indebted to her. It was indeed my great honor that the late Professor George T. Scanlon had originally agreed to write this book's introduction or foreword, but regretfully he passed away suddenly before doing so. A couple of months before he died, he wrote the following appraisal: "I must spend this coming fractured week perusing your amazing tome on Ibn Tulun. . . [for] which I am to write its introduction. My ego is pleasantly chuffed but I'll say no more. . . . I do admit that holding it gave me no end of personal satisfaction." It is without doubt that Prof. Scanlon was a great inspiration and had a strong impact on me. His thoughts and passion for Islamic Cairo will always be cherished. This book is paying homage to him.

4 – Shadow of a lamp on the Samarra-style decorations on the piers.

The book was possible by my own personal funding. Generous support was also sponsored by Mrs. Helen Bing of California, Mr. Cameron Smith of New York, and Mrs. Aphrodite Jeanne Nader of Venezuela, to whom I am most grateful. Matjaž Kačičnik took the wonderful modern photography in this book. His artistic talents excelled to their highest degrees as we were working on this book.

Jaroslaw (Jarek) Dobrowolski and Agnieszka Dobrowolska, of ARCHiNOS Architecture, Cairo, and their professional team, Joanna Dyżewska, Fatma Farouq, and Karim al-Faramawi, were responsible for the most brilliant drawings and maps, as well as their enlightening discussions and studies. They managed to transform my ideas into reality by producing the 3D renderings of the mosque of Ibn Tulun and the area around it.

I would like to thank the American University in Cairo Press for their eagerness in publishing this book. Nigel Fletcher-Jones was very encouraging. Neil Hewison was indeed the driving force behind this project. Nadine El-Hadi dealt with my manuscript with great precision. I am grateful to the staff of the Rare Books and Special Collections Library of the American University in Cairo for providing me with copies of the Creswell Photo Collection used extensively in this study. For that I owe my thanks to Ola Seif, Daad Hasan, Heba Sheta and especially Yasmine Abdalla, who went beyond her line of duty to help me.

I was privileged to use photographs from the superb private collection of Dr. Maged Farag, for which I thank him. Likewise, Barry Iverson was generous in providing me with an old nineteenth-century photograph from his unique photographic archive.

The Royal Collection Trust gave me persmissions to publish two wonderful photographs taken by the English photographer Francis Bedford in 1863. Like-wise the Musée du Louvre provided me with the rights for a beautiful painting by the nineteenth-century French artist Antoine Gros.

Great credit goes to my research assistant Nadine Issa who followed up every step I took with precise detail while I wrote this book. The same goes to Stephen Kalin, who went through the tedious task of editing most of my initial manuscript. The rest of my manuscript was done with the help of Alexandra Machaal, who worked with a high degree of interest.

My long lasting friend Seif El-Rashidi did a superb drawing of the city of al-Qata'i' years ago, during the early stages of this book. I thank him as I admire his artistic creativity. My colleague Samah El-Badrawi added to the photography of this book and I am grateful to her. I would like to thank Hind Mostafa Nabil, with whom I have had the most enlightening discussions on the issues of restorations, conservations, and preservations. Adham Nadim always came up with sparkling ideas during the course of writing this book, which I appreciate. My dear friend Iman Abdulfattah gave me her healthy criticism on several parts of this book. The same applies to my friends Dina Bakhoum and May El-Ibrashi who always had constructive ideas; I enjoyed their discussions. Ahmad El-Bendari helped me obtain information which would have been hard for me to obtain otherwise, and I would like to thank him for that.

I would like to thank my colleague and friend Fetiche Posma-Zaalouk for her graceful longstanding patience. I received most interesting feedback from her while lecturing on and at the mosque of Ibn Tulun, during our tours which started in 1997. I also owe a great deal to my colleagues—Egyptologists and tour guides—for their constant moral support. Likewise to my students and tour members, as nothing can surpass the joy of seeing their eyes glitter with fascination at the architecture of the mosque of Ibn Tulun.

To my father, who has always given me much intellectual support. I was lucky to have received a solid foundation about the architecture of Ancient Egypt from him, and without which I would have not been able to appreciate the aesthetics of Cairo's Islamic architecture. I owe him much gratitude and respect.

Much appreciation goes to my beloved wife, Hend Nadim. Her background in understanding Islamic arts and her love helped support the process of this book. I will never forget when I thought that my initial manuscript was finished, she asked me a couple of questions, which took me another six months more to answer! My son Karim, had heard of the Ibn Tulun book since he was born, hence it became more of a folkloric family legend to him. My daughter Farida, always followed up the process of this book with admiration. That is why this book is dedicated to them.

INTRODUCTION

1

One may look at the title and think: What more can this book contribute to what has already been published so far on the subject of Ahmad Ibn Tulun, his lost city, and his great mosque? It may seem like an exhausted subject, but as this book will show, there is so much yet to be discussed and argued.

I would first like to acknowledge that the greatest comprehensive study made on the mosque of Ibn Tulun was by K.A.C. Creswell. In 1920 Creswell, having felt he had adequate knowledge of Syrian architecture, drew up a proposal on the "History of the Muslim Architecture of Egypt." This proposal was submitted to the ruler of Egypt at the time–King Fu'ad I–who was known for his keen interest in the subject. The king expressed his eagerness to sponsor Creswell's work and become his patron. For that reason, Creswell dedicates his Early Muslim Architecture to King Fu'ad I in 1932. Later Creswell's works on the Muslim Architecture of Egypt continued to be sponsored by King Fu'ad's son, King Faruq, in 1940.

5 – Aerial photograph of the mosque showing some of the houses still occupying the area behind the main *mihrab* and the *qibla* wall. Photograph taken before 1943.

Creswell writes that if he were to start his *Early Muslim Architecture* with the oldest intact Muslim monument in Egypt–the mosque of Ibn Tulun–he would have had to trace all its features, which have links to earlier Islamic monuments in Syria and Iraq, and as it were, to write the first part of his subject (the mosque of Ibn Tulun) in reverse. Therefore, Creswell found that in order to understand the architecture and decoration of the mosque of Ibn Tulun, he had first to write his *Early Muslim Architecture* in such a manner that the mosques of Amr Ibn al-'As and that of Ibn Tulun would fall naturally into their proper chronological places, and that the *raison d'etre* of all their outstanding features would therefore become clear."[1] In other words, the mosque of Ibn Tulun had had the greatest impact on Creswell's monumental works in the field of Islamic architecture.

This book examines the main sources written on the subject from contemporary times until the present day. It then deals with the life and career of Ahmad Ibn Tulun, his new capital city of al-Qata'i', which he founded, and his great mosque in Cairo. It offers descriptive analyses from bibliographical, urban topographical, art historical, and social points of view. In dealing with the mosque of Ibn Tulun, the focus is more on the mosque's architecture and history than on its decoration.[2]

The first part of the book provides context and history of the man Ahmad Ibn Tulun and his city, surveying in chapter 2 the major traditional and secondary non-traditional sources. These sources deal with the history of Ahmad Ibn Tulun and his dynasty, descriptions of al-Qata'i', and finally his great mosque. Starting with contemporary historians' accounts, it moves forward into modern sources, so as to illustrate that despite numerous studies and analyses of the subject, there still remain many issues that need to be addressed.

Chapter 3 provides a brief history of Ahmad Ibn Tulun, his origins and career, as well as the dynasty he founded, in order to give background on his unique character and to show how he managed his career through the turmoil within the Abbasid caliphate and empire. Chapter 4 deals with the city of al-Qata'i', which Ibn Tulun founded as the third Islamic capital of Egypt, after Fustat and al-'Askar. It describes the city and its wonderful buildings based on the accounts and descriptions provided by the major historians, Balawi, Ibn Duqmaq, and Maqrizi, as well as others. It is important to note that the last study on the city of al-Qata'i' was written more than a century ago—in 1902—by George Salmon. It is therefore appropriate to revisit al-Qata'i' and imagine how beautiful it must have looked. This chapter provides a full description of each building, analyzes it, and compares it to others. It allows one to imagine the city as it once appeared, through reconstructions in the form of imaginative drawings and 3D bird's-eye views. It also discusses the ceremonies that took place in the city, from the palace grounds to the mosque, and at the building of Dar al-Imara, and continues with the expansions, enlargements, and transformations that were made by Ibn Tulun's son, the Amir Khumarawiya, with his fascination and love of extreme luxuries. It ends by detailing Khumarawiya's weak successors and how the Abbasid armies destroyed the city.

The second part looks at the great mosque of Ibn Tulun and is divided into nine chapters, which treat the mosque in chronological order, giving historical background on the transition from one period to another. Chapter 5 provides a description of the mosque as it is today. Chapter 6 goes back to the beginning of the mosque's existence in the Tulunid period, describing it, its location, and the reason why it was built. It discusses the different stories related to each architectural element, such as the columns and arches, the *ziyada*s, the spiral-shaped minaret, and its unusual finial. It analyzes original features: the fountain *(fawwara)* of the mosque, as described by the historians of the time, providing a reconstruction of how it would have originally looked; the text and the original location of the foundation inscriptions; and the *dikka* and the long wooden inscriptions below the ceiling. It considers the interrelation between the windows and the arches of the mosque, as well as the aesthetics and light effects within the *qibla riwaq*. It also discusses the ceremonies in the mosque, explaining how the mosque would have been used, for example during Friday prayers, and looks at the area of the *maqsura* and its relation to the building of the Dar al-Imara, located behind the mosque. The atmosphere inside the mosque and an idea of what life was like is illustrated through a new ground plan for the mosque of Ibn Tulun, along with 3D renderings of views of the mosque from different virtual angles.

Chapter 7 deals with the mosque during the short Ikhshidid period and the Fatimid age that followed, when the Fatimids came to occupy Egypt in 969. It discusses why the mosque was used and restored during the early Fatimid period. Although nothing much changed in the mosque's layout, issues such as changes to the minaret and the reason why the *maqsura* of the mosque was enlarged are worthy of attention. It also touches on the political turmoil during the reign of Caliph al-Mustansir, the coming of Badr al-Gammali to Egypt, and how the mosque was eventually used and restored to become popular during the reign of Badr al-Gammali's successor and son, the vizier al-Afdal Shahinshah. Another new ground plan and 3D renderings for this time period visualize how the mosque would have been used during this period.

Chapter 8 will explain how the Fatimid dynasty came to an end and the circumstances that led Salah al-Din to come to power and found his new dynasty of the Ayyubids. It will explain the dramatic political changes in Egypt, as well as the transformations that had occurred to the mosque of Ibn Tulun. These changes are described and analyzed and are accompanied by ground plans of the mosque and 3D renderings.

Chapter 9 starts with a short historical introduction on the transformation from the Ayyubid to the great Mamluk period. It describes the period of turmoil during Sultan al-Nasir Muhammad and the coming of Sultan Lajin to the throne of Mamluk Egypt. It explains the architectural works of Sultan Lajin within the mosque of Ibn Tulun, namely on the *mihrab* and *minbar*, and also uses the *waqfiya* of Sultan Lajin (which was not consulted earlier by scholars) to explain the usage of the different parts of the mosque (the three rooms behind the main *mihrab*). Other elements, such as the *dikka*, flat *mihrab*s, the *maqsura* area, the dominant domical *fisqiya* building in the middle of the open court, and the spiral-shaped minaret, are addressed too. It looks also to the additions made in the period after Sultan Lajin until the end of the Mamluk period. Furthermore, this chapter finds that the institutions built adjacent to the mosque, such as the *madrasa* of Amir Sarghatmish, play an essential role in the mosque's history and architecture, and therefore, the architectural relationship between these buildings is discussed. New ground plans, along with new 3D renderings, are presented to visualize how the mosque operated and to be able to picture the life both inside and outside the mosque.

Chapter 10 deals with the mosque during the Ottoman period and discusses the architectural additions to the mosque from the time the Ottomans took over Egypt in 1517 until Napoleon Bonaparte's French Expedition in 1798. This chapter provides another ground plan of the mosque, as well as 3D renderings for that period. It shows the buildings that were added around the mosque of Ibn Tulun and how it was affected by changes in the area.

Chapter 11 studies the period of Muhammad 'Ali Pasha, the founder of modern Egypt who had a long-lived dynasty of a hundred and fifty years (1805–1952). This chapter deals with the transformations that took place in the mosque of Ibn Tulun during the reign of Muhammad 'Ali Pasha and discusses the walling up of the arcades by Clot Bey and how this act (or decision) was perceived by scholars at the time. It also discusses the period of neglect that the mosque went through and that transformed it into a poorhouse. In addition, this chapter starts another line of study, which involves trying to relate to the attitude of Egypt's rulers and numerous governments toward the country's ancient antiquities, including monuments, Islamic and Coptic buildings, and heritage in particular. As such, it discusses the status of the mosque of Ibn Tulun within Egypt's historical events and deals with the emergence of the organization of the Comité de Conservation des Monuments de l'Art Arabe, reviewing the effect it had on the Islamic monuments in general. Through the reports of the Comité, this chapter also describes the state of the mosque before the Comité started its long history of restoration and of their clearing away of the buildings that were encroaching on it. These wonderful reports enable us to trace the works that took place in the mosque of Ibn Tulun from the 1890s until 1961, and this chapter surveys the yearly works of the Comité to show the changes that the mosque went through in order to bring it back to its present state. This chapter also uses old nineteenth-century archival photographs belonging to Creswell, and discusses the works by the great scholars of Egypt during the reigns of the Khedives Sa'id, Tawfiq, 'Abbas Hilmi II, Sultan Husayn Kamel, as well as those of Kings Fu'ad I and Faruq. It ends with the exile of King Faruq in 1952.

Chapter 12 deals with the presidential period of Egypt from 1952 to the present day. It details the changes that occurred in the organization of the Comité, its different names, and the different authorities that came to be in charge of the monuments of Egypt during that period. It explains how the attitude of the rulers and governments tragically affected the mosque of Ibn Tulun, despite the different restoration attempts it had gone through. It specifically addresses the mosque after the earthquake of 1992 and the move toward the recent rescuing of the monuments of Egypt, as well as looking at the mosque's latest restoration project in 2004. Looking at the mosque and Islamic monuments in the period between 2011 and 2014, it ends with its current state, after troubled times and political upheaval, and also describes the experience that visitors encounter when visiting the mosque.

Chapter 13 discusses the legacy of the mosque of Ibn Tulun, giving examples of buildings that have a symbolic visual memory of the mosque. Such examples can be found in works of art and architecture.

Part One

Ahmad Ibn Tulun and His City

The Sources

2

This chapter deals with the sources related to Ahmad Ibn Tulun, his lost city of al-Qata'i', and his great mosque. It provides an annotated bibliography on the subject from contemporaneous times until the present.

Two publications give brief surveys of sources: by Zaki Muhammad Hasan in 1933, and by his wife Sayyida Isma'il al-Kashif in the 1960s.[1] The latter considers only the medieval sources, while the former tries to examine the modern sources as well. Although it is not clearly mentioned, both sources attempt to divide the medieval sources into three categories. Here, the sources are divided into two categories.

6 – Modern mosque lamps, the stepped transitional zone of the domed *fisqiya* and the remarkable crenellations, all framed by part of a pointed arch.

I. Major Traditional Sources

The two works of the geographer and traveler Ya'qubi (d. 278 AH / 891 AD), *Tarikh al-ya'qubi* and *Kitab al-buldan*, are important as they depict the first four years of Ahmad Ibn Tulun's reign.[2] *Kitab al-buldan* is a guidebook describing the city of Samarra. As Ibn Tulun is originally from Samarra; it is useful to relate some of the buildings in al-Qata'i' to those in Samarra—Ya'qubi's account of the spiral-shaped minaret is particularly helpful.

The works of Ibn al-Daya (d. 340 AH / 951 AD) and Ibn Sa'id al-Maghribi, or al-Andalusi, (610-675 / 1213-86) are among the early sources that should be considered.[3] Ibn al-Daya's work is a biography of Ibn Tulun entitled *Sirat Ahmad Ibn Tulun*—the original manuscript is lost but the text is available in a copy by Ibn Sa'id al-Maghribi. The second work of Ibn al-Daya is *Kitab al-mukafa'a*, which provides anecdotes about Tulunid society in general.[4] Such sources are valuable for this study.

A more complete text dealing with the life and works of Ibn Tulun, which is available to us today, is that of Balawi, known as *Sirat Ahmad Ibn Tulun*.[5] It was compiled during the middle of the tenth century (Ikhshidid period) and was discovered by Muhammad Kurd 'Ali in the

Dar al-Kutub al-Zahiriya in Damascus in 1935. Balawi's manuscript is important because it is one of the oldest historical works written in Egypt. It is more detailed than that of Ibn al-Daya, though the latter was the basic source for Balawi, just as it was for Ibn Sa'id al-Maghribi (or al-Andalusi). The only difference between them is that Ibn Sa'id gives credit to Ibn al-Daya, while Balawi does not. The latter is considered a vital source for the history of Egypt and the Abbasid caliphate. Balawi records the career of Ibn Tulun and describes the city of al-Qata'i', but he does not describe the mosque of Ibn Tulun in detail, but rather narrates certain anecdotes related to it.

The description by the famous geographer Muqaddasi (d. 375 AH / 985-86 AD), known as *Ahsan al-taqasim*, provides the earliest description of the mosque of Ibn Tulun, especially the spiral-shaped minaret.[6] It is important because it is first-hand information that does not rely on any of the earlier sources. Indeed, it is the oldest surviving description of the mosque's physical features and therefore another vital document for the mosque's early history.

In the same category lies the description of the Persian traveler Nasiri Khusraw, who visited Egypt in 439 AH / 1047-48 AD and expresses his admiration for the mosque of Ibn Tulun.[7] Another traveler's account was that given by the Andalusian traveler and poet Ibn Jubayr, who visited Egypt in 578 / 1183.[8] He describes the mosque of Ibn Tulun as being a retreat for Maghribi pilgrims en route to Mecca. It is an important account as it tells us about the change of the function of the mosque into a legally and officially inhabitable place.

Another valuable source is the endowment manuscript *(waqfiya)* of Mamluk Sultan Lajin, by which there are two editions in Dar al-Watha'iq al-Misriya.[9] Both are dated Rabi' II 21, 697 / February 5, 1298 and both are in poor condition. Their surviving parts appear to have been torn or burnt, which makes them difficult to understand. However, since Sultan Lajin was not the founder of the mosque of Ibn Tulun, no description of the mosque is provided. The document provides the salaries of the appointed employees in the mosque, and by comparison to other *waqfiyas* of the same period, one can understand how the building was used and how it appeared during the period of Sultan Lajin, when it was documented in 1298. Scholars of Islamic history, art, and architecture have never consulted this *waqfiya* before, and thus it is used here for the first time in any study on the mosque of Ibn Tulun.

From the Mamluk period there are two very important and authoritative sources from well-known topographers of both Egypt and Cairo: Ibn Duqmaq (d. 809 AH / 1406 AD) and Maqrizi (d. 846 / 1442).[10] Their topographic works are important because the sources on which they rely for their works have not survived. Ibn Duqmaq quotes al-'Atimi and al-Quda'i (d. 454 / 1062), but most of his accounts follow al-Yaghmuri and Shar'i insofar as the different features of the mosque of Ibn Tulun are concerned. Ibn Duqmaq also mentions the account by Ya'qubi without giving him credit. As for Maqrizi's *Khitat*, it quotes such authorities as Ibn 'Abd al-Zahir (d. 258 / 871).[11] Moreover, Maqrizi quotes at length a source entitled *Jami' al-sira al-tuluniya* (the compiler of the biography of the Tulunids), by which he actually means the historian Balawi. Maqrizi also includes long quotations from al-Quda'i whereas Ibn Duqmaq only quotes him briefly. In addition Maqrizi quotes the historian al-Musabbahi (d. 420 / 1029). He gives a lengthy account of the restorations of Sultan Lajin to the mosque of Ibn Tulun, and he records new additions to the mosque that he must have seen. Therefore, Maqrizi was much more comprehensive than Ibn Duqmaq.

Separate chapters were dedicated to the city of al-Qata'i' and the Tulunid state, by both Ibn Duqmaq and Maqrizi. The latter gives a lengthier account than does Ibn Duqmaq. Moreover, Maqrizi chooses to include lengthy pieces of poetry which describe the social atmosphere of the city of al-Qata'i'. In doing so, he offers some hints about the architecture of the great palace of Ibn Tulun at the *maydan*.

Those great topographers and historians, Ibn Duqmaq and Maqrizi, certainly complement each other. Their invaluable records must be treated separately because the information they provide often offers different perspectives upon the same subject.

One must add to the above topographers the guidebook to the holy shrines of Cairo, by al-Sakhawi, known as *Tuhfat al-ahbab*.[12] Although his account of the mosque of Ibn Tulun is short, it is nevertheless

7 – The spectacular view from the top of the minaret of Ibn Tulun, showing the vast space of its open court. On the left is the Great Mosque of Muhammad 'Ali Pasha, built in 1848, the Muqattam Hills. The *mashhad* of al-Guyushi of the vizier Badr al-Gammali can barely be seen.

important for the location of the tomb of Ahmad Ibn Tulun, which is not mentioned in Ibn Duqmaq or Maqrizi.

There is another group of historians of the Mamluk period whose works can be grouped together because they focus on literature, the religious and social life of their period, and the provisions of biographies of the high officials of their day. These include the works of al-Nawawi (thirteenth century), al-Nuwayri (d. 733 AH / 1332 AD), Ibn Khaldun (d. 809 / 1406), al-Qalqashandi (d. 821 / 1418), al-'Ayni (d. 855 / 1451), Ibn Taghribirdi (d. 874 / 1469), Ibn Hajar al-'Asqalani (fifteenth century), and al-Suyuti (sixteenth century).[13] Most of these sources give a general history of Ibn Tulun and his successors and only mention the mosque briefly. Many of them are copies of each other. However, none of them are as accurate and precise as Ibn Duqmaq and Maqrizi. One must also bear in mind that they were compiled hundreds of years after the period of Ibn Tulun, therefore their anecdotes are frequently misleading.

During the Ottoman period, there are a few sources that can be grouped into one category. The most famous are by Evliya Çelebi, known as the *Siyahatnameh,* and Mustafa 'Ali, who wrote the *Description of Cairo of 1599*,[14] although both are thin on the subject of the mosque. In addition, the history of 'Abd al-Rahman al-Jabarti known as *'Aja'ib al-athar* is valuable as it tells of an earthquake that hit Egypt at the beginning of the nineteenth century.[15] However, it provides little information on the mosque of Ibn Tulun.

II. Secondary Non-Traditional Sources

We may consider non-traditional research to begin with the expedition of Napoleon Bonaparte to Egypt in 1213 AH / 1798 AD, which resulted in the monumental volumes known as the *Description de l'Égypte*. Research works for thirty-seven fascinating volumes were compiled in a period of less than three years, and these volumes started a new era for Egypt. The *Description* was what sparked European interest in Egypt: it encouraged Europeans to come to Egypt and explore its ancient monuments. This European fascination with Egypt was amplified under Muhammad 'Ali Pasha, the ruler of Egypt in the first half of the nineteenth century, and his reign witnessed a great influx of scholars and technicians of different fields of research who came to Egypt to document its resources and history. For example, Taco Roordaa compiled and published a biography of Ahmad Ibn Tulun in 1825, and translated the works of al-Nuwayri, Maqrizi, and al-Suyuti from Arabic into Latin.[16] It was the first attempt of its kind, but the work dealt only with the history of Ibn Tulun and did not discuss the mosque in any depth.

The monumental volumes of the *Description de l'Égypte* include studies by French scholars known as the savants—some of the 160 scientists who accompanied Napoleon's army. These were indeed the great minds of France and Europe of the eighteenth century. They were the first scholars to study the mosque of Ibn Tulun since it stopped functioning as a place for worship several decades earlier. The most extensive research was carried out by Jean Joseph Marcel, whose contribution comprised a series of engravings detailing the bands of wooden inscriptions below the ceiling of the mosque of Ibn Tulun and the two foundation inscription blocks which are completely and partially lost.[17] (Marcel was the first to record them in detail.)[18] Finally, Marcel wrote a chapter that deals with Ibn Tulun's history but, for some unknown reason, he does not describe the mosque.

The *Description* includes another study by the French topographer Edme François Jomard, whose work was more focused on describing the Citadel and the city of Cairo, which is also relevant to the mosque of Ibn Tulun.[19] Another important contribution was that of the French architect Jean Constant Protain, who contributed three engravings to *Description de l'Égypte*.[20] He presented the first ground plan of the mosque of Ibn Tulun, which showed the state of the mosque during his study. Unfortunately, Protain's work is not accompanied by a descriptive text, which would have explained many parts of the mosque that existed during his time and are not found today.

The negative aspect of the *Description* is that each chapter is dealt with separately and is not connected to the others. The chapters do not cover a single subject and the volumes of both editions are sometimes misleading. For example, in the first editions it notes that the wooden inscriptions will be discussed in the second edition, when in fact they are not. The engravings of Marcel are not described and are not referred to in his three chapters on the inscriptions. Similarly, the study of Protain is certainly of limited value, as one feels that it is unfinished because his three engravings are not discussed or his plans described.

The illustrations of the early nineteenth century French artist Pascal Coste are important and impressive, as they are based on those in the *Description de l'Égypte* but with more accuracy. Coste offers a new plan, elevations and details of the mosque of Ibn Tulun. He also adds wonderful illustrations of particular views inside the mosque. During the same period, the British artist Robert Hay adds a most important illustration, which is also based on those of Jomard in the *Description*. Equally important works are those of the French artist and historian Émile Prisse d'Avennes who helps us to comprehend the transformations that the mosque underwent during the later part of the nineteenth century.[21]

The encyclopedic studies of 'Ali Basha Mubarak, known as *Khitat al-tawfiqiya*, are the most famous Arabic source of the nineteenth century for the history of Egypt and Cairo.[22] Because of his prestigious position in the country as minister of public works and education, during the reigns of the khedives Isma'il and Tawfiq, he had all the important documents at his disposal, and most likely a well-trained staff too, and so managed to compile his monumental twenty-volume publication. Mubarak followed the same method of Ibn Duqmaq and Maqrizi by quoting all histories and accounts written before his time. It was also his practice to compile all literary and written material available on any of the buildings he discussed. However, it is strange to find that he chose to quote only a few extracts from Maqrizi concerning the mosque of Ibn Tulun. He always included the *waqfiyas* of the buildings he was discussing, but he failed to do so with the *waqfiya* of Sultan Lajin, as though he deliberately neglected the mosque of Ibn Tulun. This may have been because the mosque was in such a bad state of dilapidation at the time that he did not think to give it much attention.

No study on Islamic Cairo can neglect the works of the great pioneers in the field of Islamic art and architecture of Cairo: Edward Lane's *Cairo Fifty Years Ago*; and his nephew Stanley Lane-Poole's *The Art of the Saracens in Egypt* and *Cairo: Sketches of Its History, Monuments, and Social Life*; *History of Egypt in the Middle Ages*, as well as *The Story of Cairo*, published in the late nineteenth and early twentieth centuries.[23] They provide short histories of Ibn Tulun and descriptions of the mosque, though without analyses.

A more detailed study by Eustace Corbet, *The Life and Works of Ahmad Ibn Tulun* (1891), is the earliest major modern effort to analyze the mosque of Ibn Tulun.[24] It is a vital source as it introduces a new method of research for the study of any Islamic building, setting the pattern for analysis that was later followed by architectural historians. In 1918 Robert Williams studied the mosque, and although his work is less important than that of Corbet's, he described parts of the mosque that existed in his time and were later demolished.[25] Later publications by scholars such as Zaki Muhammad Hasan's *Les Tulunides* (1933) complement that of Corbet.[26] In fact, Hasan's study is orderly and written in a systematic way and may be considered the basic secondary source on the period of Ibn Tulun, until the late 1920s and early 1930s.

Other works such as Gaston Myogen's 1909 guidebook *Le Caire, le Nile et Memphis* provide excellent photographs of the building before its restoration.[27] The work of Yusuf Effendi Ahmad *Jami' Ahmad Ibn Tulun* (1917) is a useful document on the mosque as it provides a new ground plan before it was restored.[28] In addition, Mahmud 'Akkush's *Tarikh wa wasf al-jami' al-tuluni* in 1927 offers a good study in which he includes a record of the restoration works of the Comité de Conservation des Monuments de l'Art Arabe, starting at the end of the nineteenth century until the reign of King Fu'ad.[29]

Among the descriptive and documentary studies are the indispensable popular studies by Hasan 'Abd al-Wahhab, *Tarikh al-masajid al-athariya* (1940), as well as that of Hautecœur and Wiet, known as the *Les Mosquées du Caire* (1932).[30] The latter is most ingenious as it analyzes the proportions of the arches, which enables one to develop ideas that had not been previously approached.

Other important documents are those produced by the Ministry of Religious Endowments (Awqaf), as well as the excellent reports of the Comité de Conservation des Monuments de l'Art Arabe, which are governmental records of the restorations that took place in the mosque of Ibn Tulun from 1890 until 1956.[31] Through these documents, one may trace and understand the development of the process of restoration, although they do not offer art historical analyses of the mosque itself.

The following publications are useful because they describe and analyze the mosque in a more formal manner: Mahmud Ahmad's "al-Jami' al-Tulun" in *al-Handasa* XII; Hasan al-Basha's *al-Qahira: tarikhuha, fununuha, wa atharuha*; Ahmad Fikri's *Masajid al-Qahira wa madarisuha*; and Farid Shafi'i's article on the minaret of Ibn Tulun in *Majallat kulliyat al-adab* IV.[32]

Other studies have focused on inscriptions of the mosque of Ibn Tulun. The most important are those of Max Van Berchem's *Materiaux Pour Une Corpus Inscriptionum Arabicarum*, and Gaston Wiet's *Mémoires Publiés*, which are excellent corpora of the inscriptions in the mosque: they are documented, transcribed, translated, and sometimes transliterated.[33] They focus on several important aspects of the inscriptions of the mosque and discuss interesting points about events that are related

8 – The mosque of Ibn Tulun from the minaret of the *madrasa* of Amir Sarghatmish.

to the building and the circumstances that lie behind these events. However, the studies do not give importance to the wooden inscriptions; it is not given the attention it deserves, and therefore the works of Van Berchem and Wiet may be considered incomplete. Nevertheless, the study by Jean David-Weill, *Les bois à épigraphes jusqu'à l'époque Mamlouke*, on the wooden inscriptions can be regarded as a useful supplement to the works of Van Berchem and Wiet.[34] Moreover, Ibrahim Jum'a's study, *Dirasa fi tatawwur al-kitabat al-kufiya 'ala al-ahjar fi Misr fi-l-qurun al-khamsa al-ulla li-l-hijra*, deals with the inscriptions in the mosque from a paleographic and epigraphic point of view.[35] It makes interesting comparisons of the letters of the inscriptions with those drawn by Marcel in the *Description de l'Égypte*, but it is more technical than it is art historical. Finally, when dealing with inscriptions one must include the works of Samuel Flury, such as "Le Décor Epigraphique des Monuments Fatimides du Caire," "Samarra und die Ornamentik der Moschee des Ibn Tulun," and *Die Ornamente der Hakim-und Azhar-Moschee*, although his studies concentrate more on ornament and decoration than on the inscriptions themselves.[36]

There are also several studies that deal with the urban topography of the area in which the mosque of Ibn Tulun is located. The first was by George Salmon in 1902.[37] Apart from the historical context that he presents, his map is most interesting as it shows the area of the mosque and its urban and topographical development from the tenth to the eighteenth centuries. However, Salmon does not consider the relationship between the mosque and the palace, nor between the mosque and the rest of the city of al-Qata'i' and later that of Cairo. Moreover, Salmon's study was undertaken at the turn of the twentieth century, which means that is very much outdated.

Others within the same category are Marcel Clerget, whose texts look at the geography of Cairo.[38] James Aldridge's *Cairo* is also important as it gives a detailed history of Ahmad Ibn Tulun and al-Qata'i' based on the account by Maqrizi.[39] For the period of Khumarawiya and his extreme, luxurious life, this book is based on Aldridge's interpretation (or translation) of Maqrizi. Many other studies—'Abd al-Rahman Zaki, the article by Becker in the old edition in the *Encyclopedia of Islam*, the writings of John Michael Rogers, and Zaki Hasan in the second edition of the *Encyclopedia of Islam*—focus more generally on the Islamic city after the Ibn Tulun period.[40] As for the markets, layout of the streets, and population of Cairo, the studies of André Raymond are of utmost importance but do not deal with the period of Ibn Tulun.[41]

There is another category of sources that may be considered ancillary and contextual and that I will group by subject matter rather than by author. In archaeology, Hasan al-Hawwari examines a Tulunid period house, while Laila Ali Ibrahim considers a Tulunid period Hammam.[42] In numismatics, the early work of Oleg Grabar, *The Coinage of the Tulunids*, is useful as he provides an interpretation of Ahmad Ibn Tulun's political and religious activities through the study of the

Tulunid coinage of his time.[43] Moreover, Grabar's study is particularly important in his treatment of the foundation inscription(s) of the mosque. He discusses the official titles of Ahmad Ibn Tulun that are provided in texts and links them with Ibn Tulun's relation with the Abbasid caliph. In doing so, Grabar follows, develops, and contributes to the method initiated by Max Van Berchem and Gaston Wiet. Furthermore, Grabar compares the Tulunid coinage to the Tahirid and Aghlabid coins and examines its relationship to Abbasid coinage.

In folklore, the studies of McPherson, *The Moulids of Egypt*, and Gayer-Anderson Pasha, *Legends of the Bait al-Kiritliya*, are important as they deal with the popular folk legends that were related to the mosque of Ibn Tulun and its environs, which help us understand the different parts of the building.[44]

On the study of the spiral-shaped minaret, Doris Behrens-Abouseif's *Minarets of Cairo* and Jonathan Bloom's *Minaret: Symbol of Islam* are useful for their interpretations on the minaret of Ibn Tulun.[45] Moreover, an article by the present author "The Minaret of Ibn Tulun: Reconsidered" in *Cairo Heritage* provides a new interpretation of the minaret and suggests a new date for it.[46] Articles by Farid Shafi'i and Ghazi Muhammad on the minaret are extremely useful too.[47]

There are also guidebooks on the city of Cairo, such as Caroline Williams's *Islamic Monuments in Cairo*, which is by far the most popular guide to Islamic Cairo.[48] Older guidebooks such as Devonshire's *Rambles in Cairo,* and Dorothea Russel's *Medieval Cairo* provide short descriptions of the mosque and note elements that no longer exist.[49] Russel also romanticizes visiting the mosque at night.

Another group of beautifully illustrated publications on Islamic art and architecture mention the mosque of Ibn Tulun. Some of them give interesting descriptive commentaries on its architecture. In that category is the *Art and Architecture of Islam 650-1250* by Ettinghausen and Grabar, which notes that "[the mosque of] Ibn Tulun is perhaps the most perfectly harmonious of the ninth century Abbasid mosques."[50]

Robert Hillenbrand's *Islamic Architecture* is interesting as it discusses the size of the mosque of Ibn Tulun in relation to that of the Great Mosque of Samarra. He discusses the development of the ceilings and ways of supporting them in the early Islamic period, in particular. One would have expected more detail on the mosque of Ibn Tulun, and it is far from a comprehensive study. The reason is probably due to the massive range of monuments from all over the Islamic world that he covers in his publication and for which he should be highly credited.[51]

An invaluable source for the Islamic monuments of Cairo is that of Istvan Ormos' *Max Herz Pasha*.[52] This is indeed a wonderful compilation of the life, career, and works of this great Austro-Hungarian architect, who had such a tremendous impact on the Islamic architecture of Egypt in restoring and saving those monuments. This publication is an excellent reference to works made by the Comité from the point of view of Herz Pasha, while he was still in charge of its technical department.

9 – The conventional view from the spacious open court of the mosque of Ibn Tulun, showing the domed *fisqiya*, the spiral-shaped minaret, the arcades with their beautiful pointed arches, and the minaret and dome of the Madrasa of Amir Sarghatmish behind.

Among the most valuable sources come from K.A.C. Creswell. The K.A.C. Creswell Photo Archives, which is used extensively throughout this book,[53] is a wonderful collection of photographs taken during Creswell's work with the Comité, as well as many others taken by well-known nineteenth-century photographers, such as Pascal Sebah, Antonio Beato, and Henry Bechard. He also has photos of the Royal Egyptian Air Force and photographs taken by the Armenian photographer Lekegian. These certainly add a new dimension to our understanding of the development and evolution of the mosque's history before and after its restorations.

The most exhaustive and extensive studies on the mosque of Ibn Tulun are K.A.C. Creswell's famous and iconic works *Early Muslim Architecture* (1932–40) and *Muslim Architecture of Egypt* (1952–59).[54] These monumental studies are the culmination of all previous research works, as well as the product of all the sources cited above. Creswell's chapter on the mosque of Ibn Tulun is the most comprehensive and detailed study of the history, architecture, and decoration of the building. It provides an updated ground plan of the mosque, describes the new elevation and section of the building, includes drawings of various architectural details, and has the most precise and accurate measurements of almost every feature. Creswell describes every architectural element in the building in minute detail and also divides the building into different units, discussing each of them separately—to do so he depends heavily on the major traditional medieval sources. One of his main concerns is dating each part of the building.

Moreover, Creswell offers a wonderful comprehensive bibliography at the end of his chapter on the mosque of Ibn Tulun, which is listed in chronological order. (It does not include the text of Balawi, even though it was discovered in 1935.)[55] The bibliography lists ninety titles written by scholars and travelers in the nineteenth century and covers all fields of study related to the mosque of Ibn Tulun, including works of history, architecture, decoration, artistic illustrations, architectural surveys, early nineteenth-century photography, travelogues, collective studies, general and specific studies, urban topographic surveys, Samarran art and architecture, and guidebooks.

No doubt Creswell's study has been the primary source on the mosque of Ibn Tulun over the last seventy years or more. Yet, there are a few issues in Creswell's work that are generally overlooked. One finds that the various historical events that took place in the mosque, which had had an effect on transforming the functions of the building from one period to another, are not discussed. Moreover, he does not examine the reasons and forces behind the evolution of the mosque and its changes from one period to another. Creswell is always immersed, to an extreme degree, in minute detail without keeping an eye on the bigger-picture aspects of the mosque. The mosque of Ibn Tulun is analyzed in a formal manner, which was the norm of his methodology as well as the scholarly approach of his era. The mosque is not considered as an organic unit but rather as a series of elements, which he does not relate to one another. Creswell does not try to understand why the architectural elements in the mosque were continuously being added to or restored, nor does he envision the activities and ceremonies which took place in the mosque in each period. Moreover, he does not provide an explanation of the movement inside the building, the interior accessibility within the unified spaces of the mosque, which changed from one period to another. He does not explain who would sit where or how the different parts of the mosque were used. In other words, Creswell focuses on recording the building with utmost accuracy, but does not try to think beyond the architecture. To conclude, one may say with confidence that Creswell's studies on the mosque of Ibn Tulun are not conclusive and may not be considered to have the final word on the subject.

One may add other general works, which provide short entries of the mosque of Ibn Tulun and are useful references for other buildings within the Islamic world. These works include: Doris Behrens-Abouseif's *Islamic Architecture in Cairo: An Introduction*; *The Architecture of the Islamic World*, edited by George Michell; John Hoag's *Islamic Architecture*; Robert Hillenbrand's "Egypt," in D. Hill and L. Golvin's *The Islamic Architecture of North Africa*; and Markus Hattstein and Peter Delius's *Art and Architecture of Islam*.[56] Later publications by Richard Yeomans on the story of Islamic architecture and Islamic Cairo are mostly very general where dealing with the mosque of Ibn Tulun. However, they are beautifully illustrated and provide good photography, plans, and maps.[57] In addition, Nicolas Warner's *Monuments of Historic Cairo*, is wonderful for its up-to-date maps and plans of the city and its monuments and is indeed an invaluable source to be used.[58] Finally, it might seem surprising, but the small children's book by Fiona MacDonald and Joan Ullathome, *Ibn Tulun: The Story of a Mosque,* includes hand drawings that were most inspiring as it gave the author ideas for producing the 3D renderings in this book.[59]

From this bibliographic survey, it is clear that despite the numerous publications on the great mosque of Ibn Tulun, there are still gaps in our understanding–gaps this book seeks to fill.

Ahmad Ibn Tulun and His Successors

3

The Life of Ahmad Ibn Tulun

The tenth-century historian Balawi states that Ahmad Ibn Tulun was a Turk who was born in the month of Ramadan 220 / September 835. His mother, whose name was Qasim, was one of the slaves of his father, Tulun.[1] In the year 200 AH / 815 AD, his father Tulun, who was a Turk from Tagharghar, was taken to the Caliph al-Ma'mun by a Bukhari/Khurasani worker (*'amil*) named Nuh Ibn Asad.[2] Tulun died in 240 / 854, when Ahmad was twenty years old.[3] His mother married Yalbukha, who was close to her husband (Tulun), and he treated Ahmad Ibn Tulun as his own son.[4]

10 – The southwestern arcade *(riwaq)* showing the thick robust piers supporting the elegant pointed arches that support the high wooden ceiling of the mosque.

The Abbasid empire during the reign of Caliph al-Ma'mun (r. 813–d. 833) was vast. It extended from the Indus Valley on the east to the shores of the Atlantic Ocean, including Andalusia, in the west. It was the largest empire in the world as it was the most extensive since the time of Alexander the Great (fourth century BC). The Abbasid empire was so vast that it became hard to control from its capital city of Baghdad. The continuous intrigues, plots, and conspiracies between the different factions in the court of Baghdad and the palace city of Samarra made it even more difficult for the Abbasid caliph. Al-Ma'mun found that the only way to consolidate his power was to start a system of appanage throughout the empire. Through implementing this system, Balawi and Maqrizi tell us that the caliph was more inclined toward the Turks than the Arabs and Persians.[5]

In Egypt, the political and economic situation was unstable. The governors (*walis*) who were appointed by the Abbasid caliph did not stay long in office, and because of this many of them wanted to accumulate as much wealth as possible during their tenure in Egypt. They did so by imposing high taxes on peasants and merchants. This greatly affected the financial situation in the country, and inevitably led to the deterioration of Egypt's economy to the point of it being on the verge of collapse. Moreover, there was a dangerous threat from the Byzantines, who were taking advantage of the weakening situation in Egypt, and were ready to attack Egyptian shores at any time, although they never did.[6]

Meanwhile, it appears that the Caliph al-Ma'mun took good care of the little Turkish boy Ahmad Ibn Tulun and provided him with a good life in the palace city of Samarra (129 kilometers north of Baghdad). Balawi adds that Ibn Tulun was well brought up, unlike the Persian regiments of his time. He was known to have had high vigor and to have been very well read in literature.[7]

During his early life in Samarra, Ahmad Ibn Tulun was probably fascinated by the glorious life of the city. He would have lived in one of the palaces intended for the Turks of his class and he would have frequently gone to attend the Friday prayer at the Great Mosque of Samarra, which was founded by the Caliph al-Mutawakkil (started in 848, completed in 851). The mosque was huge, built with firebrick, and had walls which were consolidated and decorated by buttresses on its exterior walls. Its floor plan shows that it was a square within a large rectangle. It had a large open court surrounded by porticos on four sides. The latter were formed of thick rectangular piers and adorned by columns at each of their corners, which must have supported pointed arches. The mosque had a unique spiral-shaped minaret, which had always been the landmark symbolizing the city of Samarra.

Ibn Tulun would also have attended Friday prayers at the mosque of Abu Dulaf, also in Samarra, which was built later (859–61). The mosque of Abu Dulaf had the same arrangement in the layout of its plan and porticos. However, it had a section at the back side of the *qibla* wall where the caliph would go to rest or pray separately, or prepare for prayer. It too had a similar style minaret to that of the Great Mosque of al-Mutawakkil. Ahmad Ibn Tulun would have loved his life in the city of Samarra, as it was adorned with palaces, horse racing courses, and grand public buildings, and he would have admired the dynamic social and cultural life of the city. He was trained and disciplined by the military, participated in all kinds of sports activities such as horseback racing, polo games, shooting with bow and arrow, and engaged in other types of entertainment. Moreover, he must have enjoyed the ambiance of luxury that Samarra was known for, with its splendid architecture and the spectacular aspects of its royal and princely lifestyle.

Likewise, Ibn Tulun would have learned a great deal about politics while living in the Samarra palaces—being backstage to political affairs, intrigues, and controversies. Spending so much time in the palaces, Ibn Tulun would have known about both Caliph al-Ma'mun's ways of thinking, and of those who succeeded him, and so gained experience in politics. He would have been well-informed of the political agenda the caliph was following and known who had the most influence on the caliph.

Caliph al-Ma'mun died in 833 and he was succeeded by the caliphs al-Mu'tasim (833-842), al-Wathiq (842-847), al-Mutawakkil (847-861), al-Muntasir (861-862), al-Musta'in (862-866), and al-Mu'taz (866-869). Ibn Tulun lived through their reigns and witnessed all kinds of political maneuvers made by each of them. He would have learned and understood what the political inclinations within the palace were. In other words, he lived inside what one could imagine to be a political 'kitchen,' at the center of the administration of the great Abbasid empire. Living in Samarra probably had a great impact on Ibn Tulun's life and career. He must have wished to have his own 'Samarra-like' city someday.

Aside from his wonderfully intellectual and cultured life in Samarra, Ibn Tulun often went to the city of Tarsus (in south central Turkey) to learn the science of *hadith* (lectures and advice of the Prophet Muhammad). He would meet with the city's religious scholars and discuss various religious issues with them; from these experiences he managed to publish his *Kitab al-'ilm* (Book of Knowledge). He became popular and distinguished among the Turks—someone who they eventually entrusted with money and secrets.[8]

During his time in Tarsus, he approached a man called Yarjukh, who was a popular figure among the Turkish community there, and offered to marry his daughter, Majur, who later bore him his son 'Abbas and daughter Fatima.[9] On one occasion, while a caravan was on its way back from the Byzantine lands *(bilad al-Rum)*, he heard that it was in danger of an attack by Arab invaders or Bedouin *(I'rab)* and led an expedition to save those in the caravan. He then accompanied the caravan back to the caliph's quarters in Iraq, with their loads of treasures and mules, which pleased the caliph. The caliph rewarded Ibn Tulun with one thousand dinars and offered him a slave by the name of Miyas to marry. She later gave birth to his famous son and successor Abu al-Gaysh Khumarawiya in mid-Muharram 250 / Saturday, February 26, 864.[10]

Balawi also informs us that the Caliph al-Musta'in took Ibn Tulun into his favor, although he was deposed in 866.[11] His brother was to be recognized as the new Caliph al-Mu'taz, and it was decided that al-Musta'in would be exiled to the city of al-Wasit on the Tigris in Iraq, where he chose to be under the protection and guardianship of Ibn Tulun.[12] Later, Qubaiha, the mother of al-Mu'taz, sent Ahmad Ibn Tulun a message in which she offered him a deal. If he would kill al-Musta'in, whom he was protecting, she would give him the province of al-Wasit. Ibn Tulun rejected her generous offer, claiming that he would not betray a person who had trusted him for protection. This incident gained Ahmad Ibn Tulun more popularity, and his status was elevated among his people, the Turks.[13] (Al-Musta'in was later killed, but Ibn Tulun had no role in his assassination.)[14]

In 254 AH / 868 AD, al-Mu'taz, following the system of appanage, gave the province of Egypt to Bakbak, who was one of the Turkish officials in Samarra. However, Bakbak had no intention of losing his strong position in Samarra and presence in the palace as this ensured his personal status within the court and its affairs. Thus Bakbak decided to send his step-son, Ahmad Ibn Tulun, as his deputy and governor of Egypt, and granted him an army to accompany him there.[15]

Ibn Tulun entered Egypt on Ramadan 7, 254 / Wednesday, August 27, 868.[16] He found that there were two officials who were in charge of the affairs of the land. The first was Ibn al-Mudabbir, who was in charge of the land tax *(kharaj)* and was therefore the financial intendant. The second was Shukayr, whose title was the post master (*sahib al-barid*), meaning he was in charge of the correspondence between Fustat al-'Askar and Baghdad. It was obvious that both administrators were totally loyal to Baghdad.[17] Upon his arrival, both officials came out to welcome Ibn Tulun. A gift of ten thousand dinars was presented to him by Ibn al-Mudabbir, but Ibn Tulun did not wish to fall under their grip and, to their astonishment, refused the generous gift. They both knew that the new governor was going to be tough to manipulate and decided to write to the caliph asking for his removal.[18]

Ibn Tulun's main ambition was to rule Egypt and make it a completely independent state, separate from the rest of the Abbasid caliphate and empire. But he realized that his political ambition would never be achieved with the presence of these two officials, Ibn al-Mudabbir and Shukayr. He was, therefore, obliged to think of a way to get rid of them. Ibn Tulun eventually got Ibn al-Mudabbir imprisoned for life,[19] and also managed to have Shukayr removed from office—Shukayr died shortly afterward.[20] The result was that Ibn Tulun obtained full control over Egypt's financial systems, the network of posts, as well as the intelligence office and its spies. Thus, he became financially and politically independent from Baghdad, essential steps to becoming fully autonomous.[21]

In 870, al-Mu'taz died, which brought about the fall and death of Bakbak. As a result, the latter was replaced by another official named Yarjukh, who was the father-in-law of Ibn Tulun. Yarjukh continued to confer the governorship of Egypt to Ibn Tulun.

Al-Mu'tamid succeeded al-Mu'taz as caliph and also found it exceedingly difficult to control his empire. For that reason, in 256 AH / 870 AD al-Mu'tamid divided his empire between his son al-Mufawwad, who was put in charge of the eastern part of the empire, and his brother al-Muwaffaq was put in charge of the western part. In 259 / 873, Yarjukh died and Egypt was placed under the authority of the caliph's son Ja'far al-Mufawwad, under whom Ibn Tulun ruled as governor. The situation resulted in clashes between Ibn Tulun and al-Mufawwad on one side and al-Muwaffaq on the other, each of them claiming that the other was an enemy to the caliphate.

11 – The northwest and southwest arcades of the mosque, showing the thick robust piers, supporting the elegant pointed arches, which still have some of their Samarra-style stucco decorations. It also shows the high ceiling of the mosque and that the wooden Qur'anic inscription that ran below the ceiling was lost.

Tensions between Ibn Tulun and al-Mawaffaq started when al-Muwaffaq was planning to fight Zanjis and Saffarids in the east and asked Ibn Tulun for money to help him. Ibn Tulun sent him 1,200,000 dinars, an amount which al-Muwaffaq considered minute.[22] When al-Muwaffaq responded to him, Ibn Tulun sent him an insolent reply, stating that he had decided to remove and replace him (al-Muwaffaq) from his post. In response, al-Muwaffaq decided to invade Egypt in order to punish Ibn Tulun. However, Ibn Tulun's Egypt was so well defended that upon the arrival of his army, al-Muwaffaq had no choice but to withdraw.[23]

The Caliph al-Mu'tamid asked Ibn Tulun to lead an expedition to punish Ibn Sheikh, the governor of Palestine and Greater Syria (the area known as Bilad al-Sham), because he was disobedient. Ibn Sheikh had sent his son al-Mansur and one of his slave-soldiers (*ghilman*;

sing. *ghulam*) named Majur al-Afranji with an army with the orders to take over Bilad al-Sham. They arrived in Damascus and took it over and claimed themselves rulers of the whole territory in 257 / 870.[24] The caliph wrote to Ibn Mudabbir to exalt him in getting whatever Ibn Tulun needed, and Ibn Tulun managed to build up an army of strong Greek and Sudanese slaves. This situation gave Ibn Tulun a good opportunity to build an army of his own, with which he would be able to fight the rebels. He managed to buy Greek and Sudanese slaves as well as everything they needed.[25] He soon had a strong army with an expansive arsenal, which became one of the most powerful in the Near East. Due to these circumstances, Ibn Tulun reduced the annual revenue the country used to send to Baghdad, and by doing so he was able to accumulate great wealth. He used this wealth to build his new capital city of al-Qata'i', and also a well-trained and well-equipped army of Turkish, Greek, and Sudanese slaves.[26]

Ahmad Ibn Tulun took this military north to Damascus in order to fight the army of Majur al-Afranji and al-Mansur. He defeated their armies and captured both of them. He beheaded them and then nailed their bodies next to each other on wooden crosses as if crucified. He then headed back to Egypt to take care of his affairs. When Ibn Sheikh arrived in Damascus, he saw the drastic defeat of his armies and could do nothing other than accept defeat and withdraw north to Armenia.[27]

After the failure of Ibn Sheikh to protect the region of Bilad al-Sham, the Caliph al-Mu'tamid ordered Ibn Tulun to take care of that entire area.[28] A few years later, after Majur al-Afranji's death in 264 / 878, Ahmad Ibn Tulun appointed his son 'Abbas as the ruler of Bilad al-Sham. 'Abbas revolted against his father, but was unsuccessful, and therefore had to be punished. In 265 / 879, Ibn Tulun fought against the rebels in Antioch, which came under his control after its ruler Sima al-Tawil was murdered. The following year, in 880, Ibn Tulun claimed to be loyal to the caliph, forming an Ibn Tulun sub-kingdom, ruling over Egypt and Bilad al-Sham, which included Damascus and reached all the way north to Tarsus.[29] This was under the pretext of engaging in a holy war and defending the frontiers in Asia Minor against the Byzantines. Later, the Byzantine ruler would demand a peace treaty.[30]

After the Syrian campaigns, Ibn Tulun started to put his own name and titles, together with those of the caliph and his son Ja'far, on his gold coinage.[31] In 882 Ibn Tulun invited the caliph to come and live in Egypt, hoping to move the center of administration of the whole empire to Egypt and Syria. As the caliph was on his way over to Egypt, problems escalated between al-Muwaffaq and Ibn Tulun. Each was claiming that he was the caliph's protector and the other a rebel. As peace negotiations were starting to take place, Ibn Tulun fell ill, got weaker and weaker, lost his eyesight and eventually died on Dhu'l-Qa'da 10, 270 / May 10, 884, at the age of 50.[32]

Stories about Ibn Tulun

Before his death, Ahmad Ibn Tulun had developed a strange interest in spying on others. Balawi tells us that he had a habit of checking every single letter or message that was sent anywhere by reading it through first. It is for that reason that he founded an office *(diwan)* just for checking and reading letters going back and forth between Egypt and Baghdad, and probably Samarra.[33] He even sent one of his servant boys undercover into prison in order to spy on the prisoners: the boy stayed there a whole month and was rewarded at the end with two thousand dinars and ten thousand dirhams in addition to robes of honor.[34]

On another occasion it was reported that Ibn Tulun sent a Persian (al-Farisi) to spy on one of his Turkish friends. The informant searched for the house of this Turk and climbed the roof of a building across from it so that he could observe the man's activities. Apparently the man got drunk that night and began to speak ill of Ibn Tulun, saying that he would go the following morning and kill him with his own sword. Early the next morning the spy went and reported what he had seen and heard to Ibn Tulun. Ibn Tulun then waited for the man, confronted him with the story, and had him exiled to Tarsus.[35]

Balawi explains that Ahmad Ibn Tulun was very clever, to the extent that he was able to tell if someone was spying on him just by looking at his eyes. For example, he once picked out a man who was sitting in the middle of a crowd, and when Ibn Tulun went to question him, the man confessed that he was sent to spy on orders of al-Muwaffaq.[36] He also said that he had some letters to give to several people, who were close to Ibn Tulun. The man was sent to prison, and he expressed his gratitude for not having been tortured or killed by confessing that there was another spy who was present and led Ibn Tulun to him. When the other spy was brought to Ibn Tulun, he was just as truthful as the first one. He gave Ibn Tulun all the letters he was carrying and sent them back to those who wrote them, making sure that they knew that Ibn Tulun had found out about their conspiracies.[37] Ibn Tulun reportedly said that he had suspected the man was a spy because he would not keep his eyes off him.[38]

Once he identified a spy within a group of people who came to greet him, and eventually imprisoned him. Ibn Tulun was then asked whether this was a revelation. He said that it could not be so because he was not a prophet. He simply said he was just clever, and that he dreamed of this man the night before, roaming around the palace, trying to get in but being stopped.[39] Balawi adds another story in which Ibn Tulun saw a poor man from far away, felt sorry for him, and decided to send him some food. After the servant delivered the food and came back, Ibn Tulun asked for the impoverished-looking man to be brought to him. Ibn Tulun then told him to confess that he was a spy and hand over any letters he had. Surprisingly, the man did as he was told. After that, Ibn Tulun explained that he felt really sorry for the poor man at first, but when he saw the man's reaction as he was eating, he realized he was not someone who was very hungry. This raised his suspicions that turned out to be true.[40]

When Ibn Tulun fell ill, he threatened to kill all the physicians if they could not cure him—one of them died of fear and others had to take some of his medicine themselves so that he would not think they were poisoning him.[41] During his final days, he sought another physician's advice without letting his real physicians know, and this led to short-term relief.[42] He punished his original physician, who died two days after.[43]

When he lost hope of finding a cure, he would be carried every night around the palace. He would check the enclosure for any openings that people could use to sneak in and ordered them to be closed.

Feeling that his end was near, he asked people to pray for him by the mountain, so Muslims, Christians, and Jews went to pray for him.[44] He then ordered bonuses to be given to the army.[45] Ibn Tulun's advice to his son Abu al-Gaysh (Khumarawiya) was to keep paying allegiance to Caliph al-Mu'tamid.[46] He told his leaders and servants to stay together and to not let others come between them.[47] In addition, he told his son to always remember his advice and to not change the system of the country, since it was in good shape and would continue to guarantee a good life.[48] He then asked his trusted people to obey his son after his death.[49] He instructed the division of his money in his will and told his son that the monetary deposit *(wadi'a)* should remain intact. He also advised a loyal servant to keep his sons from spending too much.[50] Balawi informs us that Ibn Tulun left thirty-three children: seventeen boys and sixteen girls.[51] He also left 24,000 servants, 7,000 men, 7,000 horses used in the activities of the open parade groud of *al-maydan (al-maydaniyya)*, 3,000 camels, 1,000 mules, 350 cermonial horses (*li-rikabihi*), and 200 huge military ships (*marakib harbiyya*) with all their machines (*bi-alatiha*).[52]

Egypt enjoyed a glorious period during the reign of Ahmad Ibn Tulun. It was due to his talents and cleverness that he managed to make "administrative reforms that were directed to encouraging the peasants to cultivate their lands with zeal."[53] The prosperity of Egypt during Ibn Tulun's reign was also due to the fact that the revenues of the state were not wasted but were employed to stimulate commerce and industry and for the foundation of the new city of al-Qata'i', north of Fustat and al-'Askar, which became the new Islamic capital of Egypt.

Ibn Tulun's Successors

Ibn Tulun was succeeded by his son Khumarawiya, who expanded the Palace of al-Maydan. He added new gardens that were known for their exotic trees, flowers, and plants, as well as an exquisite zoo, where animals were brought from all over the world. Khumarawiya enjoyed many luxuries and lavish pleasures, which were never experienced or practiced before by any Islamic ruler in Egypt. Yet, he followed Ibn Tulun's policy of having a peaceful relationship with the

Abbasid caliph. Khumarawiya offered for his own daughter, whose name was Qatr al-Nada, to marry the caliph, and for that reason he built for her forty small palaces—probably luxurious tents—all the way from al-Qata'i' in Egypt to Baghdad in Iraq. The reason was that if Qatr al-Nada ever wanted to rest, she would be able to relax for a few hours or days in a palace that resembled her father's residence. While on a visit to Damascus, Khumarawiya was killed by his personal slaves. His body was brought to Egypt, where he was buried next to his father. He had ruled for twelve years and eighteen days.[54] (For the works of Khumarawiya, see chapter 4).

Khumarawiya was succeeded by the weak Abu al-'Asakir Gaysh, who was deposed and imprisoned until death. He ruled for only six months and twelve days. He was succeeded by his brother Abu Musa Harun, who was killed in battle after ruling for eight years, eight months, and a few days. The last Tulunid ruler was Shayban Ibn Ahmad Ibn Tulun. A few days after he ascended the throne, the Abbasid general Muhammad Sulayman al-Katib attacked Egypt. Terrified by the invaders, he surrendered to the general and was slaughtered, having ruled for only twelve days.[55] This was the end of the glorious dynasty of Ahmad Ibn Tulun which, according to Maqrizi (quoting the historian al-Quda'i), lasted thirty-seven years, six months, and twenty-two days.[56]

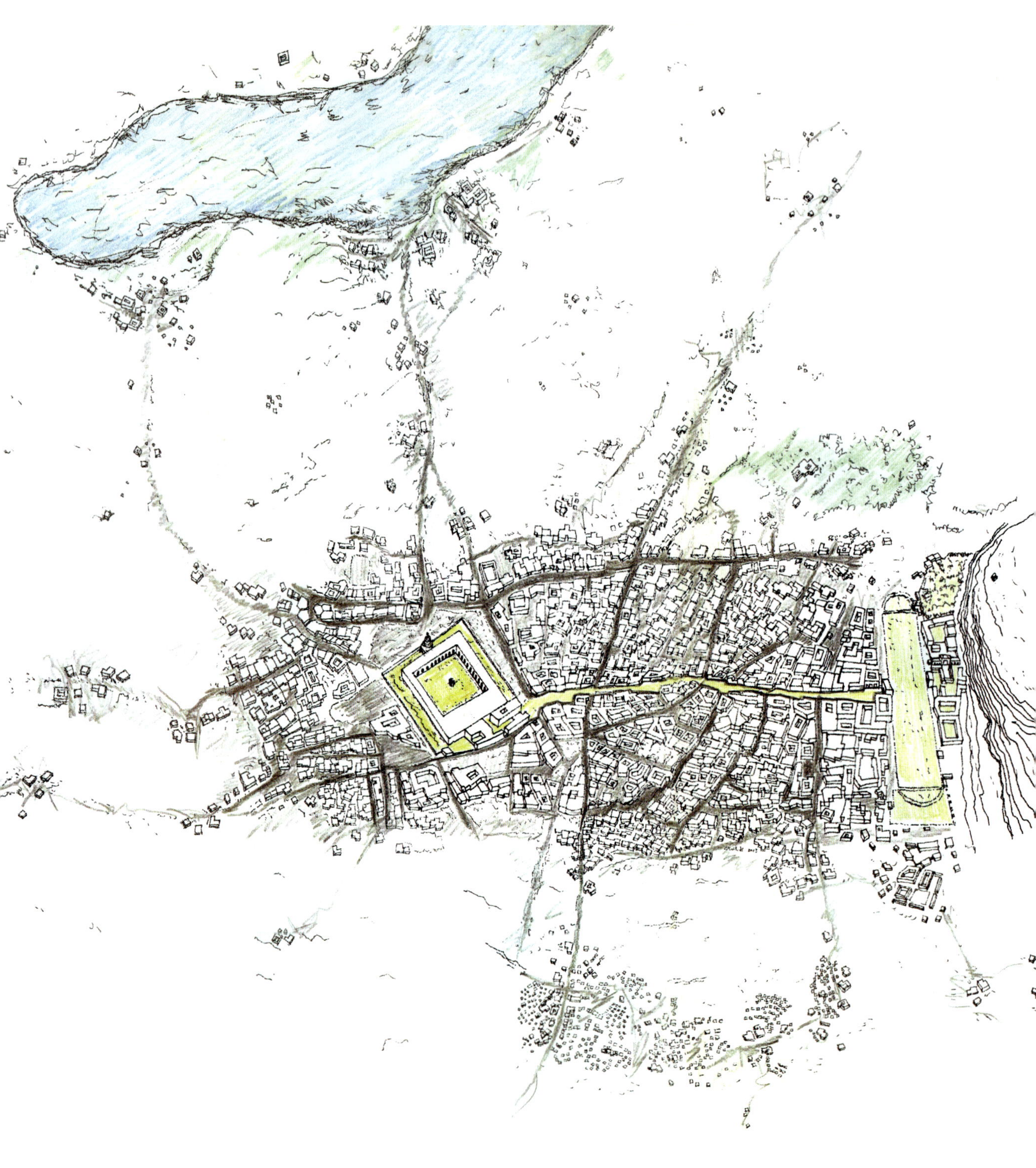

4 The Lost City of al-Qata'i'

The city of al-Qata'i' was founded by Ahmad Ibn Tulun in 256 AH / 870 AD, a few years after he established his status in Egypt.[1] The city became the third Islamic capital of Egypt after those of Fustat and al-'Askar. It contained some of the most splendid buildings that Egypt had known since the time of the Romans. The city flourished until it was totally destroyed by the Abbasid general Muhammad Sulayman al-Katib in the year 292 / 905.

Al-Qata'i' was full of wonderful buildings, some of which were symbols of Ibn Tulun's new rule in Egypt. It had a residential palace called the Palace of al-Maydan, which included an open parade ground. The main street called Shari al-A'zam (Greatest Street) led to Dar al-Imara, the administrative headquarters of the city, which was adjacent to the main mosque of Ibn Tulun. Both buildings were on top of a small rock knoll, known as Gabal Yashkur, in the center of the city. Nearby was a small tomb of Sidi Harun, and all around the mosque were bustling markets. The city of al-Qata'i' had different residential districts. It also had a hospital (*bimaristan*) and an aqueduct to supply the city with water from an ancient well. Balawi states that the city of al-Qata'i' was more developed, larger, and better advanced and urbanized—"*a'mar wa ahsan*"—than any of the cities in Bilad al-Sham.[2] (See figure 12, the general map of al-Qata'i' by Seif al-Rashidi.)

12 – A general bird's-eye view of the city of al-Qata'i', showing the approximate location of its borders. From the north is the lake of Birkat al-Fil, which no longer exisits, and to the east is the hill on which the Citadel of Cairo was later built, as well as, the possible location of the palace, open parade ground, and main street relative to the mosque of Ibn Tulun. The drawing also suggests the different residential areas of the city.

The tenth-century historian Balawi says that when Ibn Tulun returned to Egypt after defeating Ibn Sheikh in Bilad al-Sham, he found that his retinue of slaves and his army of 100,000 men had increased considerably, overcrowding the existing barracks, making them too cramped. One day he rode up to the foot of the Muqattam Hills and chose that area to build the city. He ordered his companions, slaves, and followers to start building around and close to his new palace.

City Layout

The city of al-Qata'i' was divided into streets (*sikak*, sing. *sikka*) and narrow alleys (*aziqqa*, sing. *zuqaq*), with mosques (*masajid*, sing. *masjid*), mills (*tawahin*, sing. *tahuna*), public baths (*hammamat*, sing. *hammam*) and bakeries (*afran*, sing. *furn*) as well.

The new city was divided into special districts, with each assigned to different groups who came with Ibn Tulun from Samarra. Each district was named according to the tribe, ethnic group, or social class, which inhabited it. This is probably why the city was called al-Qata'i', meaning 'districts,' 'allotments,' 'wards,' or 'quarters.'

Balawi provides an incomplete list of the districts of al-Qata'i'.[3] For example, there was a district of the servants of the palace *(al-farrashin)*, the Sudanese *(al-Sudan)*, the Nubians *(al-Nuba)*, the Greeks *(al-Rum)*, and another district named Harun, the residents of which are unclear.[4] In addition, the young slaves *(ghilman)* had their own district to live in. The idea of dividing the city into different districts according to ethnic groups was not alien to Islamic Egypt: it was done in the earlier cities of Fustat and al-'Askar and was a system followed in the city of Samarra, where Ibn Tulun grew up.[5] This made it a logical layout for the new city of al-Qata'i'.

Balawi tells of the different kinds of markets (*souq*s), in the center of the city.[6] He lists some of them: *souq al-'ayyarin*, where gold and silver were weighed; *souq al-'attarin*, which was the market of perfumers, spice dealers, and those selling medical herbs; and *souq al-bazzazin*, which was the cloth market for linen and other fabrics. Then, there were food markets, like: *souq al-famiyyin*, for selling peas; *al-jazzarin*, the butchers; *al-baqqallin*, for vegetables; and *al-shawwayyin*, for those who roasted, grilled, and barbecued on coal. In addition, there was *souq al-tabbakhin*, which was the market for cooks but also included the *sayarif*, who were the moneychangers, *al-khabbazin*, for bakers, and *al-halawayyin*, for the sweets and pastry makers.[7]

Similarly, we find the same distribution of markets in Samarra. The historian Ya'qubi mentions that in Samarra the markets were in the central area of the city and around the main congregational mosque.[8] Unfortunately, the historians do not tell us where these markets were located in al-Qata'i', but it is likely that they followed the practice established in Samarra and that the markets were located in the middle of the city and around the mosque of Ibn Tulun.

The fourteenth-century historians Ibn Duqmaq (quoting al-Quda'i) and Maqrizi both state that the city of al-Qata'i' measured one mile *(mil)* by one mile.[9] Maqrizi adds that the length of the city extended from approximately what seems to have been a famous dome called Qubbat al-Hawa (Dome of the Winds, the Atmosphere, or the Air), where the Citadel of Cairo was located, all the way to the mosque of Ibn Tulun. He adds that the width of the city began in the east from Maydan al-Rumayla, below the Citadel, to the present mosque of Zayn al-Abdin in the west.[10]

We can imagine that the city of al-Qata'i' was bordered by Saliba Street on the north, the Citadel of Cairo on the east, the hills of Qala'at al-Kabsh (near the Madrasa of Sultan Qaitbay), and an imaginary line drawn east to west through the mosque of Zayn al-Abdin on the south.[11] This leads us to conclude that the city of al-Qata'i' covered an area of one and a half kilometers in length on the north–south axis and two kilometers in length on the east–west axis.[12] This corresponds closely to the descriptions of Ibn Duqmaq and Maqrizi about the scale of the city.

The terrain of al-Qata'i' was mostly rocky, except for the northern extension, and the city was well protected by natural features. The whole site of al-Qata'i' was characterized by a series of hills, and there was a slight gradual rise toward the east, reaching the high hill on which the Citadel of Cairo was later built, and even further east were the Muqattam Hills. Also to the west of the city was a hill now known as Kiman Tulun (Mounds of Tulun) or Kiman Zinhum (Mounds of Zinhum), and another was the Manazir or Qala'at al-Kabsh (Fortress of the Ram). Toward the middle of the city was a rocky knoll known as Gabal Yashkur (Hill of Yashkur), on which the mosque of Ibn Tulun was built.

To the north, there was Birkat al-Fil al-Sughra (Small Lake of the Elephant), and Birkat al-Fil al-Kubra (Grand Lake of the Elephant), on the northwestern boundary. The northeastern boundary was left open most probably for the flow of merchant traffic and to promote expansion of the city in that direction. To the south was a considerable depression in the direction of the city of Fustat (figs. 12, 13, 14).

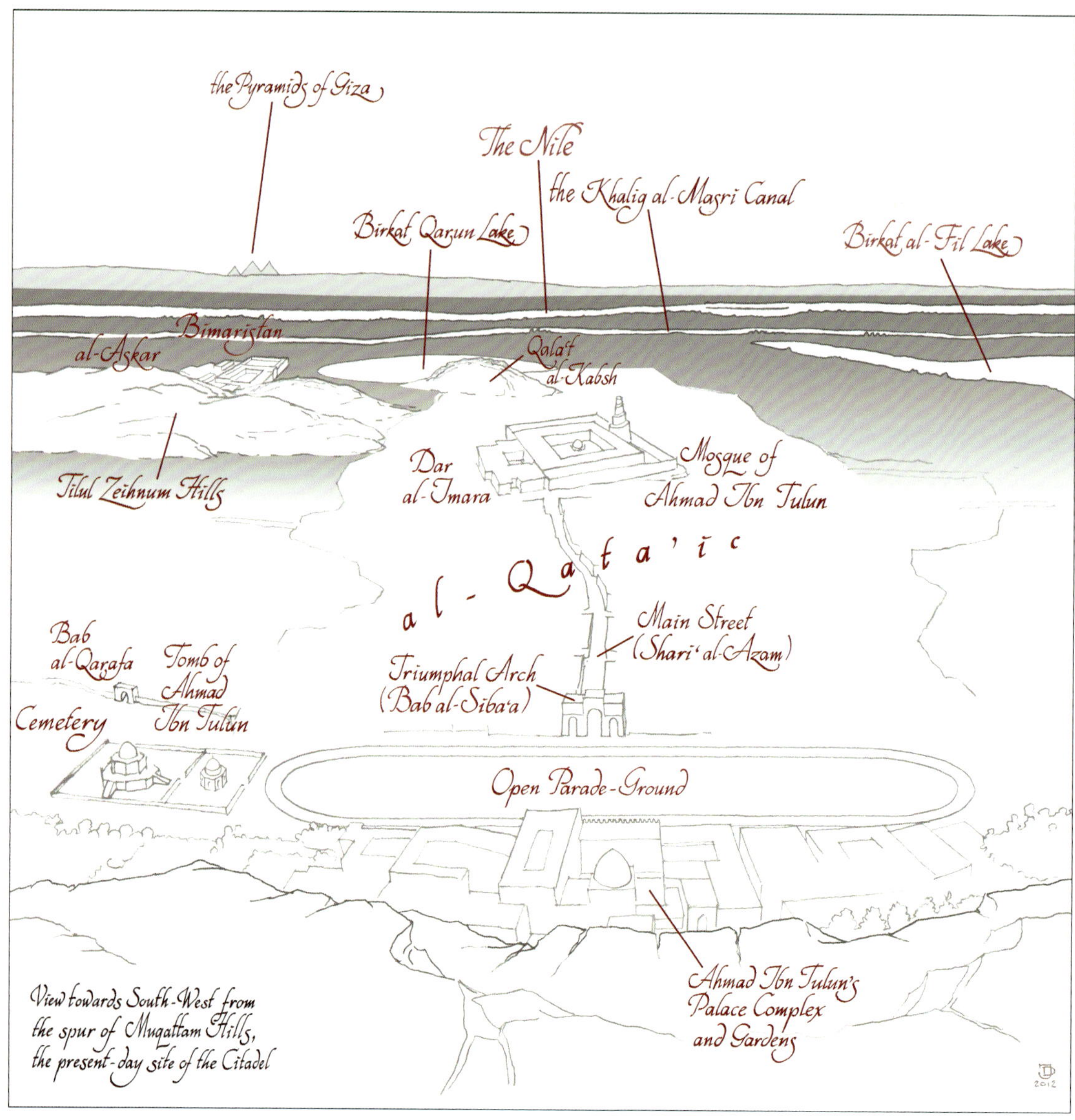

13 – Outline of the city of al-Qata'i'.

Shari' al-A'zam

Balawi describes the city of al-Qata'i' as having a main street called Shari' al-A'zam (Greatest Street),[13] which was wide and linked the palace with the mosque of Ibn Tulun.[14] His description of Bab al-Siba' (Gate of the Lion) leads us to believe that Shari' al-A'zam started from that gate, which was part of al-Maydan Palace grounds, and extended to the mosque of Ibn Tulun.

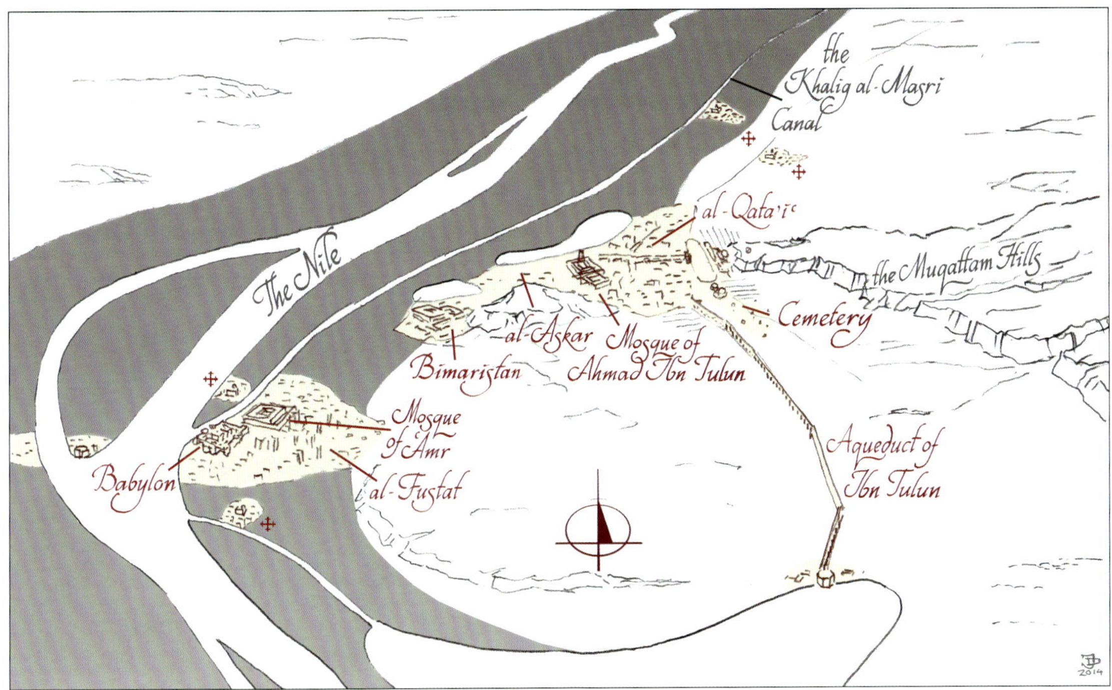

Shari' al-A'zam was the main link between the small alleys *(durub)* of the city, which branched off from the main road and, according to Balawi, the inhabitants of al-Qata'i' were identified according to a specific marker at the corner that bordered the alley in which they lived.[15] Balawi also says that Ibn Tulun used to walk along Shari' al-A'zam, that he would wind through it—"*yu'arraj minhu*"—to reach his palace.[16] Since we know that Bab al-Siba' had certain restricted ceremonies during religious feasts and festivals when Ibn Tulun assembled his troops, we may consider Shari' al-A'zam to have been the main ceremonial thoroughfare of al-Qata'i'. Thus, the street of Shari' al A'zam started from the triple arched gate of Bab al-Siba' and zigzagged all the way to the mosque and Dar al-Imara.

14 – Bird's-eye view of the city of al-Qata'i' looking north and showing the lake of Birkat al-Habash (below), from where the aqueduct of Ibn Tulun started and extended north through the older cities of Fustat and al-'Askar and onto al-Qata'i'. To the west is the River Nile and the Island of Roda with the Nilometer built on its southern tip opposite the fortress of Babylon on the east side.

From Balawi, one understands that Ibn Tulun's walk from the palace to the mosque took the form of a ceremonial procession, which is probably the reason he erected a type of honorific triple-gate arch, similar to those of the Roman period.[17] This type of ceremony probably aimed to show the power of the new regime of Ibn Tulun in Egypt. The main street of Shari' al-A'zam was directly derived from the main street in Samarra, which bore the same name and was mentioned by the traveler and historian Ya'qubi.[18] Although Ya'qubi does not describe any ceremonial processions taking place along that street in Samarra, one would expect that it was used for the same purpose since such ceremonies were an established custom.

The Aqueduct of Basatin

Ibn Tulun had an aqueduct built in the south of the city.[19] Balawi states that the water for the aqueduct came from a well that was called Abu Ibn Khalid in an area called al-Ma'afir.[20] Maqrizi, quoting al-Quda'i, tells us why this aqueduct was built. The story goes that Ibn Tulun was riding alone in the desert (southeast of the city of Fustat) and began to feel thirsty. He asked for a cup of water, and while he was drinking, the man who gave him the water asked Ibn Tulun not to drink the whole cup. When Ibn Tulun asked why, the man answered that the desert area they were in was remote and water was scarce. After Ibn Tulun reached his palace, he asked for the same man to be brought to him. He ordered him to accompany several engineers to show them a suitable place where they could build an aqueduct, which would supply water to the man's residence. In addition, Ibn Tulun gave him 1,000 dinars for the construction of the aqueduct.[21] Balawi describes the aqueduct as being built in the proper way of building—"*sahiha*."[22]

Maqrizi calls it the *qanatir* (aqueduct) of Ibn Tulun and states that it was built near an ancient well which was known as Bi'r 'Asfa ('Asfa Well). He adds that the building cost 40,000 dinars.[23] Balawi also says that Ibn Tulun built the aqueduct using money he discovered at the site of Tannur Fir'awn (Lantern of the Pharaoh) in the Muqattam Hills.[24] (The discovery of the treasure will be discussed in chapter 6.) Quoting the historian Ibn Qaratghan, Balawi adds that the aqueduct was built by al-Nasrani, a non-Muslim or Christian whom he describes as being a skillful and intelligent engineer. He adds that this was the same architect responsible for building the mosque of Ibn Tulun.[25]

There is an amusing story about the architect al-Nasrani.[26] One evening he told Ibn Tulun that he had completed the work at the aqueduct and wanted Ibn Tulun to inspect it himself. The following day Ibn Tulun rode to view the construction and was satisfied with the progress, admiring all that he had seen. While he was riding through the building site, his horse stumbled on some fresh mortar. To al-Nasrani's misfortune, Ibn Tulun interpreted the accident as a sign of evil and consequently sentenced the architect to five hundred lashes, then he was thrown in prison. He was released years later to build Ibn Tulun's mosque.[27]

The important thing about the aqueduct of Ibn Tulun is that it was among the first vast structures of its kind to be constructed in Egypt on such a large scale. However, it was not the first aqueduct in Egypt because the modern excavations of Istabl 'Antar by Roland-Pierre Gayraud show the foundations of an earlier, much smaller, pre-Tulunid aqueduct.[28] The aqueduct of Ibn Tulun was built in the south of the cities of Fustat and al-'Askar. It may be argued that it was built to serve most of the local population of these cities, as well as the newcomers who came with Ibn Tulun from Samarra to al-Qata'i', and therefore that it was purely a civil engineering project intended for a whole metropolis, not simply for the new city of al-Qata'i'. According to Balawi, the aqueduct was built for the needy and Ibn Tulun ordered it to be open all day and all night, for whoever required water.[29] The aqueduct continued to serve the population even after al-Qata'i' was destroyed. When Salah al-Din came to Egypt in the twelfth century and decided to build the Citadel of Cairo, he began building the famous Great Aqueduct along what is now the Salah Salem Road.[30] It is important to note that, unlike Ibn Tulun, Salah al-Din's aqueduct was meant to serve only the ruling class residing in the Citadel, not the population of Fustat, al-'Askar, and Qata'i'.

The building of the aqueduct of Ibn Tulun survives in very poor condition in the area known today as Bir Umm al-Sultan of Basatin, south of Cairo. It can be seen from both sides of Cairo's Ring Road, on the way to al-Tagammu' al-Khamis in New Cairo. From the south side of the Ring Road, the aqueduct's water intakes–"*ma'khaz al-miya*"– are visible, while on the north side of the Ring Road parts of the main body and the wall of arches can be seen (figs. 15, 16).[31] Thus, Egypt's

15 – The oldest aqueduct in Egypt—built by Ahmad Ibn Tulun—which today lies in ruins, in the area known as Bir Umm al-Sultan, in the south Cairo neighborhood of Basatin. The brick structure of the aqueduct runs below the modern Ring Road linking Giza to the district of New Cairo. This photograph shows the ruins of the intake-water tower, on the south side from the Ring Road encroached by surrounding homes and factories.

16 – The north extension of the aqueduct of Ahmad Ibn Tulun viewed today from the Ring Road. At a distance are the Muqattam Hills and the *mashhad* of al-Guyushi on top.

oldest, longest, and largest aqueduct is very poorly maintained today. Ugly buildings, mostly marble factories, have encroached upon it, its arches have been breached and destroyed to allow vehicles to pass through it and the area has become rundown, full of slums and squatters. No attempts have been made to restore and rescue this valuable monument of Egypt's history.[32]

The Bimaristan

Balawi mentions that among the pious and charitable acts carried out by Ibn Tulun was the building of the *bimaristan*. He adds that it was funded from the sum of one million—"*alf alf*"—dinars, which Ibn Tulun discovered in the desert and from which his mosque was also built.[33] Traveler Ibn Jubayr mentions that the *bimaristan* still existed when he visited Egypt in 580 AH / 1184 AD, but Maqrizi says it had not survived to his time.[34] Thus, quoting historian al-Kindi, Maqrizi recounts that Ibn Tulun ordered the building of the *bimaristan* in 259 / 872-73 for the infirm.[35] In addition, he says that according to the compiler of Ibn Tulun's biography *(Jami' al-sira al-tuluniya)*, meaning Balawi, it was built in 261 / 874-75, at a cost of 60,000 dinars.[36] Ibn Duqmaq and Maqrizi mention that Ibn Tulun established a few markets: a private white slave market *(souq al-raqiq al-abyad)*; an inalienable property *(habs)* market for the *bimaristan*, as well as other properties such as the *dar al-diwan*; and a market of shoemakers *(souq al-asakifa)*, together with an unnamed caravanserai *(qaisariya)*.[37]According to Maqrizi, the *bimaristan* was of special interest to Ibn Tulun. He rode there every Friday to personally inspect its warehouses and storage rooms, meet its physicians, and pass by the sick and mentally ill patients.[38]

Balawi describes the *bimaristan* as having the most precious types of drugs in its stores.[39] Well-known theriaca and antidotes found only in the treasures of kings and caliphs were also stocked in these stores. He adds that they never ran out of any of the major medicines and remedies, like laxatives. It appears that the *bimaristan* had a well-organized system. Maqrizi mentions that it incorporated two bathhouses (*hammams*), one for men and the other for women.[40] Ibn Tulun stipulated that when a patient entered the *bimaristan*, his clothes and valuables were to be kept with the superintendent and he would be lent hospital clothes instead. Patients at the *bimaristan* would be well taken care of. They would be given free medicine, food, and care from physicians until they recovered. Only when patients were able to chew and swallow chicken and a loaf of bread were they allowed to leave and given back their clothes and personal valuables.[41]

Unfortunately, there are no sources that provide any information about the architecture of this *bimaristan*. Two *bimaristans* were built in Egypt prior to that of Ibn Tulun: one was called the *bimaristan* of Zuqaq al-Qandil and the other was that of Murafir.[42] There is no specific information about them, except that they were destroyed at an early date, which may imply that they were small establishments, not significant social or architectural works, and did not have a sophisticated system like that of Ibn Tulun's *bimaristan*. Thus it is fair to say that from the time of the Islamic conquest of Egypt in 21 AH / 640–41 AD until 259 / 872 (almost 230 years), that there had not been a *bimaristan* in Egypt comparable to the one built by Ibn Tulun.

The next *bimaristan* after that of Ibn Tulun was built by Kafur al-Ikhshidi in the tenth century, after the destruction of Ibn Tulun's *bimaristan* by the Abbasids in 905. The Ikhshidids tried to revive the legacy of Ibn Tulun's glorious period, as they tried to emulate the grandeur associated with the Tulunid regime. The Fatimids did not build any *bimaristans*, but Salah al-Din converted one of the Fatimid palaces into a *bimaristan* in 567 / 1171.[43] Later, during the Mamluk period, the most famous of all *bimaristans* was that of Sultan Qalawun, built along Cairo's modern-day al-Mu'iz Street, in 683–84 / 1284–85.[44] Another *bimaristan* was also built by Sultan al-Mu'ayyad Sheikh near the Citadel of Cairo in 1420.

The idea of *bimaristans* was not a common initiative, but made an outstanding contribution to the population of Egypt. By building the *bimaristan*, Ibn Tulun was attempting to compete with the Abbasids: he was determined to show them that his new capital city was equal to theirs in Baghdad and Samarra, in both grandeur and services. Maqrizi locates the *bimaristan* of Ibn Tulun on the mounds and the desert areas of the city of al-'Askar. He specifies that it is somewhere between the mosque of Ibn Tulun and the mound of Kum al-Jarih and between Qantarat al-Sadd, which was overlooking the canal of al-Khalij, and the wall separating the Qarafa (southern cemetery) and the city of Misr.[45] In another passage he describes it as being close to the lake of Birkat Qarun.[46] George Salmon and Creswell only refer to the *bimaristan* briefly (see fig. 17).[47] Neither of them tries to locate the *bimaristan* on their maps, even though Maqrizi's description of the location of the *bimaristan* is reasonably clear.

The Dar al-Imara

When Ahmad Ibn Tulun arrived in Egypt, he resided in the administrative office building known as Dar al-Imara of the then-capital city of al-'Askar. It eventually became Ibn Tulun's private residence as well as his main administrative office.[48] After he established himself in Egypt, he started building his residential palace and left the old Dar al-Imara of al-'Askar. According to Maqrizi, Dar al-Imara was built on the southeastern side of the mosque of Ibn Tulun.[49] The historian Balawi states that Ibn Tulun entered Dar al-Imara and performed his ablutions then changed his garments and robes and perfumed himself with incense.[50] He adds that after such preparations and rituals, Ibn Tulun went out of its door to pray in the *maqsura* of the mosque.[51] Maqrizi confirms this.[52] Balawi says Dar al Imara was decorated and furnished *(furishat)* with curtains (*sutur*) and implements *(alat)* were carried to its storerooms (*khaza'inuha*) with everything that was needed and large containers (*al-awani*) filled with all kinds of drinks (*ashriba*, sing. *sharab*).[53]

The idea of having Dar al-Imara adjacent to the mosque goes back to the early Islamic period. According to Jere Bacharach, Ibn Tulun adopted local customs in constructing his most important buildings. He explains that this architectural combination of mosque-Dar al-Imara was not present in Samarra because the symbolic value of these buildings must have changed through time. Although Samarra constituted a break from the earliest traditions of the mosque-Dar al-Imara pattern, it was not immediately copied. When Ibn Tulun came to Egypt and ruled in Fustat and al-'Askar, he followed the local traditions in Egypt by linking his Dar al-Imara to his mosque.[54]

The pre-Abbasid buildings referred to by Bacharach were in fact large palaces, which functioned as both royal residences and administrative offices for the caliphs and as the setting for public audiences. However, the Dar al-Imara of Ibn Tulun was built to serve a different function from the actual palace of Ibn Tulun. It was an administrative building, which also functioned as the place where the ruler would prepare himself for the Friday prayer. At the same time, the Dar al-Imara of Ibn Tulun may also be compared with a structure discovered behind the *qibla* wall of the mosque of Abu Dulaf in Samarra, which must have had a similar function. Creswell and James Allen believe the structure behind the *qibla* wall of the mosque was designed for the caliph to pray in the mosque.[55] This may imply that the idea of having the Dar al-Imara of Ibn Tulun adjacent to his mosque was a direct influence from Samarra.

Modern Egyptian historians, such as Sayyida Ismail al-Kashif, conclude that for Ibn Tulun to build a new Dar al-Imara instead of using the old one of al-'Askar shows his eagerness to express his growing independence from the Abbasid regime. This may be an accepted interpretation because if the old Dar al-Imara was not suitable to rule from as an administrative building, Ibn Tulun could have had it enlarged or remodeled architecturally to suit his new regime. The fact that he did not do that is a sign that Ibn Tulun was seeking to establish his own power. He managed to consolidate his power and status in the country by gaining full control over the *kharaj* and his *ghilman* and *mawali* (allies from different races), as well as taking charge of the army. To demonstrate this authority, he built a grand, new Dar al-Imara as his personal seat of power.

The location of the Dar al-Imara building is said to have been behind the mosque of Ibn Tulun from the wall of the *qibla*. It does not survive today, and it is not known when this building was demolished or destroyed. We know that it was used during the Ikhshidid, Fatimid, and early Ayyubid periods, we also know that the function of the administration of Egypt moved to the Citadel of Cairo, which was begun by Salah al-Din and completed during the Mamluk period. Therefore, there is no way of knowing how this building used to look. However, since we know it was behind the mosque of Ibn Tulun, one may assume that it occupied the area behind it all the way up until the street of Tulun on the southeastern side of the mosque. One can assume it was a large building, though much smaller than the mosque itself.

George Salmon dedicates a whole chapter of his work to the Dar al-Imara of Ibn Tulun. His examination is based on the accounts

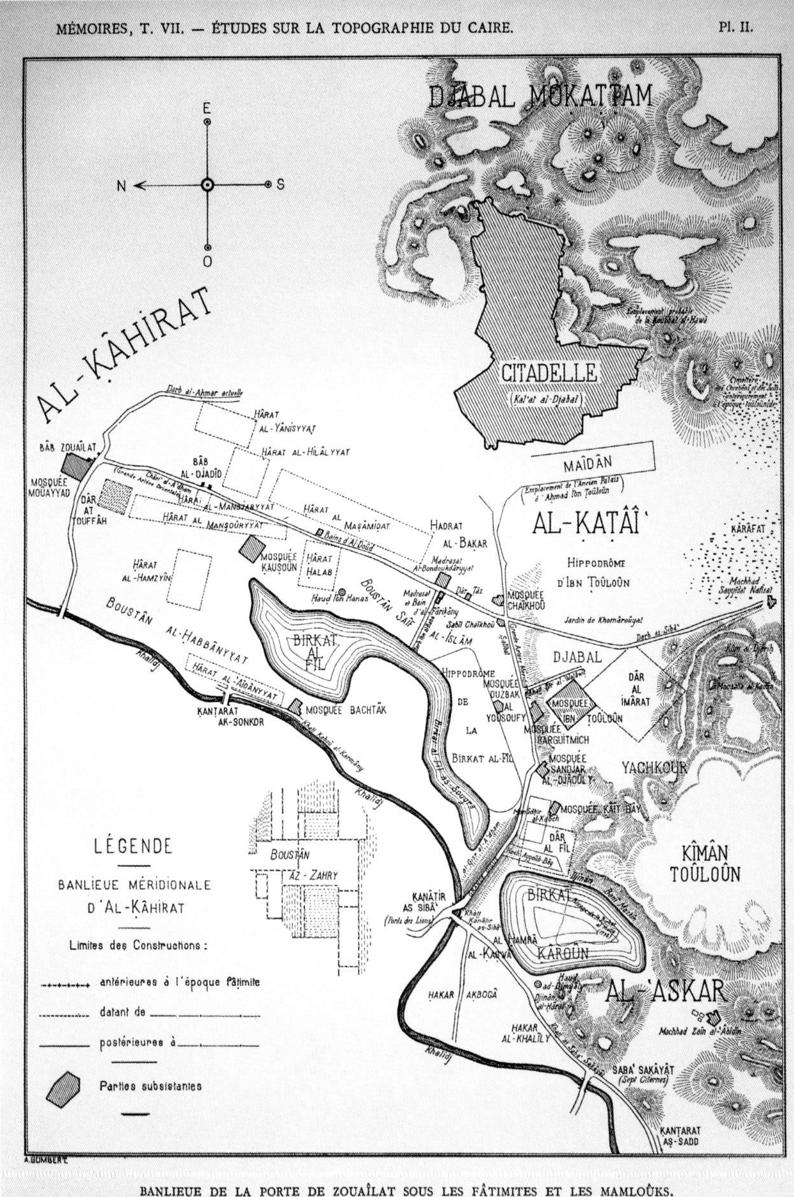

17 – Map of al-Qata'i' by George Salmon in 1902, showing the location of the palace of *al-maydan*, the open parade ground, the mosque of Ibn Tulun, and an exaggerated area of the building of Dar al-Imara. It shows al-Qata'i' relative to how the city of Cairo appeared in the later Mamluk period, which causes some confusion when studying al-Qata'i'.

provided by Ibn Duqmaq and Maqrizi. He acknowledges that there is no indication of the dimensions and size of this building and seems, in fact, to exaggerate its scale on his proposed map (fig. 17). His map shows this part of the city during the Fatimid and Mamluk times, but it is impossible to know the scale and dimensions of this building due to the lack of information.

18 – A reconstructed bird's eye view of the original Tulunid mosque and the building of Dar al-Imara behind it from an elevated eastern point. The mosque is surrounded by market stalls. The shape of the original Tunlunid spiral-shaped minaret is based on that of Samarra and is surmounted by a boat-like finial similar to that of the mausoleum of Imam al-Shafi'i. The *fawwara* in the middle of the *sahn* has a gilded wooden dome supported by circular rows of columns. Dar al-Imara is a building with an open court used by officials. Armed guards would have stood on both sides of the entrances. Nearby lies the small tomb of Sidi Harun, whose shape is based on Fatimid tombs in Aswan, the closest to the time of Ibn Tulun.

Nevertheless, when considering a reconstruction of the building of the Dar al-Imara of Ibn Tulun, one finds that it must have been limited in size in terms of the distance and length of the area behind the mosque to the street. It must have had an open court to allow light and circulation of air. If the building did not incorporate an open court, which is a traditional Cairene feature, then it would have been totally dim on the inside. Such an open court would allow the building to have windows piercing its walls, which would have been necessary for the building to be harmonious with the structure of the mosque itself. In addition, the Dar al-Imara must have had entrances on each side, with doors similar to those in the mosque. Armed guards would protect these doors, especially the southernmost door, which would have been the main royal entrance of Ibn Tulun himself. The building would have been divided into official chambers for meetings and offices for administrative purposes. In the section close to the mosque wall, there were chambers where Ibn Tulun would perform his ablutions and therefore needed a source of water.

The closest source of water available would come from the neighboring house of Bayt Amna Bint Salem and Bayt al-Kiritliya, known today as the Gayer-Anderson House/Museum. It has a famous well, known as Bi'r al-Watawit (Well of the Bats), which is the subject of folkloric legends. Physically, the well is too far away from where Ibn Tulun would have performed his ablutions before prayer.[56] Therefore, one may speculate that the water would be filled in a cistern or tank from which he would wash. Due to his high status, he would have had servants who would pour water from an ewer. He would probably change his garments in another chamber and then enter the mosque through the famous door into the *maqsura* area. In addition, Dar al-Imara would have included other halls (figs. 18, 77).

The Tomb of Sidi Harun

The Mamluk historian Ibn Duqmaq states that the tomb of the Prophet Harun (Aaron, the brother of Moses) was said to be located next to the gate of the mosque of Ibn Tulun.[57] It was known to be a place where God would answer prayers. Thus when Ibn Tulun wanted to build his mosque, he was advised to build it on Gabal Yashkur.[58] In another passage, Ibn

Duqmaq states that the Prophet Harun used to pray on the rocky area behind the mosque and the tomb of the prophet was said to be there.[59]

It is almost certain that the pre-Tulunid tomb of the Prophet Harun occupied the same spot as the present location of the tomb of Sheikh Harun al-Husayni, at the eastern corner of the mosque of Ibn Tulun, adjacent to the Gayer-Anderson House/Museum.[60] It is also possible that there was a tomb in this area before the construction of the mosque, since Ibn Tulun was advised that it was a sacred area and that it brought blessings to its people. One might also speculate that there is a relationship between the name of whoever is buried in this tomb and the Tulunid tribe called Harun, which is the tribe that accompanied Ibn Tulun when he came to Egypt. It is reasonable to believe that Ibn Tulun wanted to associate his mosque with some sort of sacredness related to prophets' legends of Gabal Yashkur and at the same time with this tomb of Sheikh Harun al-Husayni, which would have brought him more sacred blessings.

However, there probably was some confusion over time between the name of the Prophet Harun and that of Harun, the great-grandson of the Prophet Muhammad. An inscription above the tomb's portal identifies the building as the tomb *(maqam)* of Sidi Harun al-Husayni, who is also known as Harun Ibn al-Husayn, a great-grandson of the

Prophet Muhammad, the grandson of 'Ali and Fatima, and son of al-Husayn.[61] Numerous folk legends have long been related to the cult of this sheikh called Sidi Harun. For example, it was believed that the tomb of Sidi Harun al-Husayni was built during the Fatimid period.[62] He was known to be a patron saint who had brought miraculous benefits, blessings, protection, and prosperity to the adjacent house of Bayt al-Kiritliya.[63]

In reconstructing the small shrine of Sidi Harun al-Husayni, one finds that the closest domed buildings to follow from that period are those in the Fatimid cemetery in Aswan, built later in the eleventh century. It would have been a square building with a small dome on top built from firebrick. Egypt has had a long tradition of building domes, such as those found in the Coptic Christian cemetery of al-Bagawat in the Kharga Oasis (third to seventh centuries AD), where a transitional zone likely would have supported the small dome with a simple system of pendentives. The same system would have been used in the tomb of Sidi Harun. Like all shrines and tombs of the period, a *mihrab* must have been added at some point, once it became associated with a Muslim context (see figs. 18, 77).

The Maydan

The historians Ibn Duqmaq and Maqrizi state that Ibn Tulun began the foundation of his palace and hippodrome *(mal'ab)* in 256 AH / 869 AD.[64] Balawi states that Ibn Tulun built his palace, had it enlarged, improved, and beautified and then included in its grounds a magnificent open area or parade ground *(maydan)*, where polo games were played—"*yudrab fihi bi-l-sawalija.*"[65] The whole palace area was named *al-maydan* because it was a popular place for any person, young or old, to visit.[66]

Art historians have accepted the translation of the word *maydan* to be 'hippodrome.'[67] There is no doubt that hippodrome refers to either a racing course for chariots, a circus, or a theater for various entertainments. Moreover, the word hippodrome can be reserved for a place where horses ran or were trained. However, the word *maydan* has several meanings, such as public square, open space, battlefield, playground, or racecourse. Therefore, *al-maydan* should be regarded as an open space within the royal premises intended for public functions and activities—such as polo games, military parades, civil acts of charity, and public performances—and a better translation would be a parade ground.

Ibn Duqmaq and Maqrizi locate the palace of Ibn Tulun at al-Maydan al-Sultani of their time (fourteenth century), which was the great public square below where the Citadel of Cairo was later built. Maqrizi says that it was located below a domed building known as Qubbat al-Hawa (discussed below),[68] and that the site of the Maydan al-Rumayla of his time, was the area where the markets of horses, donkeys, and camels were located during his lifetime and was originally a great garden *(bustan)* during the Tulunid period. Close to this garden was the site of *al-maydan*, which at the time of Maqrizi was called *al-qubaybat* (the small domes). Therefore, the site of *al-maydan* was located somewhere between Ibn Tulun's palace and his mosque.[69]

Balawi describes *al-maydan* as having many gates (*bab*s). Each gate of the palace had a specific name and specific hours of operation.[70] He adds that on normal days these gates had certain well-known hours when they would be opened and closed.[71] The majority of the army used to enter and exit the palace area from Bab al-Maydan (Gate of the Parade Ground), which was also known as Bab al-Sawalija (Gate of the Polo Mallets). Only the upper class and the nobles, who were closely connected to Ibn Tulun, used Bab al-Khasa (Gate of the Noblemen). Bab al-Gabal (Gate of the Hill, referring to the Muqattam Hills) lead eastward, while Bab al-Daramun (Gate of Daramun) was named after a certain gatekeeper *(hajib)* who sat there. Balawi describes the gatekeeper as a gigantic, black court official whose job was to punish both male Sudanese *ghulam*s and men for their crimes. There were other gates, like Bab al-Da'naj (Gate of Da'naj), named after another gatekeeper, and Bab al-Saj (Gate of the Teak Wood), which derived its name from the wood from which the door was made.

According to Maqrizi, there was another gate called Bab al-Haram (Gate of the Private Quarters or of the Women's Quarters).[72] No one used this gate except the *harim*, the women of Ibn Tulun, as well as the female members of his family and their eunuch servants.[73] Maqrizi also states that within the palace quarters was the building of Dar al-Haram (the Women's Palace).[74] With no further information available it is not possible to suggest exactly where this building was located, but it is likely that it would have been somewhere close to Bab al-Haram. On this basis, it can be argued that Dar al-Haram was part of the great complex of al-Maydan Palace. Logically, the women of the royal family would have had their residence as close as possible to the palace used by the male members of the ruling family, as well as Ibn Tulun himself.

However, the most spectacular of all the gates was Bab al-Siba' (Gate of the Lion). Balawi describes it as being so called because it was decorated with two lions—"*sibu'ayn*"—made of stucco—"*min al-jibs*."[75] It was also know by the name of Bab al-Salah (Gate of Prayer), and Balawi relates that Ibn Tulun ordered a walled structure be erected to cut across Shari' al-A'zam, the main street of the city of al-Qata'i', leading to the mosque of Ibn Tulun.[76] Ibn Tulun would lead the way to prayer from there, which is why it was called Bab al-Salah too.

Bab al-Siba' is most interesting, as it is unrelated to anything else in Islamic Egypt. Unfortunately, there are no descriptions of this gate, except that it was adorned with the stucco lion figures. There is no way of knowing for certain how these lions were placed or how they appeared, but one may speculate that they were statues, which would have been seen from both sides of the gate. However, the fact that they were made from stucco, as confirmed by Balawi, and that no statues made of stucco could have survived from ancient Egypt into Tulunid times, rules out the idea that they could have been ancient Egyptian-style sphinxes.

Another possibility is that the lions were carved in high relief on the wall of the gate. In that case, the lion figures would have been either on one or both sides of the wall. A third possibility is that the two lion figures that decorated the walls of the gate were only of the lions' heads. This is reminiscent of the waterspouts in the Greco-Roman temples in Upper Egypt such as the temples of Horus at Edfu, Hathor at Dendera, Khnum at Esna, and the goddess Isis at Philae/Aswan. In spite of the fact that there is rarely any rain in those areas of Egypt, the lion-head decorated waterspouts were still used. Sadly, there is no way of ever knowing with certainty the nature of those wonderful stucco lion figures, which so impressed the historians who wrote about them.

Balawi adds that Ibn Tulun had three entryways piercing the wall of Bab al-Siba', each as large as any of the other gates.[77] (Maqrizi adds that these gates were set side by side and connected to each other.[78]) Thus, Bab al-Siba' must have taken the form of a triumphal, honorific arch with three openings. The ruler would walk through its central one, while his troops would use the lateral ones.[79] Indeed, Balawi describes the ceremony that took place every Friday, when Ibn Tulun left his palace and went to pray at his mosque. When Ibn Tulun assembled his troops on the Eid feast, or any other celebration, they would walk out of Bab al-Siba' in great numbers, systematically and without creating any chaos. Ibn Tulun would walk out by himself through the central gate, so that no one would crowd around him, while his troops paraded through the ones on either side.[80]

The gate of Bab al-Siba' was probably a triumphal, honorific gateway similar to those used in Roman architecture. In addition, the building would have been a replica of the triple-arched entrance of Bab al-'Amma of the Jawsaq al-Khaqani built by the Caliph al-Mutawakkil in Samarra.[81] Scholars considered the triple gate of Bab al-Siba' to have been arched, but there is no contemporary indication and no description of it being so. However, it is possible that this gate was arched only because of Bab al-'Amma of the Jawsaq al-Khaqani in Samarra and many others, which Ibn Tulun must have been to before coming to Egypt. The arrangement of having a seating area (*majlis*) on top of Bab al-Siba' is also reflective of Bab al-'Amma of the Jawsaq al-Khaqani, which had the same arrangement. Balawi adds that only part of Bab al-Siba' had survived during his time (tenth century). He says it was called the triple gates, and only one of the gates had survived, while the other two had been destroyed or incorporated into other buildings after the destruction of al-Qata'i'.[82]

Balawi also describes a *majlis* above Bab al-Siba', perhaps a pavilion in which Ibn Tulun sat to view the city of al-Qata'i'. On evenings of celebration, such as the night before the Eid, Ibn Tulun used to watch the activities of his young male servants. From this *majlis*, he was able to view the river Nile and Bab al-Madina (City Gate), behind which was a magnificent recreational ground.[83] As well as the *majlis*, Ibn Tulun built a viewing pavilion (*mandhar*), as described by Maqrizi, from where he would watch the horse parades that were known as one of the great wonders of Islam–"*'aja'ib al-Islam*."[84] In another passage, Maqrizi adds that the events at the racing course (*halabat al-sibaq*) took the form of feasts due to the amount of excessive decorations, as the *ghulams* and the military soldiers were dressed in their armor and full weaponry.[85] All kinds of people would attend a feast or religious celebration to watch the parade in which the horses showed off before the horse race started. Unfortunately, the medieval sources do not provide any descriptions of the interior of the palace or its different departments and ceremonial activities. In addition, there is no archaeological evidence of the palace, since it was completely destroyed by Muhammad Sulayman al-Katib in 292 / 904-905. Therefore, a reconstruction of the palace's interior arrangement is an impossible task.

The Tomb of Ibn Tulun

The Mamluk historian Ibn al-Zayyat (d. 813 / 1411) states that the tomb of Ibn Tulun is the smallest of the two tombs standing in the area close to Bab al-Qarafa,[86] which is today opposite Sayyida 'Aisha's shrine. Although Ibn al-Zayyat is most probably mistaken in his account and it is impossible to locate exactly where the tomb stood, we can speculate that the tomb was in that area. In Bab al-Qarafa are two intriguing domed mausoleums, one larger than the other, which are not marked on maps of Cairo and are not listed in the *Index of Mohammedan Monuments*.[87] One might expect that one of them was the tomb of Ibn Tulun, according to the above description by Ibn al-Zayyat, but by examining these two buildings, it is clear that they are nineteenth century Ottoman Turkish in their decorative style and therefore cannot be that of Ibn Tulun.[88]

It is strange that Ibn al-Zayyat's identifies the tomb of Ibn Tulun to be the smaller of the two domes in that area. There is no reason to believe that such an ambitious ruler as Ibn Tulun would choose a small tomb for himself, after he had founded an entire city to commemorate his name and founded a dynasty of his own. It is almost impossible to believe that Ibn Tulun was humble enough to choose to build a small dome, especially when a larger one was next to it. Rulers in general have large egos, and Egyptian rulers had even bigger ones. For them, size was an indicator of greatness. This tradition goes back to ancient Egypt, since which time every ruler of Egypt (pharaonic, Greco-Roman, Islamic, or modern) wanted to build a 'pyramid' of his own. It did not have to be triangular in shape, but it had to be monumental. Ibn Tulun must have been impressed by the view of the Pyramids across the Nile on the western plateau. He had a *majlis* in his palace where he may have sat and dreamed of having a similar one for himself, but did not have the know-how.[89]

It is strange that no information about Ibn Tulun's tomb is provided by Balawi, Ibn Duqmaq, Maqrizi, or any of these historians, and there is no way of knowing for certain how it would have looked. However, it is possible to hypothesize as to its appearance and location. Since Ibn Tulun grew up in Samarra, the only building the tomb might resemble is Qubbat al-Salaybiya in Samarra:[90] an octagonal domical building with pointed arched openings on each side, which was believed to be a tomb of some significance or a pavilion of some sort. One can imagine that the tomb may have been inspired by the architecture of Qubbat al-Salaybiya. This meant that the tomb of Ibn Tulun would have been a square domical building, open on four sides, with his body underground and some sort of a tombstone or cenotaph above ground, possibly bearing an inscription, which would likely be in marble and in foliated Kufic, giving the name of Ahmad Ibn Tulun, his date of birth, reign in Egypt, and date of death.[91]

One may also assume that the area where the tomb of Ibn Tulun was located used to be the main cemetery area of the city. According to the historians Ibn Duqmaq and Maqrizi, this area of al-Qata'i' was a cemetery for Christians and Jews, which Ibn Tulun ordered to be destroyed—"*hadama*."[92] This is indicated by George Salmon, as he placed the cemetery of Christians and Jews in that area (fig. 13), which would be directly south of the hippodrome of the city of al-Qata'i'.

Another possibility is that the tomb was located just on the southern part of the open parade ground. This would have been a successful location since it would have been positioned in a place in which it could be observed and seen from anywhere in the city. If so, it would suggest it was intended for the tomb to be visible from the open parade ground, which is where the population would go for the usual daily entertainment, meaning the memory of Ibn Tulun and his glorious period would be preserved. Such an idea might seem far-fetched, but the same arrangement was followed in Roman cities. A good example of such a concept is seen in the city of Antinopolis (known today as Sheikh ʻAbada), near Malawi in Upper Egypt, which was built by the Emperor Hadrian for his beloved friend Antinos. In Antinopolis, its great hippodrome was oriented toward the city's *tetra-pylon*, which was adorned with tens of statues of Antinos on its columns, so that he would always be remembered.[93] One could argue that this Roman concept was followed in Ibn Tulun's new capital city of al-Qata'iʻ. This would have created a constant visual memory that was unprecedented in Islamic Egypt and the result would have been architecturally most successful.

Qubbat al-Hawa

Balawi mentions that there was a domical building erected near the Muqattam Hills called Qubbat al-Hawa and that it overlooked the entire city. He says that it had originally been built for Caliph al-Ma'mun during his visit to Egypt, before his death in 832 AD.[94] In another passage he adds that the building belonged to Ibn Tulun and that it overlooked the Nile and all the land of the city. Maqrizi adds that this dome was built on the cliff or slope of the plateau where the Citadel of Cairo was later constructed.[95] In his description of the Citadel, Maqrizi describes the hill on which it was built as having once been occupied by the domed building of Qubbat al-Hawa, just above the palace. He quotes the historian al-Kindi to the effect that it was built in 195 AH / 810 AD.[96] He adds that Ibn Tulun used this building frequently, furnishing and decorating it in a fashion that would suit every season of the year, and that later on Ibn Tulun's son and successor Khumarawiya also used it.

It appears that Qubbat al-Hawa was used as a residence or a lounge that was open and oriented toward the strong, fresh north winds of the city. During the Tulunid period, it was a pleasure resort of sorts, where

Ibn Tulun, and later Khumarawiya, would go to enjoy a spectacular panoramic view of his royal palace and the whole city. One may visualize how the view of the city may have looked from the dome of Qubbat al-Hawa. From the hill looking toward the west, one would have the following view: The royal Palace of al-Maydan would be directly below, with the open parade ground below it. In the center of the parade ground would be the triple gate of Bab al-Siba', from which started the main street of Shari' al-A'zam, which then twined into Dar al-Imara and the mosque of Ibn Tulun, on the rock knoll of Gabal Yashkur. To the south of Gabal Yashkur were the hills of Tilal Zinhum, while to its west were those of Qala'at al-Kabsh. From the same virtual spot of Qubbat al-Hawa, one would see the lake of Birkat al-Fil, which was in the midst of agricultural lands. Farther west, one would be able to see the canal of al-Khalig, which flowed from south to north. Then there would be green agricultural lands before one would see the great width of the river Nile. On the opposite side of the Nile, there would be more of the green agricultural lands. On the horizon would be the western plateau, which was surmounted by the Pyramids of Giza, the pyramids of Abusir, the step pyramid of Saqqara, and the pyramids of Dahshur. From the same virtual spot, if one looked slightly to the lower left, one would see the domical mausoleum of Ibn Tulun, which was south of the open parade ground while farther to the west would have been the *bimaristan*. To the south would have been what was once the city of al-'Askar, and south of it would have been the tall buildings of Fustat. The view of Ibn Tulun's lost city of al-Qata'i' must have been a spectacular one (see figs. 13, 14, 19).

The Legacy of Khumarawiya

When Ahmad Ibn Tulun died in 884, he was succeeded by his legendary son Khumarawiya, who inherited the powerful wealth of his father but was weaker and indulged in the eccentricities and the extreme pleasures of life.[97] In doing so, Maqrizi says that Khumarawiya enlarged the Palace of al-Maydan and converted the open parade ground into a large exotic garden *(bustan)* that had tropical trees, roses, jasmine, lilies, and shrubs.[98] Khumarawiya hated the sight of the stalks of trees

and so ordered that every tree have its trunk and branches coated in sheets of gilded copper, which were lined with water pipes made of lead. This meant that every tree was not only a gilded lily, but also a pretty fountain running through the shady gardens.[99] In addition to the exotic trees, Khumarawiya had exotic fruits, such as apricots grafted into almonds, and an elaborate pigeon house. He built another open parade ground a short distance away from his father's, and this one had horseback racing tournaments almost every day and night.[100]

Khumarawiya also built another domical pavilion in his palace, which he called *al-dikka*, not to be confused with that of a mosque. He had it furnished with different types of furniture, curtains, and carpets, which would be removed according to the season of the year. Maqrizi says that the building matched—"*tudahi*"—that of Qubbat al-Hawa, which Ibn Tulun enjoyed sitting in to admire the great view. Khumarawiya, like his father, used *al-dikka* frequently, to take in the view of his botanical gardens and trees, as well as the desert, the River Nile, the hills, and everything else in the city. It may have been that *al-dikka* pavilion was used instead of Qubbat al-Hawa, as it was inside the palace complex and probably nearer to his residence. Although not as high as Qubbat al-Hawa, it must have still been high enough to have given Khumarawiya a good view of the area, even if the view from above at Qubbat al-Hawa must have been a much nicer one, as in figures 13 and 19.

Maqrizi continues his account to say that walls of the palace of Khumarawiya were decorated with sheets of gold studded with lapis lazuli—"*bi-l-dhahab al-mujawal bi-l-azaward*."[101] Khumarawiya was also more of a romantic person, who loved his wife Buran a great deal and erected for her a beautiful pavilion called Bayt al-Dhahab (House of Gold), which was lined entirely with gold.[102] Inside the pavilion he had wooden statues of himself, as well as his wives, which were slightly larger than life and were dressed in textiles woven with gold threads to look as if they were fully gold garments. Khumarawiya's own statue had golden trousers, while his turban was encrusted with jewels. Every evening Khumarawiya would sit on the terrace of the House of Gold or in his great *bustan* listening to poets reciting or to his favorite female slaves singing.[103]

19 – View of the city of al-Qata'i' from a virtual point where the Cairo Citadel is located.

The extent of Khumarawiya's luxurious life had no end. He "conceived what was probably the ultimate in sybaritic self-indulgence"[104] surpassing all other rulers in Egypt since. As he suffered from insomnia, his physicians advised him that he ought to be rocked gently to sleep every night. Khumarawiya took extreme measures, ordering a pool of fifty cubits in length by fifty in width in his Bayt al-Dhahab,[105] and this pool was filled with mercury (or quicksilver). He would sleep on an air-blown mattress of inflated skins that floated on top of the pool of mercury every night. The mattress was tied to the edges of the pool with silken cords. The movement of the mercury made small waves, which lapped gently to and fro, until he fell asleep.[106] Maqrizi ends his account by saying that when the moonlight shined on his pool of mercury, its reflection gave the most admirable effect.[107]

Khumarawiya's love for the exotic culminated in his magnificent zoo. He had a special house known as Bayt al-Asad (Lion House), which had cages housing a lion or a lioness.[108] Each cage had a special door where the keeper could enter to feed them, clean the cage, as well as sand the floor, and each had its own running water. Sometimes when Khumarawiya ordered that his lions be set free to play in the gardens, all of Fustat and al-Qata'i' would shake from the roars of the lions fighting and playing with each other. The lions were so well trained that they knew to go back to their quarters when the keeper called them by name.[109]

Maqrizi adds that the most extraordinary of the lions was Khumarawiya's own pet, called Zouraik (the little blue-eyed one) because it had blue eyes. He acted as his bodyguard,[110] and Khumarawiya gave him a collar of gold and would feed him chickens and goats. Zouraik slept next to his master, no matter where he was. Other than his beloved lions, Khumarawiya had chambers built for the rest of his zoo: the ponies *(bighal)*, tigers *(numur)*, leopards *(fuhud)*, giraffes *(zarafat)*, and elephants *(fiyala)*.[111] When Khumarawiya was killed in Damascus by his servants and concubines, his blue-eyed lion Zouraik was not

20 – A reconstructed bird's eye view of the original mosque of Ibn Tulun and the building of Dar al-Imara behind it from a elevated northern point. More of the market can be seen with stalls surrounding the mosque. The spiral-shaped minaret is based on the one in Samarra, but surmounted with a boat-like finial. On each side of the minaret is a rectangular building. The one on the right is the *mayda'a*, while the one on the left is the *khizanat al-sharab*. The wooden gilded dome (*fawwara*) is in the middle of the *sahn*.

there to save him. His body was brought back to al-Qata'i' where it was buried near his father, probably in the same tomb.

It is interesting to note that Khumarawiya had created a world of extravagance that Egypt had not seen since the time of the ancient Egyptians–it was a unique moment in Egypt's history. The zoo he created appears to have been well built, organized, and had well-trained animals. This idea of a zoo in a royal palace was never repeated–there is no evidence that anything similar was created during the Fatimid period, or even later, during the Mamluk period, the golden age of Islamic Egypt. However, a similarity can be seen with the ancient Egyptian New Kingdom period. On the walls of the tomb of the Vizier Rekhmyra, in the west bank of Luxor, he boasts of the great events he had seen during his career, one of such events was the presenting of animals from Africa to the king of Egypt at the time King Tutmosis III in the fifteenth century BC. The tomb shows extraordinary scenes of a baby elephant, an anteater, baboons, cheetahs, and a giraffe, which has a little monkey climbing over its neck.[112]

Khumarawiya was succeeded by his son Abu al-'Asakir Gaysh, then by Abu Musa Harun, and finally by Shayban Ibn Ahmad Ibn Tulun, who was weak and was easily deposed when the Abbasid general Muhammad Sulayman al-Katib attacked Egypt in 905.[113] The splendid city of al-Qata'i' was destroyed. Al-Katib and his troops spent four months devastating al-Qata'i', they "invaded the houses, profaned the harem, dishonored the citizens, violated the virgins, chased the women, got up to all sort of infamies, and threw people out of their homes."[114] Then, they stripped it of its wealth and opened the prisons. They also decimated the beautiful gardens and cut off the heads of most of the black troops who had been the Tulunid bodyguards. The royal Tulunid city of al-Qata'i' thereafter died a slow death. Both cities of al-'Askar and al-Qata'i' were in such a miserable state that a century and a half later a wall was built around them to hide them from the rest of the great capital of al-Qahira–Cairo.

PART TWO

THE MOSQUE OF IBN TULUN: HISTORY AND ARCHITECTURE

Construction of the mosque of Ibn Tulun began in 263 AH / 876–77 AD and was completed in Ramadan 265 AH / April–May 879, making it the primary mosque of the new city of al-Qata'i'.[1] It was the third congregational mosque built in Egypt after the mosque of 'Amr Ibn al-'As (the first mosque built in Egypt and Africa) in the city of Fustat and the mosque of al-'Askar (in the nearby city of al-'Askar). The mosque of 'Amr Ibn al-'As has been enlarged, altered, and restored over the centuries, while the mosque of al-'Askar was destroyed long ago. As a result, the mosque of Ibn Tulun is the longest surviving of these three oldest mosques in Egypt.[2]

5 The Present-Day Mosque

The mosque is located in a densely populated district of Cairo called Talun. It lies off the famous street (*shari'*) of Saliba, which is the main artery linking the Citadel of Cairo to the popular shrine and mosque of Sayyida Zaynab (see fig. 22, plan A). To the north and northwest of the mosque is the Mamluk higher religious institute (*madrasa*) of Amir Sarghatmish (1356), which is adjacent to the mosque and al-Duhdira Street.To the southwest side is the narrow alley of al-Ziyada Street. To the southeast are Tulun Street and the famous Ottoman houses of Bayt Amna Bint Salem (1540) and Bayt al-Kiritliya (1631), which together are known as the Gayer-Anderson House/Museum. The latter is also adjacent to the mosque. Finally, on the northeast side is Ahmad Ibn Tulun Street, which constitutes the main approach to the mosque (see general views of the mosque in figures 8 and 23).

21 – Close-up of the *mabkhara*-shaped finial atop the unique spiral-shaped minaret.

The mosque of Ibn Tulun was built on a rock knoll, which was known as Gabal (hill) Yashkur (figs. 16, 24). It is a typical *riwaq*-type of mosque, meaning that it consists of a large open court (*sahn*) surrounded by arcades (*riwaq*s) on all four sides (fig. 22, plan A).[1] Three sides feature two *riwaq*s, while the side oriented toward Mecca (*qibla*) consists of five *riwaq*s. Thick robust piers sustain elegant pointed arches, upon which a high wooden ceiling is supported (fig. 26). The soffits of the elegant pointed arches would have been decorated with stucco ornaments. Only those facing the *sahn* on the southwestern and northwestern sides can be seen today.[2] The spandrels of the arches have pointed windows and rosette decorations flanking those windows (fig. 28). A long wooden frieze of inscriptions runs below the ceiling of a section of the mosque (fig. 27).

A domical structure, which once acted as a fountain (*fisqiya*), dominates the middle of the *sahn* (fig. 30). The dome has a pointed-arch profile and is supported by a large, stepped transitional zone that lies

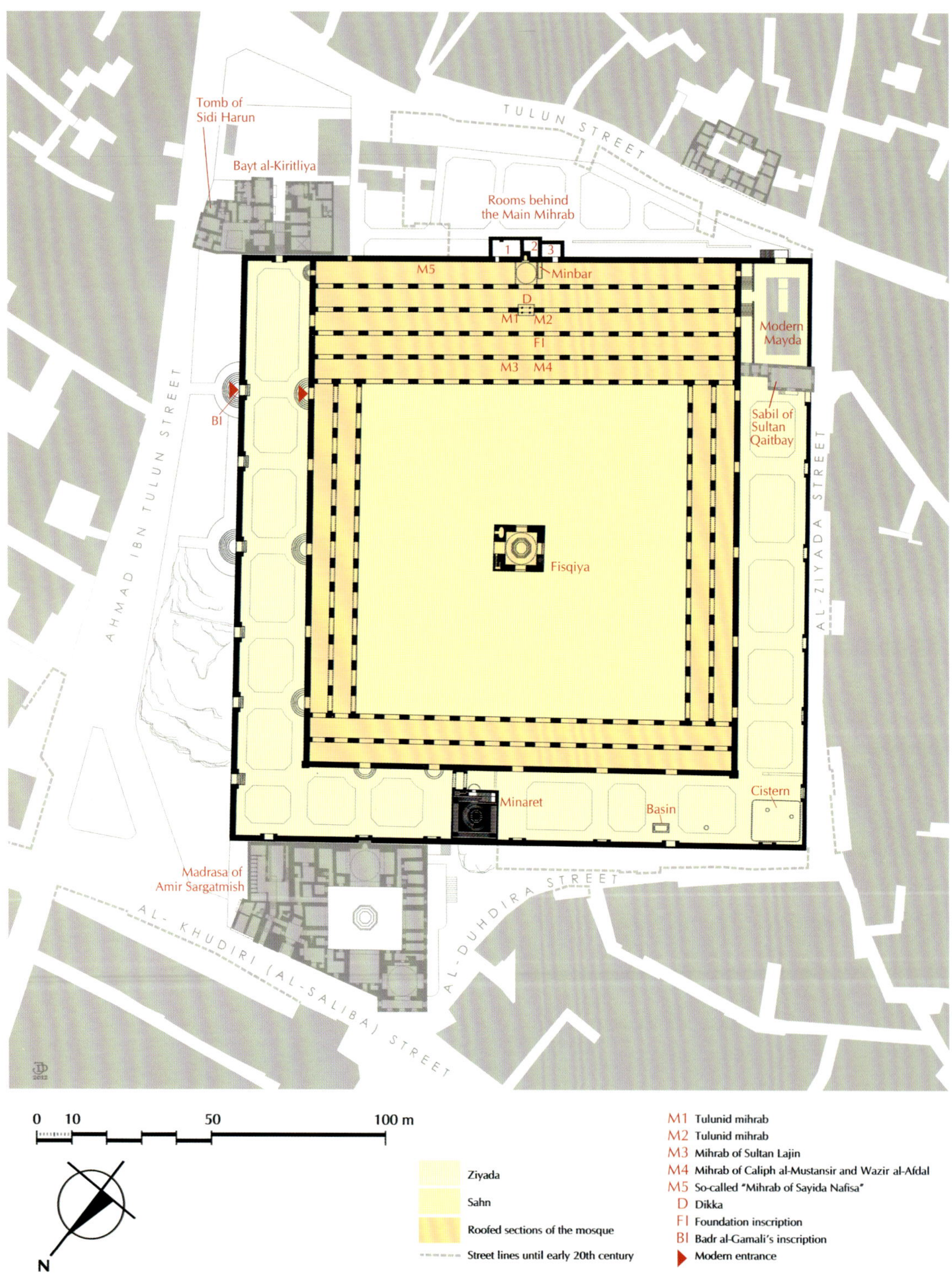

Tomb of Sidi Harun
Bayt al-Kiritliya
Rooms behind the Main Mihrab
TULUN STREET
M5
Minbar
D
M1
M2
F1
M3
M4
Modern Mayda
Sabil of Sultan Qaitbay
BI
AHMAD IBN TULUN STREET
AL-ZIYADA STREET
Fisqiya
Minaret
Basin
Cistern
Madrasa of Amir Sargatmish
AL-DUHDIRA STREET
AL-KHUDIRI (AL-SALIBA) STREET
0 10 50 100 m
N
Ziyada
Sahn
Roofed sections of the mosque
Street lines until early 20th century
M1 Tulunid mihrab
M2 Tulunid mihrab
M3 Mihrab of Sultan Lajin
M4 Mihrab of Caliph al-Mustansir and Wazir al-Afdal
M5 So-called "Mihrab of Sayida Nafisa"
D Dikka
FI Foundation inscription
BI Badr al-Gamali's inscription
Modern entrance

over a large drum. The building has pointed arched entrances on its four sides. The floor of the building is paved in stone. In the middle is an octagonal depression, which once served as a fountain (fig. 31). The dome is supported by a wonderful system of squinches (fig. 32). The floor of the whole mosque is made entirely of stone.

The walls of the mosque itself are high and have large rectangular doors, all of which are symmetrical in their arrangement, and some of which are preceded by a flight of steps from the street up to the mosque (fig. 114). The upper part of the walls is pierced by pointed, arched openings that serve as windows. Each window has a stucco grille of a different geometric or floral design. Between the windows on the exterior of the façade are niches with shell decorations, which alternate with the windows (figs. 33, 34, 35). The walls are topped on all four sides by a row of intricate remarkable crenellations that are characteristic of the mosque (fig. 36). The mosque is surrounded by another high wall on three sides (fig. 22, plan A). This outer wall features large doors that correspond to those of the inner walls, thus being symmetrical in their arrangement like those on the inner ones, and are topped by the same type of crenellations. The area between the two walls of the mosque is called a *ziyada*, which means an additional open space (figs. 8, 23, 33, 34, 35, 114).

22, plan A – The present-day mosque of Ibn Tulun and its environs.

In the middle of the *qibla* wall on the interior is the usual main niche that gives the direction to Mecca (*mihrab*) and that is flanked by four marble columns, two on each side.[3] Each pair of columns consists of a modified Corinthian capital and a two-zoned basket-like capital (figs. 37, 98). The upper part of the *mihrab* consists of a wooden conch with traces of faint paintings, while the middle part has a magnificent band of a glass mosaic Naskhi inscription. The lower part of the *mihrab* is decorated with marble panels. The *mihrab* is also decorated with stucco and has a rectangular frame. Above it is a wooden band featuring a Kufic inscription (see appendix, no. 9). The *mihrab* is not correctly oriented to Mecca, as shall be discussed later. Next to the *mihrab* is a large monumental wooden pulpit (*minbar*) used for the Friday sermon (see fig. 38). Above the *mihrab* is a small wooden dome and behind it are three rooms, which can be entered from doors along the *qibla* wall on both sides of the *mihrab* and the *minbar*. There are two smaller doors on the far ends of the same wall (fig. 22, plan A).

The *qibla riwaq* has five flat stucco *mihrabs*. Two pairs of flat *mihrabs* flank each other along the axis of the main *mihrab* (fig. 1, plan A; figs. 39–46). The fifth flat *mihrab* is located to the left of the main one (figs. 45, 46). The symmetrical flat *mihrabs* are placed on the piers flanking a high platform on columns used to deliver prayers *(dikkat al-muballigh)* on the second *riwaq* from the *qibla* wall (figs. 39–41). Two other flat *mihrabs* are located along the same axis on the fourth *riwaq* away from the *qibla* wall (figs. 42–44). Along the same axis of the main *mihrab*, on the third *riwaq* from the *qibla*, there is a marble block containing part of the foundation inscription of the mosque (fig. 22, plan A (FI); figs. 47, 48).

In the northwestern *ziyada* stands the mosque's spiral-shaped minaret (fig. 49). It is connected to the mosque proper by a bridge to the roof of the building. The passageway under the bridge is formed of large horseshoe arches (fig. 50). Creswell describes the interior of the arches as being "joined by a barrel vault, with its axis at right angles to the wall of the mosque. The vault rests on a molded cornice which is carried across the ends, where it is supported in each case by four very curious brackets, for which the French term is *modillons a copeaux*"[4] (fig. 51). The entrance to the minaret, which is also decorated with a handsome horseshoe arch, gives way immediately to the stairs of the minaret (fig. 52). The spiral-shaped minaret consists of four distinct stories: the lowest is quadrangular, the next is circular, and the final two are octagonal. The four sides of the quadrangular story are decorated with blind horseshoe-arched windows, each featuring a column decorated with spirals. The circular story is plain, while the upper stories are separated by and decorated with tiers of *muqarnas* (alveolus developed from stalactites). Above the top two stories is a shallow-ribbed dome surmounted by a copper crescent (fig. 21). An earlier minaret in Samarra inspired the spiral-shaped one of the mosque of Ibn Tulun (fig. 58).

23 – The eastern side of the mosque of Ibn Tulun from the top of an apartment building opposite.

North of the minaret are the foundations of a previous structure which takes the form of a rectangular basin (fig. 53). Farther north, in the corner of the *ziyada*, is a palm tree under which are the remains of a water cistern. On the south side of the southwestern *ziyada* is a building that once served as a fountain house *(sabil)* of Sultan Qaitbay (figs. 35, 54). Behind this building and to its south is a modern building that is currently used as the *mayda'a* (ablution place). This *mayda'a* is entered from a door in the southeast wall of the mosque (the extension of the *qibla* wall) and from another door in the *qibla riwaq* (fig. 22, plan A).

24 – The approach to the mosque along Ahmad Ibn Tulun Street, showing the main façade built directly on the hill of Gabal Yashkur.

25 – The main façade on the northeastern side of the mosque, illustrating how it is built directly over the bedrock of the hill of Gabal Yashkur, and the steps leading to the large doors of the mosque.

26 – The interior of the mosque of Ibn Tulun showing the thick robust piers, supporting pointed arches with Samarra-style stucco decorations on their soffits. The domical fountain *(fisqiya)* and the spiral-shaped minaret can also be seen through the arches.

27 – Detail of the wooden Qur'anic inscription below the ceiling of the mosque—the longest continuous inscription in the Islamic world when the mosque of Ibn Tulun was built.

28 – Details of the spandrels of the elegant pointed arches showing other pointed arched openings/windows with column-like decorations on their lower parts and rosettes flanking them on either side.

29 – One of the 128 windows that pierce the walls of the mosque of Ibn Tulun, each of which is in the shape of a pointed arch with stucco grilles of different geometric or floral designs.

30 [NEXT PAGE] – View of the interior of the mosque of Ibn Tulun, showing the dominant domical *fisqiya* in the middle of the open court and the unique spiral-shaped minaret.

31 – The interior of the domical *fisqiya* showing the octagonal depression, which once served as the basin of a fountain.

32 – The interior of the domical *fisqiya* from below, showing the sophisticated system of squinches in its transitional zone, as well as part of the stucco inscriptions from *Ayat al-Wudu'* (Verse of Ablution).

33 – The northeastern *ziyada* showing the inner walls of the mosque proper and the large rectangular doors and pointed arched windows, with alternating shell-decorated niches.

34 – The northwestern *ziyada* showing the spiral-shaped minaret and the bridge that leads to the roof of the mosque.

35 – The southwestern *ziyada* showing the Mamluk *sabil* of Sultan Qaitbay at its far end.

36 – Shadows of the remarkable crenellations reflected on the wall of the mosque—they are characteristic of the mosque of Ibn Tulun, a motif never repeated in Cairo's Islamic architecture.

37 – Detail of the main *mihrab* with a pair of columns flanking each side. Each pair has modified Corinthian capitals and two zoned basket-like capitals in the Coptic style. In the middle runs a fantastic mosaic inscription in Naskhi script of the Sunni *shahada* (bearing witness that there is no God but Allah and Muhammad is His messenger)—a masterpiece of its kind.

38 – The area of the main *mihrab* from the south (right) side of the *riwaq* showing the monumental *minbar* of Sultan Lajin (1296), the wooden dome above, and a door leading to two of the three rooms behind the main *mihrab*.

39 – Interior of the *qibla riwaq* showing the two flat stucco *mihrab*s from the Tulunid period (see fig. 22, plan A, M1 and M2), and the *dikka* between them.

40 and 41 – The flat stucco Tulunid *mihrabs*. (Left: see see fig. 22, plan A, M1; Right: fig. 22, plan A, M2).

42 – Interior of the *qibla riwaq* showing two flat stucco *mihrab*s from the Fatimid and Mamluk periods (see fig. 22, plan A, M3 and M4).

43 – Remains of a flat stucco *mihrab* (see fig. 22, plan A, M3), attributed to Sultan Lajin in 1296.

44 – The flat stucco *mihrab* of the Caliph al-Mustansir and the Vizier al-Afdal (see fig. 22, plan A, M4). According to Van Berchem, it dates to the year 1094.

45 – The interior of the *qibla riwaq* showing the so-called *mihrab* of Sayyida Nafisa, attributed to Sutlan Lajin (1296), at the far end on the *qibla* wall (see fig. 22, plan A, M5).

46 – The so-called *mihrab* of Sayyida Nafisa, attributed to Sutlan Lajin (1296) (see fig. 22, plan A, M5).

47 – The marble block containing part of the foundation inscription incorrectly placed on a pier in the *qibla riwaq* (see fig. 22, plan A, FI).

48 – Detail of the right-hand marble block containing the foundation inscription (see fig. 22, plan A, FI).

49 – The unique spiral-shaped minaret of the mosque of Ibn Tulun, which was added in stages at a later date, after the original one had fallen into ruin.

50 – The gigantic horseshoe arch that carries the bridge connecting the lower story of the spiral-shaped minaret with the roof of the mosque.

51 – The puzzling stone decorations that support a barrel vault underneath the bridge that connects the spiral-shaped minaret with the roof of the mosque, described by Creswell as "*modillon à copeaux*."

52 – The handsome horseshoe arched entrance leads to the top of the spiral-shaped minaret and the roof of the mosque.

53 – View from the top of the spiral-shaped minaret showing the northwest *ziyada* area with a reconstructed basin, which was probably part of an older *mayda'a*. A dome palm tree, above the remains of a dried-up cistern, can also be seen.

54 – The *sabil* of Sultan Qaitbay built in the southwest *ziyada* (see figs. 22, plan A; 35).

The Tulunid Period

6

Ahmad Ibn Tulun was a native of Samarra who was appointed governor *(wali)* of Egypt by the Abbasid caliph in Baghdad. As he was not Egyptian, he sought to gain the favor of the local population he was ruling over. To fulfill his political program of transforming Egypt from a mere province of the Abbasid caliphate into an independent state, he sought to legitimize his status in Egypt by any means possible. Construction of the mosque began in 263 AH / 876 AD and was completed in 265 / 878,[1] and the aim was to satisfy the need for a larger structure. According to the tenth century historian Balawi, Ahmad Ibn Tulun used to pray on Fridays in the old mosque of al-ʻAskar, which was still active during his time.[2] Al-ʻAskar mosque was the second largest state mosque built in Egypt after that of ʻAmr Ibn al-ʻAs in Fustat. But when it became too small for the rapidly growing population, Ibn Tulun ordered the new mosque built.[3] Fourteenth-century historians Ibn Duqmaq and Maqrizi report the mosque was built because the people of Egypt complained to Ibn Tulun that the large numbers of people who came for prayers made the mosque of al-ʻAskar too small for Ibn Tulun's entourage, his army of soldiers and his Sudanese slaves.[4]

55 – An example of an arch that is pointed and stilted, the first of its kind in Egypt. According to Robert Williams (*The Moslem World* VIII/3 (July 1918), 229), this type of arch was used for some two hundred years before it became common in Europe.

The limestone knoll of Gabal Yashkur was first quarried and leveled.[5] Ibn Tulun had the mosque built of lime, ashes, and well-baked red bricks extending up to the ceiling.[6] He had the structure whitewashed and decorated. The floor was furnished with mats. Lamps were hung from the ceiling by long, thick chains, and caskets of Qur'an manuscripts were brought there.[7] Scholars of jurisprudence and Qur'an reciters were appointed.[8] Historians recount that a band of amber was pasted over the entire mosque to emit a pleasant odor, which would spread among the worshipers.[9] The mosque originally had a *minbar*, later moved to another mosque.[10]

On the day of the mosque's inauguration, Ibn Tulun had prepared elaborate banquets for the poor as an expression of charity, and he provided a meal for all the people who attended. It was designated as a great and noble day.[11] However, Ibn Duqmaq says that the people refused to pray in the mosque at first.[12] One of their complaints was that they did not know the source of money used to construct the mosque,[13] and they were probably worried that it would result in higher taxes. One Friday, Ibn Tulun brought people together in the mosque and after delivering the sermon *(khutba)* and swearing in the name of God, he uttered the *shahada* and claimed that he had built the mosque from a treasure *(kanz)* he had found nearby in the Muqattam Hills.[14] Ibn Duqmaq adds that while Ibn Tulun was making his point about the source of the money, he pointed up at the minaret of his mosque to indicate that the copper boat-shaped finial *('ushari)* surmounting it had been discovered in the same treasure.[15] The people were convinced by the story and began to pray in the mosque in great numbers.[16]

Balawi confirms this account and reports that Ibn Tulun built his mosque with money God had bestowed on him and which he found on top of the Muqattam Hills at a site called Tannur Fir'awn (Pharaoh's Lantern).[17] The story goes that while Ibn Tulun was hunting in the desert, one of his young male slaves *(ghilman)* fell off his horse when the horse's foot became stuck in a hole *(fatq)*.[18] As he was clearing the sand from the hole and rescuing the horse, he discovered an enormous sum of money, estimated at one million dinars.[19] Another historian, Abu al-Mahasin Ibn Taghribirdi (d. 874 AH / 1469 AD), states that the horse, which belonged to one of Ibn Tulun's friends, got stuck in a tomb *(qabr)* in the middle of the desert, rather than in a hole.[20]

The treasure's discovery soon became widely known. Ibn Tulun informed the Caliph al-Mu'tamid of Baghdad about it, telling him that he would like to spend the money on acts of piety or charitable projects.[21] The caliph consented to Ibn Tulun's wishes.[22] This story suggests that Ibn Tulun had actually found two lucrative treasures, rather than just one. The first treasure was discovered in the Muqattam Hills and paid for the mosque as well as the aqueduct, while the second was found while Ibn Tulun was hunting in the desert and paid for the hospital *(bimaristan)*.

When Ibn Tulun decided to build a new mosque, he had certain requirements that his architects did not understand. Balawi notes that when news about the new mosque reached al-Nasrani (the imprisoned architect who had built the aqueduct in Basatin), he wrote to Ibn Tulun: "I will construct it for the Amir, God supported him, as he wishes and chooses, without columns, except the two flanking the *qibla* (meaning the *mihrab*)."[23] It seems that Ibn Tulun was impressed with what he heard. He ordered parchment to be brought to him, on which al-Nasrani drew a sketch. Ibn Tulun so admired the plans that he rewarded the architect al-Nasrani with a robe of honor, provided him 100,000 dinars for the initial construction, and promised him more funds if needed.[24]

After appointing al-Nasrani, Ibn Tulun decided to build his mosque on top of Gabal Yashkur on the northern outskirts of the cities of al-'Askar and Fustat.[25] Pious people advised Ibn Tulun to build his mosque on this site, which had both holy and folkloric legends attached to it and was a popular site for righteous people to pray.[26] According to Ibn Duqmaq and Maqrizi, this rocky knoll was believed by the local population to be the place where God spoke to the Prophet Moses, where the Burning Bush was located, and where Moses confronted Pharaoh's magicians.[27] In addition, the knoll was believed to be the landing site of the Prophet Noah's ark after the great flood and the place where the Prophet Abraham offered his sacrifice.[28] Maqrizi adds that Ibn Tulun gave orders to remove the Jewish and Christian cemeteries to build his city,[29] which had previously been at that site. However, the area on which the mosque was built was an open space that did not have any previous constructions,[30] except for a small tomb attributed to the Prophet Harun (Aaron), the brother of Moses.[31]

Ibn Duqmaq, quoting al-Yaghmuri, states that Ibn Tulun wanted to build a structure that would survive any disaster, no matter what happened in Egypt. He insisted that even if the urban center of "Misr" (Fustat and al-'Askar) burnt down or was inundated by the Nile, the mosque had to survive.[32] In fact, the whole mosque was built on the solid bedrock of Gabal Yashkur, thus protecting the mosque from flooding, fire, and earthquakes (figs. 17, 19).[33] According to popular folk legends collected by historian John Gayer-Anderson, Ibn Tulun "set the foundation of his mosque upon a living rock so that no flood has been able to shift or destroy it."[34] Islamic archaeologist George Scanlon believes that Frank Lloyd Wright used the same idea in building the Great Imperial Hotel in Tokyo in 1922.[35] Scanlon also observed during his years of excavations at Fustat that it had been used before Ibn Tulun's time.[36] It appears that this method of building directly over solid bedrock is derived from the buildings in Fustat rather than being an innovation of Ibn Tulun. Building directly on bedrock differs from building on foundations, as the former method helps a structure to be more flexible during earthquakes. Ancient structures in Egypt were usually built on a solid foundation first, but the buildings at Fustat and the mosque of Ibn Tulun were built directly onto the bedrock. This was a very successful building practice, which helped the mosque withstand earthquakes that have struck Egypt up to the present day.[37]

The *Mihrabs*

Ibn Duqmaq relates that after the mosque was completed, a group of people inquired why the (main) *mihrab* of the mosque did not follow precisely the *qibla* orientation to Mecca. Ibn Tulun explained that there was disagreement between the engineers and architects during the mosque's construction. He explained that the Prophet Muhammad appeared to him in a dream and ordered him to build the mosque this way (see its position in figure 22, plan A). Then the Prophet drew the design of the *mihrab* on the floor and ordered Ibn Tulun to trace it exactly. The next day at dawn, Ibn Tulun hurried to the mosque and went to the place where he had seen the Prophet in his dream. To his surprise, he found the design on the mosque's floor. Perceiving it as a miraculous act, he had the *mihrab* designed in that fashion. The people who had challenged him were impressed by his explanation. When they left the meeting, they spread the news around the city.[38] Based on the Prophet's design of the *mihrab*, the mosque was considered a wonderful building.[39] The exact orientation of the mosque of Ibn Tulun is 141.5 degrees southeast. The *qibla* orientation of Egypt is 136.5 degrees.[40] The deviation is thus not so great that people should refuse to pray in the mosque. In comparison to other buildings, the mosque of Ibn Tulun does not deviate much; nearly all mosques in Cairo are off by a few degrees.[41]

The Non-Use of Columns

According to Balawi, Ibn Tulun's architect al-Nasrani estimated that three hundred columns would be required to build the mosque.[42]Al-Nasrani deemed it impossible to find such a number of columns except by reaching out to expropriate columns from churches in rural areas and searching among ruins of sites that had already been destroyed. However, Ibn Tulun disapproved of this idea and became disheartened.[43] Balawi's account is rather strange as all early mosques in Egypt used columns from earlier ancient monuments, such as the original mosque of 'Amr Ibn al-'As, as well as most mosques of the Fatimid and Mamluk periods.[44] It was a common practice, so it is possible that Ibn Tulun rejected the idea because he intended to use the same type of structure as those in the mosque of al-Mutawakkil in Samarra. This mosque had rectangular piers with columns at their corners, and indeed in the mosque of Ibn Tulun there are rectangular piers with column-like decorations at the corners (figs. 10, 26).

It is well known that the ancient Egyptians invented the architectural element known as the column—it was Imhotep, the architect of the Third Dynasty King Netjerikhet (popularly known as Zoser) of the Old Kingdom period (2700 BC), who invented them. In the funerary complex of the step pyramid at Saqqara, Imhotep built columns that were engaged to the walls next to them. Hence, they were called 'engaged columns' and were the first stone columns known in history. They were tapered and built in slices placed on top of each other, constituting elegant forms. From that time, stone columns were developed in Egypt (also in the Old Kingdom period), mostly in the form of monolithic blocks of different kinds of stone found in the Nile Valley. In later periods, this method of support was exported to the Fertile Crescent and from there to Anatolia, Greece, the Mediterranean, and the Roman world. It must have been difficult for an Egyptian architect to understand exactly what Ibn Tulun was trying to explain—that he wanted rectangular piers in his mosque instead of traditional circular columns. At the same time, if Ibn Tulun had used columns from earlier destroyed churches and ancient monuments, it would have been easier for his architect than building new piers out of firebrick. Thus, one may conclude that Ibn Tulun intended to build the piers in order to emulate the mosque of al-Mutawakkil in Samarra.

Maqrizi relates that after the completion of the mosque people refused to pray in it,[45] as noted earlier, and among their complaints was the mosque's lack of columns.[46] Maqrizi also remarks that Ibn Tulun was advised not to use marble columns in his mosque,[47] with the absurd justification that marble does not withstand fire.[48] This suggests that he was looking for any excuse to avoid columns so as to imitate the Great Mosque of al-Mutawakkil in Samara. Therefore, Ibn Tulun used neither marble nor columns in his mosque, except for the columns flanking the main *mihrab* and in the *fawwara* (figs. 37, 98, 99).

The use of rectangular piers instead of circular columns was an innovation in Islamic Egypt. We may assume that the original mosque of 'Amr Ibn al-'As was built of columns taken from ancient ruins. Similarly, one would assume the same was done in the mosque of al-'Askar, as well as the smaller mosques in Fustat and al-'Askar. However, the same type of rectangular pier was later replicated in the mosques of the Fatimid Caliph al-Hakim and that of Sultan al-Zahir Baybars (known as al-Dahir).

The Pointed Arches

The rectangular piers support some of the most elegant pointed arches in the world (fig. 55). The historian Creswell mentions that the form of these arches varies only slightly in span and rise but all are pointed and stilted.[49] The stilted part has a very slight return but cannot be considered a horseshoe arch. Robert Williams argues that this type of arch was used in Arab architecture two hundred years before it became common in Europe.[50] Furthermore, the Australian-British writer James Aldridge eloquently describes the pointed arches in the mosque of Ibn Tulun as rising over the brick piers "like a ballerina's swanlike arms."[51] One can say with confidence that the mosque of Ibn Tulun was the first to use this pointed arch in Egypt.

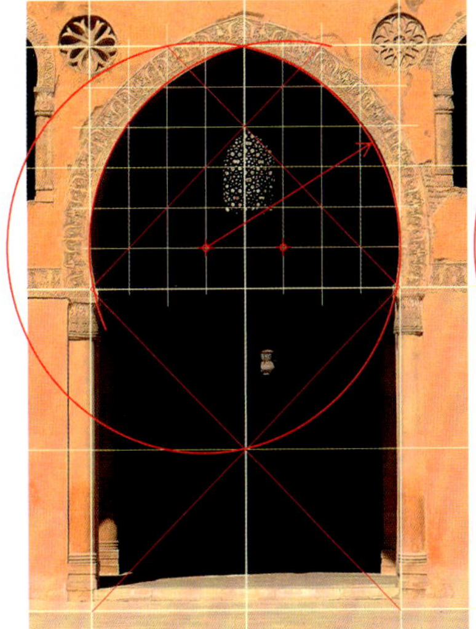

56 – The elegant pointed arches of the mosque of Ibn Tulun, with the relationships between their various parts marked.

Hautecœur and Wiet suggest that the space between the piers was meant to be a perfect square and the proportion between its piers and its arcuated space followed that of the "golden section."[52] On that subject, Jaroslaw Dobrowolski has done some useful analyses that show the relationships between the elements of the pointed arch with one another (fig. 56). This means that the arches of the mosque of Ibn Tulun were designed according to a universally recognized architectural principle of harmonious proportionality. The spaces between the pointed arches are filled with windows that pierce the walls of the mosque. The result is an unusually elegant, two-dimensional arcade (fig. 57).

Arches in the Islamic architecture of Cairo take different shapes: semicircular or barrel-vaulted as in the original (and modern) mosque of 'Amr Ibn al-'As; keel-shaped as in the mosques of al-Azhar, al-Aqmar, and al-Salih Tala'i'; and pointed horseshoe-shaped as in the mosques of Aqsunqur, Maridani, al-Mu'ayyad Sheikh, Sultan Barquq, Barsbay, Qaitbay, and al-Ghuri. Others are in the Gothic style as in the mosque of al-Husayn, opposite the mosque of al-Azhar in the Khan al-Khalili area. Although pointed arches might have been found in mosques that have not survived, such as those of Tabataba and al-Hakim,[53] the pointed arches with slight returns in the mosque of Ibn Tulun have not been duplicated in any building in Cairo since.

57 – Pointed arches in the mosque of Ibn Tulun.

Pointed-arch windows pierce the spandrels of the arches all around the mosque of Ibn Tulun (fig. 28). These windows lighten the weight of the ceiling over the piers. They are also economical, as they saved material expenses while building the mosque.[54] Furthermore, these pointed arches help illuminate the inner *riwaqs*, which are usually dim, and the windows promote the flow of air created by the northern winds, resulting in a breeze flowing from the outer court into the *riwaqs*. They are essential to the cleaning and aeration of the inner *riwaqs*. In addition to the windows, the ceiling is relatively high (ten meters in height),[55] which adds to the shade, coolness, and breezy effect throughout the mosque. It is therefore comfortable to use the mosque in both summer and winter.

The *Ziyadas*

One of the complaints that arose during the construction of the mosque was that it had become too small to pray in.[56] Egyptians approached Ibn Tulun and asked him to add additional space (or a *ziyada*). He had no choice but to oblige so he added the *ziyada* area around the mosque, which is visible today (figs. 22, plan A; 8, 23, 33-35, 114). The *ziyada* area was a common feature in the early archaic mosques of Egypt. It was added several times to the mosque of 'Amr Ibn al-'As, the first mosque built in Egypt.[57] It was echoed later on in the mosques of al-Azhar and al-Hakim. The *ziyada* has several functions. It protects the mosque and its walls from urban encroachment and everyday wear that has occurred in most of the buildings in Islamic Historic Cairo. In addition, it creates a feeling of spaciousness around the mosque, allowing worshipers to appreciate the grandeur of its walls and their decorative windows.[58] The *ziyada* is also a space where worshipers would meet and gather. It acts as a transitional buffer area, separating the interior of the mosque from the exterior. Worshipers coming to the mosque need this buffer to transition them from what their daily lives to what they will do inside the mosque. The *ziyada* adds to the sanctity of the mosque and allows seclusion from the hustle and bustle of the city and its markets. It is the area that psychologically prepares people for religious duties and piety.

The *Mayda'a* and the *Khizanat al-Sharab*

Maqrizi states that a man complained to Ibn Tulun that the mosque did not incorporate a place for ablutions (*mayda'a*).[59] Ibn Tulun responded that he did not want the mosque to be contaminated by any other structure, but he obliged this wish and ordered the *mayda'a* to be built in the *ziyada* area.[60] The *mayda'a* built in later periods must have been a reconstruction of the Tulunid one in the same location, as shall be discussed in the following chapters. The *mayda'a* was located next to the mosque's minaret and can still be seen today (fig. 22, plan A), but should not be confused with the domical structure in the middle of the open court.

Ibn Duqmaq and Maqrizi state that there was a storage area for keeping liquids called *khizanat al-sharab* located next to the *mayda'a* in the *ziyada*. This was like an apothecary where potions and medicines were kept.[61] Servants (*khaddam*) were appointed to it, as well as a physician (*tabib*) who was present on Fridays in case any accidents occurred.[62] Such an elaborate building with its sophisticated medical system did not exist in any other mosque in Egypt, and is therefore a novelty.

The Tulunid Minaret

The geographer and traveler Ya'qubi (d. 278 AH / 891 AD) relates an amusing story about the mosque's minaret. Builders asked Ibn Tulun about the style of the minaret that he wanted. It was known that Ibn Tulun was very serious and would never be unfocused during any official meeting.[63] However, during one such meeting, he played with a piece of white paper, rolling it over his finger until it was pulled out on one side and became stuck on his other finger. This scene surprised his audience, and to avoid embarrassment Ibn Tulun told his workers that he was designing this spiral shape for the minaret of his mosque. He then told his architects to construct the minaret in this shape.[64] This story may be linked to the fact that Ibn Tulun wanted a minaret built like the one in the Great Mosque of al-Mutawakkil in Samarra (known as the Malwiya, 'spiral'), and needed to explain it to his architects in Egypt, who did not know how to build it, or did not understand the concept of it being spiral (fig. 58).[65]

The historian Muqaddasi (d. 375 / 985-86) provides the earliest description of the minaret of Ibn Tulun, which he described as small, built of stone, and with its staircase on the outside.[66] Maqrizi stated that the mosque and its minaret were built with the Great Mosque in Samarra as a reference.[67] Ibn Duqmaq admires the architecture of the minaret, saying that it is one of the most unique minarets because of its external staircase whose large, spacious steps are wide enough to permit two loads of camels to ascend to its summit.[68] In another passage, Ibn Duqmaq (quoting Quda'i) adds that it was surmounted by a boat-shaped finial *(al-'ushari)*, which he claimed was part of the famous treasure that had paid for its construction.[69]

Nasiri Khusraw, who had visited Egypt in the early eleventh century, recounts that the minaret of Ibn Tulun was a freestanding structure.[70] Maqrizi says common people used to believe that the boat-shaped finial turned with the direction of the sun, but later corrects his statement to say that it actually turned with the shifting of the wind.[71] The seventeenth century historian Evliya Çelebi interpreted the boat's function as talismanic, protecting the city against catastrophic Nile floods.[72] He adds that an Ottoman *amir* used to climb to its summit on

58 – The minaret of the Great Mosque of al-Mutawakkil in Samarra, Iraq, also known as the Malwiya (spiral).

his horse, but of course the historian was referring to the present minaret and not the original Tulunid one.

Balawi relates another story about the mosque's boat-shaped finial. After the completion of the mosque, Ibn Tulun went there to pray and as he was leaving toward the fountain *(fawwara)*, the architect al-Nasrani climbed to the top of the minaret and stood next to the copper boat-shaped finial—"*al-markab al-nahas*" (actually written "*markan al-nahas*," probably by mistake). While holding it, he called to Ibn Tulun to give him security and freedom. He said he did not wish to be treated the same way, meaning he did not want to be imprisoned again, as had happened after he completed the Tulunid aqueduct of Basatin. Amused by this performance, Ibn Tulun told him to come down and mockingly called him an infidel ("*ya kafir*" in Arabic).[73] Ibn Tulun promised al-Nasrani security and freedom and then rewarded him with 10,000 dinars and robes of honor for building the mosque.[74]

Creswell suggests the boat that Ibn Tulun discovered might have been part of an ancient treasure-laden tomb. He wonders if it might have been the ark of the ancient Egyptian sun god Ra.[75] But if the treasure were a tomb, the boat would not have belonged to the sun god since ancient Egyptians usually buried luxurious items with them in order to enjoy them in the afterlife. One of the most luxurious items would have been the wooden boat, such as the one discovered near the Great Pyramid of Khufu at Giza, inaccurately called the Solar Boat. If the tomb were not a royal one, the owner might have made a model of a boat, which would become full size in the afterlife. The ark itself of the sun god Ra would never be buried in a tomb. It would have been depicted on the walls of the tombs, as is seen in the Valley of the Kings in Luxor. No examples of these copper boats were ever found. Instead, boats were used in ancient Egyptian temples to carry the statues of the gods in and out of the sanctuaries before and after visiting other temples such as at Karnak, Luxor, Dendera, Edfu, Komombo, Philae, and Abu Simbel. These boats would have been wooden and possibly gilded. Therefore, it is more likely that the copper boat-like finial on the minaret of the mosque of Ibn Tulun was a model of a true boat rather than that of the sun god Ra.

Balawi describes the boat-shaped finial as being made of copper, but no copper boat models have been found in ancient Egyptian tombs. This leads to speculation that this model boat was originally made of wood and then gilded, therefore taking the appearance of copper, especially when viewed from afar such as from the *sahn*. The finial has not survived, but the French scholar Protain illustrated it as a bird-like figure in the *Description de l'Égypte* (fig. 59).[76] By comparing this illustration with his other works on the arches of the mosque of

Ibn Tulun, it seems that there is some exaggeration in the proportions (fig. 61),[77] which is understandable as the French savants had been working under harsh conditions in Egypt and Protain must have made quick, inaccurate sketches. In another publication (1822), French surveyor Jomard describes the finial as being ten feet long, full of grain all year round and attracting many swallows.[78] Later in the nineteenth century, Pascal Coste shows it in the elevation of the mosque of Ibn Tulun.[79] However, it is a small illustration and the minaret is rather minute so its details cannot be determined.

The best illustration showing the boat-like finial is by nineteenth century British artist Robert Hay (fig. 60).[80] From its proportions, it looks closer to Jomard's description of being ten feet long. The shape is more like an actual model of boats seen in ancient Egyptian tombs. Another painting by the French artist Antoine Jean Gros shows Bonaparte visiting the plague victims in Jaffa in 1804 (fig. 62).[81] The scene is shown to be taking place in what appears to be a mosque, from its masterful architectural setting. Apart from the misery of the plagues victims, one can see an image of the spiral-shaped minaret of Ibn Tulun in the background; surprisingly it shows the finial of the minaret with a bird-like figure similar to that of Protain's. The image of the spiral-shaped minaret of Ibn Tulun is pictured even though the painting is set in Jaffa. This is different to the illustration of Prisse d'Avennes, where it looks more like a medieval oil lamp (fig. 63).[82] This was used later as the model for the finial surmounting the dome of the mausoleum of Imam al-Shafi'i (fig. 64).[83] Al-Jabarti records that the boat-shaped finial was blown off in a storm in 1693.[84] One must therefore assume that the boat illustrated by Robert Hay was a replacement made before the 1840s. Creswell states that Savigny de Moncorps and Vaujany mentioned the boat in 1869 and 1880 respectively.[85] The boat must have fallen off after that date, since nineteenth-century photographs show the minaret without a finial.[86] It was finally replaced by a crescent in 1892.[87]

The original minaret no longer survives, and the existing one was built during the Ayyubid and Mamluk periods in the twelfth and thirteenth centuries. Nevertheless, one may attempt to visualize the original minaret of Ibn Tulun. First, it must have been located on the central axis

59 – Protain's engraving in the *Description de l'Égypte* showing the area of the northwestern *ziyada*, where the present spiral-shaped minaret is located, and other buildings adjacent to it. Importantly, it shows a bird-like finial surmounting the minaret. Drawn/compiled between 1798–1801.

with the main *mihrab* of the mosque, unlike the current asymmetrical minaret.[88] Since it followed the same organization of the Great Mosque of al-Mutawakkil and the mosque of Abu Dulaf, both in Samarra, the location of the minaret would be axial with its main *mihrab*.[89] Secondly, the minaret was short as Muqadassi says, but it must have been tall enough to be seen from the mosque's interior, which means it was in

60 – Robert Hay's illustration of the northwestern *ziyada* area showing the spiral-shaped minaret and the buildings adjacent to it. It shows a different type of finial on top of the minaret. Drawn/compiled sometime before 1840.

fact relatively high. Third, it was built entirely of stone and its steps were wide enough to bear two loaded camels. Fourth, it was surmounted by the boat-shaped finial similar to that of Imam al-Shafi'i and was nearly ten feet long. A shallow dome with window openings surmounted the Malwiya minaret of Samarra. One would expect that the Tulunid minaret resembled it with the same arrangement.

61 – Protain's engraving in the *Description de l'Égypte* in which the arches are exaggerated to resemble more the Gothic style, rather than the elegant pointed arches of the mosque. Drawn/compiled between 1798–1801.

62 – Painting by the French artist Antoine Jean Gros, a masterpiece for its expressive gestures and vivid colors. Surprisingly, high on the far right-hand side is a depiction of the spiral-shaped minaret of the mosque of Ibn Tulun with the same bird-like finial as in Protain's engraving in the *Description de l'Égypte* (see fig. 59). Compiled before 1804, oil on canvas.

63 – Prisse d'Avennes' illustration of different architectural and decorative details of the mosque of Ibn Tulun showing the finial, which once surmounted the spiral-shaped minaret (before 1869), is depicted more like a medieval oil lamp.

The Tulunid Fawwara

Another impressive feature of the mosque is the large domical fountain (*fawwara*) in the middle of the open court, which supplied water for visitors to the mosque.[90] The geographer Muqaddasi (d. 375 AH / 985–86 AD) provides the earliest description of the *fawwara*. He states that the center of the mosque originally had a dome (*qubba*) with a water-wheel (*saqiya*). He describes the dome as being modeled after that of the famous well of Zamzam in Mecca.[91] Ibn Duqmaq and Maqrizi also provide descriptions of the *fawwara*, saying that it was crowned with a gilded dome that had windows on all sides.[92] They added that the roof of the *fawwara* contained sundials (*mazwalas*) and a balustrade made of teakwood.[93] The dome was supported by ten marble columns and with another sixteen columns surrounding its perimeter.

64 – The dome of the mausoleum of Imam al-Shafi'i showing the boat-like finial surmounting the dome, similar to the illustrations by Robert Hay (fig. 60) and Prisse d'Avennes (fig. 63).

The descriptions of Muqaddasi, Ibn Duqmaq, and Maqrizi are of great interest as they help one imagine how the original *fawwara* might have looked and therefore permit the following attempt to imaginatively reconstruct the mosque. The *fawwara* was crowned with a dome likely made of wood then covered with a layer of plaster and gilded, as was the case with most of the domes of that era. The contour of the dome might have been the same as in the pointed arches of the mosque, but historians do not provide any such details. Below the dome was a marble basin, which measured four cubits in diameter, with a *fawwara* in the center that jetted water. The floor of the fountain was paved with marble.[94]

It is recorded that the gilded dome was supported directly by ten columns. Corbet suggested in 1890 that the dome was supported by two columns at each angle forming a pentagon of ten marble columns surrounded by sixteen others in an octagonal colonnade around it.[95] One might have imagined the columns to have been arranged in a circle but historians report that the roof of the dome contained sundials, meaning they were supported or hung on flat walls. By comparing structures of that era, it would make sense that the flat surface where the sundials were placed was octagonal in shape. In architectural terms, that area would have been the 'transitional zone' of the dome. Therefore, one may deduce that the columns were arranged in an octagonal form, rather than a circular one (fig. 65).

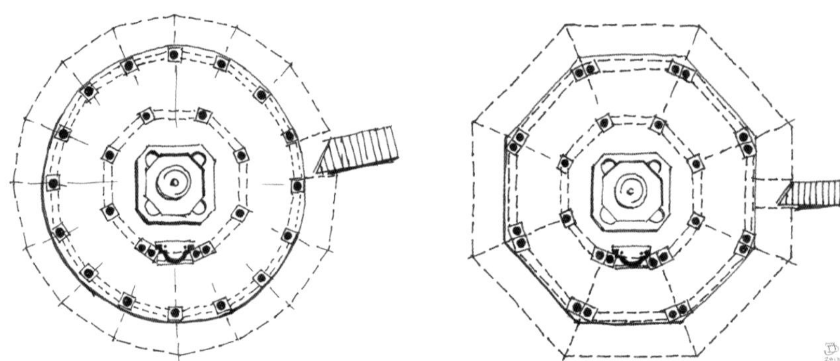

65 – Sketch of the two possibilities of how the plan of the original Tulunid *fawwara* of the mosque of Ibn Tulun would have been designed. From the descriptions of medieval historians it would be logical to deduce that the circular plan would not have been as successful as the octagonal one.

Below the dome was a marble basin, which measured four cubits in diameter, with a *fawwara* in the center that jetted water. The floor of the fountain was paved with marble.[96] The columns used in the *fawwara* were probably recycled from earlier pre-Islamic monuments, similar to those found in the *mihrab* (one with a basket-like look and the other semi-Corinthian). One may assume that the columns were brought from a dilapidated church, which might also be the same case here in the *fawwara*, and that these columns were from the same church (or ruin site) where those of the *mihrab* were taken. Hence, we will consider that the columns of the *fawwara* were also made to look like them, as in the reconstructed section in figure 65.

Since the transitional zone was octagonal, it would make sense that there were only eight columns. However, historians claim that Ibn Tulun made it mandatory for small children to pray in the *fawwara* of the mosque, which indicates that there might have been a simple portable *mihrab* on its *qibla* side. If this were true, one might assume that there were eight columns at each corner, with an additional two columns in the direction of the *qibla*. These extra columns would have supported a small flat *mihrab*, as was added in the *qibla riwaq* area of the mosque of ʿAmr Ibn al-ʿAs in 1050.[97] On that basis, we may imagine that this *mihrab* was, in fact, made of wood and perhaps it was portable like those used in later mosques and shrines.[98]

Historians claim that the dome had sundials and a balustrade made of teakwood. The sundials must have been hung or placed on the sides of an octagonal dome, which also had windows. The fact that they were placed on the top and that the top had a balustrade of teakwood

66 – A section of the original ninth-century Tulunid *fawwara* of the mosque of Ibn Tulun, reconstructed from the descriptions of medieval historians. There are two rows of columns arranged in concentric circles. The columns must have supported pointed arches, all of which support a dome, which for structural reasons had to be a double shell. The call to prayer would have been announced from atop the *fawwara*, where sundials were also situated. Therefore, it had to have had a wooden flight of steps leading to the drum.

suggests there must have been a staircase or ladder, which reached the top of the structure. The use of sundials is of particular interest, as they would be used only by the person who determined the exact time of prayer (*al-miqati* or *al-muwaqqit*). That job was usually assigned to the muezzin of the mosque. After he performed the call to prayer (*adhan*), he would check the times of the following prayers on the sundials. This could imply that the *fawwara* was used to announce the *adhan*. Although Ibn Duqmaq does not mention whether the *adhan* was ever called from the top of this *fawwara*, which is puzzling, Maqrizi provides additional insights about the *fawwara*, describing it as a decorated dome (*qubba muzawwaqa*) from which the call to prayer was announced.[99] Strangely, he adds that the call to prayer was also announced elsewhere on the stairs. The presence of sundials here would suggest that the *adhan* was announced. As for why it would be announced from the top of the *fawwara* rather than the spiral minaret, in the Mamluk period the *adhan* was announced from the domical *fisqiya* structure, which is present today, because the minaret was totally unsuccessful for that purpose.[100] It is interesting therefore to consider whether the spiral-shaped Tulunid minaret of the mosque was similarly unsuccessful.

Ibn Tulun required small children to pray in the *fawwara* of the mosque.[101] Male worshipers who prayed in the mosque would take their children with them, but to preserve the prestige and respect of the area inside the *maqsura*, the children stayed outside and were accompanied by young *ghilman* servants while their fathers were listening to the Friday sermon *(khutba)*. After prayers, the children would attend an assembly of the scholar al-Rabi' Ibn Sulayman who would give them religious lessons.[102]

Maqrizi describes a paper maker *(warraq)* and a few *ghilman* servants praying with the children in the *fawwara*.[103] The presence of *ghilman* makes sense, as they were probably serving the children who were using the *fawwara*. To keep the children calm, the paper maker would give them paper to write on, and then they would pray inside the *fawwara* area and around its fountain. After the prayer, the children would attend a lesson or assembly, given by a teacher named al-Rabi' Ibn Sulayman and using the paper provided by the *warraq*. It should be noted that this is one of the first mentions of paper in Islamic Cairo, before which time Egyptians were using papyrus and parchment. Since paper was a precious item back then, it needed to be carried by a special person, the *warraq*. Using a *fawwara* area for small children to pray in may have been an innovation in mosque functions, as it was not known in earlier architecture of Islamic Egypt.

The Inscriptions

The Foundation Inscriptions

The mosque of Ibn Tulun had two foundation inscriptions. 'Ali Basha Mubarak mentions that a marble block with Kufic inscriptions was found inside the door of the mosque facing the place for ablutions *(mayda'a)*.[104] He adds that it provided the date of the mosque's founding in Ramadan 265 / April–May 878.[105] 'Ali Basha Mubarak does not specify which door it was or where the marble block was found, but according to Creswell, Sir Gardner Wilkinson made a drawing between 1833 and 1860 showing two inscription slabs that were still affixed to the central piers of the *riwaq* facing the *sahn*.[106] Karl Baedeker confirms that "to the middle piers, which fell in 1814, were attached marble tablets with Kufy inscriptions which recorded the date of building: these also have gone to ruin."[107] This leads us to believe that the door which is referred to by 'Ali Basha Mubarak could have been part of one of the blocked arches of the *riwaq* (of the *qibla* side) facing the *sahn* and not one of the lateral entrances or doors in the wall of the mosque proper. In addition, his description of the block found facing the *mayda'a* means it was facing the domed *fisqiya* of Sultan Lajin, which currently lies in the middle of the *sahn*.

Corbet says that the two blocks were formerly attached to the two middle piers on the outside line of the south colonnade, and that though their former existence was on record, they had disappeared for many years. In the summer of 1890, the foundation inscription was discovered while clearing away some of the structures that were added later. It has been fixed on the pier to the right of the *mihrab* in the second (surviving) line from the court, and consists of a slab of coarse-grained white marble.[108] However, it is complete at the top and bottom. Its reproduction is interesting, since it is one of the oldest Arabic inscriptions in Egypt.[109] It is mostly Qur'anic but also contains the date and a historical portion (see appendix, no. 12).[110]

Jean Joseph Marcel published drawings of two foundation blocks made of marble in the *Description de L'Égypte* (figs. 67, 68).[111] Marcel authored another study on the mosque of Ibn Tulun in a separate publication,[112] where he states: "Ahmed [Ibn Tulun] had placed these two inaugural inscriptions on the two pillars of the arcade in which the *qibla* [meaning the *mihrab*] was placed: I had the good fortune to discover these two inscriptions that had disappeared under a thick coating of plaster at the time of the fall of the Tulunid Dynasty."[113]

During the restoration in 1890 carried out by the Comité de Conservation des Monuments de l'Art Arabe, part of the mosque's original foundation inscription was uncovered. Owing to its historical importance, the members of the Comité decided to have the marble foundation inscription fixed on one of the piers in the *qibla riwaq*. But it was only the right half of the marble blocks described by Marcel (fig. 47, 48, 67). The other half is lost. The second set of blocks that Marcel published is also lost (fig. 68). The texts of the two inscriptions are identical.

67 – Marcel's engraving in the *Description de l'Égypte* showing the original marble blocks containing the complete foundation inscription, which in his time was cracked into two halves. The right-hand block still survives (see figs. 47, 48; 22, plan A, FI). Drawn sometime between 1798–1801.

A puzzling aspect of the foundation blocks is that one would have expected them to be removed or destroyed by Muhammad Sulayman al-Katib, after his conquest and destruction of the city of Qata'i', as they must have included the names and titles of Ahmad Ibn Tulun and the Abbasid general intended to eliminate all traces of the Tulunid Dynasty. However, medieval historians do not provide any information

68 – Marcel's other engraving in the *Description de l'Égypte* showing the lost marble blocks containing the second foundation inscription, which was identical to that in figure 67. Drawn sometime between 1798–1801.

about the inscription. Karl Baedeker and Sir Gardner Wilkinson saw them fixed on the central piers of the *riwaq* facing the *sahn*. Is it possible that the two foundation blocks were actually leaning on the piers, rather than fixed to them? In this regard, one must remember that when Marcel saw them at the end of the eighteenth century, they had been cracked. How then is it possible that they were fixed on two piers?

Van Berchem made two interesting remarks about the text of the inscriptions. The first is that from line 16 of the text the mosque is identified by the term *masjid*, which was usually applied to such congregational buildings; the term *jami'* was only used later.[114] We find that medieval historians such as Balawi, Muqaddasi, Ibn Duqmaq, Maqrizi, and others use the term *jami'* for the mosque rather than the term *masjid*. Moreover, a mosque could only be identified as a congregational mosque (*jami'*) if it had a *khutba* delivered on Fridays.

Maqrizi relates that the mosque had a *khutba* delivered on Fridays during the time of Ibn Tulun. He recounts an incident when the preacher (*khatib*) Yalbugha al-Balkhi invocated—"*da'a*"—to the Abbasid Caliph al-Mu'tamid and his son and forgot to mention Ahmad Ibn Tulun at the end of his sermon. As he was coming down the steps of the pulpit (*minbar*), Ibn Tulun gave orders to al-Khadim (who was probably one of his servants) to have the *khatib* beaten five hundred blows. He realized his mistake and went back up and began invocating to Ahmad Ibn Tulun, exaggerating his gratitude, and pleading for longer than the *khutba* itself. As a result, Ibn Tulun gave instructions to convert the blows into dinars instead. The *khatib* was extremely relieved and thanked God for his own safety, and the people also congratulated him.[115]

Thus, one should not understand from the use of the term *masjid* in the foundation inscription that the mosque was built as a private mosque. It was surely a congregational mosque intended for Ibn Tulun and his entourage, his army and followers from Samarra, and the whole population of Misr (al-Fustat and al-'Askar). It was the new state mosque of Egypt, and it differs from later mosques, such as al-Azhar, which was originally intended for the ruling class living in the enclosed private city of al-Qahira. One must conclude that at the time the mosque of Ibn Tulun was indeed a congregational mosque, but that the meaning of the terms *masjid* and *jami'* had not yet been formalized.

Van Berchem makes a second remark about the titles on line 14 of the foundation inscription. He says that such a title was not used until the time of Salah al-Din at the Citadel in Cairo. He explains that all titles include "amir al-mu'minin" in the sovereign power of the caliph. In this regard, Oleg Grabar wonders whether, at this time, this expression of "mawla amir al-mu'minin" was a statement of a certain personal relation between the caliph and the Amir Ahmad Ibn Tulun or whether it was in fact an official title.[116]

About the Qur'anic quotations, Grabar says:

> The inscription as a document consists essentially in the emphasis given in it to religious themes not usually found in construction inscriptions. Apart from the quotations used usually as (II, 256; IX 18; XXIV, 36–38), we have quotations (XLVIII, 29; III, 106) which are less common on building inscriptions and which emphasize the duty of the Muslim against the infidel, thus pointing once more to the importance given by Ibn Tulun to the religious motivations of his acts and to the Holy War. Expressions such as *tasniyat al-Din* and *ulfat al-mu'minin* within the inscription itself give it an exhortative quality which was common enough on mosque inscriptions but whose emphasis relates it to later Seljuk and Ayyubid inscriptions, at a time when the main task of the rulers was to restore the spiritual unity of the Islamic community."[117]

Gaston Wiet connects the foundation inscription with the treasure found by Ibn Tulun, pointing to the following expression (on line 16): "from the revenues of the pure and legal source which God has bestowed him with." Wiet remarks that Van Berchem did not compare this expression with the legend of the treasure.[118] However, his interpretation is that the inscription indicates that Ibn Tulun built the mosque out of legitimate funds and did not employ the revenues of the state in the construction. He adds that this type of expression was frequent in the Arabic epigraphy, where the founder of a monument often engraves an inscription in stone stating that the funds or money spent for construction were his own.[119]

The text of the foundation inscription shows that Ibn Tulun was trying to equate his own name and titles with that of the Abbasid Caliph al-Mu'tamid, but at the same time he was constrained by prescribed rules. He wanted to claim autonomy but until he gained independence from the caliphate he had to act within certain parameters. However, as recounted by Maqrizi, he became furious when his name was not mentioned after that of the caliph at the end of the *khutba*, and he

69 – A reconstructed image of the original ninth-century placement of the marble foundation inscription blocks. They were placed on the outer piers of the arches, along the axis of the main *mihrab*, facing the *sahn* in a symmetric order for aesthetic purposes and so as to be seen by worshipers.

added the title of "mawla amir al-mu'minin" on the inscription and later on gold coins under the name of the caliph. Ibn Tulun gained his full independence from the caliphate in 266 AH / 880 AD.

The entire mosque displays excellent examples of stuccowork. Ibn Tulun could have used stucco or even limestone for his foundation inscription. But marble is coarse and more expensive and lasts much longer than stucco, which is fragile and disintegrates quickly. Thus an inscription carved in marble would have been an appropriate expression of Ibn Tulun's new position and status in Egypt. Aesthetically, the placement of the marble foundation blocks on the two central piers adds to the idea of centrality and to the symmetrical arrangement of the *sahn* of the mosque. The desire to maintain balance and harmony also probably accounts for the placement of the two flat *mihrab*s during the Tulunid period and two more during the Fatimid period. The central placement of the foundation blocks on the central piers indicates that Ibn Tulun wanted to display his foundation inscriptions to the court and all the different social classes and races entering his mosque. A reconstruction of the original placement of the foundation inscription blocks is shown in figure 69.

The Wooden Inscriptions Below the Ceiling

Among the most interesting features in the mosque of Ibn Tulun is the carved wooden inscription below the ceiling of the mosque. About 30 centimeters below the ceiling is a carved frieze of sycamore wood running around the entire mosque, which contains a Qur'anic inscription (see fig. 27). The frieze is divided into three equal registers by carved borders. The upper and lower registers are blank, while the middle one contains an inscription in Kufic letters which is entirely Qur'anic. It begins with the *basmallah* followed by chapter *(sura)* I and then continues with a large portion of *sura* II until verse *(aya)* 156.[120] Unfortunately, the frieze was partially destroyed or lost after *aya* 156, but since there is no break in the text, this implies that the original idea was to have the entire Qur'an inscribed from beginning to end.

In the late eighteenth century, the French art historian Jean Joseph Marcel was the first to admire and record those wooden inscriptions after they had fallen off, and managed to produce them in wonderful engravings in the *Description de l'Égypte* (figs. 81, 87, 97; appendix, nos. 13 and 14).[121]

Inscriptions in earlier buildings were more political than religious. At the Dome of the Rock in Jerusalem, the Great Mosque of Qairawan, the Nilometer on Roda Island in Cairo, and even in the mosque of al-Hakim later on, specific verses were chosen to impress the population of newly conquered lands or to reflect the character of these new rulers or invaders. However, no special verses were chosen for the inscription in the mosque of Ibn Tulun, and despite its incomplete state, it later became popular in folkloric accounts that the mosque contained the whole Qur'an. Such a lengthy Qur'anic inscription is not found elsewhere in the Islamic world before the period of the mosque of Ibn Tulun. We do not know if the mosque of al-'Askar had any inscriptions, as it was destroyed and we have no records of it. Therefore, the Qur'anic inscription is another feature that adds more of a holy and unique character to the mosque of Ibn Tulun.

The frieze is scattered in different places. Great lengths of it are either blank spaces or broken or restored fragments. Most of the fragments have fallen off over the centuries. The inscription does not begin at the far side of the *riwaq* on the south side but rather just above the tenth window of the mosque's *qibla* wall, which is quite curious. One may assume that the blank space, which precedes the *basmallah*, originally contained a foundation inscription, including a dedicatory and a titular text of Ibn Tulun.[122] It is possible that when the Abbasids conquered Egypt in 292 AH / 905 AD and destroyed the city of al-Qata'i', they removed the part of the inscription that must have contained the name of Ahmad Ibn Tulun.

Such acts were part of political culture, throughout the history of Egypt and the caliphate. They took place at the Nilometer where the name of the caliph was removed from the inscriptions, and the Dome of the Rock in Jerusalem where the Abbasids removed the name of 'Abd al-Malik and replaced it with that of the Caliph al-Ma'mun. One would expect the name of Ibn Tulun to have been replaced by the name of the new conqueror, but for some reason it was not and therefore remains blank.

Since the inscription is so high up on the wall, it is difficult to read with the naked eye. It is also now grayish-brown in color, rendering it even more difficult to identify the letters. Many fragments are lost, and the *riwaq* is dimly lit. In addition, the contrast between the light from the open court and the darkness of the *riwaq*s poses further difficulties in viewing the inscription. There is no direct evidence to support the idea that the inscription was once painted or gilded in its original state, but this seems likely, judging from manuscripts from the same period.[123]

The *Dikka*

A high platform on columns used to deliver prayers (*dikka*) is located between the central piers where the two flat Tulunid *mihrab*s are positioned (M1 and M2 in fig. 22, plan A (D); fig. 39). It consists of a platform with a wooden balustrade. Four marble columns with *muqarnas*-style capitals, which became common only during the Mamluk period, support the *dikka*, suggesting that the original Tulunid *dikka* had been destroyed. It also has a portable ladder that leads to the platform. Unfortunately, medieval historians neither refer to the *dikka* of the mosque of Ibn Tulun, nor do modern scholars discuss it. However, from the style of its capitals, one may conclude that it was added sometime during the Mamluk period, as shall be discussed later.[124]

Someone called the *muballigh* would echo what the imam announced during Friday prayers using the *dikka*. In the time of the Prophet, when Muslims would pray in great numbers in the open air, worshipers praying far from the Prophet could not hear what he was saying, so someone would stand on a stool and repeat what the Prophet was saying. It became a tradition within mosques to repeat the imam's words and developed into an important architectural element. Between prayers, the *muballigh* would sit in the *dikka* and recite the Qur'an.[125]

The Windows and Movement Within the Mosque

The upper parts of the mosque's walls are pierced by 128 windows (most of which have been restored), with the same form as the pointed arches but without the slight returns (fig. 71).[126] Each window has a stucco grille with different geometric or floral designs. Creswell discovered irregularity in the distribution and placement of the windows:[127] They are spaced and positioned in a way that does not correspond to the axes of the courtyard's arches; rather, pointed arches facing the open court are off-center (fig. 57). Walking around the interior of the mosque, one is inclined to center the windows with the pointed arches in front of them. As one does so, it seems that the building is moving. The eyes are guided from side to side so that the windows are centered with the arches. As one moves throughout the building, new visual perspectives emerge. The more one moves around, the more one admires the beauty of the mosque's architectural serenity and the power of its remarkable simplicity.

The effect is slightly different in the *qibla riwaq*. There the windows are centered diagonally with the entire depth of the arches, producing another remarkable effect.[128] Walking into the *qibla riwaq*, one moves unintentionally toward the *mihrab* area to take position in the rows of worshipers during prayer times. One does not make 90-degree sharp-angled curves but rather moves on diagonally. While doing so, one looks ahead and finds a window leading the eye to the final destination (fig. 70). The windows do not provide a sufficient amount of light inside the mosque. However, in the early morning the

70 – The windows of the *qibla* wall are diagonally centered through the arches of the *qibla riwaq*.

sun shines through the grilles of the stucco windows into the *qibla riwaq*. As the sun moves, it shines onto the piers, arches and floor of the *riwaq*. Its rays illuminate the outlines of the windows and their different geometric designs. As the sun rises further, it shines alternately on the piers and the floor between the piers (figs. 71-76). This

71–75 [PAGES 121 TO 126] – The sun shining through the windows of the *qibla* wall of the mosque is reflected on the floor and walls of the *qibla riwaq*.

affects the lighting in the *riwaq*: the floor is decorated along the full *riwaq*, creating a superb result, which could be described as a 'carpet of light' (fig. 75). This lighting effect illuminates the entire *riwaq*, and the light is indirectly reflected upward to illuminate the whole mosque's interior.

Did this lighting effect exist when the mosque was originally built? Did the architect plan it? Unfortunately, the available sources do not provide answers. Yet, the carpet of light is certainly a magnificent, dramatic effect unknown elsewhere in the Islamic world until the ninth century. The wooden inscription below the ceiling could only be read thanks to this lighting phenomenon. Could the architect al-Nasrani have created this unusual visual effect intentionally? Unfortunately, due to the lack of historical sources, this will never be known.

The Area of the Maqsura

The mosque of Ibn Tulun had a *maqsura* that has not survived. The *maqsura* is the enclosed area in a mosque reserved for the ruler or patron and his entourage to congregate. It is in front of the *mihrab* and usually made of turned wood. It is known that Ibn Tulun used to come from his palace to Dar al-Imara where he changed his garments, then performed his ablutions and perfumed himself with incense.[129] Only then did he enter the mosque, passing through the connecting door from Dar al-Imara to the interior of the mosque, into the *maqsura* area, which was on the left side of the main *mihrab* and *minbar* (figs. 22, plan A (1); 100).[130]

There is another door on the right side of the *mihrab*, which was used by the preacher *(khatib)* to enter the mosque and walk directly to the *minbar* to deliver his speech. This door was located just below the tenth window on the *qibla* wall, where the wooden Qur'anic inscription below the mosque's ceiling starts. Ibn Tulun had ordered copies of the Qu'ran manuscripts *(masahif)* to be transported to the mosque. One may assume that there was a library *(khizanat kutub)* in which these books were held. Behind that door is a room where he would prepare his speech by reading or conducting research; hence, it incorporated a library (figs. 22, plan A (2, 3); 38). This room was the hall of the preacher *(qa'at al-khataba)*, which was actually the *khatib*'s office. One might imagine Ibn Tulun sitting in front of the *mihrab* during prayer time. Beside him would be the *khatib* of the mosque and then his army of bodyguards. This mass of important people would occupy the whole area of the *maqsura*, which would be bordered by a wonderful screen in turned wood (figs. 69, 77).

The French architects Pascal Coste and Prisse d'Avennes include a *maqsura* in their nineteenth century plans of the mosque of Ibn Tulun, but the architects' plans are not identical.[131] It is strange that no other plans show this *maqsura*. (However, one should be cautious when studying such small details on plans, because they are often inaccurate.)[132] Still, the *maqsura* need not have been the original one of Ibn Tulun and may have been added during the French architects' time without being recorded.

The area of the *maqsura* can be assumed to have been bordered from the part below the tenth window of the *qibla* wall (from the right) and in a symmetrical order on the other side. The start of the inscription here may indicate that the rest of the inscription until that point, meaning the *basmallah*, might have been followed by the titles and praises of the founder Ahmad Ibn Tulun, which would have been removed when al-Katib destroyed al-Qata'i'. The closest existing *maqsura* screens, which are comparable to that of Ibn Tulun's, are in the mosques of Maridani (1340) and al-Azhar (1470s), the latter added by Sultan Qaitbay. Other *maqsuras* existed in the mosques of al-Zahir Baybars I (1269), al-Nasir

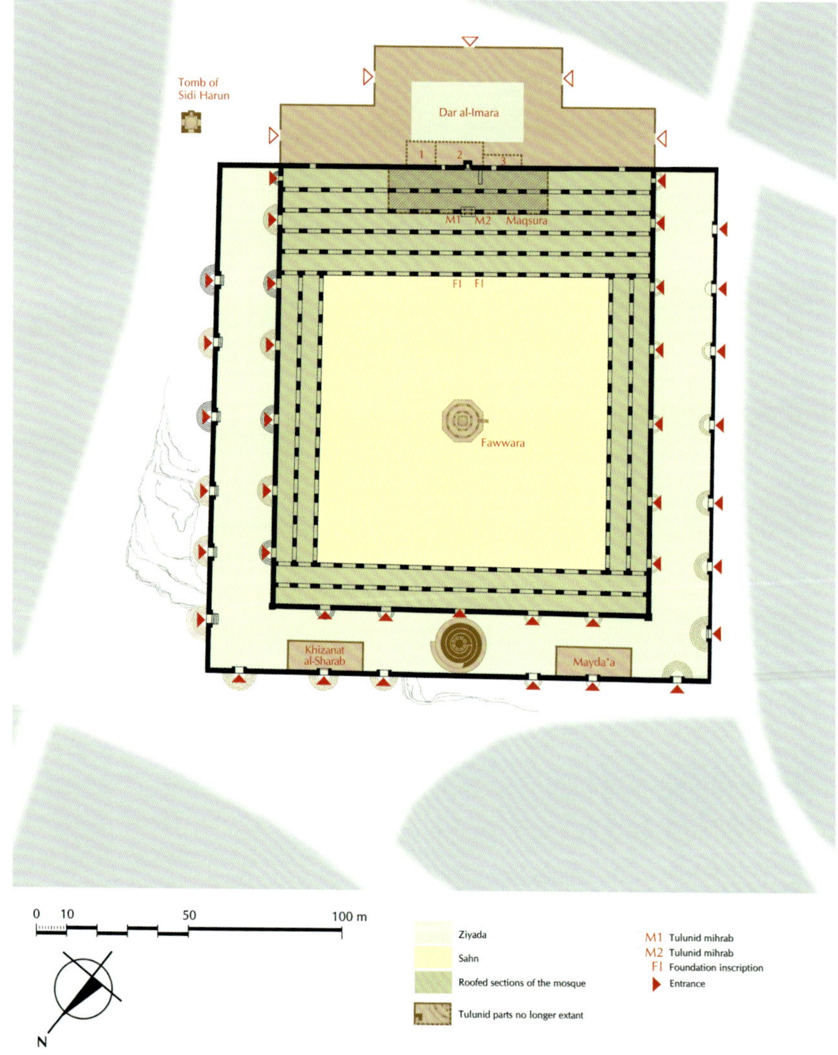

76, plan B – A reconstructed plan of the original mosque of Ibn Tulun in the ninth century. It is a rectangle within a square, as it is today. The mosque proper is surrounded by a *ziyada* on three sides and the original spiral-shaped minaret stands on the same axis of the main *mihrab*. Two buildings stand symmetrical on both sides of the minaret: the *mayda'a* is on the right, while the clinic–pharmacy *(khizanat al-sharab)* is on the left. The original Tulunid *fawwara* in the middle of the *sahn* is on the same axis as the main *mihrab*. The shaded area in the *qibla riwaq* indicates the area of the *maqsura*. Dar al-Imara is limited by the size of the area behind the mosque and present-day Tulun Street, and is depicted as symmetrical with an open court in the middle of the building. The three rooms behind the main *mihrab* would be part of Dar al-Imara. Nearby lies the small tomb of Sidi Harun. Its plan and shape is based on the Fatimid tombs in Aswan, which are the closest to the period of Ibn Tulun.

77 – Bird's-eye view reconstruction of the mosque of Ibn Tulun and the Dar al-Imara. The roof of the *qibla riwaq* is peeled back to show the parameter of the original Tulunid *maqsura*, where Ibn Tulun and his entourage would have sat during prayer time. A wooden screen would have bordered the *maqsura* area. Dar al-Imara is depicted as a symmetrical building, relative to the mosque. However, if it were entirely roofed then it would have been totally dark or dim on the inside, and for this reason, it is logical to include an open court to provide it with light and air.

Muhammad at the Citadel (1335), and Amir Aqsunqur (1346) along the Darb al-Ahmar. However, large domes would have covered them.

The Influence of the Great Mosque of Samarra

It is a known fact that the Samarran Great Mosque of al-Mutawakkil directly influenced the mosque of Ibn Tulun. The Great Mosque was the largest mosque in the world and still is one of the largest mosques ever built. According to Robert Hillenbrand, the Great Mosque of Samarra accommodated almost 100,000 worshipers.[133] The mosque of Ibn Tulun, including the space of the *riwaq*s and the courtyard, could accommodate no more that 20,000 worshipers. However, by excluding the courtyard and only counting the size of the *riwaq*s, the number would be around 10,000 worshipers.[134] It is therefore one of the largest spaces among the Islamic monuments of Cairo. Indeed, as outlined above, a *ziyada* was created on three sides to make sure there was enough space for prayer.

As has been explained in this chapter, the plan for the mosque was imported from Samarra, but its architecture differed in several important ways. The piers did not have columns on their corners like those at Samarra but rather column-like decorations. The pointed arches in the mosque of Ibn Tulun had slight returns. The foundation inscriptions and their placement were also unique, as well as the long wooden Qur'anic inscriptions running below the ceiling, and the gilded domed *fawwara* in the middle of the *sahn*. The Tulunid spiral-shaped minaret would have been on the same axis of the main *mihrab*, also as in Samarra. Finally, the two structures of the *mayda'a* and the medical clinic (*khizanat al-sharab*) were also novelties in the Islamic architecture of Cairo. These would have been next to the Tulunid spiral-shaped minaret. Considering the aesthetics and symmetry of the mosque's architecture, one may assume that these two structures lay on both sides of the Tulunid spiral-shaped minaret. A reconstruction of the plan of the mosque of Ibn Tulun, relative to the adjacent Dar al-Imara and the tomb of Sidi Harun, can be seen in figure 76, plan B.

Creswell states that the scheme of the façade of the mosque of Ibn Tulun does not resemble that of the Great Mosque of al-Mutawakkil or that of Abu Dulaf of Samarra.[135] The reason he gives is that the mosque of Ibn Tulun does not have the bastions on the exterior façades like the others. He adds that the only feature of the façade that resembles the mosque in Samarra is the small circles in the squares below the remarkable crenellations. In addition, the windows of the façade in no way resemble those of the Great Mosque. However, in the mosque of Ibn Tulun the windows, with their pair of engaged columns on the exterior and the interior of the façades, resemble those of the mosque of 'Amr ibn al-'As, but they lack the transverse beams. Hence, the space between the windows is filled with fluted niches, and it is because of this that Creswell believes the façade is more Egyptian than Samarran.[136] In other words, the façades of the mosque of Ibn Tulun are 'in the spirit of' those of the mosque of 'Amr Ibn al-'As.[137] And, when we say Egyptian in spirit, we actually mean inspired by Coptic style.

FRIDAYS IN THE MOSQUE OF IBN TULUN

Imagining the scene on Fridays, one sees the Tulunid ruler arriving at Dar al-Imara after a ceremonial procession from his palace. He enters from a private entrance made especially for him, finely furnished with curtains and all kinds of utensils, implements, and equipment. He would prepare for prayer by performing the ablution, powdering himself with incense, and changing his garments and robes.

Meanwhile, members of the royal family, courtiers, high officials, and military leaders would enter the mosque from the lateral entrances of the *qibla riwaq*. The army would divide itself into ethnic groups, and the native Egyptians would proceed systematically through the other entrances on the three sides of the mosque. All these people would either arrive on foot or on their horses, camels, and donkeys. They would leave their animals outside the mosque walls, probably on the lowest point of the slope of Gabal Yashkur, as seen in the bird's eye view of figure 20.

Important people occupied the *maqsura*, which was bordered by a screen of turned wood that prevented people gathered outside the *maqsura* from seeing those inside. However, they would face the same direction since it was emphasized by the two Tulunid flat *mihrab*s on the central piers outside the *maqsura*, which symbolize the main *mihrab*. Before the prayers began, the people would gather in the *ziyada* area. Slowly, they would head inside to perform the ablutions next to the spiral-shaped minaret. Then they would enter the mosque proper and take their seats on the ground for the sermon. High officials would be allowed to walk into the *maqsura* area, which must have had entrances on three sides. As they entered the *maqsura*, servants, attendants, and bodyguards would check that worshipers did not hold any weapons that might threaten the ruler. They would walk in, sit down, and wait. As they sat, they might chat to those next to them.

If one of the worshipers fell ill or were injured for any reason, he would be taken to the *khizanat al-sharab*, which was built close to the *mayda'a* and spiral-shaped minaret (fig. 76, plan B). After everyone was seated and the *adhan* was called from the minaret or the top of

78 – A reconstruction of the interior of the mosque of Ibn Tulun showing the original Tulunid *fawwara* with its gilded dome supported on two rows of concentric columns. A muezzin stands atop the drum of the dome, having checked the sundial placed behind him on the octagonal transitional zone between the windows of the dome. Children are sitting to receive a lesson given by a private teacher, with a *warraq* to provide the paper. In the background stands the original Tulunid spiral-shaped minaret.

the gilded dome of the *fawwara*, Ibn Tulun would enter through the door on the left side of the main *mihrab* and walk to the first row in the center, in front the main *mihrab*. Next to him would be his family, high-ranking officials, and administrators of the court along with royal bodyguards.

The last one to enter the congregation would be the mosque's *khatib*. He would enter from the door opposite to that from which the ruler entered (meaning the door on the right side of the main *mihrab* and *minbar*). Behind that door is the *qa'at al-khataba* used by the *khatib*. From there, he would walk into the *maqsura* area of the mosque and climb the steps of the *minbar*. It is not known whether he would greet the ruler before climbing the steps or only after delivering his *khutba*. The *khatib* would end the *khutba* in the name of the ruler Ahmad Ibn Tulun (and the Abbasid caliph). He would then descend and go directly to the *mihrab* to lead the prayer itself. This is when the *khatib* becomes the leader of the prayer (imam) of the mosque. During the prayer, the *muballigh* would echo what the imam had said for the benefit of those out of earshot.

Children (whether orphans or those there with their fathers) remained in the *fawwara* in the middle of the *sahn* with their *ghilman* and supervisors. There they sat under a wonderfully decorated wooden dome, as shown in figure 78. When they became bored, a *warraq* would give them paper to keep them busy until the sermon was finished. After the prayer, a teacher would then give the children a lesson, for which they would also use this paper.

After the prayer, Ibn Tulun would inspect and supervise different activities. There was probably another grand procession back to the royal palace. One assumes that the same entrances would also be used as exits. The spaces around the mosque would then also have acted as markets where people would buy food and fruits, and for the rest of the day the markets would have witnessed tremendous activity. The mosque of Ibn Tulun was built as part of the great architectural and political program, which Ibn Tulun had designed. The mosque was a great architectural statement of splendid ceremonials that glorified its founder, Ahmad Ibn Tulun.

7

The Ikhshidid and Fatimid Periods

The Tulunid dynasty came to an end in 905 AD with the invasion of the Abbasid general Muhammad Sulayman al-Katib. The entire city of al-Qata'i' was destroyed except for two buildings—Dar al-Imara and the mosque of Ibn Tulun. A few years later, the Ikhshidid dynasty established its rule and Ibn Tughrul founded a new regime, which was a sub-dynasty of the Abbasids, just as Ahmad Ibn Tulun had done earlier. The Ikhshidids sought to revive the glory of the Tulunid period, through political power, but few building activities took place during that time except for the mosque of Tabataba.

79 – The marble inscription of Badr al-Gammali above the main entrance of the mosque.

During the Ikhshidid period, the building of Dar al-Imara started to function again and returned as the center of Egypt's administration. The mosque remained because of its religious sanctity, and its proximity to Dar al-Imara was an important factor in its survival and continued operation during the Ikhshidid period. There is no information about how the mosque was used, or if anything differed in how it was used compared with the Tulunid period, but it lost some of its purpose as there were no longer weekly ceremonies or processions and army parades that culminated in a grand finale at the mosque. Nor was there a rich and dynamic local population who prayed in the mosque. The mosque of Ibn Tulun entered a period of neglect and decline. The Ikhshidids' rule was short-lived, as they were weak and could not resist the influence and underground movement of the Shi'a who sought to establish an independent state of their own in Egypt. A new era began with the advent of the Fatimid dynasty.

Fatimid Rule in Egypt

In 969, the Fatimid General Gawhar al-Siqilli (the Sicilian) entered Egypt, as part of the conquest orchestrated by Caliph al-Mu'iz. He founded a new capital for Islamic Egypt—the city of al-Qahira (Cairo) to be the fourth capital after Fustat, al-'Askar, and al-Qata'i' (fig. 80).[1] This was different to the earlier capitals (of Fustat, al-'Askar, and al-Qata'i') and was fortified to protect the Fatimid caliph and his entourage in two large palaces adorned with rich furnishings and a great treasury. The city was planned with a celebrated ceremonial boulevard called al-Qasaba, meaning 'windpipe,' which is known today as al-Mu'iz Street. Around the middle of that street was a vast plaza called Bayn al-Qasrayn (literally: between the two palaces). This plaza accommodated 10,000 troops of the Fatimid army. Their treasuries were considered to contain some of the richest artifacts imported from all over the world. The palaces were the residences of the Fatimid rulers and also housed administrative functions. Scholars once believed al-Qahira was forbidden to anyone other than the Fatimid ruling family and their entourage, but modern research proves that was not so, as markets were set up on special occasions in the Bayn al-Qasrayn area.[2]

The Fatimids claimed to be direct descendants of Fatima, the daughter of the Prophet Muhammad and wife of Imam 'Ali ibn Abi Talib, the Prophet's cousin and the youngest convert to Islam. 'Ali was the fourth of the Rashidun (Rightly Guided) Caliphs who ruled the Muslim community after the Prophet's death. Civil war broke out within the community after the death of 'Ali and the martyrdom of his son al-Husayn. The followers of 'Ali, known as the Shi'a, were expelled from Arabia and fled in different directions. Those who fled to North Africa founded the city of al-Mahdiya, in what is modern Tunisia, and became known as the Fatimids.

The Fatimids were followers of the Isma'ili sect of Shi'ism and owners of an ambitious program to spread their doctrine throughout the Muslim world. Until this time, the majority of Egyptians followed Sunni doctrine, making Egypt a prime target for the spread of Shi'i thought, politics, and military authority. Soon after the Fatimid invasion of Egypt and the founding of al-Qahira, a new program of teachings was

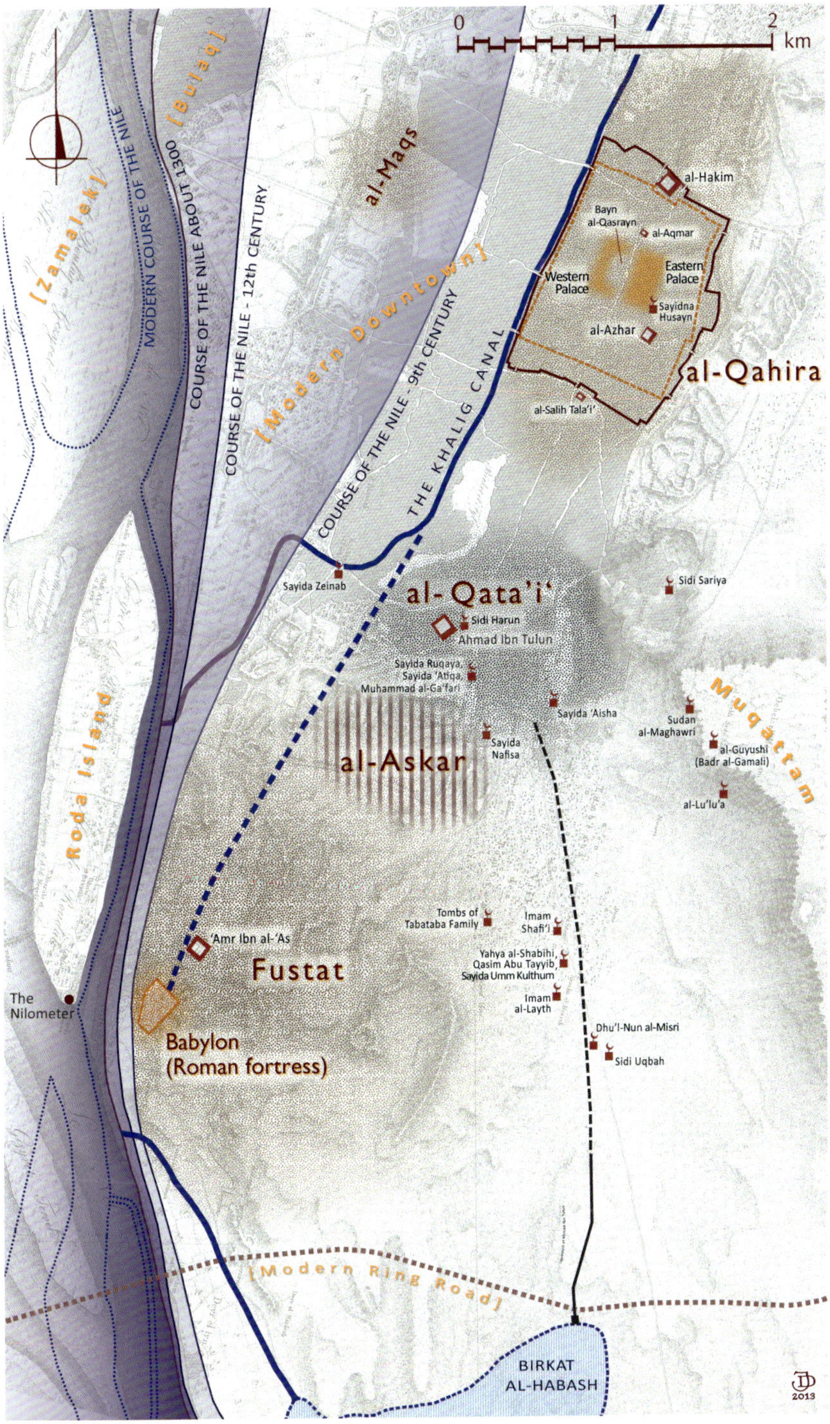

80 – The Islamic capitals of Egypt and their monuments in the year 1170 AD.

established in the mosque of al-Azhar by a minister *(wazir)* known as Ya'qub Ibn Killis, a Jewish convert to Islam. He is credited with the formation of the religious teaching system *(madrasa)* at al-Azhar in 989.[3]

The Fatimids built small domed shrines called *mashhads* over the burial places of the Prophet Muhammad's descendants including al-Husayn, Sayyida Zaynab, Sayyida Ruqayya, and Sayyida 'Aisha.[4] These memorials became the regional focus for *mulids*—festivals marking the anniversaries of the saints' deaths. These festivities became popular among local Egyptians particularly in rural areas, enabling the ruling Fatimids to quickly gain support in Egypt.[5] It must also be noted that the mosque of Ibn Tulun had received significant attention during the Fatimid period due to its closeness to some of the major holy Shi'i shrines that the Fatimids had erected in the nearby cemeteries (fig. 80).[6] It was inevitable that visitors to those shrines would require a place to worship, and probably a drink of water from the *fawwara*. The mosque of Ibn Tulun was the ideal place for this.

The Fatimids also built important mosques throughout al-Qahira, such as those of al-Azhar (970 AD), al-Hakim (990–1013), al-Aqmar (1125) and al-Salih al-Tala'i' (1160) (fig. 80).[7] These mosques were mostly for the use of the Fatimids and their armies and Egyptians did not pray in them—part of Caliph al-Mu'iz's program to maintain distance from the local population and to separate the newly built city of al-Qahira from Fustat, al-'Askar, and what remained of al-Qata'i'. The Fatimid mosques were rather small and could not accommodate large enough numbers and so al-Mu'iz had to use older, larger mosques for prayer and as places to make political announcements, one of which was the mosque of Ibn Tulun. As a result the mosque and the area around it were centers of significant activity during the Fatimid period. Maqrizi confirms that the mosque of Ibn Tulun was used during the reign of Caliph al-Mu'iz and that in 363 AH / 973 AD he appointed Ya'qub Ibn Killis and 'Asluj Ibn al-Hasan to take charge of the land tax *(kharaj)* in Dar al-Imara.[8] Maqrizi also adds that they announced the land estates *(diya')* from the *minbar* of the mosque. While the city of al-Qahira, was being built, Egypt continued to be administered from Dar al-Imara, behind the mosque of Ibn Tulun, and this carried on even after al-Qahira was founded. It was far from the urban centers of the new city and the older city of Fustat. It was also mid-way between the royal palace city of al-Qahira and Fustat. Therefore, it was convenient for the new Fatimid regime to use it as the main administrative office.

Fatimid Mosques

The trend of building mosques in the Fatimid period was different than in previous times. The mosque of al-Azhar was founded by Gawhar al-Siqilli for Caliph al-Mu'iz and his entourage so that they could pray near the two great Fatimid palaces (of the Bayn al-Qasrayn area). Caliph al-Mu'iz's son, Caliph al-'Aziz, promoted crafts and arts and used his observatories and libraries constantly. In addition, he used the mosques of 'Amr Ibn al-'As and Ibn Tulun regularly, and when the *fawwara* at the latter mosque was burnt he restored it and built a new one. Hence, the mosque was also associated with him. Later, al-'Aziz's son, Caliph al-Hakim bought these mosques from their owners (descendants and inheritors of Ibn Tulun and 'Amr). Nevertheless, he built a huge mosque outside the walled city of al-Qahira, which still bears his name (fig. 80).

Later on, in 526 AH / 1132 AD, Caliph al-Hafiz, son of al-Hakim, ordered construction to take place in the mosque of Ibn Tulun.[9] A wooden panel, an image of which the French scholar Jean Joseph Marcel published in the *Description de l'Égypte*, displays al-Hafiz's name and the date (fig. 81; appendix, no. 6).[10] It is not known where Marcel found this inscription, and there is no mention of the type of construction work that was done by Caliph al-Hafiz.[11]

The Maqsura of Fatima al-Zahra'

The historian Ibn Duqmaq states that a man had a dream in which he envisioned Fatima al-Zahra' praying in the mosque. This story became so popular among the local population that people raced to pray in the same spot in the mosque where Fatima al-Zahra' was thought to have prayed in the dream. Ibn Duqmaq does not provide a date for these events. However, one must assume that it happened

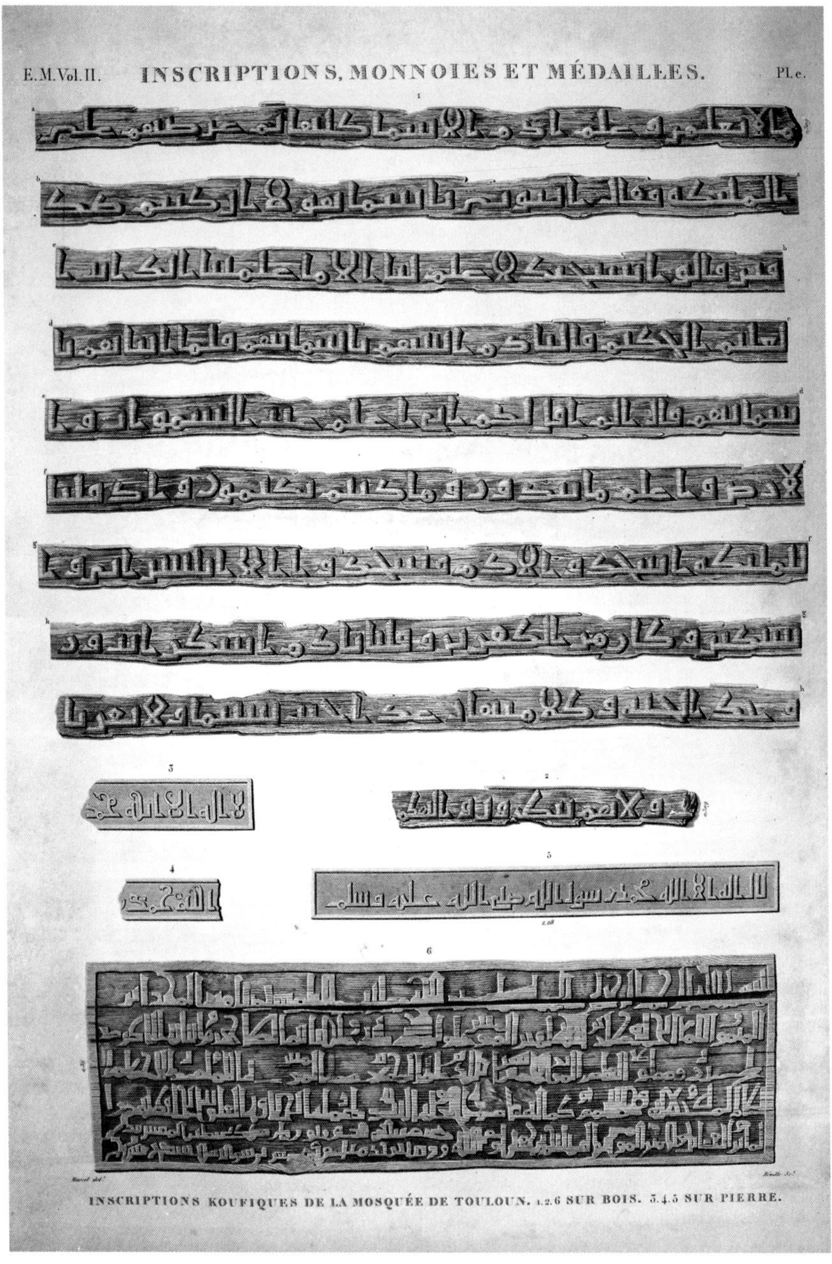

81 – Marcel's engraving in the *Description de l'Égypte* showing different bands of the wooden Qur'anic inscriptions below the ceiling of the mosque and a large rectangular wooden panel with the name of the Caliph al-Hafiz li-Din Allah, who ordered unknown construction work to be done in the mosque. Drawn between 1798–1801.

during the Fatimid period, because Fatima al-Zahra' was not only the daughter of the Prophet Muhammad but also the mother of al-Hasan and al-Husayn. She is venerated as the holy figure from which the Fatimids claim to have descended. In addition, she was directly related to two men who had been martyred in early Islam—her husband, Imam 'Ali, and her son, Sayyidna al-Husayn. Such saintly ideas were not prominent in Egypt before the Fatimid period. Only with the spread of Shi'i Islam would she have been elevated to a holy status. In other words, the *maqsura* must have been connected to the Fatimid context. The alleged *maqsura* of Fatima al-Zahra' is not referred to in Maqrizi or any later source, nor does it physically survive in the mosque today—only Ibn Duqmaq mentions it—and there is no indication as to where it would have originally been located. If it had existed, it would have been for a relatively short period of time during the Fatimid period.

The only feature that can be related to the *maqsura* of Fatima al-Zahra' is the so-called *mihrab* of Sayyida Nafisa, which is located on the left side of the main *mihrab* along the *qibla* wall (fig. 22, plan A (M5) and figs. 45, 46). This is a curious flat *mihrab* attributed to Sultan Lajin in 1296 (see appendix, no. 7). No explanation has been offered as to why it was built at all and in that particular place, which suggests that the *mihrab* of Sultan Lajin may have replaced an older Fatimid one. This might have been enclosed by an older maqsura from the Fatimid period named after al-Sayyida Fatima al-Zahra'.

With the mosque of Ibn Tulun's long history of deterioration and revivals, the names of popular features may have been forgotten. Many legends related to the building have also been forgotten. One may therefore consider that because of the proximity of the mosque-shrine of Sayyida Nafisa, to the south along al-Khalifa Street (fig. 80), the latter's name must have been linked in popular folk legends to that particular quarter of the city. These legends continued to be passed down until the name of Sayyida Nafisa eventually replaced that of Fatima al-Zahra'. Thus, the claimed *maqsura* of Fatima al-Zahra' was renamed for Sayyida Nafisa, and the *mihrab* in that *maqsura* became known as the *mihrab* of al-Sayyida Nafisa. This suggests that the *maqsura* of Fatima al-Zahra' was a small area incorporating a *mihrab* with the same name located around the area of the so-called *mihrab* of Sayyida Nafisa.[12] If there was in fact a *maqsura* built in the name of Fatima al-Zahra', it would have been smaller than the Tulunid *maqsura* and similar to the Fatimid one.

Fatimid Works in the Mosque of Ibn Tulun

Ibn Duqmaq, quoting al-Quda'i, says that the original (Tulunid) *fawwara* (fountain) in the middle of the *sahn* (open court) of the mosque of Ibn Tulun burned down on the evening of Thursday, Jumada II 10, 279 / October 17, 892.[13] Later on, the Fatimid caliph al-'Aziz bi-Allah ordered a new *fawwara* built by in the month of Muharram 385 / 995.[14] The date of the fire was later corrected by Maqrizi as the year 385 AH / 995 AD rather than 279 / 892 because that would have meant that the *fawwara* was burnt only nine years after Ibn Tulun's death in 270 / 883.[15] Consequently his successor and son, Amir Khumarawiya, would have automatically rebuilt the *fawwara*. It is therefore more reasonable that the *fawwara* burned down in 385 / 995, because Caliph al-'Aziz decided to build a new one immediately after the fire.[16] Historians do not provide a description of this new *fawwara* of Caliph al-'Aziz.

Caliph al-Mu'iz li-Din Allah charged the vizier Ya'qub Ibn Killis with all financial affairs of the empire. Later, his son Caliph al-'Aziz bi-Allah ordered Ibn Killis to add a new *fawwara* to the middle of the *sahn* of the mosque of 'Amr Ibn al-'As.[17] On top of that *fawwara* was a dome used as a treasury *(bayt al-mal)* of the Fatimid Empire. Ibn Killis and al-'Aziz thought there was no better place to keep the treasury than in the mosque, since it belonged to the people and not the ruling class. By doing so, Ibn Killis and al-'Aziz gained the favor of the Egyptians whom they had recently conquered.

The Fatimid caliphs continued to visit the mosque of Ibn Tulun on a regular basis. The Persian traveler Nasiri Khusraw (1004–1088), who visited Cairo between 1047 and 1048, recounts that Caliph al-Hakim bought the mosque from the inheritors of Ibn Tulun for 30,000 dinars.[18] Shortly thereafter, al-Hakim was surprised to hear that the descendants of Ibn Tulun had started to demolish the mosque's minaret. When he inquired what they were doing, they explained that they had sold him the mosque but not the minaret, and that they wanted to use the stone of the minaret.[19] Al-Hakim wisely ended the argument by paying them an additional sum of 5,000 dinars, and everyone was satisfied.[20] Nasiri Khusraw's story seems strange, especially since no other historian refers to it. Jonathan Bloom and Doris Behrens-Abouseif believe the story may be related to the folktales of the legendary figure Goha.[21] There is no doubt that the mosque of Ibn Tulun was still in use during the time of al-Hakim (386–411 / 996–1020) and that it was important enough for him to purchase it.

The mosque of Ibn Tulun's status as public or private was not always clear during the Fatimid period and historians do not provide much information about this point. In general, a mosque cannot be purchased or sold since it is the house of God, which would suggest that Nasiri's story is false. However, Caliph al-Hakim bi-Amr Allah was eager to buy Cairo's older mosques and it is known that in the year 1013 he purchased the mosque of 'Amr Ibn al-'As for 100,000 dinars from its descendants.[22] Thus there is reason to believe that there is some truth to the story and that the caliph did actually purchase the two important mosques—'Amr Ibn al-'As and Ibn Tulun—in Cairo. It is also likely that al-Hakim, being something of a protector of Islamic heritage, would have bought the land surrounding the mosque of Ibn Tulun to rescue the building from further deterioration.[23] The motives for these purchases are unclear, as is much surrounding the reign of this controversial ruler. Why would he spend such extravagant sums to buy two great mosques, which had been imbued with importance by his Fatimid predecessors? In fact, he had built a large mosque in his own name outside the early walls of al-Qahira, at Bab al-Futuh. There is reason to believe that the issue of buying an older mosque might have been another effort to gain popularity among the Egyptian people.

Al-Hakim was known to be involved in numerous political intrigues between the Sunnis and Shi'a and between the Jews and Egyptian Copts. He did not have a straightforward policy toward any of the religious factions and thus remained mysterious to a large degree.[24] However, the preservation of the mosque and its environs did not last long, after the disappearance of al-Hakim in 1021. (He went horse riding on the Muqattam Hills and mysteriously never returned. His body was never found and he was probably assassinated as a result of a conspiracy organized by his influential sister Sitt al-Mulk.) The mosque of Ibn Tulun entered another period of neglect and decline.

From an architectural-historical viewpoint, Creswell suggests the presence of an upper story implies that the minaret was seriously damaged during the time of al-Hakim.[25] However, a story related by Maqrizi, quoting Ibn Tuwayr (d. 617 / 1220), says that during the Nile Festival *(wafa' al-nil)* in 461 / 1067, a long cord was tied between the boat-shaped finial on top of the minaret and the street. An entertainer dressed as a cavalier and holding a lance and shield did acrobatic performances as he rolled down the rope to the street where the caliph was sitting.[26] This suggests that a tower still existed in the eleventh century.

Ghazi Muhammad believes the freestanding nature of the minaret of Ibn Tulun encouraged its inheritor's claim to it as independent property. He argues that their attempt to destroy the minaret may have damaged it to such an extent that al-Hakim had to reconstruct it and attach it to the mosque. Yet no source mentions such a project. Ghazi Muhammad bases his argument on the fact that the minaret was in excellent condition during the late Fatimid period; for example, in the year 461 / 1068 it was used for acrobatic performances in the story above.[27]

The Age of Badr al-Gammali and al-Afdal Shahinshah

During the 1060s, the Fatimids lived through a poor economic period due to several consecutive years of low Nile floods.[28] The result was that the Fatimid state imposed high prices on goods,[29] causing riots throughout Egypt in 460 AH / 1067 AD by ethnic Turkish troops against the African guards of Caliph al-Mustansir. When the chief of the Turkish troops achieved victory, his army began to loot the treasuries of the palace and the great library.[30] Conditions deteriorated rapidly, and a great famine followed these events in 467 / 1074.[31]

The historian Maqrizi says that the cities of al-Qata'i' and al-'Askar had already fallen into ruin by the start of the reign of Caliph al-Mustansir (Safar 470 / August-September 1077). Nobody was living in the area where the mosque of Ibn Tulun was located, because the surroundings were severely dilapidated.[32] Part of the mosque was actually burned and destroyed during the riots described above.[33] Caliph al-Mustansir's only option was to ask for assistance from Syria. The Armenian governor of

82 – Close-up of the marble inscription of Badr al-Gammali, in graceful foliated Kufic script, below the remarkable crenellations.

Acre (in the Holy Land), Badr al-Gammali, brought his troops to Egypt and restored order throughout the country.

Badr al-Gammali revived the *kharaj* to improve the financial and economic conditions of his new regime controlling Egypt. Tax records may have been kept in the Dar al-Imara building itself and one could argue that Badr al-Gammali wanted to revive the functions of Dar al-Imara for that purpose. In doing so, he restored the area of the mosque and put up his own inscription over the main entrance.[34] Scholarly research proves that Badr al-Gammali ordered this restoration right after he came to Egypt, pacifying both Upper and Lower Egypt.[35]

The inscription over the mosque's modern entrance (figs. 79, 82) indicates that this area was the most damaged part, suggesting that the riots were aimed at the destruction of Dar al-Imara, which is adjacent to that side of the mosque.[36] This means the part of the mosque which had suffered most was that area under the inscription and part of the wall where the main modern entrance is located as well as part of the northern *ziyada*. However, since the medieval historians did not mention this restoration, it probably did not amount to much.[37] The placement of that inscription shows that this entrance must have been the most frequently used due to its close proximity to Dar al-Imara.

There is no doubt that Badr al-Gammali had the greatest impact on Egypt during the Fatimid period due to his political, military, and architectural accomplishments. After consolidating his power in Egypt, he built new fortifications around the city in stone rather than firebrick and enlarged the city on all sides, incorporating the mosque of al-Hakim in the process. Hence, the famous gates of al-Qahira were built: Bab al-Futuh (Gate of Conquest) and Bab al-Nasr (Gate of Victory) in the north; and Bab Zuwayla in the south (fig. 80). Armenian architects whom Badr al-Gammali had brought with him built these splendid gates, which show traces of their Armenian influence. The city of al-Qahira thus became well fortified and up-to-date in all methods of defense. Badr al-Gammali's walls were the most advanced fortifications of military architectural projects until the eleventh century.

Badr al-Gammali is also known for his small memorial tomb *(mashhad)* on top of the Muqqatam Hills overlooking the city of Fustat and its cemetery of al-Qarafa (fig. 83). He adopted the title of Amir al-Guyushi (General or Prince of the Armies). After Badr al-Gammali's death in 1094, his son al-Afdal Shahinshah succeeded him as vizier. At the time, the *kharaj* and *diya'* were still administered from Dar al-Imara, and the mosque was constantly in use.[38] On one of the piers in the *qibla riwaq*, a flat stucco *mihrab* is fixed and bears the name of Caliph al-Mustansir. It was added by Vizier al-Afdal Shahinshah (fig. 22, plan A (M4); 42, 44).[39] The *mihrab* has been well studied by Van Berchem, who dates it to 485 / 1094.[40]

Like the other flat *mihrab*s, this one generates questions when it comes to function: why was it placed here? An explanation might be that the entourage increased tremendously during the Fatimid period, and therefore the *maqsura* had to be enlarged. Since the mosque was frequently used by the Fatimids to announce the *kharaj*, the old Tulunid *maqsura* became too small or simply deteriorated from a long period of neglect after the destruction of al-Qata'i'. When the mosque was revived again during the Fatimid period, the *maqsura* area had

83 – The *mashhad* of Amir al-Guyushi of Badr al-Gammali atop the Muqqatam Hills, where it could be viewed from anywhere in the capital city of al-Qahira. Today it is dwarfed by tall telecomunication and satellite antenae around it.

to be expanded. To indicate the direction of the *qibla* and the main *mihrab*, this one was therefore added.

It is impossible to believe that this *mihrab* stood on its own. The Fatimids were known for their strong adherence to artistic aesthetics and symmetry was important to their designs. It is therefore likely that another *mihrab* was added at the same time on the left-hand side to achieve symmetry. This second *mihrab* would have been almost identical to it and is attributed to Sultan Lajin (fig. 22, plan A; 42).[41] It must have replaced another one that was contemporary with that of al-Afdal's and symmetrical to it. One may assume that the earlier Fatimid *mihrab* had deteriorated badly, and therefore Sultan Lajin restored it. Both *mihrab*s indicated the direction and orientation of the main *mihrab*, which could not be seen because of the high wooden screen of the *maqsura* that connected them.

The *mihrab* of al-Afdal has a rectangular frame with an upside-down U-shaped band enclosing two horizontal bands above an arched frame, which encloses a smaller arch. A large inscription around the exterior gives the patron's titles, and Qur'anic inscriptions cover the borders of the inner arch (see appendix, no. 4). There is also a small historical inscription across the top and a restored inscription in large Kufic script on the innermost arch. There is no date on the *mihrab*, but since it mentions al-Mustansir and al-Afdal the date is limited to 487 / 1094.[42]

The *mihrab* of al-Afdal is an excellent example of Fatimid stuccowork, but the designer seems not to have been very skilled, because the letters are crowded at the corners due to the placement of the caliph and the vizier's names prominently on the top right and top left respectively. A more talented designer would have designed the whole *mihrab* with the inscriptions on paper before working with plaster to avoid such a problem.[43] Scholars believe the scheme of the decoration of this *mihrab* is probably a combination of native Egyptian and Persian styles.[44] The *mihrab* of al-Afdal had deteriorated by the beginning of the twentieth century and a copy was made and exhibited in the Arab Museum in Cairo, known today as the Museum of Islamic Art.[45]

It is strange that during his twenty-year tenure, al-Afdal built neither a mosque that bore his name nor a *mashhad* for himself like his father Badr al-Gammali did. His sole contribution to the architecture of Cairo was the *mihrab* in the mosque of Ibn Tulun. One reason for this might be that he was heavily engaged in political and military confrontations with the Seljuk Turks who were taking control of Bilad al-Sham (modern-day Syria, Lebanon, Jordan, and Palestine). Al-Afdal was worried the Seljuk invaders would eventually make their way into Egypt to revive Sunni doctrine. His fear reached the extent that when he heard about the first Crusades, he marched to Palestine with his troops to pave the way for the Crusaders to capture Jerusalem.[46] In that sense, he actually preferred to help the Crusaders rather than the Seljuks. It appears that al-Afdal decided to focus on his political career

84 – Rendered image of the mosque during the Fatimid period. Removing the roof shows the limits of the newly enlarged *maqsura* area, which was defined by a wooden screen.

and was satisfied with his addition of a *mihrab* to the mosque of Ibn Tulun by expanding the area of *maqsura* for a larger Fatimid entourage (fig. 84). Bloom suggests that by erecting this *mihrab,* al-Afdal made a public statement without going through the expense of building and endowing a new mosque.[47] Badr al-Gammali and al-Afdal did not need to build mosques which bore their names as they were only viziers (*wazirs*) and did not have caliphal blood. The mosque of Ibn Tulun was suitable for them to 'take over' after it had been neglected for long periods. The mosque became directly associated with them rather than with the ruler of their time, Caliph al-Mustansir.

Later in the Fatimid period, the vizier Ma'mun al-Bata'ihi built the mosque of al-Aqmar in 1125 along the main Qasaba, which is known today as al-Mu'iz Street (fig. 80). At the end of the Fatimid period, the vizier al-Salih al-Tala'i' built his mosque outside Bab Zuwayla. It seems that the memory of Badr al-Gammali and his son al-Afdal were both attached so strongly to the mosque of Ibn Tulun that the later Fatimid rulers had no option but to build new mosques that were relatively small in size. In other words, they were unable to overshadow the mosque of Ibn Tulun.

Fridays during the Fatimid Period

One would assume that the rituals of Friday prayer in the mosque of Ibn Tulun would not have changed much during the Ikhshidid and early Fatimid periods. The Fatimid caliph would parade to the mosque in an elaborate ceremony from the fortified city of al-Qahira in a procession known as *shaq al-Qahira* (processional ceremony through Cairo). He would enter the Dar al-Imara, which was still in use. Once inside, he would see about affairs, perform his ablutions, change his garments, fumigate his body with incense, then put on perfume and walk into the mosque via the door to the left of the main *mihrab*, similar to what Ibn Tulun used to do earlier. The *khatib* of the mosque would use the other door to ascend the *minbar* for the Friday sermon. As in earlier times, the armies and local population would enter through the doors on the three sides of the mosque into the *ziyada* area. They would use the *mayda'a* for ablutions before congregating inside the *riwaq*s. There is no indication that the medical clinic was still in use. If anyone wanted a drink of water, he would use the *fawwara*. The same procedure and ceremony would have probably continued through the reigns of the caliphs al-Mu'iz, al-'Aziz, al-Hakim, al-Hafiz, and al-Mustansir.

Badr al-Gammali and his Armenian entourage probably used the entrance on the northeast wall of the mosque above which he had placed his marble inscription (indicated as B1 in fig. 9, plan A; see also figs. 79, 82). Given Badr al-Gammali's status in the ruling hierarchy, he would have performed a ritual separately from the caliph. This would have given his entry into the mosque of Ibn Tulun more attention in front of his army and the local population. Consequently, Badr al-Gammali would walk up the first flight of steps and through the *ziyada* area to gather with more officials waiting to greet him before continuing up the second flight of steps of the mosque's interior. Then he would walk through the *riwaq*s to the area of the old Tulunid *maqsura* or what had remained of it. Finally, he would sit next to or behind the caliph.

The rituals might have developed further during the tenure of Badr al-Gammali's son, Vizier al-Afdal Shahinshah who would have used the same entrance as his father. He would have walked up the two flights of stairs via the *ziyada* and instead of walking into the old Tulunid *maqsura*,

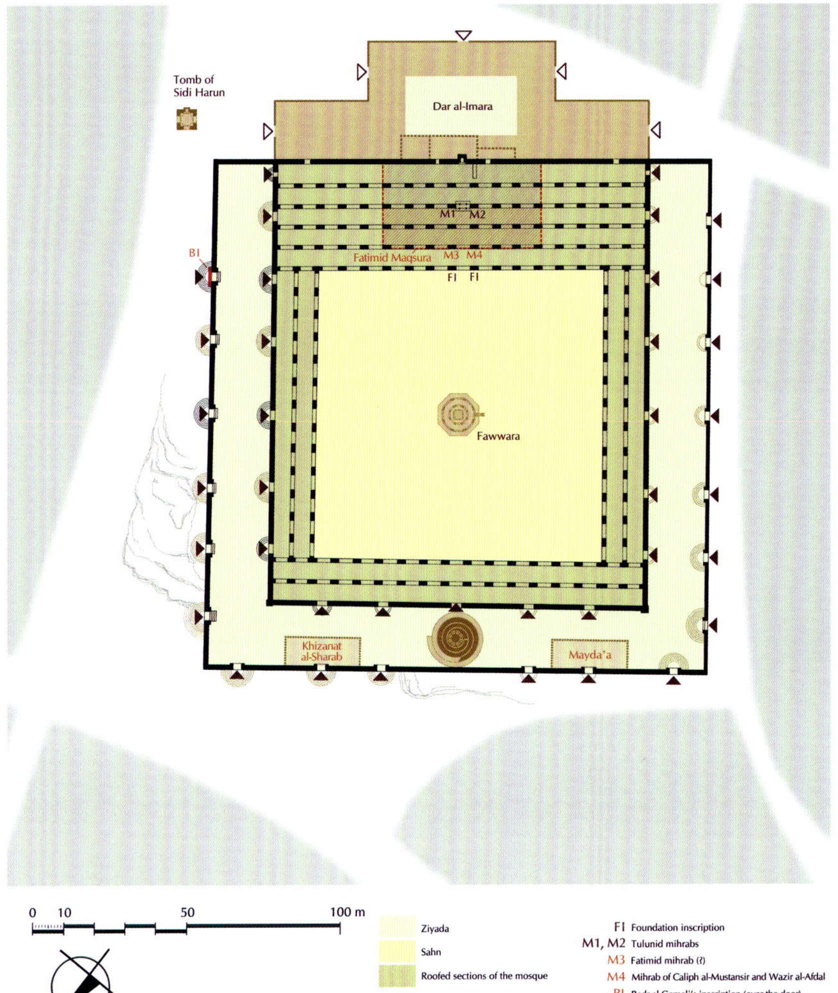

85, plan B – Reconstructed plan of the mosque of Ibn Tulun during the Fatimid period.

he would have walked into the new Fatimid one which was restricted by the two flat *mihrab*s, which he had founded. The *maqsura* of the mosque would have been much wider and larger than the old Tulunid one to accommodate the increasing numbers of the entourage and high officials of the court. After the Friday prayer, the *wazir* would ascend the *minbar* of the mosque to call out for the *kharaj* and *diya'*—the tax collections. One may imagine a reconstruction of the wooden screen bordering the area of the *maqsura* area during the Fatimid period in a bird's-eye view in figure 84. Consequently, a ground plan for the mosque of Ibn Tulun during the Fatimid period may be put forward, as in figure 85, plan B.

The Ayyubid Period

8

Low Nile flooding during the 1160s created great difficulties for the Fatimids. Internal civil strife combined with external threats from the Crusaders, who had established their Latin kingdoms along the western coast of the Holy Land and Bilad al-Sham, brought chaos to Egypt and its Fatimid rulers. This included King Amalric's attack on Fustat in 1168-69, which led to the burning of the city—ordered by the Fatimid vizier Shawar to stop it falling into the invaders' hands. The Fatimids were desperate and requested assistance from the Zangid atabeks of Bilad al-Sham. The popular general Shirkuh, who was under the command of Nur al-Din Zangi, was asked to restore order to Egypt. Among the army generals of Shirkuh was his nephew, Salah al-Din Yusuf (known as Saladin of the Crusades). Upon arriving in Egypt, they arrested and executed Shawar, and shortly afterward, in 1169, Shirkuh died suddenly and Salah al-Din assumed control. Amalric retreated to Jerusalem. Fustat was neither invaded nor destroyed by the Crusaders; it was the Fatimids who burned it down. It fell into ruin, never to regain its former prominence.[1] Salah al-Din managed to restore order to the country and, like Badr al-Gammali before him, he became the real ruler of Egypt. During the process, Salah al-Din revived the Sunni tradition and created a new regime known as the Ayyubid dynasty with al-Qahira as its capital.[2]

86 – Light is reflected on the piers of the *qibla riwaq*.

However, as a great military commander, Salah al-Din did not spend any leisure time in Egypt. To the contrary, once he established his status in Egypt, he returned to his hometown of Damascus where he lived until his death in 1193. Salah al-Din defeated the Crusaders in the Battle of Hittin (1187) near the Sea of Galilee (Lake Tabariya) and regained the city of Jerusalem.

With the advent of Salah al-Din's rule in 568 AH / 1172 AD, the mosque of Ibn Tulun was neglected as a formal mosque. After consolidating his power in Egypt, Salah al-Din began the foundation of the Citadel of Cairo. He also allowed the local Egyptian populace to enter the great Fatimid palaces at Bayn al-Qasrayn, which resulted in their looting and eventual destruction, as well as the destruction of surrounding buildings. While the Citadel was being built, Salah al-Din converted one of the Fatimid palaces in the area of Bayn al-Qasrayn into his private residence and the headquarters of the administration of Egypt.[3] The administration was later moved to the Citadel, which became the administrative headquarters for Egypt and the entire Ayyubid Empire—and remained so for all rulers of Egypt until the Palace of Abdin was built in the 1860s—as well as the place in which royal public audiences were held. Thus, Dar al-Imara behind the mosque of Ibn Tulun was no longer used as an administrative center.

Transformation of the Mosque

The traveler and historian Ibn Jubayr (1145-1217) recounts that Salah al-Din made the mosque of Ibn Tulun a place for the foreigners *(ghuraba)* coming from the western lands of Barbary and Spain—"*min al-maghariba*"—to live and attend lectures.[4] This account is important to the history of the mosque of Ibn Tulun because it documents that Salah al-Din changed the mosque's function from a place of worship into an official place of habitation[5]—he transformed it into a sort of caravanserai or hostel for pilgrims. Maqrizi confirms this, saying that they came to stay with their camels and baggage as they passed through Egypt during the Hajj pilgrimage journeys.[6] At that time, Cairo was heavily urbanized, so large enclosed spaces were scarce. The mosque of Ibn Tulun was already neglected, so it made sense that from the 570s / 1180s onward the mosque was used as a shelter for Maghribis.[7]

Ibn Jubayr adds that Salah al-Din granted them a monthly allowance and created an incentive for them to use the mosque by allowing them to have their own rules and regulations, with no interference from government authorities,[8] and even that the Maghribis could appoint someone from their own community to act as their ruler.[9] However, Salah al-Din, being a talented politician, had a further motive in that he sought to isolate these Maghribis from the rest of the Egyptian

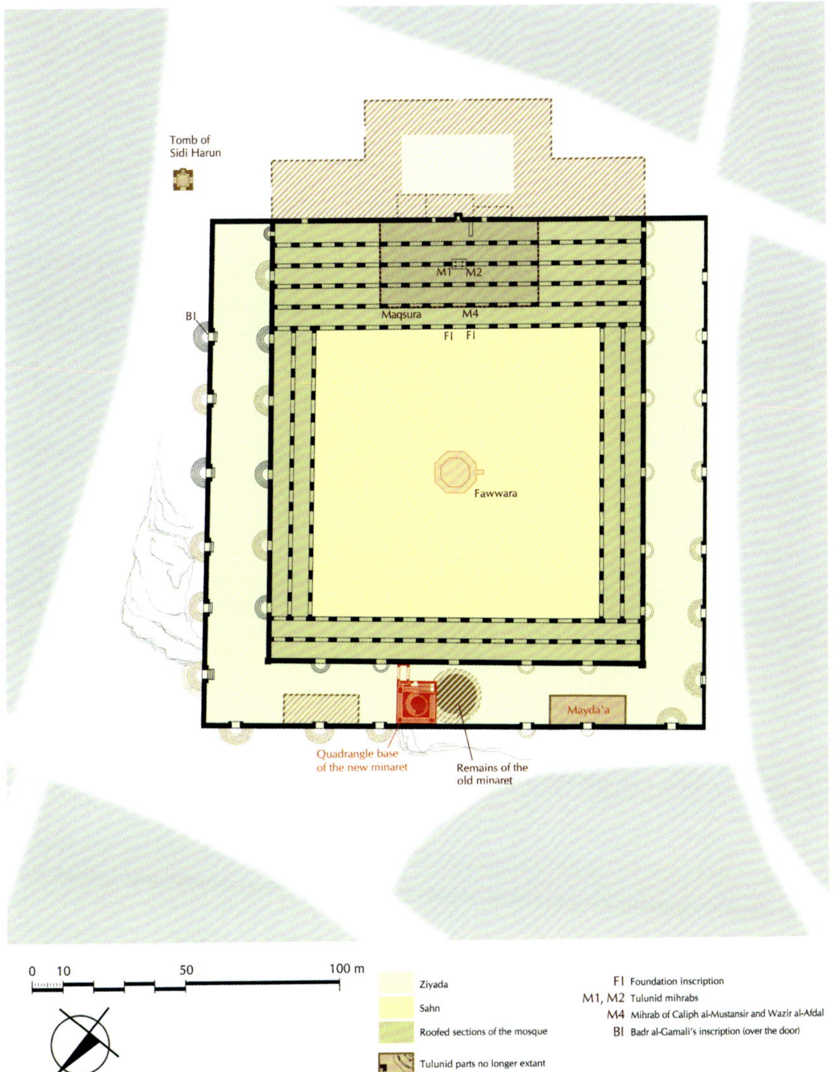

87, plan D – Reconstructed plan of the mosque during the Ayyubid period.

population in order to control their activities and dealings. Already facing the threat of the third Crusade, he was cautious about the North Africans, from whom the Fatimid Shi'i regime originated, and sought to avoid the risk that they might have wanted to regain their power in Egypt.[10] Furthermore, if they had been scattered throughout the city, it would have been difficult to control them and to collect taxes or customs for crossing through Egypt on the way to Mecca.

As for the mosque's architecture, as argued in *The Minaret of Ibn Tulun Reconsidered*, the lower part of its minaret might have been built

88 – Bird's-eye-view reconstruction of the mosque from the north.

during the Ayyubid period,[11] as the two blind windows with horseshoe arch decorations on the lower quadrangle must have been made by a Maghribi-Andalusian architect who was living in the mosque during the Ayyubid period. This argument is supported by the fact that the blind arches are horizontally centered on a quadrangular base but vertically off-center in relation to the height of the minaret. This implies that these decorations were designed for the lower quadrangular level without concern for the symmetry of the minaret's elevation, which also suggests that the lower and upper stories were not built simultaneously. Therefore, it seems that the horseshoe decorations would have been made at the same time as the quadrangle story.[12]

The same study says that since Ibn Jubayr did not mention or describe the minaret, the original Tulunid minaret must no longer have been standing during the second half of the twelfth century.[13] By that time, the original minaret must have been dilapidated or partially destroyed. The new Maghribi community wanted to add a structure for the call to prayer, so they built the square quadrangle and decorated it with horseshoes, marking the mosque's new identity as belonging to a Maghribi community (figs. 50, 52).

Within the same context, the bridge connecting the minaret to the roof of the mosque is both interesting and puzzling (fig. 50). A gigantic horseshoe arch supports the bridge underneath which are decorated patterns described by Creswell as *modillon a copeaux* (fig. 51). The entrance of the minaret is decorated by a handsome horseshoe arch, which has no equivalent in Cairo's Islamic architecture. Corbet suggested that the bridge connecting the minaret with the roof of the mosque was a later addition and probably dates to the time of Lajin in 1296. However, if Sultan Lajin had built it, he would have included an inscription to that effect just as in the case of the *minbar* and the domed *fisqiya* in the middle of the *sahn*. The decorations of the *modillon a copeaux*, under the bridge, was a foreign element, which was common in western Islamic architecture, as well as in Central Asia, but not in Egypt.[14] The presence of the *modillion a copeaux* and the horseshoe entrance to the minaret as well as the entire structure of the bridge may have been the product of the North African-Spanish architects who were inhabiting the mosque during that period—and therefore may be attributed to the Ayyubid period. During the Ayyubid period, the quadrangular—and perhaps the circular—stories of the mosque's minaret were built. The decorative features of the horseshoe arches can be interpreted as part of a Maghribi propaganda effort intended to symbolize and publicize their presence. These decorations gave the mosque its new identity and character. After Salah al-Din, the mosque continued to be used as a shelter. The historian Maqrizi says that during the early years of Sultan al-Kamil (615-35 / 1218-38) the minaret of Ibn Tulun was always illuminated on the evening of the middle of the month of Sha'ban, a tradition that was later abandoned.[15] The notion that the minaret was illuminated shows that the building was used during that period and great effort would have been made in order to light it up.

Salah al-Din had a great impact on the mosque of Ibn Tulun. He revived the function of the building as a mosque and introduced a *madrasa* curriculum for the benefit of the resident Maghribi community.[16] The mosque of Ibn Tulun during the Ayyubid period was transformed partially from a place of worship into a residential area. This was due to its large enclosed space—a facility that Salah al-Din could exploit for a completely different purpose.

One might imagine the mosque of Ibn Tulun during the Ayyubid period as an enclosed area full of foreign-looking people from North Africa and Andalusia. The markets remained around the mosque

89 – Bird's-eye-view reconstruction of the mosque during the Ayyubid period showing the quadrangular first story of the newly built minaret from an elevated eastern point.

90 – Reconstruction of the interior of the mosque during the Ayyubid period showing the quadrangular first story of the newly built minaret, which is decorated with double blind horseshoe windows defining the mosque's new identity as being Maghribi/North African/Andalusian. (It is not known how the *fawwara* would have looked and is therefore faded.)

for buying food and goods. The *ziyada* area was the place to register Maghribi pilgrims who were arriving and departing. The *riwaq*s might have been walled up or separated by thick tent material to house the Maghribi pilgrims. The *fawwara* of al-'Aziz might have been functioning still as a source of drinking water. The *qibla riwaq* would have been used for prayer. Somewhere in the mosque would have been a meeting place used to settle disputes between the inhabitants. Ibn Jubayr's account mentions that Salah al-Din gave the Maghribis the freedom to appoint whoever they wished to oversee their affairs. Elsewhere in the mosque would be the *madrasa* where they would hold classes about Sunni doctrine and jurisprudence. The mosque would have still had the *mayda'a* in the *ziyada* area near the minaret, but the old Tulunid minaret would have been partially demolished and probably not visible from the open court inside the mosque. Another tower was built adjacent to it, which was the quadrangular base of the current minaret. It is not known if the second circular shaft was built or completed by that time, but the horseshoe arch decorations or blind windows were visible from the quadrangular four sides, giving the mosque its new Maghribi identity.

If one imagines a reconstruction of how the mosque would have appeared during the Ayyubid period, from the open court looking toward the minaret, one would only see the quadrangle of the new minaret; and almost none of the old Tulunid spiral would be visible (fig. 90). Furthermore, one may imagine how the mosque would have appeared during the Ayyubid period in the bird's-eye views presented in figures 88 and 89 and the new ground plan of the mosque in figure 87, plan D.

The Mamluk Period

9

Medieval historians give the impression that not much activity was taking place in the mosque of Ibn Tulun through the last phase of the Ayyubid period. The last Ayyubid ruler, Sultan al-Salih Nagm al-Din Ayyub, had started importing young boys from the area between the Caspian and the Black Sea, who became known as the Mamluks. This was a large, sophisticated corps of bodyguards who developed into strong armies. They were loyal to no one but their master–the sultan. Great celebrities emerged from this body of elite men–such as Aqtay, Qutuz, Aybak, Baybars and Qalawun – who became the masterminds of all the political and military events that took place in the years that followed. Equally important and close to the sultan was his shrewd Armenian wife, the famous Shagar al-Durr, and his son, Turan Shah.

91 – The dominant domical *fisqiya* in the middle of the open court *(sahn)*.

The French King Louis IX led the seventh Crusade, which attacked Egypt from the Mediterranean port of Damietta. The Mamluk forces of Sultan al-Salih Nagm fought against the Crusader army. In the Battle of Fariskur (1260), near the modern-day town of al-Mansura, they managed to defeat and capture the French king. Instead of killing him, they asked for a large ransom for his release. Meanwhile, Sultan al-Salih fell ill and died. His son Turan Shah wanted to take over his rule, but the Mamluks had him killed. The sultan's wife Shagar al-Durr became queen of the Mamluks. To legalize her status, she married one of the Mamluk generals–Aybak. He was assassinated shortly after. Then, Shagar al-Durr's own slaves killed her in one of the most famous assassinations in history: She was beaten to death with wooden clogs. General Qutuz, who feared the Mongol invasion from the east, took over as the Mongols invaded and destroyed the city of Baghdad–the capital of the Abbasid caliphate–and swept through the area of Bilad al-Sham. Qutuz and Baybars joined their armies and met the Mongols, and at 'Ain Jalut, in Palestine, a fierce battle took place. The

Mamluks dealt the Mongols their worst defeat ever. On their way back to al-Qahira, Baybars asked Qutuz to reward him with the governorship of Acre (in the Holy Land), but Qutuz refused so Baybars killed him before they reached the gates of the city. Baybars was recognized as the new Mamluk sultan and was received in al-Qahira as the victorious leader. A new era began: the Mamluk period, best described as the 'golden age' of Islamic Egypt.

Sultan al-Zahir Baybars did not give much attention to the mosque of Ibn Tulun. He was engaged with his own affairs against the Crusaders in Bilad al-Sham. Like Salah al-Din a century earlier, Sultan Baybars did not stay in Egypt long. He took Damascus as his central base and military headquarters, from where he attacked and conquered every Crusader castle in the area.[1] In Egypt, Sultan Baybars was busy building his huge mosque, which still bears his name: the mosque of al-Dahir outside the walled city of al-Qahira. Within the city, in the area of Bayn al-Qasrayn, Sultan Baybars erected a handsome *madrasa* adjacent to the complex of his master, Sultan al-Salih Nagm al-Din Ayyub, in the area of the eastern Fatimid palace.[2]

The mosque of Ibn Tulun was not given any architectural attention because of the other contemporary building taking place elsewhere. However, according to Maqrizi, Sultan al-Zahir Baybars ordered bread to be distributed from the mosque of Ibn Tulun to the various small prayer areas without minarets *(zawiyas)*.[3] Thus it appears that a bakery must have been added to the mosque during his reign. It would likely have been located close to the spiral-shaped minaret in the *ziyada* area, which was close to the urbanized area, rather than the back area where the building of the Dar al-Imara used to stand. Upon the death of Sultan Baybars, his companion Qalawun succeeded him as sultan. Qalawun sought to consolidate the power of the Mamluks, which Baybars had established over Egypt and the region of Bilad al-Sham. At his capital city of al-Qahira, in the area of Bayn al-Qasrayn, Sultan Qalawun founded a fantastic complex incorporating a mosque-*madrasa*, domed mausoleum, and a huge *bimaristan*, which was opposite those of Sultan al-Salih Nagm al-Din Ayyub and Sultan Baybars. The intense building activity during Sultan Qalawun's reign is probably the reason why there is no mention of any architectural projects in the mosque of Ibn Tulun.

The reign of Sultan Qalawun's son, Sultan al-Nasir Muhammad, was a period of turmoil, as the Mamluks fought among themselves to become sultan. The long reign of Sultan al-Nasir Muhammad (1293-1342) was interrupted three times by periods of exile. During his second exile, the rivalry between the Mamluks reached its peak. The sultan's brother, al-Ashraf Khalil, known as the most treacherous Mamluk, was cruel and therefore disliked, so his Mamluks killed him.

Sultan Lajin's Additions and Restorations in Ibn Tulun's Mosque

During this period, the Mamluk Amir Husam al-Din Lajin escaped and hid in the ruins of the old Tulunid spiral-shaped minaret of the mosque of Ibn Tulun.[4] Maqrizi states that Lajin lived in a poor state, alone and miserable. He describes the mosque as uninhabited, deserted, and abandoned.[5] Ibn Duqmaq adds that Amir Lajin lived there for a whole year.[6] However, Maqrizi says that at night, only one lamp was lit, and no one went up the minaret to announce the call to prayer. Instead the *muezzins* announced it from the door of the mosque.[7] This may suggest that the minaret was in poor condition, and the congregation was very small. In any case, during the period of his hiding, Lajin vowed that if God rescued him and made him sultan, he would restore the mosque and revive its glory,[8] giving it a large endowment deed (*waqf*).[9]

When Lajin ascended the throne, he kept his promise and restored the mosque. One might wonder why Sultan Lajin decided to use, add to, and restore the mosque of Ibn Tulun when the city had so much space and land available. The distribution of mosques, *madrasas*, *khankas*, and tombs in the city would have easily allowed him to build a mosque-*madrasa* in the area of Bayn al-Qasrayn, or outside the city walls in the area of al-Husaniya, or along the Darb al-Ahmar, but he did not (fig. 92). The fact that he did not and instead used the mosque of Ibn Tulun suggests that he wanted to use the existing building, as it was grand, famous, and quite monumental. In fact, one may consider that Sultan Lajin had the same intentions as that of Badr al-Gammali

92 – Mamluk Cairo in the year 1299.

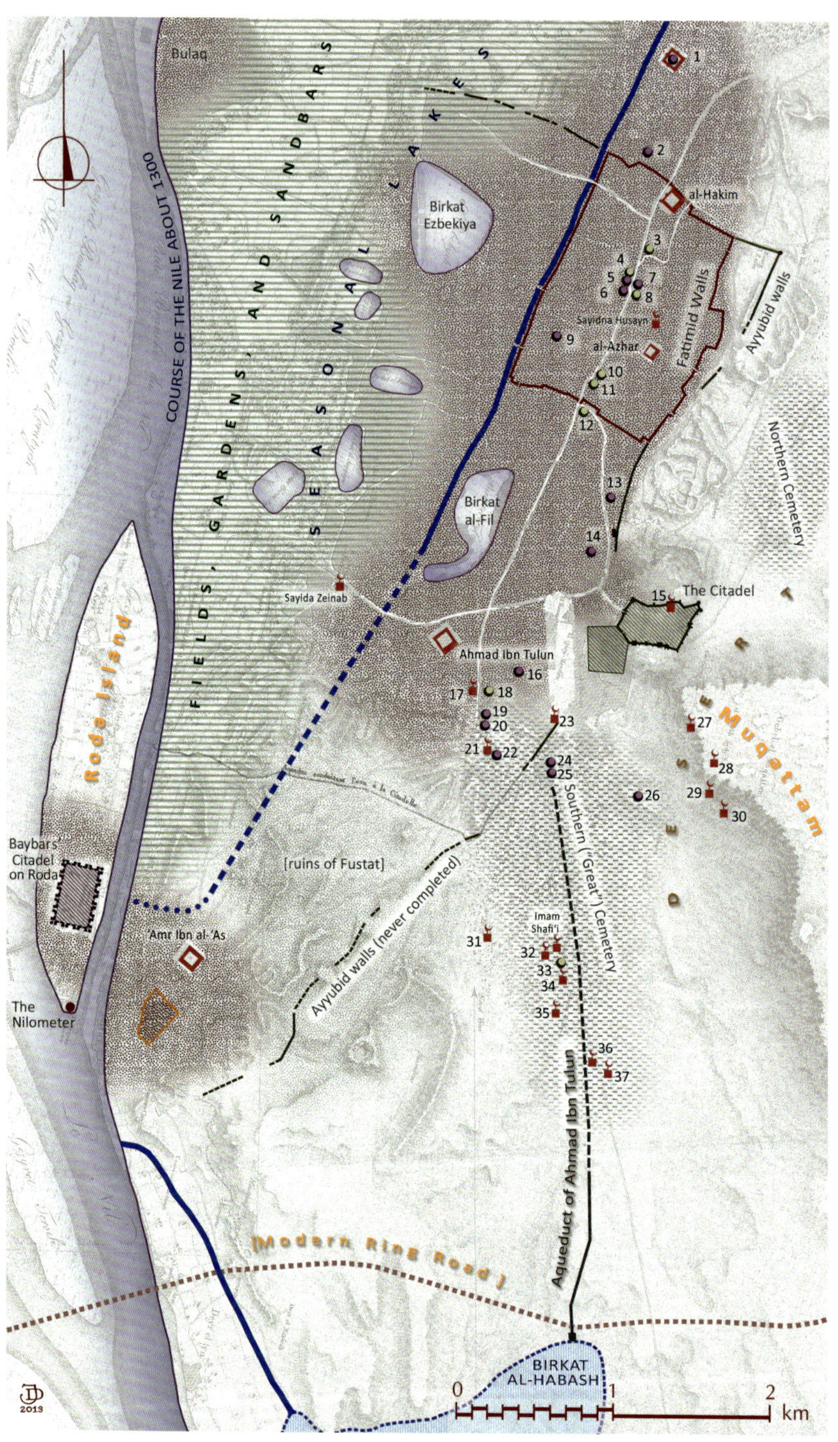

Legend for figure 92

1	Mosque of al-Zahir Baybars:	1	(1266-69)
2	Madrasa al-Mazhariya (doors preserved):	8	(1298)
3	al-Aqmar mosque:	33	(1125)
4	Madrasa al-Kamiliya:	428	(1125)
5	Madrasa of al-Nasir Muhammad:	44	(1295-1304)
6	Complex of al-Mansur Qalawun:	43	(1284-85)
7	Madrasa of al-Zahir Baybars:	37	(1262-63)
8	Madrasa and tomb of al-Salih Ayyub:	38	(1243-50)
9	Mausoleum of Husam al-Din Turuntay:	590	(1290)
10	al-Fakahani mosque:	[with 109]	(12th cent.)
11	Sam Ibn Nuh mosque	[unlisted]	(before 11th cent.)
12	al-Salih al-Tala'i' mosque:	116	(1160)
13	Zawiya al-Hunud:	237	(1260)
14	Between 13 and 14: Palace of Alin Aq:	249	(1293)
15	Ribat of Ahmad Ibn Sulayman:	245	(1291)
16	Mashhad of Sidi Sariya:	[with 142]	(Fatimid)
17	al-Baqli mosque (minaret survives):	156	(1297)
17	Mashhad of Sayyida Ruqayya:	273	(1133)
	mausoleums of Sayyida 'Atiqa and Muhammad al-Ga'fari:	333	(1120-25)
18	Mausoleum of Shagar al-Durr:	169	(1250)
19	Tomb and minaret of Fatima Khatun:	274	(1283-84)
20	Mausoleum of al-Ashraf Khalil:	275	(1288)
21	Sayyida Nafisa shrine	[unlisted]	(Fatimid or earlier)
22	Tombs "of 'Abbasid Caliphs":	276	(1242-43)
23	Sayyida 'Aisha shrine	[with 378]	(Fatimid or earlier)
24	Mausoleum of Mustafa Pasha:	279	(1267-73)
25	Madrasa and tomb of Zayn al-Din Yusuf:	172	(1298)
26	Qubbat al-Sawabi:	296	(1285-86)
27	Cave of Sudan al-Maghawri:	517	(1030)
28	Mashhad al-Guyushi:	304	(1085)
29	Mashhad Ihwat Yusuf al-Asbat:	301	(12th cent.)
30	Mosque of al-Lu'lu'a:	515	(1016)
31	Tombs of the Tabataba family:	563	(10th cent.)
32	Mausoleum of al-Hasawati:	315	(12th cent.)
33	Mausoleum of Isma'il Ibn Tha'lab	282	(1216)
34	Mashhad of Yahya al-Shabihi:	285	(1150)
	and mausoleums of Qasim Abu Tayyib:	284	(12th cent.)
	and of Umm Kulthum:	516	(1122)
35	Mosque and tomb of Imam al-Layth:	[with 286]	(Fatimid or earlier)
36	Tombs of Dhu l'Nun Misri	[unlisted]	
	and three other prominent sheikhs	(?-early)	
37	Mosque and tomb of Sidi 'Uqba	[with 535]	(Fatimid or earlier)

and his son the vizier al-Afdal. The mosque must also have had some sentimental value, since he had lived and hid inside it for at least a year. One may assume that at some point during his hiding, he walked around it and felt pity at its state of dilapidation, and at the same time, admired its architecture and its grandeur. His work on the mosque was certainly impressive, successful, and has had a positive mark in the history of the mosque.

He entrusted the work to Amir 'Alam al-Din (Sangar) al-Dawadari al-Salihi, who restored it extremely well. In addition, he installed the teachings of *fiqh* (jurisprudence), *hadith* (lectures, speeches, and advice of the Prophet Muhammad), *tafsir* (interpretations of the holy Qur'an), *tibb* (medicine), and other subjects.[10] Sultan Lajin also appointed a teacher of religious guidance *(sheikh mi'ad)*.[11] The endowment established a fixed income for the preacher *(khatib)* of the mosque. Lastly, Lajin appointed an *imam* to the mosque with a regular salary, in addition to more *muezzins* and attendants *(farrashin)*. Ibn Duqmaq tells us that Sultan Lajin also created a special *waqf* for roosters to be kept in a special area on top of the mosque's roof to determine prayer times for the *muezzins*.[12] Ibn Duqmaq adds that the mosque was in its best possible condition during his time.[13] Maqrizi estimates the cost of the restoration at 20,000 dinars.[14]

Sultan Lajin was generous in his restoration. He bought land as a perpetual endowment for the mosque, and he paid Amir Sangar to build the mosque and gave him strict orders not to use forced labor to build it.[15] Sultan Lajin also forbade having taskmasters for the workmen, and he bought everything at full price.[16] Displaying more of this generosity, Sultan Lajin informed Amir Sangar that he would pay everything from his own budget.[17] In this way, the village of Minyat Anduna in Giza was endowed. Furthermore, Sultan Lajin bought all the land behind the mosque, which once contained the building of Dar al-Imara.[18]

In restoring the mosque, Sultan Lajin removed debris and had the mosque paved and whitewashed.[19] The structure of the mosque was also well restored, but not changed then or at any time during the Mamluk period. However, Maqrizi says that Sultan Lajin had the structure well consolidated by restoring its walls. [20] Creswell's examination

93 – View of the rear part of the mosque showing the three rooms behind the main *mihrab*, (see fig. 22, plan A, 1, 2, 3).

of the mosque's 128 windows shows that some of the windows are decorated with stucco ornaments, which are typical of the thirteenth and early fourteenth century.[21] Accordingly, Creswell correctly attributes a few windows to works of Sultan Lajin in 696 / 1296.[22]

The Rooms Behind the Main *Mihrab*

On the right and left sides of the main *mihrab* and *minbar*, there are two doors leading to three rooms behind the *qibla* wall (figs. 22, plan A (1, 2, 3); 93). These are believed to be part of the old Dar al-Imara (where Ibn Tulun would have gone from the palace to renew his ablutions and prepare for prayer, before entering the mosque's *maqsura* area through a door) and Maqrizi specifies that the door of Dar al-Imara was part of the *qibla* wall.[23] Maqrizi adds that this area fell into ruin after the Fatimid period, and that this area was then bought and monopolized by Amir Sangar al-Dawadari at the time of Sultan Lajin in 696 AH / 1296 AD.[24] The present rooms are not related to the Dar al-Imara of Ibn Tulun, nor did they exist when Sultan Lajin came to Egypt. However, they were later restored or added by him, and a small *diwan* (lounge area or office) may have been built in its place.

Creswell describes the rooms as having large, elaborate corbels that supported a ceiling, which appear "like the foreparts of gigantic locusts" (fig. 94). He adds that in 1934, Marcais showed that they were a local version of a type of corbel used in Muslim Spain, and there are many examples of buildings that use it.[25] However, a similar type of corbel can also be found in Central Asia.[26] None of the modern historians who have studied the mosque of Ibn Tulun have analyzed the functions of these rooms behind the main *mihrab*. The *waqfiya* document of Sultan Lajin does not refer to a Dar al-Imara in that area. In fact, the *waqfiya* mentions that there was a mill built behind the mosque on its southern limit (meaning the *qibla* wall).[27] It adds that near the mill was a door close to the *minbar*, which was used by the mosque's preacher *(khatib)* to enter and exit on Fridays. The *waqfiya* also specifies a job for a librarian in charge of preserving books and manuscripts and for arranging and categorizing them.[28] Therefore, there must have been a library somewhere in this part of the mosque.

94 – An example of the wooden corbels, from the rooms behind the main *mihrab*, which according to Creswell appear like the foreparts of gigantic locusts.

The *waqfiya* of Sultan Lajin is torn and missing parts, making it difficult to pinpoint the library *(khizanat al-kutub)*. Another edition of the *waqfiya* of Sultan Lajin (no. 17) states that the room was used by scholars of the four rights of Sunni law/scholars of jurisprudence (*faqihs*) and teachers (*mudarrisin*), and intended as a *khatib*'s office *(qa'at al-khataba)*.[29] This makes sense since, as in Tulunid times, the room where the *khatib* would get ready for his Friday *khutba* would be his main office in the mosque, the *qa'at al-khataba*. The room next to it would be his *khizanat al-kutub*, where he would conduct research to prepare his sermon.[30] At Friday prayers, he would walk out of the *qa'at al-khataba* directly to the *minbar*, where he would deliver his Friday sermon, just as during the Tulunid period.

One could therefore conclude that the door used by the *khatib* of the mosque is that on the right side of the *minbar* (fig. 22, plan A) and that the door on the right side of the *minbar* would have been the one leading to his office. Consequently, the *qa'at al-khataba* would correspond to [3] in figure 22, plan A, while the *khizanat al-kutub* would correspond to [2]. At the same time, one may speculate that earlier in the Tulunid period, the ruler Ibn Tulun would have exclusively used the third room–[1] of figure 22, plan A–on the left side of the *mihrab* during his time (see also fig. 85, plan C). It must have also been used later during the Fatimid period by high officials, such as Ya'qub Ibn Killis and 'Asluj, before reading out the taxes from the *minbar*, right after the Friday prayers. Similarly, in the Mamluk period, Sultan Lajin must have utilized it during his Friday prayers.

The *Dikka*

Between the two central piers, where the two flat Tulunid *mihrab*s are located, lies the *dikka*. The platform is supported by four marble columns (fig. 39), has a balustrade made of wood, and its columns have *muqarnas*-style capitals, which were common during the Mamluk period. It also has a portable ladder that leads up to the platform. Unfortunately, medieval historians and modern scholars do not refer to the *dikka* of the mosque of Ibn Tulun, but from the style of its capitals, one may conclude that it was added sometime during the Mamluk period. It was believed to be among the works of Sultan Lajin of 696 / 1296,[31] but there is no inscription or any other proof that it was among his works.

The placement of the *dikka* between the two piers of the two flat Tulunid *mihrab*s is rather puzzling. The location of the *dikka* indicates that it would have been in the middle of the *maqsura* area, where the ruler and high officials would be sitting during prayer time. If the Qur'anic reciter (*muqri'*) or the *muballigh* was delivering the imam's sermon from the *dikka*, then the other worshipers, the common people, and military soldiers in the mosque who were outside the *maqsura* area would not be able to hear. The only possible reason why this *dikka* was located in that particular spot would have been for security reasons. The period of Sultan Lajin was a time of turmoil and constant infighting among the Mamluks. One can imagine the bodyguards would climb this *dikka* to protect the sultan during prayer times, a time when assassinations took place.

The Domical *Fisqiya* in the Middle of the *Sahn*

Among the major additions of Sultan Lajin was the large domical building in the center of the open court (*sahn*) (fig. 91). A faded wooden inscription at the summit of the southeastern corner of its drum confirms that he founded it in 1296 (see appendix, no. 11). The inscription states the following: "Has ordered the construction of this

95 – Photograph by Gaston Migeon of the interior of the open court of the mosque showing the domical *fisqiya* with a room on its drum used for the call to prayer. The arched entryways into the building and the arcades were completely walled up by Clot Bey in the nineteenth century. Photograph taken before 1892.

blessed dome, and fountain, and the noble sundials, our Lord, the Sultan al-Malik al-Mansur Husam al-Duniya wa-l-Din Lajin al-Mansuri, may his victory exalted, in the year six and ninety and six hundred."[32]

It is a solidly built domical structure of stone and brick with all four sides open, including the *qibla* side. The lower story is not quite square, the extra length being due to a thickening on the northeastern side where there is a staircase of twenty-five steps lit by two splayed windows like arrow slits, which once served a small room, now destroyed, at the east corner.[33] The small room can be seen in nineteenth-century photographs of the mosque (fig. 95). They show a room the same height as the transitional zone of the dome, which was built of fire bricks and wood and had a slight projection, with a large open rectangular window facing the *sahn* on the *qibla* side. The photographs show that the room had a flat top, but it is not clear whether its roof existed at the time of the photographs. The room would have been reached by a flight of steps, which could be accessed from a side door in the northeastern opening of the building. Once on top, a brick walled passage with two small square windows on the southwestern side would look through and onto the *sahn* (fig. 110). The room had a rectangular entrance which seems to have had a door. The room had three windows on the

96 – Photograph by Pascal Sebah of the interior of the open court of the mosque showing the domical *fisqiya* with its entrances walled up, the room used for the call for to prayer, and a structure built in front of it. It also shows the walled-up arches of Clot Bey. Photograph taken between the 1870s and 1892.

upper southeastern wall. The room as well as the whole domical building appears to have been in a poor state and therefore, was removed in the early twentieth century. On the lower side (northeastern wall), there is a small oval-shaped room, which has a domical roof about the same height as the drum, which is used today as a storage place. This room cannot be seen from the outside.

The wooden inscription mentions a sundial, which has not survived. However, the sundial was studied and published by Marcel in the *Description*.[34] It is not known where and how this sundial was placed in the building, but it must have had some connection to the room, which was once on top of the platform of the building (fig. 97).[35] The small room on the platform of the building is a strange architectural feature. If one compares this building with the earlier Tulunid *fawwara*, the only possible function is for the call to prayer *(adhan)*. However, the *waqfiya* of Sultan Lajin does not mention anything about the *adhan*, but does refer to the timekeeper and employee in charge of the sundial *(sa'ati)*.[36] This leaves no doubt that the small room on the platform was used by the *sa'ati* while observing different times of day on the sundial.

The square drum of the domical building is high and originally had a row of stepped crenellations (figs. 95, 96, 110).[37] These crenellations have disappeared. On top of the square drum there is a stepped zone of transition, which is octagonal, and a plain dome. The profile of the dome is pointed in sections, almost identical to the pointed arches of the mosque. Illustrations by earlier scholars such as Protain in the *Description de l'Égypte*, Pascal Coste, Mahmud 'Akkush, and Creswell, as well as by the Ministry of Awqaf, show that it is a double dome.[38] Both the zone of transition and the dome are made of brick, and the latter retains its bronze finial. Internally, the four walls are plain with traces of plaster coating. The wooden frieze, from which all decoration has disappeared, runs immediately below the system of squinches of its transitional zone. The squinches consist of different tiers of alveoli-like niche *(muqarnas)* decorations, separated by tall, narrow windows (fig. 32). The upper tier, which forms part of the dome, is topped by a great stucco band of Qur'anic inscription: *sura* IV:43, in Naskhi letters; and another concentric inscription giving *sura* V:6, at the apex of the dome.[39] The architectural sophistication of this dome is overwhelming, known only in the mausolea of the Mamluk period (known as the period of Sultan al-Nasir Muhammad). The squinch system is seen in the *madrasa* of Sultan al-Nasir Muhammad at Bayn al-Qasrayn and the nearby mausolea of Salar and Sangar al-Gawli.[40] The fact that the architecture of this dome is similar to that of mausolea of the Mamluk period makes this dome unique in the mosque architecture of Mamluk Cairo.

The floor of the present *fisqiya*, located in the middle of the *sahn*, was once paved with marble, mostly in long strips obtained by sawing columns, which Creswell saw in 1916. But a modern pavement has since replaced all this. In the center is an octagonal basin of stone, 85 centimeters deep, with a block for a jet of water in the middle.[41] A comparison of the Tulunid *fawwara* and the Lajin *fisqiya* reveals that both buildings were fountain pavilions with domes and intended for sundial observation. The Tulunid building was also used for the

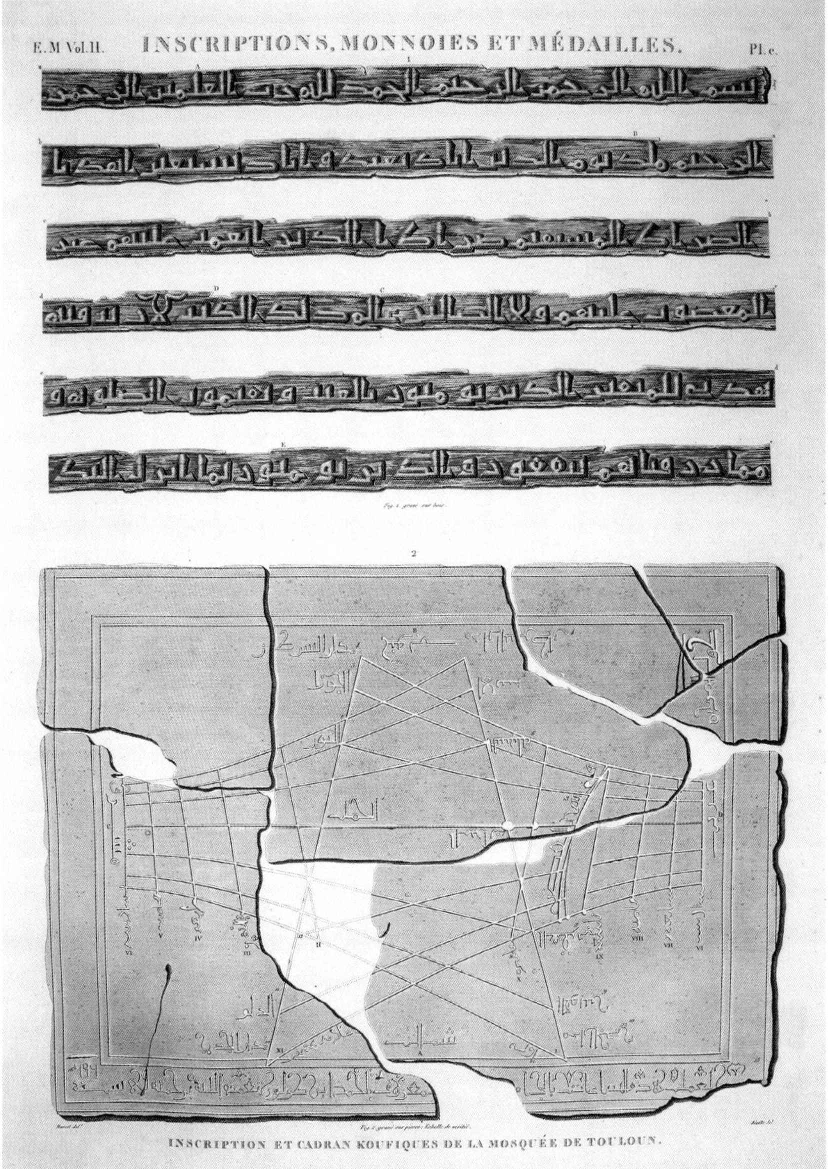

97 – Marcel's engraving in the *Description de l'Égypte* showing the bands of wooden Qur'anic inscriptions that were below the ceiling of the mosque. It also shows a sundial that was found in the domical *fisqiya* that had been cracked. Compiled between 1798 and 1801.

call to prayer. The *waqfiya* of Sultan Lajin, however, does not refer to the function of the *fisqiya*, except that it was intended as a place for ablutions *(mayda'a)*.[42] Aesthetically, the present domed *fisqiya* is a dominant architectural feature of the mosque. The profile of its dome and its pointed arched entrances or openings harmonize visually with the horizontality of the whole building. It accentuates the concentricity of the building and is the focal point for anyone entering the mosque.

The Main *Mihrab*

Among Sultan Lajin's restoration works was the main *mihrab*, which is large and concave (fig. 98). It is made of several kinds of materials including stucco decoration on the outer part and spandrels, above which is a wooden band of Kufic inscription and a larger wooden plank with traces of faded paintings decorating it. The upper part of the *mihrab* has a wooden conch with traces of faded painted, both of which are in bad condition. The middle part has a band of glass mosaic of the highest quality that displays the *shahada* (bearing witness that there is one God and Muhammad is His Prophet) written in a fantastic Naskhi script (see appendix, no. 8). The lower part of the border is made completely of marble, which is typical of the Mamluk period. The most distinctive feature of the *mihrab* is the two flanking marble columns on either side with their distinguished Coptic-style capitals, which are Tulunid (fig. 37). Creswell rightly argues that the main *mihrab* is among the great restoration works of Sultan Lajin in 696 AH / 1296 AD.[43] It is also one of only four *mihrab*s in Cairo decorated with faience mosaics.[44] It is the most developed and a masterpiece in itself because of the combination of four materials—stucco, wood, glass mosaics, and marble—in one architectural feature.

The small wooden dome above the main *mihrab* area is not from the original mosque of Ibn Tulun (fig. 99). It was probably built during the time of Sultan Lajin in 696 / 1296. When compared with other domes of the period, its transitional zone includes a squinch system that is identical to that of the small dome at the complex of Salar and Sangar, near to the mosque of Ibn Tulun.[45] As stated by historians, Sultan Lajin appointed Amir Sangar al-Dawadari to be in charge of the affairs and work in the mosque. One may assume or deduce that the Amir Sangar al-Dawadari must have employed the same architect for his building as well and used this dome as a model for his own, which was later made in stone.

The dome above the main *mihrab* allows additional light into the area of the *mihrab* and *minbar*, which is usually dim. The ruler or high official would sit in that area of the mosque, and therefore it had to be well lit and provided with good air circulation. There is reason to believe that this dome replaced an earlier one as well, built sometime during the Fatimid period. Having a dome over the *mihrab* area was a common practice in

98 – The main *mihrab* of the mosque, which is divided into several parts: the upper part is a wooden conch with some traces of painting in bad condition; the middle part is a band of mosaic Naskhi inscription of the highest quality; and the lower part is decorated with marble panels. The *mihrab* is flanked by a pair of columns on either side—the only columns in the mosque. The spandrels of the *mihrab* are in stucco, above them is a band of Kufic inscription, and above that is a rectangular piece of wood with traces of faded painted decorations.

Fatimid mosques, such as at al-Azhar and al-Hakim. During the Mamluk period, this feature was magnified in order to create a large dome covering the area of the *mihrab*, which became enclosed by a wooden screen. This area was known as the *maqsura* area, where a sultan and high officials would sit while attending Friday prayers.[46] Knowing the architectural and restoration works of the rulers and high officials who used the mosque

99 – The main *mihrab* and the monumental *minbar* and the wooden dome above.

of Ibn Tulun (Ya'qub Ibn Killis, Caliph al-'Aziz, Caliph al-Hakim, Badr al-Gammali, and al-Afdal Shahinshah) leads us to the conclusion that the dome might have been originally added during the Fatimid period. When Sultan Lajin took the throne of Egypt, the small Fatimid dome must have deteriorated badly enough that a new one was made. It is also possible that it was constructed as an experimental model in wood for the small dome of the complex of Salar and Sangar, and then added to Ibn Tulun.

There is also the flat *mihrab* on the left side of al-Afdal's (figs. 42–44), which according to its inscriptions, was ordered by Sultan Lajin (see appendix, no. 5).[47] This *mihrab* would have been replaced by another one which was symmetrical and contemporary to that of al-Afdal. The earlier Fatimid *mihrab* must have fallen into disrepair, and therefore Lajin decided to restore it. This project was probably undertaken in order to replace the old Fatimid *maqsura* with a new Mamluk one. In other words, Sultan Lajin decided to use the same *maqsura* area of the Fatimid times that had been set up by the vizier al-Afdal.

A wooden screen acting as a *maqsura* to separate officials from ordinary worshipers was later adopted in the mosque of al-Tunbugha al-Maridani (1340) and the mosque of al-Azhar (1468–1495). However, in those mosques, the *maqsura* separated the entire *qibla riwaq* from the *sahn*, rather than just a smaller section of the *qibla riwaq*. Such a feature was not found in Islamic architecture in Cairo after the Mamluk period. Another feature that is attributed to Sultan Lajin is the *mihrab* of Sayyida Nafisa, which is located on the left side of the *qibla* wall (figs. 45, 46). Creswell, Corbet, and Van Berchem have identified it as a contribution of Sultan Lajin in 696 / 1296.[48] (This *mihrab* and its *maqsura* area are discussed in chapter 9.) We may assume that since Sultan Lajin had restored this *mihrab*, its small *maqsura* would still have been used until his time. However, it is not known why there would be a separate *maqsura* in that part of the mosque.

The Monumental *Minbar*

Among the other restorations of Sultan Lajin was the *minbar* (pulpit), which is located on the right side of the *mihrab* (figs. 38, 100). As stated earlier, this is not the original *minbar* of the mosque, as this was moved earlier. The *minbar* is made of wood and bears an inscription stating that it was made by order of Sultan Lajin in 696 AH / 1296 AD.[49] It was restored in 1914.

Owing to its curiously large size, it will be referred to as the monumental *minbar*. Creswell mentions it briefly, but does not discuss it in depth in his study of the mosque.[50] The monumental *minbar* blocks one of the windows in the upper wall of the mosque and also the *qibla* wall above. At the same time, the *minbar* is directly placed in front of a brick pier. It is made of teakwood, while its decorative panels are inlaid with ebony and the balustrade is made of boxwood.[51] Gloria Karnouk describes the monumental *minbar* as following the late thirteenth-century style of Sultan al-Nasir Muhammad.[52] She adds that the entrance has a stilted arch, above which are several tiers of *muqarnas* crowned by trefoil crenellations. The doors of the *minbar* open to the back. They bear inscriptions on bronze bands nailed to them, which show that they were the work of the Comité during the reign of the Khedive 'Abbas Hilmi II in 1332 AH / 1913–1914 AD (appendix, no. 10). There is a step that leads up to another flight of eleven steps, which then leads to a platform for sitting. The platform is covered with a canopy that is decorated with *muqarnas* and topped by crenellations. It is crowned by a bulbous, domed finial and copper crescent, the first to appear on *minbar*s in Cairo and similar to those on the minarets of the period. The triangular sides of the *minbar* have wooden balustrades decorated with turned wood, which have metal hinges of different shapes. The triangular sides are decorated with geometric designs, which have floral patterns.[53] The designs on the sides of the *minbar* are masterful examples of woodcarving in Cairo's Islamic architecture (fig. 101).

The monumental *minbar* is an imposing feature of the mosque. Visually and physically, it projects outward, almost blocking the entire *riwaq* where it stands (fig. 100). This relationship is uncommon, since there is a tendency in the mosques of Cairo to emphasize harmonious proportions between the *minbar* and the *riwaq* or, more frequently, in the *iwans*. The exaggeration in size is unnecessary here. It does not help the *khatib* deliver his Friday sermon and, in fact, it makes it difficult for him to even see his audience.

However, this exaggeration in size may have been deliberate. If the *khatib* was expected to be seen by the audience, then his speech would turn out to be more of a theatrical performance rather than simply a vocal message. There is a more practical reason as well: Assassinations in Islamic history were sometimes committed during or after prayer times. This issue had to be considered when planning the layout of a mosque. Indeed, very few of the Mamluk sultans died a natural death, and during

the period of Sultan Lajin, there was infighting between his Mamluk emirs and those of Sultan al-Nasir Muhammad, who was in exile and was constantly threatening Sultan Lajin. Therefore, the shape and size of the *minbar* may have been intended in part to safeguard the ruler's security.

Since this *minbar* was made by Sultan Lajin in 696 AH / 1296 AD, it might have been large enough to secure one side of the area where the sultan would be praying, right in front of the *mihrab*. This speculation is based on the fact that when a ruler or any high official prayed in the mosque, he would sit in the area directly in front of the *mihrab* with his entourage surrounding him. Such a monumental structure would protect him as long as a security guard stood directly in front of the *minbar*'s door, between the door and the pier. The same idea of security might also relate to the original *minbar* of Ibn Tulun, which was mentioned by medieval historians, although none of them describe its size. When Ibn Tulun went to pray in the mosque, he would sit in the same area right in front of the main *mihrab* and could have been well protected by his *minbar*, just as Sultan Lajin was later on.

100 – The area of the main *mihrab* from the east (left) side of the *riwaq* showing the monumental *minbar* of Sultan Lajin (1296), the wooden dome above, and a door leading to one of three rooms behind the main *mihrab*.

101 [NEXT PAGE] – Details of the geometric patterns on the monumental minbar.

102 – Reconstruction of the interior of the mosque during the reign of Sultan Lajin in 1296.

103 and 104 – Reconstructed bird's-eye view of the mosque during the reign of Sultan Lajin in 1296, seen from the east (above) and the south (below).

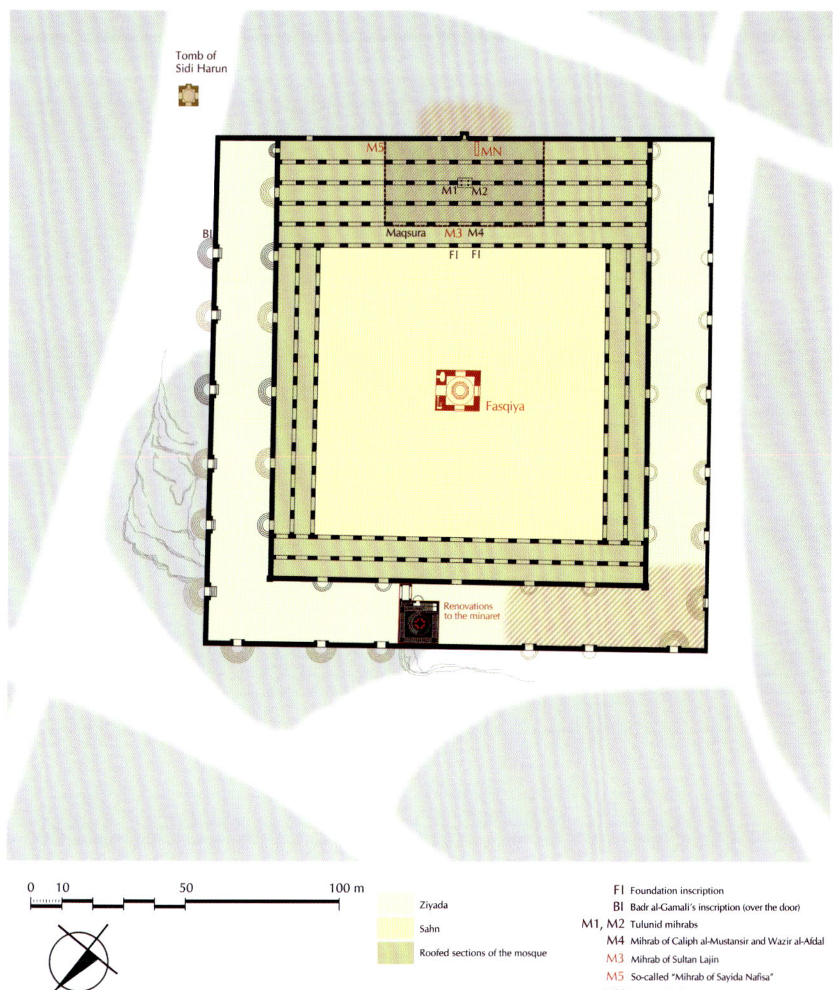

105 , plan E – The mosque of Ibn Tulun during the reign of Sultan Lajin, in the year 1296.

The Spiral-Shaped Minaret

The spiral-shaped minaret is also attributed to Sultan Lajin. The original had fallen or deteriorated so badly that another one was built next to it. However, this minaret was not as complete as the one seen today, consisting only of the lower quadrangular base. It is not known when the circular shaft was added. However, one is inclined to date it to the Ayyubid period as it is rare to find minarets with circular shafts in the Mamluk period, except for that of Sultan Baybars al-Jashankir, built in 1307-10. The upper *mabkhara* (incense burner)-shaped finial with its ribbed dome helmet could have been attributed to Sultan Lajin. Creswell, Salmon, and Hautecœur believe it was built by Sultan Lajin after the architect Patricolo conducted an archaeological test in 1920,[54] showing a hole which can be seen in the minaret's northwestern side (fig. 49). Doris Behrens-Abouseif disagrees with Creswell's attribution of the entire minaret to Sultan Lajin, on the basis that if he really had built it, it would have been in the typical Mamluk style, which is not the case.[55] Behrens-Abouseif adds that minarets added to pre-existing structures were usually inscribed with foundation inscriptions to acknowledge the sponsor's contribution, which is not the case with the minaret of Ibn Tulun.

By comparing the shape of the *mabkhara* that surmounts the minaret of Ibn Tulun (fig. 21), one might think it was added during Lajin's time but that there was a reason he did not record his inscription—perhaps he was killed immediately after it was completed. It was typical of the period to have inscriptions on the minarets. The closest minarets with inscriptions are those of Salar and Sangar al-Gawli (703 AH / 1303–4 AD), near the mosque of Ibn Tulun (along Saliba Street), and later that of Sultan Baybars al-Gashankir (1307–10) and Hasan Sadaqa/Sunqur Sa'di (715 / 1315–21).[56] Since we know that Sultan Lajin had appointed Amir Salar to oversee the works in the mosque, this may lead us to believe that it was the same architect who would have been responsible for it.

The Minarets of Qadi Karim al-Din

Maqrizi states that during the reign of Sultan al-Nasir Muhammad (693–741 AH / 1293–1340 AD), a judge *(qadi)* called Karim al-Din al-Kabir had to restore two minarets in the mosque of Ibn Tulun.[57] Historian and government official 'Ali Basha Mubarak confirms that the mosque of Ibn Tulun once had three minarets, two of which were still standing on the southeastern side by the nineteenth century. He adds that these minarets were built of brick and had staircases on the inside, distinguishing them from the spiral-shaped one.[58] One could conclude that the minarets were already there and Qadi Karim al-Din had restored them. However, we have no information as to when these minarets were built. No scholars prior to 'Ali Basha Mubarak mention anything about the two minarets of Qadi Karim al-Din except for Pascal Coste who shows one of them (on the eastern corner) in an elevation of the mosque.[59]

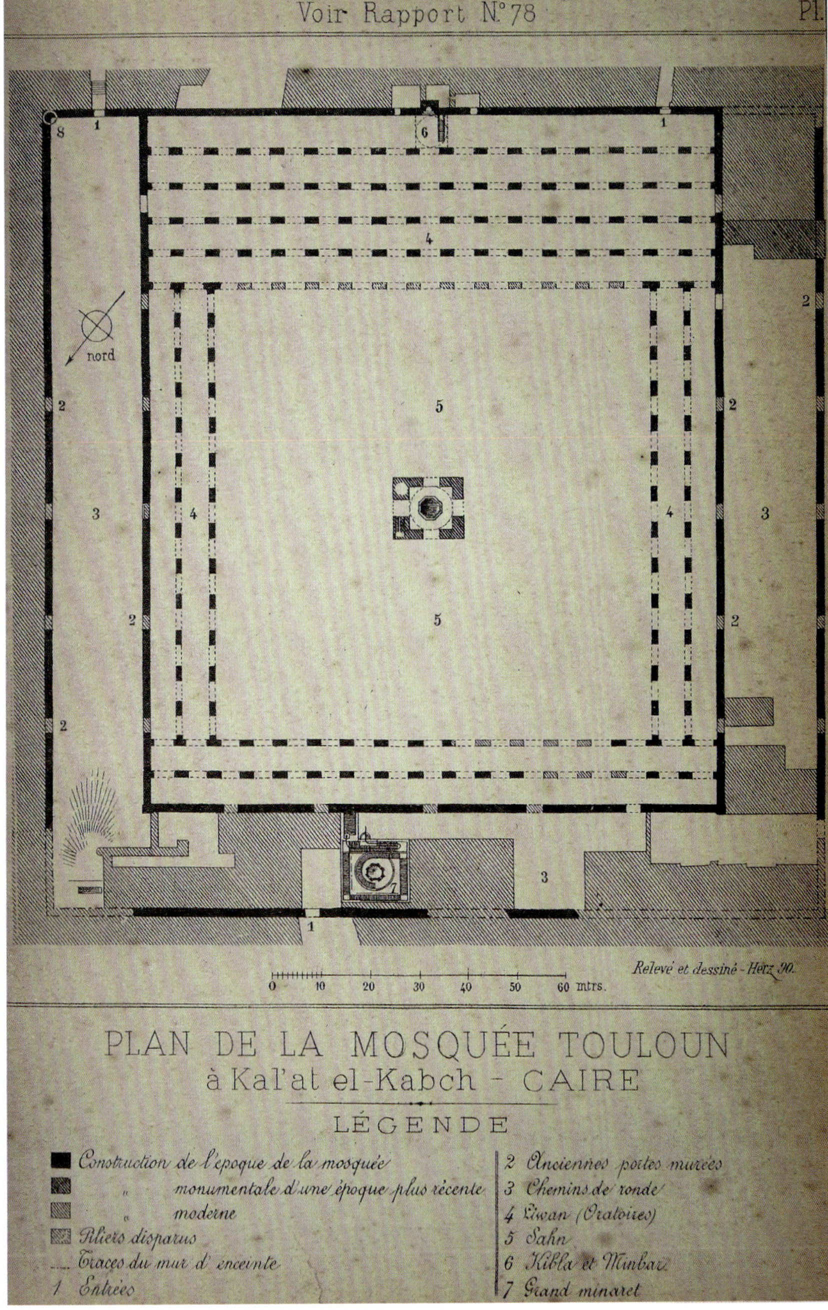

106 – Herz Pasha's plan of the mosque of Ibn Tulun in 1890.

107 [NEXT PAGE] – Photograph by G. Lekegian, taken from the top of the minaret of Ibn Tulun, showing the lost minaret of the Qadi Karim al-Din, part of a broken pier of the then-missing arcade of the *qibla riwaq* facing the *sahn* which had fallen in 1877. Photographed taken between 1877 and 1920.

108 [NEXT PAGE] – The mosque of Ibn Tulun from the minaret of Amir Sarghatmish. On the left is the dense building encroaching on the mosque from Ahmad Ibn Tulun Street, which allowed no access to the mosque from that side. It also shows the now-missing minaret of Qadi Karim al-Din before it was demolished. Photograph taken before 1934.

However, the same minaret is indicated—though depicted incorrectly—in the 1890 plan of Herz Bey (fig. 106),[60] and numerous photographs show that this minaret was still standing at the eastern corner of the mosque proper (figs. 107, 108).[61]

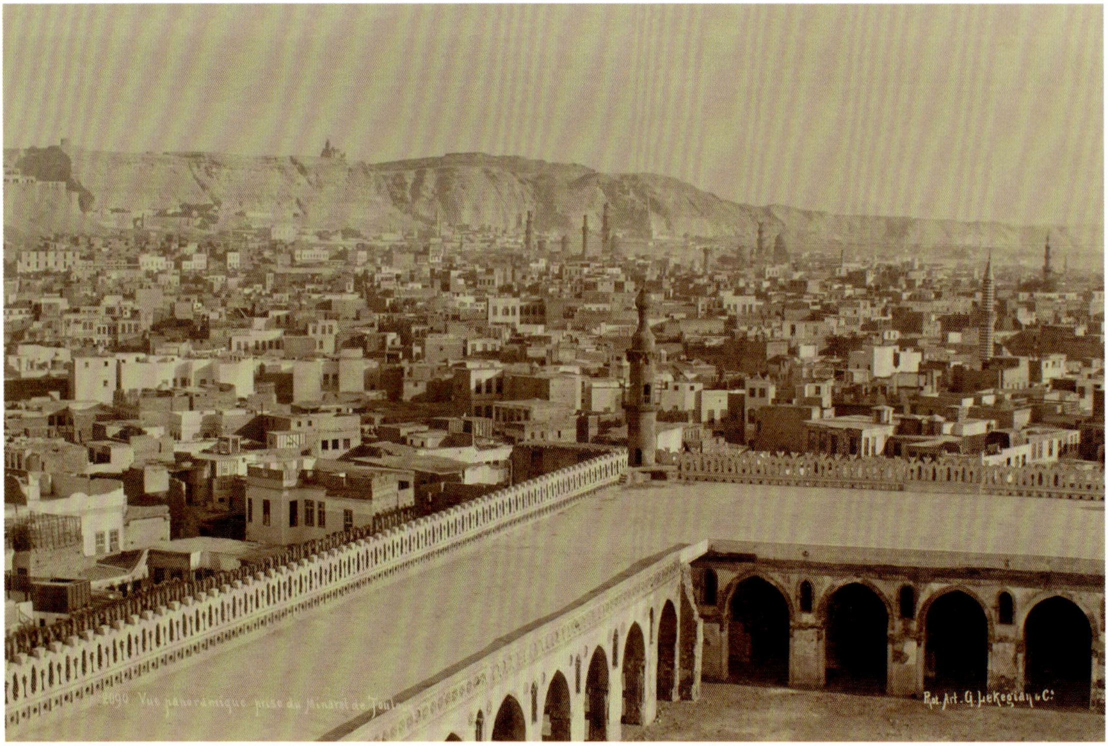
2090 Vue panoramique prise du Minaret de Touloun
Phot. Art. G. Lekegian & C°

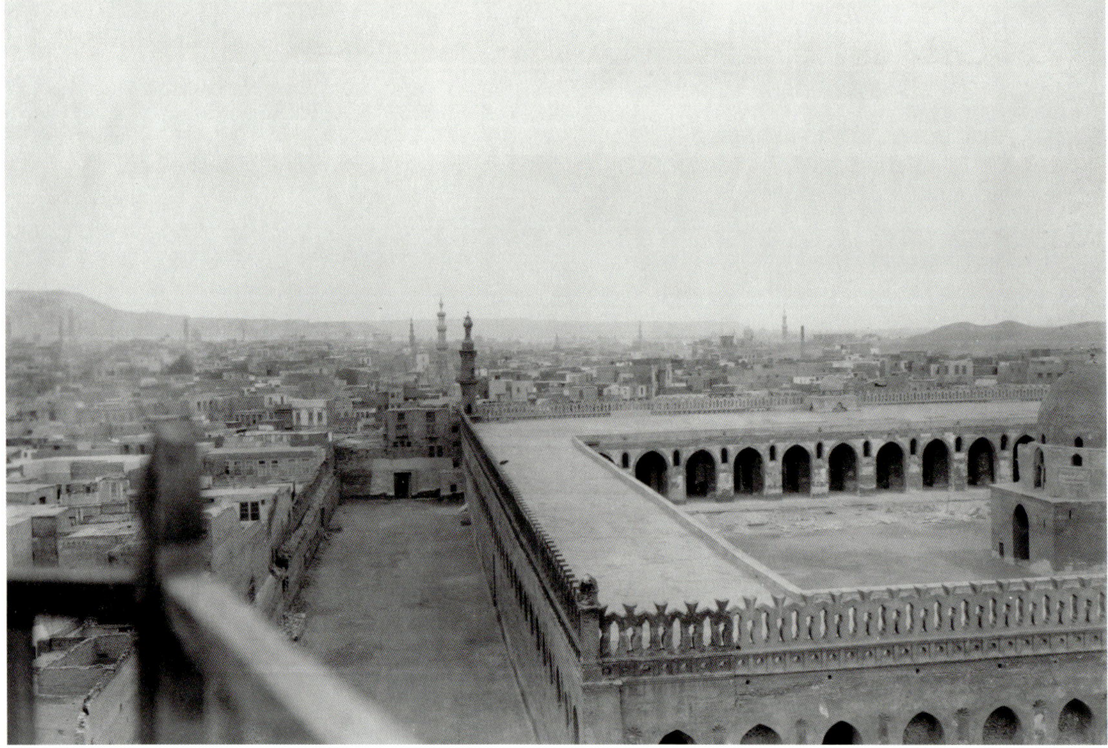

109 – Photograph by the Armenian nineteenth-century photographer G. Lekegian showing the domical *fisqiya*, the missing arcade of the *qibla riwaq*, and the lost minaret of Qadi Karim al-Din. Photograph taken between 1877 and 1929.

The eastern minaret once consisted of three stories, two of which were plain, circular shafts with a balcony between them and a bulbous dome on top, which probably was surmounted by a copper crescent. The lower shaft had an opening on its northwestern side, which led into an interior staircase, according to 'Ali Basha Mubarak. A plain cavetto cornice supported the balcony. It had at least one opening and a wooden railing. Several tiers of *muqarnas* supported the bulbous dome top. It was approximately eleven meters in height. This minaret was demolished by the Comité de Conservation des Monuments de l'Art Arabe in 1934.[62]

'Ali Basha Mubarak stated that the mosque had three minarets, indicating that there was one still standing at the southern corner of the mosque during his time (late nineteenth century). The southern minaret can be seen in a photograph by Francis Bedford in 1862

110 – Photograph by Francis Bedford, taken from the roof of the mosque looking south and showing the interior of the open court and the domical *fisqiya* with its entrances fenced up by wooden beams and bricks. Photograph taken on March 25, 1862.

(fig. 110). It can also be seen in an illustration by Stanley Lane-Poole sometime before 1886, which was probably drawn at the same time, shows a minaret standing at that location.[63] An undated nineteenth-century photograph by Pascal Sebah shows that this minaret was still standing.[64]

The southern corner minaret appears to have almost the same as the eastern one. It too consisted of three stories. However, the lower was octagonal with keel-arched windows on each side, with one of them being blocked or blind. The middle shaft was also plain and circular with a balcony between them and an elongated finial that probably had a dome that was lost on top. In addition, it had what seems like a very tall rod on top. However, it probably would have been surmounted by a copper crescent. A fragile wooden staircase leads to its lower octagonal shaft, which had a keel-arched entrance that led into an interior staircase. A plain cavetto cornice supported the balcony, and no openings can be seen although it had a poor quality wooden railing. Unlike the eastern minaret, no tiers of *muqarnas* can be seen supporting the finial, though another plain cavetto cornice does.

Strangely, is that the minaret is not built or located directly at the corner of the mosque proper, but rather on what seems like a wooden corbel that was attached to a house or structure that was encroaching the mosque at the time, from behind it. One can see that the crenellations are gone, and the circular designs below them had also deterioarated and the base of the minaret seems to be behind these crenellations (fig. 110). One would expect that it was the same height as the eastern minaret, i.e. approximately, 11 meters high. This must have collapsed sometime after 1886.[65]

The *Mayda'a*

Maqrizi reports that in 793 AH / 1390 AD the northwestern *riwaq* of the mosque, which is adjacent to the minaret, was restored by al-Ubayd Ibn Muhammad Ibn Abd al-Huwaydi. He adds that this man also founded a *mayda'a* (place for ablutions) alongside the old one.[66] Some time before 1918, the British scholar Robert Williams saw this structure and described it as

> rectangular in plan, measuring about 42 feet by 35 feet [14 meters by 11.6 meters]. In the center is a large reservoir at each of the four corners of which are built up stone columns, with slightly molded bases and caps. These columns at one time supported a roof, some of the beams remain. At the four angles of the reservoir are semicircular, backed seats cut in the stone. Around the reservoir is a gangway abutting on which are the remains of twenty water closets. The place is full of dust and refuse, is used in fact as a dustbin for the house built against its back.[67]

This description corresponds to the plan of Pascal Coste, which refers to a structure as the "cour des latrines," meaning the *mayda'a*, located on the western side of the minaret. It can also be seen in the plans of Yusuf Ahmad and Mahmud 'Akkush.[68] These plans show the *mayda'a* in the same location. Yusuf Ahmad and 'Akkush state that this building had a waterwheel (*saqiya*), which was functioning during their time (early twentieth century). The plan of Pascal Coste indicates that there was a *saqiya* on the northern side of the minaret. An old photograph in Creswell's photo album (fig. 111) shows part of a wooden wheel, which was probably the remains of the *saqiya* referred to above. Although not functioning at the time of the photograph, it would have supplied water to the *mayda'a* of the mosque.

Yusuf Ahmad briefly mentions that this building was the original *mayda'a* of the mosque, while there was another one built on the southwestern part of the mosque, which must have been the *mayda'a* of al-Huwaydi. This is confusing, because Yusuf Ahmad does not refer to the plans which he provides and does not describe these structures;

111 – Photograph of the northeastern *ziyada* showing the lost minaret of Qadi Karim al-Din, at the eastern corner of the mosque proper, and the remains of a wooden waterwheel (bottom left), which must have been used in the *mayda'a* nearby. Photograph taken before 1934.

he only mentions them briefly. Moreover, the plan does not include a legend. None of the historians tell us that there was a *mayda'a* on the southwestern side. At the same time there is a structure on that side which appears to have had four pillars. However, there is no indication of a water reservoir in its center. To conclude, there is neither historical nor archaeological evidence to support the claim that there was a *mayda'a* on the southwestern *ziyada* of the mosque. This leads us to conclude that the *mayda'a* of al-Huwaydi was in fact the building indicated in the plans of Pascal Coste, Yusuf Ahmad, and 'Akkush.

One can recognize the entrance of the *mayda'a* of al-Huwaydi in the illustrations by Protain and Robert Hay. The illustration by Protain (fig. 59) shows a man just about to enter a structure. Since the man is carrying a water container, it would be reasonable to consider that the structure is related to water. This leads us to believe that this is the *mayda'a* built by al-Huwaydi. The illustration of Robert Hay (fig. 60) shows the same building but in a rather deteriorated state. Moreover, the *mayda'a* of al-Huwaydi is not shown in the plans of Protain, Prisse d'Avennes, and Herz Pasha (fig. 106).

At present, in the western part of the minaret of the northwestern *ziyada*, there is a newly restored/rebuilt rectangular structure, which indicates a water basin, which may have been that in the center of the *mayda'a* of al-Huwaydi (figs. 22, plan A; 53). The latrines surrounding it had been destroyed or demolished at a later date. Since Maqrizi states that the new *mayda'a* had been built alongside the original one, we believe that the smaller rectangular structure was in fact the central basin for the original *mayda'a* built by Ibn Tulun, which must have deteriorated and been restored several times. In addition, it is almost certain that the *mayda'a* of al-Huwaydi was not functioning by 1840, when Robert Hay published his illustration (fig. 60), which is why it was built over and then inhabited by people and forgotten. The ruins seen today were the result of the clearing and cleaning which took place under the direction of the Comité de Conservation des Monuments de l'Art Arabe.

The addition of the northwestern *riwaq* and the *mayda'a* of al-Huwaydi leads us to conclude that they were the result of rapid population growth and urbanization in the southern quarters of the city by 1400. By the late fourteenth century, the mosque needed repair and maintenance. A logical explanation would be that the northwestern *riwaq* and the area of the *ziyada* near the minaret were so encroached upon and heavily inhabited at that time that they became damaged and required restoration, and hence, had to be upgraded.[69]

The *Sabil-Maktab*

Maqrizi notes that Sultan Lajin also erected a *maktab* next to the mosque, the purpose of which was to teach Muslim orphans the holy Qur'an.[70] This type of building was popular in Cairo during the Mamluk and Ottoman periods. The only building that can be related to this *maktab* is the *sabil* of Sultan Qaitbay, (figs. 22, plan A; 35, 54) built in what would seem a remote part of the mosque, at the end of the southwestern *ziyada*. Creswell believes that this *maktab* is the *sabil* of Sultan Qaitbay and bases this on the building being attributed to Sultan Qaitbay by the historian al-Sakhawi, who speaks of a man named Rayhan al-Zanji al-Halabi being appointed in the mosque to take charge of this *sabil*.[71] There are two facts that Creswell bases his argument on. First, he fixes the date of the appointment of Rayhan al-Zanji al-Halabi between the date of Sultan Qaitbay's accession to the throne in 873 AH / 1468 AD and the year when al-Sakhawi gives for the death of Rayhan al-Zanji al-Halabi, 887 / 1482. Second, the style of the entrance bay is in keeping with this period.

However, Corbet believes this *maktab* is a *sabil-kuttab* built by Sultan Lajin.[72] He describes it as being ruined, without any inscriptions. He adds that it had a door that was blocked from the outside of the *ziyada*.[73] There is no proof that Sultan Qaitbay built this *sabil* anew or simply restored the earlier structure of Sultan Lajin, as unfortunately we have no information about Sultan Qaitbay's work in the mosque of Ibn Tulun, except that he had appointed Rayhan al-Zanji al-Halabi to be in charge of this *sabil*.

Sultan Qaitbay is known to have been a great patron of architecture—the greatest of all Mamluk sultans. He built mosques, *madrasas*, *wakalas*, and *sabil-kuttabs*. He gave his amirs properties, which enabled them to erect buildings as they wished everywhere in Cairo and across Egypt. Sultan Qaitbay may therefore be considered the 'Hadrian of the Mamluks' for his passion for architectural patronage and activities. Sultan Qaitbay produced *waqf*s for most of the buildings he ordered to be erected.

After constructing such a prominent building in the mosque of Ibn Tulun, which was located in a densely populated quarter of Cairo, why was it not recorded with an inscription on the building? No such inscriptions survived, so if there had been any, they must have been lost. In addition, contemporary historians such as Ibn Iyas would have certainly recorded such restorations by Sultan Qaitbay, but Ibn Iyas does not mention any such building activity in the mosque of Ibn Tulun. There are reasons why Sultan Qaitbay may have built it in the mosque of Ibn Tulun, the first being overpopulation of that area of Cairo. A second reason would be that the *sabil*'s window grilles lie exactly in front of the alley leading to the mosque-*madrasa* of Sultan Qaitbay in the area of Qala'at al-Kabsh (fig. 112). When coming from

112 – The *sabil-kuttab* of Sultan Qaitbay, as seen in the approach to the mosque from the area of Qala'at al-Kabsh, where the mosque of Sultan Qaitbay is located.

the Qal'a, down the alley, one would be immediately struck by the *sabil* of Sultan Qaitbay. However, it is most likely that the *maktab* that was built by Sultan Lajin in 1296 had deteriorated over time with the rest of the mosque. With the heavy increase in population in that area of Cairo, it would have been restored and repaired by Sultan Qaitbay sometime between 873-887 / 1468-1482.

The *Madrasa* of Amir Sarghatmish

The Mamluk Amir Sarghatmish, around 1350, must have upgraded the area around the mosque on the north and eastern sides. He might have wanted this upgrade since he had erected a superb complex adjacent to the mosque of Ibn Tulun on the northwestern side, directly on Saliba Street (fig. 22, plan A). The complex of Amir Sarghatmish is an excellent example of Cairene Mamluk architecture, displaying all the elements of this architectural style in its tripartite portal with handsome tiers of *muqarnas* and a vestibule that leads to an open court via a bent entrance corridor. The building is an *iwan* type, with a mausoleum on one of its sides. The building has two onion-shaped domes, each with the most graceful profile. One was built over the *qibla iwan* and the other over the tomb of Amir Sarghatmish. However, the most outstanding feature of the building is the placement of its minaret. The minaret consists of three stories–an octagonal shaft, balcony, and another octagonal shaft–and is surmounted with a pavilion-like structure, with an onion-shaped finial supported on columns. The onion-shaped minaret was introduced in Egypt in the mosque of Amir Maridani in 1340 and became part of standard Mamluk architecture in Cairo. The minaret of Amir Sarghatmish with its harmonious proportions is visually centered along Saliba Street, so that it could be seen from both sides of the street, and is placed so it can be seen as one walks through the main entrance of the mosque of Ibn Tulun; once in the *ziyada* area this minaret with its superb proportions is visible. The result is a stunningly successful visual effect. It tends to give the impression that the minaret of Amir Sarghatmish is in fact that of the mosque of Ibn Tulun, rather than the unique spiral-shaped one that cannot be seen from that part of the *ziyada* (fig. 114). In other words, the minaret of Amir Sarghatmish

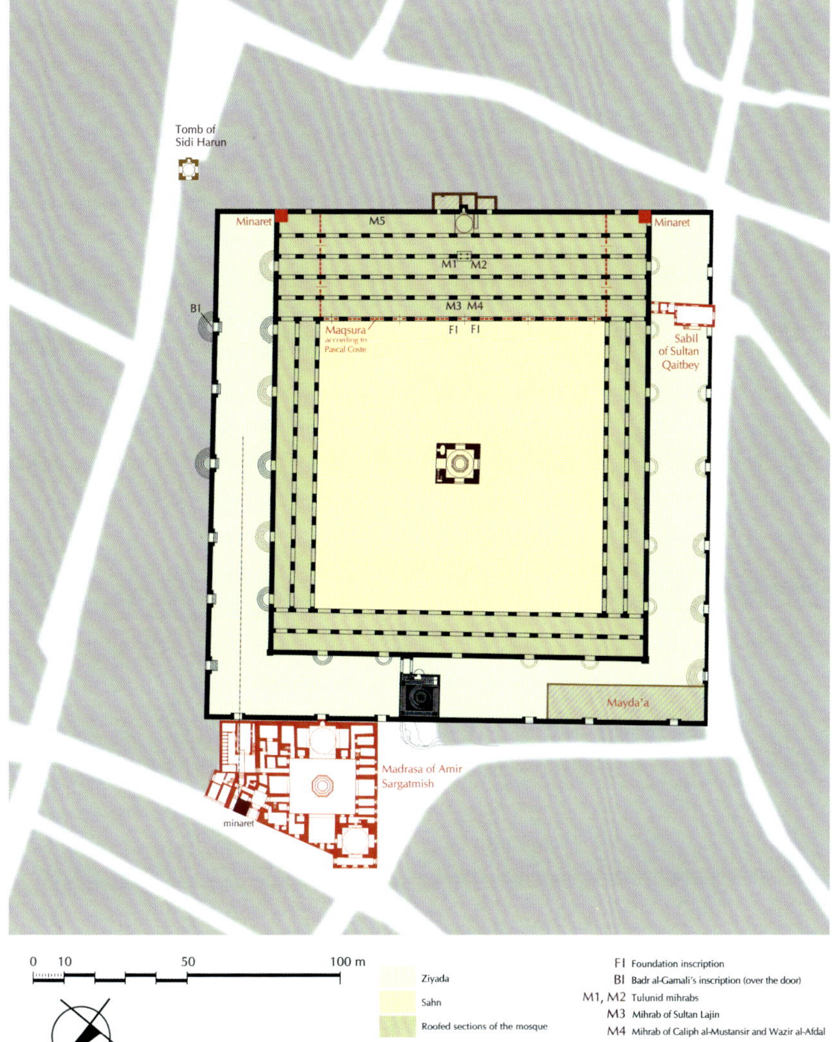

113, plan F – The mosque of Ibn Tulun and its environs, at the end of the Mamluk period. It shows the two minarets of Qadi Karim al-Din on the extremities of the *qibla* wall, an enlarged *maqsura* area, according to the plan of Pascal Coste, and the *mayda'a*. It also shows the addition of the *madrasa* of Amir Sarghatmish, built adjacent to the mosque on the northwestern side. Most distinct is the placement of the minaret of Amir Sarghatmish along a central axis with the *ziyada* (marked by a dotted line).

visually usurps that of Ibn Tulun (figs. 113, plan F; 114). One may therefore consider the *madrasa* of Amir Sarghatmish to be an important component added to Ibn Tulun's mosque in the fourteenth century, although it was outside the mosque's premises.

There is no doubt that the mosque of Ibn Tulun had reached its splendid peak and had revived its glorious past, during the short-lived reign of Sultan Lajin and one can visualize how the interior of the mosque might have appeared during the period of Sultan Lajin (1296), as in the reconstruction of the interior of the mosque in

114 – The northeastern *ziyada* showing showing the entrances with doors preceeded by flights of steps and at the far end the spectacular minaret of the *madrasa* of Amir Sarghatmish centered within the *ziyada*. This powerful visual effect accentuates how the minaret visually usurps that of Ibn Tulun.

figure 102. Bird's-eye views of how the mosque may have looked after the new spiral-shaped minaret was completed and the domical *fisqiya* of Sultan Lajin was built can be seen in figures 102 and 103, and a reconstruction of the ground plan of the mosque after Sultan Lajin made his additions in 1296 is shown in figure 105, plan E. One can also imagine how the mosque of Ibn Tulun might have appeared at the end of the Mamluk period in reconstruction renderings in figures 115 and 116, as well as a reconstructed ground plan of the mosque at the end of the Mamluk era in figure 113, plan F.

The splendor of the Mamluk period came to an end during the reign of Sultan al-Ghuri. The discovery of the route of the Cape of Good Hope by Vasco Da Gama, which enabled marine trade traffic to circulate around Africa instead of taking the land routes through Palestine and Bilad al-Sham, dealt an economic blow to the Mamluk treasury. During the late fifteenth century, the Ottomans and the Safavids competed fiercely, while the Mamluks became a weak power in the Near East. When

115 and 116 – Reconstructed bird's-eye view from the east (above) and the north (below) of the mosque during the end of the Mamluk period. The madrasa of Amir Sarghatmish and the two minarets of Qadi Karim al-Din can be seen on the edges of the qibla wall, and the mayda'a can be seen next to the minaret, which was then complete.

the Ottomans attacked the Safavids, the old Mamluk Sultan al-Ghuri sent troops to support the Safavids. Instead of fighting the Safavids, the Ottoman Sultan Selim I attacked the Mamluks in Bilad al-Sham. The Ottomans defeated the Mamluks in the decisive battle of Marj Dabiq, north of Aleppo, where Sultan al-Ghuri lost his life. In Cairo, al-Ghuri's nephew Tuman Bay reluctantly accepted the throne but he was too weak to stand up to the Ottomans. The Mamluks were not as up-to-date with methods of war as the Ottomans, who bribed the Mamluk amirs with high posts in the new regime–for example, Amir Khayir Bak who betrayed the sultan. As a result, Sultan Tuman Bay was captured and hanged on Bab Zuwayla in 1517. Selim I declared Egypt an Ottoman province, and Cairo ceased to be the capital of an empire.

10 The Ottoman Period

The Ottoman period of Egypt was dynamic. Trade and merchants from all over the world directed commercial life to Egypt. Cairo was crowded with bustling markets adorned by *wakala*s and *khanqa*s (commercial buildings), hotels (*funduq*s), *sabil-kuttab*s, shrines, and *madrasa*-mosques. Due to intense building activity in Cairo, little attention was paid to the mosque of Ibn Tulun during this period. According to 'Ali Basha Mubarak, there was a small *zawiya*, in a state of ruin near the mosque's stone spiral minaret, and this *zawiya* included the tomb of a man named Sheikh al-Bushi, but he does not provide a date for this tomb.[1] Yusuf Ahmad describes this building in 1917 as being a small prayer area (*musallah*) with a tomb next to the minaret.[2] He says the building had a door, above which was a Qur'anic inscription followed by the name of the founder Sheikh Sharaf al-Din al-Madini and the month Rajab 930 / May 1524.[3]

117 – The ruins in the northwestern *ziyada* and the spiral-shaped minaret, along with the remains of the tomb and *zawiya* of Sheikh al-Bushi or al-Madini. Photograph taken before 1943.

Robert Williams describes a building in the same location in 1918, saying it contained a tomb belonging to a sheikh by the name of al-Bushi and not Sharaf al-Din al-Madini.[4] This is strange because the name of the founder is usually found on an inscription rather than in a written historical source like that of 'Ali Basha Mubarak. Since there are no other similar structures in that area of the mosque—except for the old *mayda'a* in the *ziyada* area (further to the west)—one may assume that Williams is referring to the *zawiya* of Sheikh al-Bushi (as described by 'Ali Basha Mubarak). The names are written in almost the same way—*Sheikh al-Bushi* and *Sheikh al-Madini*—and it is possible that 'Ali Mubarak copied the name of al-Madini in the same way as that of al-Bushi by mistake. One can only conclude that Sheikh al-Bushi was the popular name for Sheikh Sharaf al-Din al-Madini. There are no historical sources about this person or why he built his *zawiya* and tomb in the *ziyada* area next to the minaret of Ibn Tulun. The historian of the early Ottoman period of Egypt, Ibn Iyas, ends his history in 928 AH /

1522 AD, two years before this *zawiya* was built, and says nothing about Sheikh al-Bushi or Sheikh al-Madini.

The *zawiya* and tomb of Sheikh al-Bushi or al-Madini is the building shown next to the minaret of Ibn Tulun in both Protain's illustration and that of Robert Hay (figs. 59, 60).[5] The fact that it was well illustrated shows that it was in use during the eighteenth and nineteenth centuries. Williams describes the *zawiya* as a dilapidated building, which had four rooms of different sizes.[6] The largest room was divided into three aisles by two rows of columns, which supported a roof. He identifies the room as a small mosque because it had a *mihrab*, which at that time had been dismantled. He adds that in another room there was a shrine with the tomb of Sheikh al-Bushi. Above the burial was a wooden platform, which had been covered with a faded cloth and had a dusty green turban on a post as its head. He adds that the main door of the building and part of the roof had been repaired with pieces of the Kufic inscription, boards that had been torn from the frieze below the ceiling of the mosque.[7] Finally, Williams says that the worshipers at the shrine of Sheikh al-Bushi were very few during his days.[8]

The description of Robert Williams is identical to what can be seen in the plans of Mahmud 'Akkush, Yusuf Ahmad, and Creswell.[9] In addition, old photographs in Creswell's photo album also show the *zawiya* and the tomb of Sheikh al-Bushi or al-Madini in a dilapidated and ruined state (figs. 117, 118, 130).[10]

However, the Egyptian scholar Hasan 'Abd al-Wahhab mentions that the building was later demolished in 1943.[11] The fact that this building was erected next to the minaret of Ibn Tulun in 930 / 1524 shows that this area was active and functioning well right after the Ottoman conquest of Egypt in 923 / 1517. It must have played a vital role in the social, religious, and urban growth of the surrounding district. It reflects a new kind of piety connected with the memory of holy men like Sheikh al-Bushi or al-Madini.

It appears that there were no activities taking place in the mosque of Ibn Tulun during the Ottoman period. However, in 1540 an Egyptian woman by the name of Amna Bint Salem built a house behind the eastern corner of the mosque and adjacent to it. She must have been rich in

118 – Photograph of the remains of the *zawiya* and tomb of Sheikh al-Bushi (or al-Madini) next to the spiral-shaped minaret. Photograph taken before 1943.

order to afford such an elaborate traditional Cairene house, which was probably for her and her family. It had a well, known as Bi'r al-Watawit (Well of the Bats), famous for the folk legends related to it, and had incorporated the small domed tomb of Sheikh Harun al-Husayni (Sidi Harun), who was the local saint of the area. About ninety years later, in 1631, another house known as Bayt al-Kiritliya—the house of the woman from Crete—was built adjacent to both Amna Bint Salem and the mosque. This woman must have been a foreigner from Crete involved in trade.

The two houses were built on the location of the old Dar al-Imara, separated by a narrow alley, and were both later bought by Gayer-Anderson in the 1930s. Today they are known as the Gayer-Anderson House/Museum. Although both houses were built outside the walls of the mosque of Ibn Tulun, they became part of the life and history of its large complex (fig. 119).

Historians do not mention anything about the mosque of Ibn Tulun during the Ottoman period until 'Ali Basha Mubarak, who says that sometime during the governorship of the Ottoman *wali* Muhammad Bey Abu al-Dhahab (1187–89 / 1773–75) the mosque of Ibn Tulun was turned into a workshop for the manufacture of wooden girdles.[12] However, the source on which 'Ali Basha Mubarak relies for this information is not known, because the Ottoman historian al-Jabarti does not mention this function or activity while dealing with the period of Muhammad Bey Abu al-Dhahab.[13] It is unclear whether 'Ali Basha Mubarak means that there was a factory built in the area of the mosque or that the mosque was converted into a large workshop. Nor is it clear whether the whole mosque or only part of it was used in this way. However, it would seem unlikely that the mosque—or even part of it—would be used for such a strange function, unless the whole mosque was in such a bad state of ruin that it was only useful for its large space and craftsmen decided to use it as a workshop. This would mean the mosque was no longer functioning as a place for prayer.

The period of Muhammad Bey Abu al-Dhahab was full of political disputes and civil wars between the Mamluk regiments and the Ottoman regime. His master 'Ali Bey al-Kabir and his comrade Murad Bey had revolted against the Ottomans and started to gain control over the Hijaz and Syria to form a united force to defeat the Ottoman regime and expel it from the area. The Ottomans sent an army to crush 'Ali Bey al-Kabir and Murad Bey, though they fled to Upper Egypt where they gained control over that territory. Egypt was therefore divided between the Mamluks in Upper Egypt and the Ottomans in Lower Egypt, with Cairo as their capital. At the same time, the Ottomans faced a crisis in Europe from the Hapsburgs and the Russians. The Ottoman *wali* left Egypt to deal with that situation, allowing 'Ali Bey al-Kabir and Murad Bey to regain control over Lower Egypt and then the whole of Egypt.

This history might explain why the mosque of Ibn Tulun was given little attention during the Ottoman period, despite the fact that the governorship of 'Abd al-Rahman Katkhuda in the 1770s was the most dynamic period of architectural projects under the Ottomans.

In 1798, Napoleon Bonaparte invaded Egypt in a campaign known as the French Expedition. His intensions were simple: to obstruct all communications between Britain and India. Upon setting foot in Egypt, the

119 – Reconstructed bird's-eye view from the east of the mosque during the Ottoman period, after the houses of Bayt Amna Bint Salem and Bayt al-Kiritliya (known today as the Gayer-Anderson House/ Museum) were built.

highly organized French army, clad in elegant uniforms with starched collars and using the world's finest technology, fought against the chaotic, unorganized Mamluk army who were using outdated weaponry. The Mamluks were defeated in a battle that supposedly took place at the Pyramids of Giza but actually took place in the suburb district of Imbaba, near Giza. This marked the final military defeat in the history of the Mamluks. Accompanying Bonaparte to Egypt was an army of learned men known as the *savants,* who constituted the main body of scholars of the institution he founded known as l'Insitut d'Égypte. These men recorded everything in Egypt, including its geography, topography, flora, fauna, history, ethnic groups, monuments, and all aspects of its social life. The studies were published in the monumental volumes of the *Description de l'Égypte*.

With regard to the mosque of Ibn Tulun, several studies were made by Marcel, Jomard, and Protain, which have been discussed throughout this study, on the mosque's inscriptions and architecture, as well as the fabulous engravings which portrayed life taking place inside it. Among the armies sent by the Ottoman Sultan to fight against Bonaparte was an Albanian regiment led by a young Albanian named Muhammad 'Ali. When the French Expedition failed in 1801, different factions sought to rule Egypt. Muhammad 'Ali won, became the new Ottoman *wali* of Egypt, and changed the country's history altogether.

The Muhammad 'Ali Period

11

Muhammad 'Ali Pasha ruled Egypt from 1805 to 1848. He was the father and founder of Egypt's modern period. He sought to modernize Egypt in every field to enable it to compete with the British, French, and Ottomans. His policy was to use European methods of administration and technologies to revolutionize Egypt. For almost three hundred years, the Ottomans had ruled Egypt, during which time it became underdeveloped and stagnant in all fields of life and culture. Muhammad 'Ali sought to develop Egypt through agriculture, culture, architecture, arts, education, sciences, and technology. He introduced modern European methods to make the Egyptian military the strongest in the Near East. In 1229–30 AH / 1814 AD, during the early years under Muhammad 'Ali, an earthquake hit Egypt.[1] Al-Jabarti mentions that the aftershocks continued for days, causing damage to the mosque of al-Azhar.[2] It seems that the earthquake also damaged the mosque of Ibn Tulun because Karl Baedeker mentions that the *riwaq* facing the *sahn* on the *qibla* side had suffered badly and its middle piers collapsed.[3]

120 – The *sahn* of the mosque after it was cleared from mounds of rubble and sand and finally leveled and with new paths put in. It also shows the domical *fisqiya* after the room on its drum had been removed, (see figs. 95, 96). Photograph taken circa. 1950.

Some of Muhammad 'Ali's greatest achievements were in healthcare and medicine. He employed a Frenchman named Clot Bey to develop the medical education and system in Egypt. Clot Bey became known as the 'Father of Medicine in Egypt' (fig. 121). He was credited with building the Hospital of Abu Za'bal in 1827, which later moved to new the Hospital of Qasr al-'Aini in 1837. His achievements allowed him to convince Muhammad 'Ali to convert the mosque of Ibn Tulun into an asylum for lunatics in 1846, which later was converted into a poorhouse.[4] He had the beautifully designed pointed arches of the mosque walled up (figs. 95, 96), destroying the essence of the pointed arches

121 – Antoine Clot Bey (1793–1868), the Frenchman known as the 'Father of Medicine in Egypt,' who convinced Muhammad 'Ali to convert the mosque of Ibn Tulun into a poorhouse and ordered the pointed arches to be entirely walled up.

and the beauty of their harmonious proportionality, and cells were constructed in the *riwaqs* to accommodate the poor.[5]

Around the same period, Rhone recounts that Muhammad 'Ali's son, Ibrahim Pasha, established a military hospital in the mosque of Ibn Tulun, which was subsequently converted into a salt magazine.[6] A blacksmith's workshop was established in the mosque at an unknown date and, in 1846, the mosque was converted into a pauper asylum upon Clot Bey's suggestion.[7] It remained so for almost three decades after the death of Muhammad 'Ali, until about 1880.[8] Prisse d'Avennes discusses the mosque's conversion into a poorhouse and accuses Clot Bey of walling up the beautifully designed pointed arches,[9] which he describes as "an act of vandalism, masked by the pretext of philanthropy."[10] On the same grounds, Corbet finds it unfortunate that the man known as the father of medical studies in Egypt would be connected with such a shocking act of vandalism.[11]

Muhammad 'Ali seems to have been disinterested in maintaining the mosque of Ibn Tulun as a place for prayer, since he allowed Clot Bey to spoil the building. Another interesting perspective is that the use of the mosque of Ibn Tulun as a shelter might reflect Muhammad Ali's attempt to centralize poor relief services. By using the mosque as a shelter he fulfilled his obligation toward charity, providing assistance for the needy, such as, abandoned children, free hospital treatment, as well as free passage for pilgrims traveling home from the Hajj.[12]

Muhammad 'Ali Pasha's main objective was to modernize Egypt, and he did everything he could to do so. He encouraged European engineers, technicians, scientists, and entrepreneurs from every field to work for him. Apart from making a good living in Egypt, Muhammad 'Ali allowed them to explore and exploit Egypt's antiquities and take them back to Europe. Rather than drawing attention to Egyptian heritage, his policy ignored (or even denied) the past, and did not treat it with any respect, by allowing it to be abused. Until the nineteenth century, there were no regulations over the use of the ancient Coptic and Islamic monuments.[13] There were no rules for the trade of Egyptian antiquities. In 1835, Muhammad 'Ali made the first step toward control of this trade with a decree banning the unauthorized removal of antiquities from the country.[14] This decree also designated a building in the Ezbekiya Gardens in Cairo as a storehouse for artifacts. These artifacts and antiquities were given away as gifts to foreign dignitaries,[15] although it is not known who gave these gifts or whether they were given before or after the decree was passed. The most famous gift was the obelisk of Ramesses II taken from the temple of Luxor and given to King Louis Philippe of France. It stands to this day in La Place de la Concorde in Paris.

Muhammad 'Ali Pasha died in 1848, a year after abdicating to his eldest son, Ibrahim Pasha, on account of mental illness. Ibrahim Pasha is considered the greatest warrior of the nineteenth century. Trained under the Frenchman Soliman al-Faransawi, he led the armies of Egypt into the Sudan, Hijaz, Syria, and Palestine, gaining control over these lands. He eventually became a threat to the Ottoman sultan in Istanbul, forcing the sultan to ally with the superpowers of Europe, who managed to fight Ibrahim Pasha and Muhammad 'Ali and defeated their navy at Navarino in 1832. Ibrahim Pasha's reign was short-lived; he died just a few months before his father, and right after taking power in 1848. Ibrahim Pasha was succeded by his brother, 'Abbas Hilmi I, who pursued policies contrary to his father's and opposed European colonization of Egypt. He was known as a man who did not favor education, and therefore closed the schools that his father had founded.

In 1850, the traveler Patterson saw the mosque of Ibn Tulun and wrote, "It was now sadly out of repair, and is being poorly repaired and patched up into dwellings for dervishes and their families (on three sides of the court) by the present pasha ['Abbas Hilmi]."[16] 'Abbas Hilmi I showed the ugliest form of his disinterest in Egyptian antiquities when he decided to give all that remained of the Ezbekiya collection of antiquities to the Austrian Archduke Maximilian.[17] It is therefore no surprise that the antiquities and monuments continued to suffer terribly. By 1856, the lawyer and economist Nassau Senior visited the mosque and said that there were 100 families living in it.[18] He added that the *sahn* contained a grove of palms and sycamore trees, as can be seen in Protain's illustration in figure 61 and Francis Bedford's photograph in

122 – Muhammad Sa'id Pasha approved the creation of the Services des Antiquities in 1858.

figure 110).[19] The mosque of Ibn Tulun and the poorhouse were neither improved nor given much attention during that period.

A few months before he died in 1854, 'Abbas Hilmi I had the railway built between Alexandria and the town of Kafr al-Zayat on the Rosetta branch of the Nile—the first in Egypt and the entire Near East. After his death, his son Sa'id took over Egypt as a shaky and unconfident ruler. In 1856, he extended the railway to Cairo and later, in 1858, to Suez. Sa'id Pasha also proclaimed the firman for the digging of the Suez Canal, which changed the entire history of Egypt and the region. Sa'id Pasha was a well-educated man (fig. 122) and his training in Europe made him appreciate Egyptian culture and heritage. So in 1858, he created the Service des Antiquités (Antiquities Service) to stem the illicit trade in Egyptian artifacts and appointed the French Egyptologist Auguste Mariette Pasha as the director. This was the first time that there was a governmental department working to save the antiquities of Egypt. The Antiquities Service was responsible for carrying out its own excavations and also for approving and supervising foreign archaeological missions.

In 1862, the photographer Francis Bedford was commissioned by Queen Victoria to accompany her eldest son, the Prince of Wales and Crown Prince Edward VII, on a tour of the Near East. During his stay in Cairo, he visited the mosque of Ibn Tulun and took some great photographs, which are considered some of the oldest-surviving images. His invaluable work shows the dilapidated state of the mosque of Ibn Tulun (see fig. 110), while another photograph taken from the top of the minaret of Ibn Tulun looks toward the Citadel of Cairo and the mosque of Muhammad 'Ali (fig. 123).[20] In spite of being an attractive view of the city, with the buildings topped by an incredible number of wind catchers, one also sees a huge structure and the large amount of buildings that had encroached on the area of the mosque. Upon careful examination, one can see a small rectangular window, at the lower left-hand side of the image, and trace the row of remarkable crenellations that are on top of its exterior northeastern *ziyada* wall, which had been entirely covered up. At that time (1862), there was no access to the mosque from that side (cf. figs. 8, 23, 24).

The same year (1862), Lucile, Lady Duff Gordon, the English author and translator visited the mosque of Ibn Tulun and described it, in a letter dated November 11, 1862, as being a vast poorhouse.[21] With great detail, she described two of the three lodgings that she had visited. One had several Turkish families that had partitioned off a larger room with mats hung from ropes. Each section of the lodgings had "as many bits of carpet, mat, and patchwork as the poor owner could collect."[22] A young boy explained to her how he slept, ate, and cooked in this small space. Most of the people living with him were either blind or lame. Another lodge was like an Arab hut, stuck against the lovely arches of the mosque, and it was inhabited by people poorer than the other one. It did not have mats or carpets to serve as mattresses and therefore the people had to sleep on the floor or on piles of rocks. As Lady Duff Gordon left, she gave a woman a few coins that were received with a loud melee, as the women in the hut scambled to claim the coins. During her tour of the mosque, she was moved by the poverty she witnessed and the lack of physical comfort afforded to the poor.[23]

In 1863, Auguste Mariette Pasha created the first national museum of Egyptian antiquities in the Cairene suburb of Bulaq, overlooking the river Nile. This became the nucleus of the Egyptian Museum of Antiquities, located in what is today's Tahrir Square and was the first museum built in the entire Near East. Sa'id Pasha died the same year and was succeeded by his nephew Isma'il Pasha, who later gained the new title of Khedive. Khedive Isma'il was well educated, ambitious, and rich, which enabled him to follow the policies of his father and grandfather but with caution so that he would not repeat their mistakes.

Khedive Isma'il was responsible for the Europeanization of Egypt, as the modernization process of Muhammad 'Ali was revived. During his reign, the Suez Canal, and other canals, were dug and inaugurated. The new European district of today's downtown Cairo was founded. This new area was called al-Isma'iliya Quarter, and it was laid out according to French principles of city planning. He built Abdin Palace, which would replace the citadel as the new seat of the rulers of Egypt, based on European-style architecture. In addition, the Gezira Palace and the Mena Palace were built during his reign and later converted

123 – Photograph by Francis Bedford, showing the spectacular view from the top of the minaret of Ibn Tulun, looking toward the mosque of Muhammad 'Ali atop the Citadel of Cairo. It shows massive encroachment of parasitic houses over the area of the northeastern *ziyada* wall of the mosque; the crenellations of the outer *ziyada* wall can hardly be seen as they have been entirely built over, not allowing access to the mosque from that side (see figs. 8, 23, 24).

124 – Prisse d'Avennes' engraving showing the area of the main *mihrab* and *minbar*, and the wooden dome above them. It also shows the soffits of the arches were still decorated with stucco designs at that time and the ceiling still existed during the 1860s. Compiled before 1869.

to hotels: the Marriott Hotel and the Mena House Hotel respectively). Wide boulevards were cut through the medieval quarters of Cairo. It was a period of renaissance, glory, and splendor.

Yet during the reign of Khedive Isma'il, the mosque of Ibn Tulun was not given any attention and continued to be used as a poorhouse. It was neglected and continued to deteriorate. Sometime before 1869, the French artist Prisse d'Avennes made a wonderful engraving of the *qibla riwaq*, and the area of the *mihrab* and *minbar* (fig. 124).[24] In 1877, Karl Baedeker says that that the *riwaq* facing the *sahn* on the *qibla* side totally fell off, having suffered badly for over twenty years after its middle piers had collapsed (figs. 107, 109).[25]

Isma'il's policies did not suit the European superpowers. Egypt had accrued large foreign debts, forcing it to sell the Suez Canal Company to Britain and France. In 1879, Isma'il was exiled to Istanbul where he lived until his death in 1895. His son Tawfiq took over (fig. 125), but was weak and could not maintain his father's policies. He faced pressure from Europe, and the debt crisis led to the British occupation of Egypt. The khedive had no choice but to accept Britain and France's decisions. However, one of the few great achievements of Khedive Tawfiq was that in 1881 he managed to establish the Comité de Conservation des Monuments de l'Art Arabe by firman, which turned out to be important and at the same time extremely effective. The Comité was a body within the Ministry of Religious Endowments (*Awqaf*).[26] It was an Egyptian institution, but was known by its French name as the Comité, and was divided into two sub-committees, each with a specific role. The task of the first commission was to provide a complete inventory of every Islamic and Coptic monument in Egypt and to specify those monuments most urgently in need of attention. The second, called the technical commission, would then visit the monuments and recommend a particular course of action, basing its decision on the monument's condition and its architectural or artistic value.[27]

125 – Khedive Tawfiq, who issued a decree in 1881 for the formation of the Comité de Conservation des Monuments de l'Art Arabe.

Khedive Tawfiq would set up meetings with members of the Comité to discuss the state of the monuments. They would create a budget for the projects, according to priorities, and then restoration works would start. The most significant success of these projects was the Comité's reports, which were annual or sometimes covered a few years at a time. The reports are indeed invaluable sources and indispensable for the study of any monument in Egypt. The Comité published all the restoration, preservation, and conservation works that took place on Islamic monuments in Cairo from 1890 until 1961 (a period of seventy-one years). These reports show the state of the mosque of Ibn Tulun when the Comité started their restoration in the 1880s and the extent of work

126 – Photograph by G. Lekegian showing the interior of the *qibla riwaq* without a ceiling and a broken arch of the missing *riwaq* that fell in 1877. On the right is a wall built between the piers. Photograph taken between 1887 and 1929.

127 – Photograph by Pascal Sebah showing the state of the mosque during the nineteenth century when it was used as a poorhouse. People lived in structures built with brick walls or fences between the piers of the mosque. Date unknown.

done to bring it to its present state. One can therefore trace the development of these restorations and learn about projects that were intended for the mosque but were never accomplished. However, these reports do not offer any form of art-historical analysis of the building itself.

Khedive Tawfiq had good intensions toward Egypt's heritage, but he also had many internal problems to resolve. The Egyptian army officers wanted to be treated and paid equally to the Turko-Circassian regiments. This caused a revolt led by the Egyptian general Ahmad 'Urabi, who challenged the khedive in front of his residence at Abdin Palace, demanding equal rights. The khedive obliged and a new government was established according to requests of 'Urabi, who was appointed minister of war. While, the Ottoman sultan hesitated to back anyone, but Britain and France refused to acknowledge the new government. The result was foreign intervention through the bombardment of the city of Alexandria by the British. Egyptian forces withdrew to al-Tell al-Kabir where 'Urabi was defeated by the British army and then exiled. These events led to the British military occupation of Egypt in 1882.

Meanwhile, the mosque of Ibn Tulun continued to be used as a poorhouse until 1880.[28] Istvan Ormos says that Franz Pasha closed the mosque and evicted the ill and the vagabonds.[29] In 1882-83, the mosque was still closed because the ceiling was expected to collapse. The mosque was examined and a report was presented to the Comité, which urged a new tiled roof and ceiling be built. The mosque ceiling had been damaged, probably as a result of the arches being walled up. The beams of the ceiling were broken and many pieces of the wooden inscriptions below the ceiling had fallen off or become detached (figs. 126, 127, 137-139). The Comité also stated that the *minbar* was completely ruined as a result of humidity and recommended it be isolated from the ground to prevent further deterioration (fig. 128). The Comité advised that wooden panels should be consolidated, and it warned of the need to remove the walls of the modern constructions. In addition, it recommended that the huts, which were built in the open courts (meaning the *sahn* and the *ziyada* areas) should be demolished, and that these areas should be cleared of the rubble and dirt which covered these areas. The mosque was architecturally surveyed, and wood and iron were bought for the rebuilding process.

In 1884, the members of the Comité recommended the complete removal of the walls erected by Clot Bey. In 1888, Stanley Lane-Poole described the mosque

128 – Photograph by G. Lekegian showing the monumental *minbar*, with its beautiful wooden panels missing. Herz Pasha later restored the *minbar* in 1913. Photograph taken between 1887 and 1913.

> Unfortunately its impressive quadrangle is defaced by the bricking-up of most of the arches to shelter the beggars and "casuals" of Cairo, who infest and disfigure the noble building. Ugly whitewashed walls now take the place of the cloisters on all sides but the east, and it is only there, in the liwan or sanctuary, that the original beauty of the design can be in some degree appreciated."[30]

'Ali Basha Mubarak says that the mosque accommodated an "ample crowd" of poor people, who had inflicted considerable pollution, destruction, and decay upon the fine monument and built in it

129 – The main entrance of the mosque, while the semicircular steps were being built. Photograph taken between 1929 and 1940.

for themselves shanties and shackles.[31] In 1888, it was suggested that all measures should be taken against the influx of the parasitic houses into the mosque and the walling up of the *riwaqs* (fig. 130). In addition, the windows of the houses, which at the time were also those of the mosque, that looked through the fine stucco window grilles into the mosque were constantly being broken and therefore had to be repaired.

In 1890, members of the Comité undertook careful re-examination of the mosque under the direction of Austro-Hungarian architect and engineer Max Herz, who later became director of the Arab Museum in 1892 and then director of the Comité de Conservation des Monuments de l'Art Arabe in 1901 (fig. 131). An extensive report was made of the dire state of the mosque and was accompanied by a new ground plan by (or supervised by) Herz Bey (fig. 106). The report provides information about the mosque's state of deterioration, its history and documents, and the desperate need for restoration. For example, the report notes that the principal façade of the mosque was

130 – The area of the northwestern *ziyada* showing the encroachment of parasitic houses on the mosque in the early 1940s. Photographed before 1943.

once adorned on one side by a vast public place, but by that time the street could not be seen because of the number of buildings occupying it (see fig. 5). It adds that since there was a fee to visit the mosque, some audacious neighbors used to allow visitors into the mosque—probably at a reduced price—by inviting them to enter through their homes. Once they were in, they would climb through a broken window (that was later blocked up) and find themselves on top of the *minbar* of the mosque, where they would walk down its steps.[32] In the same year (1890), Herz Pasha managed to demolish the parasitic structures, which consisted mainly of the walls occupying the interior of the arcades that had been erected by Clot Bey.[33]

While clearing the sand and rubble, several sculptured pieces of sycamore wood with Kufic inscriptions, which had been detached from the ceiling of the mosque, were found and later transferred to the Arab Museum.[34] The following year (1891) two more wooden pieces from the inscription and another piece from the *minbar* (probably a geometric panel) were found and taken to the Arab Museum.[35] The crenellations were also repaired and the roof was reinforced. [36] Only a small part of the old ceiling was saved during the restoration and conservation works.[37] The same year, Corbet published his detailed study on the mosque of Ibn Tulun. He explains that, "Its deterioration was rapidly progressing under the hands of a couple hundred of the most ignorant and filthy of the whole population."[38]

131 – Max Herz Pasha, the Austro-Hungarian architect who had the greatest impact on the restoration of the mosque of Ibn Tulun and most of the monuments of Islamic Cairo during the period between 1890 and 1914.

In 1892, the Comité continued renovations on the mosque, including the dome over the *mihrab* and its windows, a new ceiling, the upper part of the minaret, and the addition of a crescent to its finial. The famous *al-'ushari* copper boat-like finial had blown away during a storm at the beginning of the century. It also examined the area (rooms) behind the main *mihrab* and worked on the restoration of the *fisqiya*, *minbar*, and *dikka*, as well as the re-establishment of the *sahn*.[39]

Khedive Tawfiq died in 1892 at the age of 39 and was succeeded by his son 'Abbas Hilmi II (fig. 132). The new khedive was an energetic ruler who resented the British and sought to fight them through interior resistance. He encouraged Egyptians to create political parties for the first time and also encouraged arts and culture. During his reign, the Greco-Roman Museum of Alexandria was created in 1892. This was followed by the inauguration of the Egyptian Museum of Antiquities in Tahrir Square—a project that was completed by the French Egyptologist Gaston Maspero after it had been initiated by Auguste Mariette Pasha. In the same year (1902), the new building of the Arab Museum (known today as the Museum of Islamic Art) was erected and its first director was the Austrian architect, Julius Franz, who was later succeeded by Max Herz Bey. A few years later, in 1908, the Egyptian Marcos Samaika Pasha founded the Coptic Museum. The Egyptian Geological Museum was also built during the same period.

During the reign of 'Abbas Hilmi II, Egypt witnessed a dynamic cultural and political revolution like never before. Unlike Isma'il, who allowed Europeans to occupy and control most of Egypt's intellectual and cultural life, Khedive 'Abbas Hilmi II encouraged Egyptians to take part. Therefore, the Comité members consisted of European technicians, scholars, and specialists, as well as a new set of Egyptian elite, who were highly educated (mostly in Europe) and came back to apply their experiences in Egypt. During this time there was a spark of cultural awareness among Egyptians, as many began to appreciate their heritage for the first time in Egypt's modern history. In 1894, a map (not a plan) of the area around the mosque was made under the supervision of Herz Pasha, who was then the director of the Arab Museum.[40] During that year, one of the old doors on the southern side of the mosque collapsed. The Comité decided to pave a new street to clear the eastern façade (Tulun Street) and repair the rooms behind the main *mihrab*, adding a new ceiling to them (fig. 93).[41]

In 1902, the German architect Julius Franz Pasha, who was head of the technical department of the Ministry of Awqaf, suggested that the Comité make a copy of the stucco decorations of the Fatimid *mihrab* of al-Afdal to be analyzed (fig. 41).[42] It seems that without a ceiling, this part of the mosque was highly exposed to weather conditions, and with the amount of rain in wintertime, the stucco of this wonderful *mihrab* was deteriorating, and would have been completely destroyed. Hence, it was logical for Franz Pasha to make that suggestion. The same year, Herz Pasha became head of the technical department of the Comité. He was therefore in charge of all restoration works carried out by the Comité, until he was forced to leave Egypt in 1914.

In 1907, the members of the Comité noticed that the eastern minaret (of Qadi Karim al-Din) had tilted slightly (figs. 109).[43] Two years later, E. Klippel examined the same minaret—under the guidance of Herz Pasha—to see the extent of its inclination.[44] The reason for the attention to the minaret may have been no more than the safety of the people living around the mosque. In 1908, the Comité decided to build a small wooden roof (shelter) over the Fatimid *mihrab* of al-Afdal to protect it from the weather. By that time, the whole ceiling of the *qibla riwaq* had been destroyed (figs. 137, 138). In the same year it was also decided that a new copy of the *mihrab* of al-Afdal would be made and placed in the Arab Museum.[45]

In 1910, Herz Pasha removed the paintings covering the stucco decorations.[46] The same year, Diwan al-Awqaf presented a major project to accommodate students of al-Azhar inside the mosque of Ibn Tulun, but fortunately the Comité rejected it.[47] In 1914, the restoration of the *minbar* was completed. It was also determined that the small minaret of Qadi Karim al-Din had to be consolidated. It was inclining due to the lack of a solid foundation and because it was resting directly on the wooden ceiling of the mosque, which was badly deteriorated.[48]

132 –Khedive 'Abbas Hilmi II, whose reign witnessed a spark of cultural awareness among Egyptians in appreciating their heritage for the first time in modern history. He was exiled from Egypt in 1914.

The year 1914 was an unfortunate one in Egypt's history. Khedive 'Abbas Hilmi II was exiled. Like his father (Isma'il), Khedive 'Abbas Hilmi II's policies did not suit the superpowers of Europe, especially the British. While visiting Istanbul in 1914 (the year the First World War broke out and Egypt became a British protectorate), he learned of his removal from power, and lived in Switzerland until he died in 1944. The eldest member of the royal family, Husayn Kamel, who later took the title of Sultan, succeeded Khedive 'Abbas Hilmi II to the throne.

Sultan Husayn Kamel was old and weak; he could not stand up against the British occupation. Great changes were reshaping the policies and geography of the Near East–such as the Arab Revolt in the Hijaz and Bilad al-Sham and the Sykes-Picot Agreement–and Sultan Husayn Kamel was unlucky to be caught in the middle of the politics and military affairs of this time. The First World War led foreigners of Austro-Hungarian origin living in Egypt to be considered enemies of the British; Herz Pasha was forced out of British-controlled Egypt, which created a huge gap in the history of the Comité. The flow of funds stopped and works that Herz Pasha had started were not completed.

In 1915, the British architect Robert Williams asked permission from the Comité to set up scaffolds in the mosque of Ibn Tulun to study

133 – The encroachment of buildings on the area of the northwestern *ziyada*. Photograph taken before 1943.

134 – Fu'ad I, the king of Egypt and Sudan (1917–36), took pride in Egypt's heritage, history, and monuments in general, but he also had a special interest in the mosque of Ibn Tulun. He was the first ruler to attend the Friday prayer there since the Mamluks (1250–1517).

the inscriptions below the ceiling and the ornaments in the soffits of the arches (figs. 10, 26, 27).[49] In 1916, the Comité decided to pave a street near the northern corner (known today as Ahmad Ibn Tulun Street). During the same year, Achille Patricolo—who had succeeded Herz Pasha as director of the Antiquities Service—removed some of the ornaments of two arches on the *qibla riwaq*,[50] while the arcade facing the *sahn* on the *qibla riwaq* collapsed completely. However, all in all, we find that little work was done in the mosque of Ibn Tulun during the years that followed Herz Pasha's departure from Egypt.

After a short reign, Sultan Husayn Kamel died in 1917 and was succeeded by King Fu'ad I (fig. 134). A year after his accession to the throne of Egypt, on Rajab 22, 1336 / May 3, 1918, King Fu'ad attended Friday prayer at the mosque of Ibn Tulun.[51] This marked the first time that a ruler of Egypt visited and prayed in the mosque of Ibn Tulun since the reign of Sultan Lajin during the Mamluk period. King Fu'ad I had a personal interest in the mosque. When he learned (and probably saw) the buildings crowding and encroaching on its outskirts, he ordered the expropriation of these buildings so the *riwaq*s could return to their original form. He also wanted the mosque to be free of inhabitants. The area was cleared, and the walls of the mosque were made independent. The mosque was isolated on all four sides by a space of

135 – The encroachment of buildings on the mosque around the area of the spiral-shaped minaret and the wall of the mosque along al-Duhdayra Street. Photograph taken before 1929.

136 – The exterior walls of the northern corner of the mosque and the dense parasitic buildings encroaching on the mosque. On the right is part of the wall of the *madrasa* of Amir Sarghatmish. On the left are walls that had been removed in order to give easy access to the mosque from Ahmad Ibn Tulun Street. Photograph taken before 1929.

at least twenty meters, apart from the small square *maydan* or roundabout in front of it.[52] King Fu'ad's visit to the mosque of Ibn Tulun and his attendance during the Friday prayer was such a huge event that two houses adjacent to the *madrasa* of Sarghatmish, which were encroaching on the mosque, were ordered to be demolished to make appropriate space around it. (figs. 135, 136). During their demolition, a few of the original steps in front of the large entrances that had once given access to the mosque from that side were discovered.[53]

In the following year, the 1919 revolution took place against the British occupation; the people backed the popular nationalist leader and prime minister Sa'd Zaghlul, who was demanding Egypt's independence. During this time, no major activities took place in the mosque of Ibn Tulun. In 1920, when the revolution was over and affairs went back to normal, the Comité adopted measures regarding the expropriation of the buildings adjacent to the mosque behind the *qibla* wall (the area where Dar al-Imara used to stand).[54] In addition, the Comité bought the bazaars on the left side of the mosque's main entrance.[55] Old aerial photos show the mosque after some of the parasitic houses were demolished, while those in the area of Dar al-Imara were still there (figs. 5).

The Comité focused most on the encroachment of houses on the mosque and was trying to demolish them systematically year after year. Another issue was the constant removal of debris, rubble, and sand from the mosque, which was an essential activity due to its accumulation over years of neglect. In 1924, the southwestern *ziyada* had deteriorated badly because a large number of damaged cars were dumped in that area of the mosque. This part of the mosque became a dumping ground for people living in the houses around it. Public hygiene demanded that many of the breaches made in the *ziyada* walls be completely closed.[56] In addition, there was an attempt to restore the *sabil* of Lajin (also known as the *sabil* of Sultan Qaitbay) (fig. 54). At the same time, there was an ongoing effort to remove the accumulated rubble from the adjacent houses on the eastern side, behind the *qibla* wall (figs. 5).[57]

In 1927, the Comité reconstructed the ceiling of the mosque, which had been totally destroyed (figs. 137–139). They did so using wooden beams covered by reinforced concrete. This decision was based on the "solidity and economic values of that method." Specially made tiles then covered the roof. The tiles were originally going to be made in the town of al-Ma'sara, where the main factory for tile work in Egypt was located, but it was decided that new square ceramic tiles had to be specially made in the French town of Marseille and exported to Egypt.[58] (These tiles were removed and replaced by newer ones in the restoration works of 2004.)

137 – Photograph by L. Fiorillo showing the interior of the *qibla riwaq* with no ceiling. Photograph taken early 1900s.

138 – Photograph by H. Bechard showing the interior of the *qibla riwaq* with no ceiling, with only four *riwaq*s left after the outer one facing the *sahn* had fallen off in 1877. Photograph taken before 1887.

Les ruines de la Mosquée Touloun N° 164 Pl III.
Photog. Artistique G. Lekegian & Cie

In 1928, more debris was removed from the *ziyada* area and reconstruction was conducted on the missing walls and arches in the *qibla riwaq*. During the process of clearing, a flight of steps was discovered in front of the main entrance of the mosque. The marble-inscribed plaque of Badr al-Gammali, above the main entrance of the mosque used today, was found (figs. 79, 82). More excavations were made in front of the other entrances to see if there were similar plaques as well, but nothing was found. In addition, a pathway was made and a garden with trees was planted in the *ziyada* area directly in front of the mosque.[59]

In 1929, construction works included putting the walls in place, opening blocked entrances and doors, and repairing the base of the minaret and the part of the bridge linking the minaret with the roof. A complete photographic survey of the mosque and the wooden inscription below the ceiling was also conducted. Finally, the missing arcade facing the *sahn*, which had fallen in 1877, was totally rebuilt.[60] In 1930, six wooden pieces with Kufic inscriptions were discovered by Edmond Pauty and presented to the Arab Museum to be studied, published, and displayed.[61]

It is clear that King Fu'ad was well educated and had a keen interest in Egypt's history and heritage. The years of his reign marked a high degree of energetic work in the restoration and preservation of Egyptian monuments. The mosque of Ibn Tulun had much work done in clearing away what was around it, which allowed for better accessibility. More studies were carried out on the architecture and decoration of the mosque as well. One of King Fu'ad's great achievements was to personally sponsor the works of the iconic scholar K.A.C. Creswell (fig. 140). In 1932, Creswell published the first of five volumes of his *Early Muslim Architecture*; the second was published in 1940. His later work, *Muslim Architecture of Egypt*, was published from 1949 to 1969. These publications are among the most famous and outstanding in the field of Islamic architecture and had it not been for King Fu'ad, Creswell might not have been able to publish his monumental studies.

In 1933, the Comité requested four palm trees be planted in the *sahn* of the mosque, but this was not carried out. There had been trees in the *sahn*, as can be seen in Protain's illustration in the *Description*

139 – Photograph by G. Lekegian showing part of the *qibla riwaq* without a ceiling, as well as part of an arch of the arcade, which faced the open court and was completely broken by that time. It shows the spaces between the piers and their arches had been built up with firebricks. The main entrance of the mosque would be to the left side of the wall, which is hidden by the piers, and further left would be the open court. Photographed taken between 1887 and 1927.

140 – K.A.C. Creswell, who published monumental works in Islamic architecture and decoration, which were sponsored by King Fu'ad and later by his son King Faruq.

de l'Égypte (fig. 61), as well as others including a sycamore tree was seen by Nassau Senior in 1882, as can be seen in Francis Bedford's photograph of 1862 (fig. 110). These trees must have been removed sometime between 1882 and the 1930s. It is indeed a shame that they were removed by the Comité, as they gave the mosque a very pleasant atmosphere, such as they once did in the mosques of al-Mu'ayyad Sheikh at Bab Zuwayla, and the mosque of Aqsunqur, and still do at the "suavee mosque of Maridani," along the Darb al-Ahmar.[62]

In the same year (1933), the Comité proposed the demolition of more modern constructions near the minaret and two other houses on the façades as well as the construction of a new ceiling for the *sabil* of Sultan Qaitbay. The proposal was approved and the area behind the *qibla* wall (where Dar al-Imara used to stand) was cleared away.[63] In 1934, the small minaret of Qadi Karim al-Din was demolished due to its severe inclination that had become a danger to public safety (figs. 141, 142).[64]

In 1936, Egypt became semi-independent. The British evacuated the country, leaving only a military presence in the Suez Canal zone. The Comité moved from the authority of the Ministry of Awqaf to the Ministry of Education.[65] The same year, King Fu'ad I died and was succeeded by his teenage son King Faruq (fig. 143). In 1940, the Comité

141 – Image by an unknown photographer showing the mosque when it was inhabited and used as a poorhouse. Photograph taken ca. 1860s.

142 – The northeastern *ziyada* area of the mosque with structures built on the left side and huts at the far end, in front of the main entrance of the mosque. The lost minaret of Qadi Karim al-Din is vaguely visible on the far end. Photograph taken before 1934.

proposed the introduction of electrical lamps in the mosque, which were installed by LEBON and Co. seven years later.[66] In the same year, Creswell proposed that the Comité should inspect the cypress trees that were planted in the *ziyada* area. An irrigation canal was dug to impress the members of the Comité during their visit, but a couple of years later, the trees were removed because their irrigation endangered the foundation of the mosque's walls.[67]

In 1943, the Fatimid *mihrab* of al-Afdal was restored because it had deteriorated badly. The restorers relied on the copy of this *mihrab*, which was made for the Arab Museum in 1908.[68] During the same year, the Comité built a water reservoir in the *ziyada* of the mosque, which can be seen today at the western corner of the *ziyada* area, though the water has long since dried up (fig. 53).[69] This cistern must have been reconstructed over the site of the original Tulunid and Mamluk ones. This was the best location for a water reservoir, which would feed the fountain of the *fawwara* and *fisqiya*. Water ran downhill from there probably in a specially made canal or duct and sprung out of the fountain. In 1944, the Comité blocked some of the windows of the wall proper of the mosque because they had been badly damaged by children throwing stones.[70] The report does not specify which windows were blocked, but just that they were near the western side of the mosque.[71]

143 – King Faruq, the last king of Egypt (1936-52), had a great interest in history and monuments of Egypt. He, like his father, attended Friday prayer at the mosque of Ibn Tulun.

Between 1947 and 1948 the Comité built a new wall for the mosque on the western extremity of the *ziyada* and added the crenellations on top. It completed the rest of the wall on the southwestern side in the following year.[72] The Second World War broke out in 1939, and Egypt was caught in the middle, with the British still occupying the Suez Canal zone and the German Nazis approaching from the west to fight the British in Libya and the Western Desert of Egypt, where the famous battle of El Alamain took place. At the same time, Egyptian resistance by a group of young officers, calling themselves the Free Officers, was growing. They resented Faruq's corruption and increasing British interference in Egyptian politics. There was tension between the political parties in Egypt, and when a government was elected, the British ambassador forced the king to appoint a new prime minister, one who would be more allied to the British. When King Faruq obliged, the young officers took it as a sign of humiliation and were determined to remove him from power.

It is clear that, like his father, King Faruq gave great attention to and was interested in Egyptian monuments. He made it a point to attend Friday prayer in the famous mosques of Egypt. It was for that reason that in 1946, the Egyptian scholar Hasan 'Abd al-Wahhab made an invaluable descriptive and historical publication in two volumes in Arabic on the mosques where the king attended the Friday prayer.[73]

In 1950, the Comité proposed paving the entire area of the *sahn* with stone, arguing that the northern wind blew excessive dust into the *qibla riwaq*. The proposal was received with caution due to its extreme cost. A compromise was reached to cover the area of the *sahn* with small stone pebbles. This was agreed upon but never realized. The *sahn* was leveled and new paths were created (fig. 120).[74] Later on these paths would disappear and instead be paved. Similar paths can be seen in the plan of Pascal Coste, and the remains of one of those paths can be seen in Francis Bedford's photograph from 1862 (fig. 110).[75] The latter shows that the only remaining path was that from the domical *fisqiya* to the *qibla riwaq* along the central axis of the mosque. During the same year, the door of the *minbar* was set in place.[76]

Between 1950 and 1951, the Comité repaired the two chambers behind the *mihrab* (fig. 93) and the ceilings of these rooms in order to save the wonderful wooden corbels, which were described by Creswell as the "foreparts of gigantic locusts" (fig. 94). In addition, the stucco windows were restored, and the three *ziyada* walls were completed. The walls of the *sabil* of Lajin were also restored.[77] Looking back now, one may conclude that during the reign of King Faruq, under the enormous tasks of the Comité, the mosque of Ibn Tulun had reached its present state.

The Presidential Era

12

On July 23, 1952, the Free Officers surrounded the royal palace of Abdin with tanks and demanded King Faruq's immediate departure from Egypt. Faruq was exiled to Europe where he lived between Italy, France, and Switzerland until his death in 1965. The military coup had so much backing and support from the Egyptian population that it was seen as a revolution ending the rule of the Muhammad 'Ali dynasty, which had lasted for almost 150 years. Egypt became a presidential republic, with General Muhammad Naguib as the first president of Egypt. A new era had begun.

During the early years of the presidential era (1951 and 1952), some minor repairs were made by the Comité de Conservation des Monuments l'Art Arabe to the tympanum of an arch in the northern *riwaq* and the consolidation of stucco decorations of some arches.[1] Sometime after 1952, a new *mayda'a* was built in the southeastern part of the *ziyada*, just behind the *sabil* of Sultan Qaitbay. This *mayda'a* has an entrance on the southeastern side of the street and two interior entrances that lead from the *qibla riwaq*. The growing population justified building this new *mayda'a*, which is still standing and in use until today, having been restored several times (fig. 22, plan A).

144 – Photograph of the spiral-shaped minaret being consolidated by scaffolds after its upper part was seriously weakened by the earthquake that struck Egypt in October 1992. The scaffolds on the lower quadrangular story were removed in 1993. Photograph taken in 1993.

President Gamal 'Abd al-Nasser

In 1953, President Naguib was forced out of his position and put under house arrest until his death in 1984. Gamal 'Abd al-Nasser became the second president of Egypt. The same year, Mustafa 'Amer became the first Egyptian director of the Antiquities Service, after European scholars had headed it for almost a century. From that time on, it became a fully Egyptian-run authority.

In 1960, the Antiquities Service became a part of the Ministry of Culture, having been under the Ministry of Education since 1936. The following year the Comité was dissolved and became a permanent committee for Islamic and Coptic monuments within the Antiquities Service. The main interest of the Antiquities Service was salvaging Nubia, south of Aswan, which was going to be submerged under the waters of what would become Lake Nasser. UNESCO launched a worldwide campaign for monuments like the Temples of Abu Simbel, Philae, and Wadi al-Subu'a. Attention was focused more on the ancient Egyptian monuments and sites than the Islamic and Coptic monuments of Cairo.

Thus, the mosque of Ibn Tulun, along with other Islamic and Coptic monuments, were entirely neglected, their maintenance and upkeep ignored. The last report published by the Comité was in 1961,[2] which had a tragic effect, as the changes and evolution of the monuments were no longer recorded. There has been a great loss of knowledge and documentation about the monuments, which has led to a loss of awareness about antiquities. All interests toward the welfare of the monuments was almost gone, especially with the mosque of Ibn Tulun. One should, at this point, remember that the negative impact of the work of the Comité was that it was concerned only with the monuments, regardless of the surrounding areas and their services, and that it did not encourage any participation by the communities living around the monuments they were restoring. In other words, they did not try to educate or increase the awareness of the neighboring people.[3]

The only addition to the mosque of Ibn Tulun was an air-raid shelter built at the front, in the northeastern part of the mosque. This was in 1967, following the Six Day War, but it was removed in 1986.

President Anwar al-Sadat

In 1970, 'Abd al-Nasser died and Anwar al-Sadat became president, inheriting the heavy burdens that 'Abd al-Nasser left behind. The same year, the Antiquities Service, headed by Egyptologist Gamal Mukhtar, was renamed the Egyptian Antiquities Organization (EAO). During the early years of Sadat, little activity took place in the mosque of Ibn Tulun as the main focus was to regain Sinai, which Sadat did with the signing of the Camp David Accords with Israel in 1978.

145 – The mosque from the top of the minaret showing the pathways that led to the present domical *fisqiya*, which were added by the Egyptian Antiquities Organization during the 1980s. Photograph taken in 1993.

There was then some space and time for the Islamic monuments to regain some attention. In 1978 and 1979, the EAO, headed by Egyptologist Shehata Adam, started a long restoration process in the mosque of Ibn Tulun. The driving force behind the restoration was Egypt's first lady Jehan al-Sadat, who was interested in cultural awareness. The restoration included repair of the stucco windows and the pointed arches with their stucco decorations, whitewashing the lower parts of the piers facing the *sahn*, repairing and adding a new pavement for the entire building, paving the ground of the *sahn* with pebbles, and adding new pathways in the *sahn* that led to the present *fisqiya* (fig. 145).

Other works by the EAO included the restoration of the present *fisqiya* and the entire ceiling of the mosque, tiling the roof, adding electric fixtures for the newly made glass lamps, installing the dome over the main *mihrab*, and cleaning the *ziyada*s and the entire area around the mosque, as well as other works in the *sabil* of Lajin. Thus, the mosque of Ibn Tulun was given a facelift. One may say that the most important aspect of this phase of restoration was the cleaning and clearing away of rubble within the mosque, while the whitewashed piers also gave the building a striking but strange look. It was relatively well renovated, but was not given an ongoing maintenance plan–it did not last long before it needed another wave of restorations two decades later.

The 1970s witnessed some serious restoration works by foreign institutions in collaboration with the EAO on the monuments of Islamic Cairo.[4] In 1971 the Polish Institute embarked on restoring the complex of Amir Qurqumas in the Northern Cemetery.[5] A couple of years later (1973), the German Archaeological Institute in Cairo under Phillip Speiser started the major restoration of important buildings in the area of Darb al-Qirmiz, to include: the mosque of Tatar al-Higaziya, the palace of Amir Bishtak, and the *sabil-kuttab* of ʻAbd al-Rahman Katkhuda. The project later expanded to include the *madrasa* and mausoleum of Sultan Salih Nagm al-Din Ayyub, and the *madrasa* of Sultan al-Nasir Muhammad along al-Muʻiz Street.[6] The Darb al-Qirmiz project was probably the first major serious restoration work that was done in Islamic Cairo. They were successful projects except for the Bishtak palace which, apart from some art exhibits, was neglected and never rehabilitated. It was left to deteriorate for decades.[7] In 1976, the Italian Cultural Institute began to restore the Mehlevi Dervish convent and the buildings around it.[8] Within the same period, the Egyptian government allowed the Bohra Ismaʻili sect from India and Pakistan to restore Fatimid mosque and shrines, such as the mosque of al-Hakim and al-Aqmar.[9]

The mosque of Ibn Tulun also benefited greatly from the renewed interest in Egyptian culture and history that came from the boom in tourism following the peace treaty with Israel. The King Tutankhamun exhibition that traveled to the United States encouraged masses of American tourists to visit Egypt. In 1978, the German Archaeological Institute, together with the Goethe Institute and the EAO, hosted a conference about the architectural conservation and urban development of Historic Cairo. A couple of years later, in 1980, the First International Conference for the Conservation of Islamic Cairo was held in Cairo under the patronage of the minister of cultural affairs and the first lady

Jehan al-Sadat.[10] The same year, the World Bank gave Egypt a large amount of money in the form of a grant for the documentation and rescue of the historic zone of Cairo. As a result, a comprehensive inventory of historic buildings was made, which was the first of its kind.[11]

President Hosni Mubarak

In 1981, President Sadat was assassinated while attending a military parade. His vice president, Hosni Mubarak, was elected by the Egyptian parliament as the fourth president of Egypt. In 1982, Egyptologist Ahmad Qadri became the new director of the EAO. Caroline Williams describes him as "the strong-willed and imaginative Director."[12] He gave special attention to the Islamic and Coptic monuments of Egypt, launching a campaign to restore them. His method was to focus on one area, and he used students and youth to do the work. He started with a grand restoration project of the Citadel of Cairo, followed by other monuments of Islamic Cairo. Although there was controversy about his methods, whether positive or negative, Ahmad Qadri triggered a sense of cultural awareness among young Egyptian university students and new graduates for the first time in the twentieth century. Qadri's project resulted in the Citadel of Cairo becoming the most frequently visited Islamic site by both foreign tourists and Egyptian visitors.

In the first half of the 1980s the Royal Danish Restoration Academy reconstructed the Jawhariya Madrasa in al-Azhar mosque and the Institut Francais d'Archaeologie Orientale (IFAO) in Cairo started the restoration of the Ottoman houses of Bayt al-Harawi and Bayt al-Sinnary.[13]

In 1986, with the intense impact of tourism on Egypt's economy, the EAO carried out more works in the mosque of Ibn Tulun to facilitate tour group visits. The EAO added an iron fence around the area of the mosque to prevent people from spoiling the walls and entrances. It is interesting to note that this iron fence in fact created a new *ziyada* area for the mosque, giving it two *ziyada* areas. In addition, the EAO restored the ceiling, isolated the roof, and added waterspouts for rainwater to pour directly onto the area of the *sahn*. It had the quadrangular areas in the *ziyada*s sanded over and cleared away the rubble accumulating around them.

In 1992, one of the worst earthquakes in Egypt's history hit, and Cairo's monuments were badly damaged. Most of the city's minarets shook and were in danger of falling. The EAO, under the direction of the Egyptologist Muhammad Ibrahim Bakr, consolidated the monuments that had been affected by supporting them with scaffolds. Little could be done to fix the affected monuments due to a lack of funds for proper restoration. Although most of the mosque of Ibn Tulun did not suffer much, the upper part of the spiral minaret was severely affected. As a result, the EAO ordered that scaffolds should consolidate the minaret.[14] It is interesting to note that in spite of the earthquake, the walls of the mosque were not seriously at risk. This was the result of their having been built directly over the bedrock, making them well balanced during earthquakes (fig. 144).

Ironically, the 1992 earthquake had a positive effect on Egyptians' cultural awareness. The American Research Center in Egypt (ARCE) organized a conference on the status of externally supported conservation projects and the work undertaken by their Egyptian colleagues. As a result, the United States Agency for International Development (USAID) started a series of major grants for the conservation and preservation of Egypt's heritage. ARCE's work has included architectural preservation, the conservation of decorative elements, the design and installation of visitors' centers, and improvements to water management infrastructures that protect the monuments from decay. It was also decided to follow a preservation method through documentation rather than just conservation.[15] Funds poured into Egypt, partly via USAID, for huge restoration projects in Islamic Cairo.

In 1992, the project of al-Azhar Park began in the area of Darb al-Ahmar, which was funded by a donation of US$30 million given by the Aga Khan to the city of Cairo. Caroline Williams considers it to be one of the most complex and diversified examples of a multi-dimensional and integrated urban rehabilitation program.[16] Along with the development of the project, a series of archaeological and restoration projects took place, and the result was the largest green area to overlook the historic city of Cairo, and highly successful excavations of the area of Darb al-Ahmar and the eastern Ayyubid walls. Great restoration projects took place in the area of Darb al-Ahmar, such as the *madrasa* of Umm al-Sultan Sha'ban and the mosques of Aslam al-Silahdar and Aqsunqur (the Blue Mosque), restored by Dina Bakhoum.[17] The park was completed and opened in 2004, and should be considered one of the most successful projects in the historic zone.

Bright and energetic architects and scholars led great restoration projects that were funded by ARCE in the 1990s, such as Nairy Hampikian at Bab Zuwayla, Hoda Abd al-Hamid at the *zawiya* of Farag Ibn Barquq, Agnieszka Dobrowolska at the *wakala* of Nafisa al-Bayda and the *sabil* of Tusun Basha, and Alaa al-Habashi at Bayt al-Razzaz. In 1994, presidential decree number 82 changed the name of the Egyptian Antiquities Organization to the Supreme Council of Antiquities (SCA).[18] However, it was still under the authority of the Ministry of Culture. Its first secretary-general was the Egyptologist Mohammed Abdel Halim Nur el-Din. During his tenure, he studied the problems facing the monuments of Islamic Cairo. In 1994, Egyptian scholars such as the folklorist Dr. Asaad Nadim and his family initiated a non-governmental project to restore the seventeenth-century house/museum of Bayt al-Suhaymi, in collaboration with the SCA and the Ministry of Culture. US $3 million was granted by the Arab Fund for Economic and Social Development, which is based in Kuwait, for the project. The success of the project resulted in not only the restoration of the house "but included the historical context and the urban residential environment as well in the restoration concept."[19] Ultimately, other monuments and residential houses along the alley of Darb al-Asfar in the Gamaliya Quarter were restored and upgraded. The project also introduced a new concept: the social component of restoration. This was achieved by raising the awareness of people in the neighborhood about the importance of the monuments and how to value them. The project, completed in 2000, introduced new strategies and methods in restoration, which were taken as the model for a larger national restoration project: Historic Cairo (discussed below).

The Suhaymi project was an urban redevelopment project, which was the first of its kind within Historic Cairo.[20] It was one of the very few restoration works conducted by a non-governmental organization.

The reason for this is that prior to that project there was no cooperation between the antiquities authorities and NGOs. In addition, bureaucratic rules would prevent proposals for projects from being accepted. Collaboration with people who were actually interested in preserving their monuments was almost nil and never encouraged. Hence, there were hardly any restoration projects carried out by private individuals or entrepreneurs.[21]

With the rise of terrorism in the early 1990s, tourism faced tough times. The government was not giving attention to the upkeep of the monuments, especially the mosque of Ibn Tulun, which had deteriorated badly due to a lack of maintenance. The state of the mosque was such that the northeastern *ziyada* area was in very poor condition and was covered with fallen tall wild palm reeds, which made it hard to walk through the mosque. Moreover, the defective sewage system in the urban district of Tulun often caused flooding around the mosque. The *ziyada* area was deserted and inhabited only by stray animals.[22] It had become a dangerous place and affected the hygiene of the entire neighborhood.

The problem facing the mosque of Ibn Tulun, as well as the rest of the Islamic monuments, is the various authorities that have jurisdiction over them. The first authority is the SCA, which is in charge of the structure itself. Their most important concern is to ensure the monument does not collapse. As long as that is the case, they do not address other issues. The second authority is the Ministry of Religious Endowments (Awqaf), which owns the land where the building lies. Their responsibilities include cleaning the mosque and seeing that it is suitable for conducting prayers. The ministry appoints the *muezzin* and *khatib* of the mosque, as well as the cleaners and sweepers. The third is the city council, which is part of the governorate of Cairo. Their jurisdiction lies within the area around the monument, making sure it allows people to access the mosque easily, that there is good parking, and that any garbage around the monuments is removed. They are also responsible for providing, removing, and replacing the lamps for electricity, and paving streets and sidewalks. The fourth authority, introduced in the 1990s, is the tourist police. They make sure that no harm happens to the building, such as looting, both inside and outside the monument. They have the right to check people walking in and out of the building. Thus, we find that there are different departments who feel they are in charge of the monuments. No single department in the Egyptian government oversees all four authorities. In the midst of all this the monuments deteriorate and ultimately no one carries the blame. The result is that the mosque of Ibn Tulun, as well as other monuments, become the victims of these authoritarian departments.

The project of Historic Cairo, known in Arabic as *Mashru' al-Qahira al-tarikhiya*, was probably the largest restoration project ever undertaken in the history of Islamic Egypt.[23] The aim of the project was to transform the historic zone of the city into an open-air museum. It focused on the main street of the Fatimid City, known today as al-Mu'iz Street. This was the main windpipe *(qasaba)* of al-Qahira, which starts in the north from Bab al-Futuh and ends in the south at Bab Zuwayla. The project restored the street to its original level during the Mamluk and Ottoman eras. The street's sewage, water, electrical, and phone systems were fixed. In addition, all the monuments on both sides of the street were restored. A new lighting system was installed so visitors could take a stroll in the evenings. Above all, the project was meant to close the street to traffic, in order to transform it into a pedestrian walkway. People from all over came to admire the beauty and magnificent architecture of Islamic Cairo, and this became an attractive and popular area to visit. Cultural awareness in Egypt had reached a new high.

Within the wake of the Historic Cairo project, in 2002, the SCA, under the leadership of its director Egyptologist Gaballah Ali Gaballah, started another phase of the restoration of the mosque of Ibn Tulun. The same year, Gaballah retired and Egyptologist Zahi Hawass filled his post. The Historic Cairo project was more of a project belonging to the Ministry of Culture.

In 2002, the restoration of the *sabil* of Tusun Pasha near Bab Zuwayla was completed. This became the nucleus of other restoration projects by restorer Agnieska Dobrowolska. Thanks to her, the *sabil* of Nafisa al-Bayda behind Bab Zuwayla and the *sabil* of Mustafa Pasha were restored too.[24] The problem with these relatively small but wonderful projects is that there was never a plan to rehabilitate those buildings. This is probably due to the realization that it would be hard to figure out who would have the power or the authority to decide how they should be later used.

During the same year, the mosque of Ibn Tulun was featured in a publication that consisted of a well-documented and technical report.[25] It concluded that the minaret and foundations of the monument were structurally safe, but showed the severe damage and destruction the mosque had suffered. A geotechnical study of the foundation soil showed that the walls and piers had been seriously affected, while another study showed the increase of humidity in the walls of the mosque, resulting from poor water supply and sewage leakages from nearby houses.[26] The same report showed more cracks and cavities in the walls and piers of the mosque. Horizontal cracks were found in the ceiling of the mosque and the concrete roof added earlier by the Comité. All the elements mentioned above were treated, in addition to the restoration of some of the windows and cracks in the walls. A waterproof polyethylene layer was placed around the foundations, a new drainage system was added to protect the walls from underground water leakage, and the salts were removed.[27]

The mosque of Ibn Tulun was fully restored at a cost of US$2.5 million in 2004. An elegant publication was distributed on the occasion of its inauguration.[28] The structure was well consolidated. The cracks in the brick walls and piers were filled. The ceiling was restored, and a newly isolated roofing system and new waterspouts were added. The *mihrab*s, the *minbar*, the dome above the *mihrab*, and the rooms behind them were all restored. The stucco was also restored, and new stone flooring was installed. The area of the *ziyada* was cleaned up and garbage was removed.

The mosque was given another new look with the addition of a vast stone platform/pavement covering the entire area of the open court. The idea was to apply a complete layer of damp proofing sheets below the entire area of the courtyard. In order to achieve this, it was necessary to use electrical equipment for cutting into the bedrock. The removal of the gravel layer, which had acted as a natural filter since the 1920s and blocked the natural breathing of the rock, led to the accumulation of humidity, as a result of the increase of the amount of water stored within the rock underneath the mosque area. This water mainly came from the leakage of nearby water sources and sewage systems. Thus the humidity levels increased significantly along the internal and external walls of the mosque, as well as along the piers. In addition, the increase in the water content and humidity inside the rock had an effect on the rate of swelling of the rock beneath. After that, the façades of the mosque were injected with 'wacker.'[29] A new lighting system was added in the flooring of the mosque and in all the pointed arched windows. Next, strong light fixtures were inserted along the area of the *ziyada*, open court, the domical *fisqiya* in the middle of the mosque, and the spiral-shaped minaret. The mosque looked glamorous and especially magical in the evenings.[30]

However, these changes disturbed scholars, students, and aficionados of Islamic architecture—in particular the idea of covering the entire open court with stone. To them, the mosque of Ibn Tulun was special for its old look preserved by the peaceful, tranquil, beautiful, and harmonious arcades. Caroline Williams was surprised that the mosque of Ibn Tulun—the single most important monument in Cairo that had survived without any major alterations since the ninth century—was being restored with such interventions.[31] She confirms that the earthquake of 1992 did not affect the building, and adds that the exterior walls that had stood for more than one thousand years were being injected with a consolidant, despite the fact the contractor of the project had confirmed their structural integrity. Williams adds that all the layers of plaster had been removed and replaced, simply for the sake of the money involved. Finally, she laments the fact that the restoration project was not being documented and therefore, all possibility of establishing a history of the earlier layers had been lost.[32]

The Mubarak era, which lasted thirty years, had also put its stamp on the history of the mosque of Ibn Tulun. The changes reflected the mentality of the era: showy and rich but at the same time lacking knowledge and appreciation of the value of serene, simple, tasteful architecture and proportions. As much as Clot Bey in the nineteenth century had committed the most shameful act of vandalism by walling up the beautiful pointed arches of the mosque, here was another act of vandalism which would change the entire appearance of the mosque of Ibn Tulun. As for the lights, there is no doubt they are impressive, but few people visit the mosque at night, which begs the question: Why was it done? Was the mosque of Ibn Tulun going to be used as a backdrop for evening functions? The mosque closes its doors right after the evening prayer, so lights would not serve any special purpose. The only explanation is that the mosque might have been intended for other functions. In the midst of the political tensions facing Egypt and the Mubarak regime, the government of Egypt was eager to protect tourism by any means. Thus, there was heavy security, with a visible presence, in all tourist sites all over the country.

In 2010, the experience of visiting the mosque of Ibn Tulun was interesting and illustrated how the whole organization of employees in the mosque was full of tension, and at the same time fragile and ineffective. Ahmad Ibn Tulun Street was barricaded from all sides. From Saliba Street, no vehicles were allowed in, except those for tourism or of local residents. People had to show their IDs as they walked along the street. If you were visiting the mosque as a tourist, another policeman holding a heavy dossier would approach you and ask the name of the tour agency you were with, what hotel you were staying in, the name of the tour guide and his mobile number, the name of the driver and his mobile number, and the license plate of the car/van/bus. He would then ask where you were coming from, and where you were heading after your visit to the mosque. As you walked past the iron fence surrounding the mosque, another policeman would be sitting, holding a machine gun. He would ask you to open your bags for security measures. Behind him would be a temporary wooden office, with one or two officers sitting inside. You had to go through an electric X-ray machine, similar to those found in hotels, airports, and high-end restaurants in Egypt. The X-ray machine seemed totally out of place. After that, you would walk up the steps into the *ziyada* area and enjoy the peace, tranquility, and the spacious isolation of the mosque. As you looked at the grandeur of the walls and space of the *ziyada*, you would see to your right the powerful minaret of Amir Sarghatmish, almost visually centered within the space of the *ziyada*. You could easily mistake it for the minaret of Ibn Tulun, and not of another mosque. You would then walk up the second flight of steps that lead into the mosque proper and its *riwaqs*. There you would find another set of employees, seated at the entrance. One of them would be another security guard. who would be holding his walkie-talkie, set at high pitch to project its distorted sound around the tranquil atmosphere of the mosque and to show his importance. He too would ask another set of questions as the policeman outside the mosque did. After that, if you wanted to enter further, you would find two other men, who tie cloth coverings onto your shoes, while sitting on the floor. They usually would be Awqaf employees, who make most of their living from the tips they receive from visitors and guides. After that, there would be another employee sitting, exuding authority—he would be the antiquities employee. After that you would enjoy the beauty of the mosque's architecture by walking round, admiring its wonderful visual perspectives. If you had the time, you would ask to climb the spiral-shaped minaret and maybe have a stroll on the roof of the mosque. The view from the top of the minaret is striking and spectacular.

Post-2011

The January 25, 2011, revolution ousted President Mubarak after three decades in power. This revolution, which had a noble cause, negatively affected Egypt's monuments (Ancient, Greco-Roman, Coptic, and Islamic). During the early days of the revolution, the Egyptian Museum of Antiquities was looted. When news about this spread, young Egyptian protesters formed a human chain to protect the museum from further pillaging. This was a sign that the revolution was taking its correct path: Young Egyptians were aware of the value of their heritage.

In 2012, Muhammad Morsi of the Muslim Brotherhood became the president of Egypt, but the following year, on June 30, 2013, he too was ousted with another revolution. During Morsi's year in office, Egypt's monuments suffered burglary and lootings. Storage houses and museums full of ancient antiquities were robbed and destroyed, stolen antiquities were sold on the international market and al-Mu'iz Street of historic Cairo became more of a garage for cars and trucks than a pedestrian street. Its light fixtures, which when lit up gave the area a magical effect at night, were vandalized or stolen.

In the midst of these events and the collapse of security forces, the mosque of Ibn Tulun went through a phase of vandalism as well. Its light fixtures were sabotaged, as floodlight lamps were destroyed and electrical cables were looted. In the early months of 2014, efforts were made by the government to revive al-Mu'iz Street by bringing it back to being a pedestrian-only area and reviving its beauty. This would allow for some optimism for this glorious historic zone.

One should add that the Megawra Society, headed by May Al-Ibrashi, is an energetic group that beams a ray of light into Egypt's heritage and cultural awareness. It is an architectural hub for young Egyptian students and architects serving the community around the area of al-Khalifa, where the mosque of Ibn Tulun is located. It is a place for young people to meet and debate on the field of architecture and urbanism. It focuses on art, theory, praxis, and cultural heritage and also on promoting sustainability and social responsibility in the built environment.[33] It is an active society that pushes for the welfare of education of ordinary people and is aimed at increasing the cultural awareness of the people living in the area of al-Khalifa. One of their earlier events took place in November 2012, in the mosque of Ibn Tulun after it was restored and had a huge attendance by the neighboring community.[34] In the past, the monuments conditions depended on the government's efforts to keep them safe and standing. This policy has proved to be inefficient because without the participation of the communities surrounding the buildings the monuments will decay and might even disappear. It should no longer be that the government fixes and saves the monuments. It will be the private sector along with the rise of community awareness that will save these monuments–the activities of the Megawra Society in the mosque of Ibn Tulun make a good argument for this.

During the last decades, an interesting phenomenon has taken place in the mosque of Ibn Tulun. A group of worshipers of the Bohra sect, who are recognized by their Pakistani-Indian-style costumes, visit the mosque of Ibn Tulun every Friday morning, before the noon

prayer. Interestingly, they don't attend the Friday prayers, but rather worship in front of the Fatimid *mihrab* of the Caliph al-Mustansir and the Vizier al-Afdal (fig. 146). They arrive in groups of different numbers of men, women, and children. They usually attend a lecture by their leader, after which some of them are seen taking their photographs next to the *mihrab*. Furthermore, some of the women tend to kiss the Fatimid *mihrab*.

146 – A group of worshippers from the Bohra sect, who regularly visit the mosque of Ibn Tulun on Friday mornings, to perform the interesting phenomenon of only praying in front of—and to—the Fatimid *mihrab* of the Caliph al-Mustansir and the vizier al-Afdal.

Today the mosque might seem as though it is drifting through another period of dilapidation. This is not new for the mosque of Ibn Tulun. It has certainly gone through worse periods during its centuries of survival. However, only time will tell whether or not this generation of Egyptians will be respectful enough of Ibn Tulun's glorious architecture. Regardless of what happens, another phase in the mosque's history of restorations will soon begin.

THE LEGACY OF IBN TULUN

13

There are several works of art and architecture that echo or resemble the mosque of Ibn Tulun, both inside and outside of Egypt. During the early nineteenth century, the French architect Pascal Coste came to Egypt because he was commissioned to design and build the mosque of Muhammad 'Ali Pasha, who was the ruler of Egypt at that time. He wished to build the mosque in a typical Neo-Mamluk style, which characterized the style of Cairo's Islamic architecture during the Mamluk period (1250-1517). In order to meet this difficult task, Pascal Coste had to study Cairo's mosques. During the process, he drew a new plan of the mosque of Ibn Tulun, adding new elevations as well as details of its decorative features. He made a wonderful lithograph showing the open court of the mosque, with the domical *fisqiya* and spiral-shaped minaret, looking through the arches of the *qibla riwaq* (fig. 148). It is worth noting that the same scene was illustrated earlier by Protain in the *Description de l'Égypte* (fig. 59). However, the latter shows the arches in a more gothic style rather than a pointed one. Pascal Coste must have had a reason for making this particular painting from the same angle as Protain's illustration. It is important to mention that Pascal Coste was one of the first artists or architects to show the pointed arches of the mosque of Ibn Tulun in their actual shape and style. Nevertheless, the angle from which he supposedly stood to create this painting is an absolutely impossible one. In addition, he brilliantly shows the wooden inscription below the ceiling of the mosque. The same scene was later copied as an engraving by Marcel.[1]

One can say that the works by Jomard, Marcel, and Protain in the *Description de l'Égypte* sought to document the mosque of Ibn Tulun as it appeared during their time. They did not, however, attempt to include an artistic value to their subjects. We find that Coste tried to

147 – The free-standing minaret of the mosque opposite the chic resort of Hacienda,on the North Coast of Egypt, resembles that of Ibn Tulun.

148 [NEXT PAGE] – Lithograph by Pascal Coste looking out at the open court through the *qibla riwaq* of the mosque. It shows the domical *fisqiya* and spiral-shaped minaret. The main subjects of the painting are the shapes of the pointed arches and the wooden inscription below the ceiling of the mosque.

149 – Painting by British artist Reginald Barratt showing an Egyptian standing against the *qibla* wall of the mosque of Ibn Tulun and details of the mosque's architectural decorations.

follow the same trend, however he added an artistic side to his subject by imagining such an impossible angle, as he simply wanted to show the mosque from the most beautiful perspective. Later, the British artist Robert Hay adds a most important illustration of the spiral-shaped minaret and the area around it (fig. 60). He bases his illustration on that by Jomard in the *Description*, which is purely recording what was there at the time, without adding a dramatic effect that would make it appealing to the viewer. It is another documentation of the building. Similarly, the works of French artist and historian Émile Prisse d'Avennes (figs. 63, 124) also follow the same trend but help us to comprehend the transformations that the mosque underwent during the later part of the nineteenth century.

Antoine Gros' painted masterpiece shows Bonaparte visiting the plague survivors in Jaffa (which was then part of Palestine) (fig. 62). The subject of the painting is indeed sad and dramatic. The painting shows Bonaparte inspecting the survivors, in what seems like the architecture of a mosque with arches and columns. However, on the far upper horizon, it strangely shows the spiral-shaped minaret of the mosque of Ibn Tulun. One wonders why Antoine Gros would show the minaret of Ibn Tulun in a painting that is supposed to depict Jaffa. One explanation could be that the artist visited Egypt during his trip to the Near East and either mixed up his sketches or deliberately added the minaret as something he remembered as having an effect on him. One may also say that the unique shape of the spiral minaret of Ibn Tulun had left a deep impression on Gros' visual memory, to the extent that he included it in his wonderful painting.

Another painting is by the British artist Reginald Barratt published in 1907 (fig. 149).[2] It shows a man wearing traditional Egyptian dress, standing and looking downward at the floor, suggesting that he is in the middle of prayer. On the left side of the worshiper is a decoration resembling the main *mihrab* of the mosque of Ibn Tulun, with the Coptic-style columns flanking it and the wonderful band of mosaic inscriptions. High above the man's head is one of the windows that pierce the wall of the mosque. The painting is strange in many ways. First, it shows the man in the process of prayer, standing up with his

150 – An Egyptian five-pound note from 1973 (still in use) with an illustration of the mosque of Ibn Tulun, includes the domical *fisqiya* in the middle of the *sahn*, and the *madrasa* of Amir Sarghatmish with an almost exaggerated Mughal-style dome.

151 – An Egyptian five-pound note from 2013, with an illustration of the mosque of Ibn Tulun, omitting the domical *fisqiya* from view, and elongating the finial of the spiral-shaped minaret of Ibn Tulun, as well as keeping the Mughal-style dome in the *madrasa* of Amir Sarghatmish.

back to the *qibla* wall. He is therefore standing in the wrong position because while praying, one should be facing the *qibla* wall and not giving it one's back. The second issue is that the angle which this painting depicts shows another impossibility, as the monumental *minbar* of the mosque would have been where the man is standing, but it is not seen in the painting. Therefore, both the angle and the orientation of the worshiper are incorrect. Again, the only explanation would be that Barratt made a few sketches of the items in his paintings while in Egypt and then incorrectly compiled them after arriving home in Europe. Due to his lack of knowledge of the culture of Egypt and Islam, it is easy to see how he would have made these mistakes. In spite of this, the mosque of Ibn Tulun must have had a positive impression on the artist. Whatever the appreciation of this work of art, the general impression that it gives is of peace and tranquility inside the mosque—an effect which is still felt in the mosque today.

In 1973 and 1978, two new five-pound notes were issued in Egypt (fig. 150). They show a view from the roof of the mosque of Ibn Tulun, with the domical *fisqiya* in the middle of the *sahn*, the spiral-shaped minaret and the *madrasa* of Amir Sarghatmish with an almost Mughal-style exaggeration of its bulbous dome. Several decades later (in 2013), a newer version of the scene was made in the same five-pound note (fig. 151), omitting the domical *fisqiya* from its view and showing the spiral-shaped minaret of Ibn Tulun with its elongated finial, while at the same time keeping the same Mughal-style dome in the *madrasa* of Amir Sarghatmish, without correcting it. It is worth noting that Egyptian paper currency usually has an ancient Egyptian theme on one side, with an Islamic scene on the other.

In late 1977, some scenes of the famous movie *The Spy Who Loved Me*, staring Roger Moore as the British agent James Bond, were shot in Egypt. Exciting action took place, with the monuments of Egypt acting as the backdrops for these scenes. One of the most thrilling sequences was shot showing the hero walking through the beautiful *riwaq*s of the mosque of Ibn Tulun. Another scene showed a fierce fight with a villain on top of the terrace of the houses of Amna Bint Salem and Bayt al-Kiritliya, now the Gayer-Anderson Museum. The interesting aspect of the scene is that it takes place with the spiral-shaped minaret of Ibn Tulun and that of Amir Sarghatmish in the background. These minarets and mosque are special and unique, and would have been chosen for those scenes as symbols of Islamic Cairo.

During the last ten years many mosques have been built in different parts of Egypt, and four mosques especially conjure up a memory of the minaret of the mosque of Ibn Tulun—especially the freestanding minaret with a staircase on the outside. One is at gate number six of the famous Marina resort near El Alamain on the North Coast (fig. 152). Farther along the North Coast is another mosque built opposite the chic resort of Hacienda, which is small and has another freestanding minaret, closely resembling that of Ibn Tulun (fig. 147). Another mosque was built in the newly developed governmental and business compound known as Smart Village on Giza's outskirts along the Cairo-Alexandria desert road (fig. 153). The mosque is small and

152 – The mosque at gate six of the popular Marina resort on the North Coast of Egypt.

153 – The mosque in the Smart Village complex on the outskirts of Giza showing a minaret with an iron staircase circling around its minaret.

154 – A mosque in Sixth of October City, west of Giza, showing a minaret with its staircase on the outside like Ibn Tulun, though more cubical in shape.

is intended to serve the employees and workers of that area. Its minaret also has a staircase on the outside, though the staircase is not built of stone, brick, or cement, but rather of iron. The fourth is a newly built mosque in the Sixth of October City, west of Giza (fig. 154). It too has a minaret with a staircase on the outside, like the others, but it is more square and cubical than round and circular.

There is no doubt that the symbolism of the mosque of Ibn Tulun lies in its unusual spiral-shaped minaret. Most of the works of art such as that of Protain and Robert Hay, and even Antoine Gros, focus on the minaret, while those of Pascal Coste, Prisse d'Avennes and the Barratt painting conjure up memories of its interior architecture. Nevertheless, the legacy of Ibn Tulun will long survive.[3]

155 [NEXT PAGE] – Detail of the marble block containing the foundation inscription.

156 [PAGE 266] – Detail of the interior of the domical *fisqiya*.

157 [PAGE 274] – Detail of the Samarra-style decorations on the piers.

Appendix: The Arabic Inscriptions of the Mosque of Ibn Tulun

1. The Tulunid *Mihrab* M1 (fig. 40)

لا إله إلا الله محمد رسول الله

2. The Tulunid *Mihrab* M2 (fig. 41)

لا إله إلا الله محمد رسول الله

3. The Inscription of Badr al-Gamali BI (fig. 82)

بسملة.... C.IX, 18

نصر من الله وفتح قريب لعبد الله ووليه معد أبي تميم الإمام المستنصر بالله أمير المؤمنين صلوات الله عليه وعلى أبائه الطاهرين وأبنائه الأكرمين

أمر بتجديد هذا الباب وما يليه عند عدوان النار على أبدعه المارقون فيه السيد الأجل أمير الجيوش سيف الإسلام ناصر الإمام أبو النجم بدر المستنصري

أدام الله قدرته وإلى كلمته ابتغاء ثواب الله وطلب مرضاته وذلك في صفر سنة سبعين وأربعمائة الحمد لله وصلواته على سيدنا محمد النبي وآله الطاهرين وسلم تسليماً

4. The Mihrab of Sultan Lajin M3 (fig. 43)

بسم الله الرحمن الرحيم أمر بإنشاء هذا المحراب المبارك مولانا السلطان الملك المنصور حسام الدنيا والدين لاجين سلطان الإسلام والسلملين....

5. The Mihrab of the Vizier al-Afdal and the Caliph al-Mustansir M4 (fig. 44)

On the right side

بسملة....أمر بإنشاء هذا المحراب خليفة فتى مولانا وسيدنا الإمام

On the upper side

المستنصر بالله أمير المؤمنين صلوات الله عليه وعلى أبائه الطاهرين

On the left side

وأبنائه المنتظرين السيد الأجل الأفضل سيف الإمام جلال الإسلام شرف الأنام ناصر الدين خليل. أمير المؤمنين....

On a small line below the upper one

ثقة الأمام فخر الأحكام القاسم عبد الحاكم ابن وهيب بن عبد الرحمن

On the middle line

لا اله إلا الله محمد رسول الله علي ولي الله

6. The Inscription of the Caliph al-Hafiz li-Din Allah, copied in the *Description de l'Égypte* (fig. 81)

بسملة....مما أمر بإنشائه عبد الله ووليه مولانا وسيدنا عبد المجيد أبي

الميمون الأمام الحافظ لدين الله أمير المؤمنين صلوات الله عليه وعلي أبائه الطاهرين وأبنائه الأكرمين

علي يد(؟؟) عبده (؟) ومملوكه القاضي المؤيد (؟) الأمير سراج الدين علي (؟) المح (....) ين المؤمنين الأمام وعمدة (؟) الأحكام

أطال (أدام؟) (الل)ه جلاله وخلد (؟) (أمره و(؟) كماله...خلافه العلوية الحافظية درا (؟)

لماير والقبائل (؟) ولي (؟) أمير المؤمنين أبو الثريا نجم بن جعفر....الله....في شوال (؟) سنة ست (؟) وعشرين (؟) (وخمسمائة)

7. The so-called *Mihrab* of the Sayyida Nafisa M5 (fig. 46)

قد نري تقلب وجهك في السماء

فسبح بحمد ربك وكن من الساجدين واعبد ربك حتى يأتيك اليقين

8. The Main *Mihrab* (fig. 37)

لا اله إلا الله محمد رسول الله

9. The wooden inscription above the Main *Mihrab* (fig. 98)

لا اله إلا الله محمد رسول الله

10. The Monumental *Minbar* (fig. 99)

أمر بعمل هذا المنبر المبارك مولانا السلطان الملك المنصور حسامنة ست ٢ الدنيا لاجين المنصوري وتسعين وستمائة

On the right door

تجدد هذا المنبر المبارك في عصر خديو مصر المعظم الحاج عباس حلمي الثاني ادام الله أيامه

On the left door

وذلك بمباشرة لجنة حفظ الآثار العربية سنة اثنين وثلاثون وثلاثمائة بعد الألف من الهجرة النبوية

11. The faded wooden inscription on the domical *fisqiya* (fig. 99)

أمر بإنشاء هذه القبة المباركة والفسية والساعات الشريفة مولانا السلطان الملك المنصور حسام الدنيا (1) والدين لاجين المنصوري

في سنة ست(؟) وتسعين وستمائة

12. The surviving inscriptions of the marble Foundation Blocks FI (fig. 48)

Marcel had copied their full texts before their destruction in the Description, (figs. 67, 68)

(1-14) بسملة c.II, 256: XLVIII, 29: III, 106 (fragment): IX, 18....

Line 1	...أمر الأمير أبو العباس أحمد بن طولون مولي أمير المؤ
Line 2	منين أدام الله له العز والكرامة والنعمة التامة (؟) في الآخرة والأو
Line 3	لى ببناء هذا المسجد المبارك الميمو(ن) من خالص ما أفاء الله عليه وطيبه
Line 4	لجماعه المسلمين ابتغاء رضوان الله والدا/(ر) الآخرة وإيثار(ا) لما فيه تسنية الدين
Line 5	وألفه المؤمنين ورغبة في عمارة بي/(وت) الله وأداء فرضة وتلاوة كت(ا)
Line 6	به ومداومة ذكره اذ يقول الله تقدس/(و) تعالي في بيوت أذ(ن) الله أن ترفع و
Line 7	يذكر فيها اسمه يسبح له فيها بالعدو والآصال رجال لا تلهيهم تجارة ولا بيع عن
Line 8	ذكر الله واقام الصلوة وايتآء الزكوة يخا/(ف)ون يوما تتقلب فيه القلوب والأبصار
Line 9	ليجزيهم الله أحسن ما عملوا ويزيدهم من/(ف)ضله والله يرزق من يشآء بغير حساب
Line 10	في شهر رمضان من سنة خمسة وستين وما(ئ)تين./سبحان ربك رب العزة عما يصفون و سلم على المرسلين والحمد الله رب العالمين. الله/(م) صلى على محمد وعلى آل محمد وارحم محمدا
Line 11	وآل محمد وبارك على محمد وعلى آل محمد كا(فضل) ما صليت وترحمت وباركت على إبراهيم
Line 12	
Line 13	..../ وعلى آل إبراهيم وأنعم أنك حميد مجيد.

13. The fragments of the wooden inscriptions below the ceiling of the mosque that are recorded by Marcel, *Description*, Plate C (fig. 97)

Row a-b	بسم الله الرحمن الرحيم الحمد لله رب العالمين الرحمن
Row b-c	الرحيم مالك يوم الدين إياك نعبد وإياك نستعين اهدنا
Row c-d	الصراط المستقيم صراط الذين أنعمت عليهم غير
Row d-e	المغضوب عليهم ولا الضالين. ألم ذلك الكتب لا ريب فيه
Row e-f	هدى للمتقين يؤمنون بالغيب ويقيمون الصلوه و
Row f-g	مما رزقناهم ينفقون والذين يؤمنون بما انزل اليك

Row g-h	فزادهم الله مرضا ولهم عذاب اليم بما كانوا يكذ
Row h-i	بون واذا قيل لهم لا تفسدوا في الأرض قالو
Row i	نما نحن مطحون الا أنهم هم المفسدون ولكن لا
Row k-l	يشعرون واذا قيل لهم آمنوا كما آمن الناس قالوا
Row l-m	ا أنؤمن كما آمن السفهاء الا انهم هم السفهاء
Row m-n	لكن واذا لقو الذين آمنوا قالوا آمنا واذ
Row n	خلوا إلى شيطينهم قالوا نا معكم نحن مست

14. Marcel's Plate E (1)

The fragments of the wooden inscriptions below the ceiling of the mosque that are recorded by Marcel, *Description*, Plate E (1) (fig. 81)

Row a-a	ما لا تعملون وعلم آدم الأسماء كلها ثم عرضهم على
Row a-b	الملئكة فقال ائتوني بأسماء هؤلاء إن كنتم صد
Row b-c	قين قالوا سبحانك لا علم لنا الا ما علمتنا انك انت
Row c-d	العليم الحكيم قل يا آدم أنبئهم بأسمائهم فلما أنبأهم بأ
Row d-e	سمائهم قال ألم أقل لكم اني اعلم غيب السموات وا
Row e-f	لأرض اعلم ما تبدون وما تكتمون واذا قلنا
Row f-g	للملائكة اسجدوا لآدم فسجدوا الا ابليس أبي وا
Row g-h	ستكبر وكان من الكافرين وقلنا يا آدم اسكن انت وز
Row h	وجك الجنة وكلا منهما رغدا حيث شئتما ولا تقربا

Glossary

adhan: call to prayer

al-'ushari: the boat-like finial surmounting the minaret

al-muwaqqit: the officer who keeps time; known as the timer

amir: prince or a general in an army

atabeks: lords ruling the Levant in the eleventh and twelfth centuries

awqaf: see *waqf*

aya: a verse in the Qur'an

basmala: the opening chapter of the Qur'an, starting with the name of Allah

bayt al-mal: treasury

bimaristan: hospital

da'i: preacher

dikka: a high platform in a mosque from which the prayer is repeated

dinars: coinage in medieval times

diwan: sitting area, lounge, or office

diya': owned pieces of land

faqih: scholar of jurisprudence

farrashin: sweepers or cleaners

fatq: crack, hole, gorge

fawwara: fountain

fiqh: jurisprudence

fisqiya: fountain jetting water

funduq: hotel

ghilman: boy servants

ghuraba: foreigners

hadith: lectures or speeches uttered by the Prophet Muhammad that constitute the second major source of Islamic studies

imam: leader of the prayer

iwan: a huge vaulted hall

jami': Friday congregational mosque

kafir: disbeliever in religion or atheist

kanz: treasure

khadam: servants

khanqa: commercial building in the urban fabric of a city. Also, a caravanserai if the building lies in a deserted area, outside an urban fabric

kharaj: land or property tax

khatib: preacher in a mosque on Friday, also known as an imam

khizanat kutub: library

khizanat sharab: a sort of a pharmacy, apothecary, or medical clinic

khutba: Friday sermon during the Friday noon prayer

kursi: lectern where a reader sits to read the holy Qur'an

kuttab: school for teaching the Qur'an by heart to small children

mabkhara: incense burner

madrasa: high institute/school for education

maktab: school for teaching the Qur'an

malwiya: spiral-shaped

maqsura: an area where the ruler and his entourage sit, usually surrounded by a wooden screen.

markab al-nahas: copper boat-like shape

masahif: a Qur'anic manuscript (plural of *mushaf*)

mashhad: memorial

masjid: mosque

mayda'a: ablutions place in a mosque

mazwala: sundial used to provide time of day

mihrab: niche that gives the orientation to Mecca

min al-maghariba: from the Morroccons, North Africans, Spanish, or Andalusians

minbar: pulpit from which the imam gives his sermon on Fridays

miqati: the person who determined the exact prayer time

muballigh: the person who repeats what is said during the Friday prayers, for those who are far from the imam and cannot hear him

mudarrisin: teachers

muezzin: the person who calls the people to pray, usually from the top of a minaret (today through a microphone and loudspeaker)

mulid: festival marking the anniversary of a holy man

muqarnas: alveolus, stalactites without their drops, honey-comb-like decorations

muqri': reciter of the Qur'an

musallah: prayer area

muzawwaqa: decorated

Naskhi: cursive Arabic script

qa'at al-khataba: hall or office of the *khatib* (preacher)

qabr: tomb

qadi: judge

qibla: orientation to Mecca

qubba: dome or domical building, or tomb

riwaq: columned area with arches, that support a flat ceiling

sa'ati: a timer, or someone specialized in clocks, or sundials

sabil: public fountain house, common within the city

sahn: open court

saqiya: waterwheel

shahada: bearing witness that there is no god but Allah and the Prophet Muhammad as His messenger

sura: chapter

tabib: physician

tafsir: religious interpretations

tibb: the science of medicine

wafa' al-nil: an Egyptian festival that is celebrated since ancient Egyptian times

wakala: commercial building in the urban center, a caravanserai outside the urban center

wali: governor

waqf (pl. *awqaf*): religious endowment

waqfiya: religious endowment deed

warraq: paper provider

wazir: vizier or prime minister

zawiya: a small place for prayer that has no a minaret, can be a corner of a street or alley

ziyada: an additional area

Figure Credits

Line drawing by ARCHiNOS Architecture, Cairo; concept by Tarek Swelim: 13, 19

Map made with the technical help of Jaroslaw Dobrowolski at ARCHiNOS Architecture, Cairo; concept by Tarek Swelim: 14, 22 plan A, 56, 65, 76 plan B, 85 plan C, 87 plan D, 92, 113 plan F

Rendering made with the technical help of Agnieszka Dobrowolska, Joanna Dyżewska, Fatma Farouq, and Karim al-Faramawi at ARCHiNOS Architecture, Cairo; concept by Tarek Swelim: 18, 20, 66, 69, 77, 78, 80, 84, 88-90, 102-104, 105 plan E, 115, 116, 119

Pascal Coste, *Architecture Arabe Ou Monuments Du Kaire*, plate II: 148

Francis Bedford, *Cities, Sights, and Citadels of the Near East*. Photograph courtesy of Royal Collection Trust © Her Majesty Queen Elizabeth II 2014: 110, 123

Creswell Photo Collection, the Rare Books and Special Collections Library, The American University in Cairo: 58 (plate 21 c/5 C3), 107 (A9, plate 1), 109 (A9, plate 3E), 111 (A8, plate 47 B), 117 (A9, plate 41 B), 118 (A9, plate 42 D), 130 (A9, plate 41 D), 137 (A8, plate 56), 138 (A8, plate 57), 126 (A8, plate 59 C), 139 (A8, plate 59 B), 129 (A8, plate 47 C), 128 (A9, plate 34 B), 108 (A8, plate 46 A), 120 (A20, plate 11 B), 133 (A8, plate 46 C), 129 135 (A8, plate 46 B), 136 (A9, plate 44 A), 5 (A8, plate 43), 142 (A8, plate 56 B)

Photograph by Samah Elbadrawi: 15, 16, 83, 121, 147, 152-154

From the private collection of Dr. Maged Farag: 122, 125, 132, 134, 143

Robert Hay, *Illustrations of Cairo*, plate V, Courtesy of the Rare Books and Special Collections Library, The American University in Cairo: 60

From the private collection of Barry Iverson, Albumen Print: 141

Photograph by Matjaž Kačičnik: 1-4, 6-11, 21, 23-55, 57, 64, 70-75, 79, 82, 86, 91, 93, 94, 98-101, 112, 114, 146, 155-157

Musée du Louvre, Paris: 62

Marcel, *Description de l'Égypte*, vol. II, *Planches, État Moderne*, courtesy of the Rare Books and Special Collections Library, The American University in Cairo: 67 (plate F), 68 (plate G), 81 (plare E), 97 (plate C)

D.S. Margoliouth, *Cairo, Jerusalem and Damascus, three chief cities of Egyptian sultans* (New York: Dodd Mead & Co, 1907): 149

Gaston Migeon, *Le Caire, le Nil et Memphis*, page 42: 95

Protain, *Description de l'Égypte*, vol. I, *Planches, État Moderne,* plate 29. Courtesy of the Rare Books and Special Collections Library, The American University in Cairo: 59

Protain, *Description de l'Égypte*, vol. I, *Planches, État Moderne,* plate 31. Courtesy of the Rare Books and Special Collections Library, The American University in Cairo: 61

The Rare Books and Special Collections Library, The American University in Cairo: 63 (Prisse d'Avennes, *L'Art arabe* I, plate II) 106 (Comité de Conservation de l'Art Arabe, *Exercise 1890*, plate I); 124 (*al-Musawwar*, 29 July, 1937), 131 (Istvan Ormos, *Max Herz Pasha 1856-1919*, 46, figure 7), 140

Drawing by Seif El-Rashidi; concept by Tarek Swelim: 12

George Salmon, *Etudes sur la Topographie du Caire*, plate II: 17

Photograph by Tarek Swelim: 144, 145

Pascal Sebah, *Egypt*: 127

Pascal Sebah, *Description de l'Égypte*, Volume 15. Courtesy of the Rare Books and Special Collections Library, The American University in Cairo: 96

BIBLIOGRAPHY

MEDIEVAL SOURCES

al-'Asqalani, Ibn Hajar. *Inba' al-ghumr bi-anba' al-'umr*. Cairo, 1973.

al-'Ayni, Badr al-Din. *'Iqd al-juman fi tarikh ahl al-aaman*, 762-855 AH /1360-1451 AD. 23 vols. Cairo: Dar al-Kutub al-Misriya, Tarikh no. 1584.

al-Balawi, Abu Muhammad 'Abd Allah Ibn Muhammad al-Madini. *Sirat Ahmad Ibn Tulun*. Edited by Muhammad Kurd 'Ali. Cairo: Maktabat al-Thaqafa al-Diniya, circa 1939.

Ibn al-Daya, Abu Ja'far Ahmad Ibn Yusuf al-Katib. *Kitab al-mukafa'a*. Edited by Amin 'Abd al-'Aziz. Cairo: al-Maktaba al-Adabiya, 1914.

Ibn Duqmaq, Sarim al-Din Ibrahim Ibn Muhammad Ibn Aydamur al-'Alla'i al-Misri. *Kitab al-intisar li-wasitat 'iqd al-amsar*. Edited by K. Vollers. Beirut: Markaz al-Mawsu'at al-'Alamiya, 1893.

Ibn Jubayr, Muhammad Ibn Ahmad. *Rihlat Ibn Jubayr*. Beirut: Dār Ṣadir lil-Ṭibā'ah wa-al-Nashr, 1959.

———. *The Travels of Ibn Jubayr*. Translated and edited by R.J.C. Broadhurst. London: J. Cape, 1952.

Ibn Khaldun, 'Abd al-Rahman. *Tarikh Ibn Khaldun*. Beirut: Mu'assasat al-A'lami, 1971.

Ibn Taghribirdi, Jamal al-Din Abu al-Mahasin Yusuf al-Atabki. *Al-nujum al-zahira fi muluk Misr wa-l-Qahira*. 16 vols. Cairo: Matbạ'at Dār al-Kutub al-Misriyah, 1929-1972.

Ibn al-Zayyat, Shams al-Din Abu 'Abd Allah Muhammad Ibn Nasir al-Din al-Ansari. *al-Kawakib al-sayyara fi tartib al-ziyara*. Baghdad: Maktabat al-Muthanna, 1968.

al-Jabarti, 'Abd al-Rahman. *'Aja'ib al-athar fi al-tarajim wa-l-akhbar*. 4 vols. Beirut: Dar al-Gil, n.d.

al-Maghribi, Ibn Sa'id. *al-Mughrib fi hula al-Maghrib, kitab al-durr al-maknum fi hulay dawlat Bani Tulun*. Text and German translation by K. Vollers. Semitistische Studien I. Berlin: 1894-95.

———*al-Mughrib fī ḥulá al-maghrib, al-nujūm al-zāhirah fī ḥulá ḥaḍrat al-Qāhirah*. Edited by H. Nassar. Cairo: Matḅa'at Dār al-Kutub, 1970.

al-Maqrizi, Taqi al-Din Ahmad. *Kitab al-suluk li-ma'rifat duwwal al-muluk*. Edited by Mustafa Ziyada. 4 vols. in 12. Cairo: Matba'at Lajnat al-Ta'lif, 1934-1972.

———. *Al-maw'iz w-al-i'tibar fi dhikr al-khitat w-al-athar al-ma'ruf bi-l-khitat al-maqriziya*. Edited by Ayman Fu'ad Sayyid. 4 vols. London: Mu'assasat al-Furqan lil-Turath al-Islami, 2002.

al-Maqaddasi, Shams al-Din Abi 'Abd Allah Muhammad Ibn Ahmad Ibn Abi Bakr al-Banna' al-Shami al-Muqaddasi al-Ma'ruf bi-l-Bashari. *Ahsan al-taqasim fi ma'rifat al-aqalim*. Edited by M.J. De Goeje. Bibliotheca Georgraphorum Arabicarum. Leiden: Brill, 1967.

———. *Ahsanu-t-Taqasim fi Ma'rifati-l-Aqalim*, known as *al-Muqaddasi*. Translated by G.S.A. Ranking and R.F. Azoo. Calcutta: Baptist Mission Press, 1897.

Khusraw. *Safarnama*. Translated and edited by Yahiya Khashshab. Cairo: Matba'at Lajnat al-Ta'lif wa-l-Tarjama wa-l-Nashr, 1945.

———. *Sefer nameh*. Translated and edited by Charles Schefer. Paris: E. Leroux, 1881.

al-Nawawi, *Tahdhib al-asma'*. Boettingen, 1842-47.

al-Nuwayri, Shihab al-Din Ahmad. *Nihayat al-arb fi funun al-adab*, edited by Ahmad Zaki Pasha. Cairo: Dar al-Kutub al-Misriya, 1923-60.

al-Qalqashandi, Abu al-'Abbas Ahmad Ibn 'Ali. *Subh al-a'sha fi sina'at al-insha'*. Vol. III. Cairo: al-Matba'a al-Amiriya, 1913-17.

al-Sakhawi, Muhammad Ibn 'Abd al-Rahman. *Tuhfat al-aḥbāb wa bughyat al-ṭullāb fī al-khitat wa-l-mazārāt, wa-l-tarājim wa-l-biqā' al-mubārakāt*. Edited by Ahmad Nash'at, Mahmud Rabi', and Hasan Qasim. Cairo: Matba'at al-'Ulum wa-l-Adab, 1937.

al-Sakhawi, Shams al-Din. *al-Daw' al-lami' li-ahl al-qarn al-tasi'*. 5 vols. Cairo: Manshurat Dar Maktabat al-Hayat, 1966.

al-Suyuti, Jalal al-Din 'Abd al-Rahman. *Husn al-muhadara fi tarikh Misr wa-l-Qahira*. Edited by Muhammad Abu al-Fadl Ibrahim. 2 vols. Cairo: Dar Ihiya' al-Kutub al-'Arabiya, 1968.

al-Ya'qubi, Ahmad Ibn Abi Ya'qub Ibn Wadih. *Kitab al-buldan*. Najaf, al-Matba'at al-Haydariya, 1957.

———. *Tarikh al-Ya'qubi*. 2 vols. Beirut: Dar Sadir, 1960.

———. *Ya'kubi: Les Pays*. Translated by Gaston Wiet. Cairo: IFAO, 1937.

Modern Sources

'Abd al-Wahhab, Hasan. "al-'Imara al-islamiya: jami' Ibn Tulun." *al-'Imara* II (1940): 105–12.

———. *Tarikh al-masajid al-athariya allati sulla fiha faridat al-jum'a al-salih Faruq al-awwal*. 2 vols. Cairo: Matba'at Dar al-Kutub al-Misriya, 1946.

Ahmad, Mahmud. "al-Jami' al-tuluni." *al-Handasa* XII (Misr: Matba'at al-I'timad bi-Shari' Hasan al-Akbar, 1932), 402–11.

Ahmad, Yusuf Effendi. *Jami' Ahmad Ibn Tulun*. Cairo: Matba'at al-Taraqi, 1917.

———. *al-Khatt al-kufi*. Cairo: Matba'at Hijazi, 1939.

'Akkush, Mahmud. *Tarikh wa qasf al-jami' al-tuluni*. Cairo: Matba'at Dar al-Kutub al-Misriya, 1927.

Aldridge, James. *Cairo*. London: Macmillan, 1970.

Allen, James, and K.A.C. Creswell. *A Short Account of Early Muslim Architecture*. Cairo: The American University in Cairo Press, 1989.

Amin, Muhammad. *Fihris watha'iq al-Qahira hatta nihayyat 'asr salatin al-mamalik*, Catalogue des documents d'archives du Caire. Cairo: IFAO, 1981.

Arnold, Sir Thomas W., and Professor Adolf Grohmann. *The Islamic Book: A Contribution to Its Art and History from the VII-XVIII Century*. Paris: The Pegasus Press; New York: Harcourt, Brace and Company, 1929.

Al-Asad, Mohammad. *Restoration of Ahmad Ibn Tulun Mosque, Cairo, Egypt*. 2007 On Site Review. Cairo: The Aga Khan Award Publications, May 2007, http://archnet.org/system/publications/contents/1575/original/FLS1819.pdf?1384750740.

Baedeker, Karl. *Egypt: Handbook for Travellers*. 1st part. Leipzig: Karl Baedeker, 1885.

Bacharach, Jere L. "Administrative Complexes, Palaces, and Citadels: Changes in the Loci of Medieval Muslim Rule." In *The Ottoman City and its Parts Urban Structure and Social Order*, edited by Irene Bierma, Rifa'at Abou-El-Haj, and Donald Preziosi, 111–28. New Rochelle, NY: A.D. Caratzas, 1991.

———. "Conserving Historic Cairo's Splendid Legacy." In *Preserving Egypt's Cultural Heritage*, edited by Randi Danforth. Cairo: American Research Center in Egypt, 2010.

———, ed. *The Restoration and Conservation of Islamic Monuments in Egypt*. Cairo: The American University in Cairo Press, 1995.

Bakhoum, Dina Ishak. "The Madrasa of Umm al-Sultan Sha'ban before and after Creswell," *Creswell Photographs Re-examined, New Perspectives on Islamic Architecture*, edited by Bernard O'Kane, 99–120. Cairo: The American University in Cairo Press, 2009.

al-Basha, Hasan. *al-Qahira: tarikhuha, fununuha wa atharuha*. Cairo: Dar al-Kitab al-Jadid, 1970.

Becker, C.H. "Cairo." In *The Encyclopedia of Islam*. 815–26 1st ed. Leiden: E.J. Brill, 1913.

———. "Egypt." In *The Encyclopedia of Islam*, 4–23. 1st ed. Leiden: E.J. Brill, 1927.

Bedford, Francis. *Cities, Sights, and Citadels of the Near East: Francis Bedford's Nineteenth-Century Photographs of Egypt, the Levant, and Constantinople*. Cairo: The American University in Cairo Press, 2014.

Behrens-Abouseif, Doris. *Cairo of the Mamluks: A History of the Architecture and its Culture*. Cairo: The American University in Cairo Press, 2007.

———. *Islamic Architecture in Cairo: An Introduction*. Cairo: The American University in Cairo Press, 1989.

———. *The Minarets of Cairo*. Cairo: The American University in Cairo Press, 1985.

Van Berchem, Max. *Matériaux pour un Corpus Inscriptionum Arabicarum*. 1st part, Égypte. Cairo: IFAO, 1894–1903.

Bloom, Jonathan M. "Al-Ma'mun's blue Koran?" *Revue des Études Islamiques* LIV (1986): 59–65.

———. *Arts of the City Victorious: Islamic Art and Architecture in Fatimid North Africa and Egypt*. Cairo: The American University in Cairo Press, in association with the Institute of Ismaili Studies, 2008.

———. *Minaret, Symbol of Islam*. Oxford Studies in Islamic Art VII. Oxford: Oxford University Press, 1989.

Brentjes, B. "Zu Einigen Samanischen and Nachsamanidischen Holzbildwerken des Seravschantales im Westen Tadshikistans." *Central Asiatic Journal* 15 (1971): 295–97.

Casanova, Paul, trans. *Livre des admonitions et de l'observation pour l'histoire des quartiers et des monuments ou descriptions historique et topographique de l'Égypte*. Cairo: IFAO, 1920.

Çelebi, Evliya. *Seyahatnamesi*. Edited by S.A. Kahraman, Y. Dagli, and R. Dankoff. 10 vols. Istanbul: Yapı Kredi Yayınları, 2005.

Clerget, Marcel, *Le Caire: étude de géographie urbaine et historie économique*. 2 vols. Cairo: Imprimerie E. and R. Schindler, 1934.

Comité de Conservation des Monuments de l'Art Arabe: Procès verbaux des séances. Rapport de la deuxième commission. 41 vols. Cairo, 1882-1945.

Corbet, Eustace K. "The Life And Works of Ahmad Ibn Tulun." *Journal of the Royal Asiatic Society* (1891): 527-62.

Coste, Pascal. *Architecture arabe ou monuments du Kaire*. Paris: Firmin Didot Freres, 1839.

Creswell, K.A.C. *A Brief Chronology of the Muhammadan Monuments of Egypt to ad 1517*. Cairo: IFAO XVI, 1919.

———. *Early Muslim Architecture. Umayyads ad 622-750*. 2 vols. Oxford: The Clarendon Press, 1932 and 1969; New York: Hacker Art Books, 1979.

———. *Muslim Architecture of Egypt*. 2 vols. Oxford: The Clarendon Press, 1952; New York: Hacker Art Books, 1978.

———. "Some Newly Discovered Tulunide Ornament." *The Burlington Magazine* XXXV (November 1919): 180-88.

David-Weill, M. Jean. *Les bois à épigraphes jusqu'à l'époque Mamlouke*. Catalogue général du Musée Arabe du Caire. 2 vols. Cairo: IFAO, 1931.

Devonshire, Henriette Caroline. *Rambles in Cairo*. Cairo: E. and Schindler, 1931.

Dobrowolska, Agnieszka, and Jaroslaw Dobrowolski. *The Sultan's Fountain: An Imperial Story of Cairo, Istanbul, and Amsterdam*. (Cairo: The American University Press, 2005).

Dobrowolski, Jaroslaw. "A Polish-Egyptian Restoration Project at the Eastern Cemetery in Cairo." In *The Restoration and Conservation of Islamic Monuments in Egypt*, edited by Jere Bacharach, 76-79. Cairo: The American University Press, 1995.

Ebers, George Moritz. *Egypt: Descriptive, Historical and Picturesque*. Translated from German by Clara Bell. 2 vols. London: Cassell, Petter, and Galpur, 1881-82.

Erner, Mine. *Managing Egypt's Poor and the Politics of Benevolence 1800-1952*. Princeton: Princeton University Press, 2003.

Ettinghausen, Richard, and Oleg Grabar. *The Art and Architecture of Islam 650-1250*. London: Penguin Books Harmondsworth, 1987.

Fanfoni, Guiseppe. "The Italian-Egyptian Restoration Center's Work in the Mevlevi Complex in Cairo." In *The Restoration and Conservation of Islamic Monuments in Egypt*, edited by Jere Bacharach, 59-75. Cairo: The American University Press, 1995.

Fikri, Ahmad. *Masajid al-Qahira wa madarisuha*. Cairo: Dar al-Ma'arif, 1961.

Flury, Samuel. "Le décor épigraphique des monuments fatimides du Caire." *Syria* XVII (1912): 365-76.

———. "Samara und die Ornamentik der Moschee des Ibn Tulun." *Der Islam* IV (1913): 421-32.

———. *Die Ornamente der Hakim-und Ashar-Moschee*. Heidelberg: C. Winter, 1912.

Franz Pasha, Julius. *Kairo von Franz Pascha*. Leipzig: E.A. Seemann, 1903.

Gayer-Anderson, R.G. John. *Legends of the Bait al-Kretliya, "Asatir Bayt al-Kritliyya," as told by Sheikh Sulaiman al-Kretil*. Ipswich, UK: East Anglian Daily Times Co. Ltd., 1951.

Gayet, Albery Jean. *L'Art Arabe*. Paris: Libraries-Imprimeries Reunies, 1893.

Gayraud, Roland-Pierre, et al. "Istabl 'Antar (Fostat) 1987-1989: Rapport de fouilles." Annales Islamologiques XXV, 57-87. Cairo: IFAO, 1991.

Gordon, Matthew. "Ibn Tulun, al-Qata'i' and the Legacy of Samarra." In *Hundert Jahre Grabungen in Samarra* (Beitrage zur Islamischen Kunst und Archaologie, Bd. 4), edited by Julia Gonnella, Rania Abdellatif, and Simone Struth, fur das Museum fur Islamische Kunst, 63-77. Berlin, Wiesbaden 2014: Dr. Ludwig Reichert Verlag.

———. "Ahmad ibn Tulun and the Politics of Defence." In *Islamic Cultures, Islamic Contexts, Essays in Honor of Professor Patricia Crone*, edited by Behnam Sadeghi, Asad Q. Ahmed, Adam Silverstein, and Robert Hoyland, 229-56. Brill: Leiden/Boston 2015.

Grabar, Oleg. *The Coinage of the Tulunids*. New York: The American Numismatic Society, 1958.

———. "The Umayyad Dome of the Rock." *Ars Orientalis* III (1959): 52-55.

Grohmann, A. "Die Baunschrift der Moschee des Ahmed Ibn Tulun." In *Studies in Islamic Art and Architecture in Honour of Professor K.A.C. Creswell.* Cairo: The American University in Cairo Press, 1965.

A Guide of the Gayer-Anderson Pasha Museum Bayt El-Kredlea, Ibn Tulun, Cairo. Cairo: Government Press, 1946.

Hampikian, Nairy. "The Restoration of the Mausoleum of al-Salih Najm al-Din Ayyub." In *The Restoration and Conservation of Islamic Monuments in Egypt*, edited by Jere Bacharach, 46-58. Cairo: The American University Press, 1995.

——. "The Mausoleum of Sultan al-Salih Najm al-Din." In *A Future for the Past Restorations in Islamic Cairo 1973-2004*, edited by Wolfgang Mayer and Philipp Speiser, with contributions by Nairy Hampikian, Sylvie Denoix, Nelly Hanna, May Al-Ibrashy, and Giorgio Nogara, 121-28. Mainz: Verlag Philipp Von Zabern, 2007.

——. "The Minaret of the Salihiya Madrasa." In *A Future for the Past, Restorations in Islamic Cairo 1973-2004*, edited by Wolfgang Mayer and Philipp Speiser, with contributions by Nairy Hampikian, Sylvie Denoix, Nelly Hanna, May Al-Ibrashy, and Giorgio Nogara 129-38. Mainz: Verlag Philipp Von Zabern, 2007.

Hasan, Zaki Muhammad. "Ahmad B. Tulun." In *The Encyclopedia of Islam*, 278-79. 2nd ed. Leiden: E.J. Brill, 1960.

——. *Les tulunides, études de l'Égypte musulmane à la fin du IXe siècle, 868-905.* Paris: Établissement Busson, 1933.

Hattstein, Markus and Peter Delius, eds. *Islam: Art and Architecture.* Cologne: Könemann, 2004.

Hautecœur, Louis and Gaston Wiet. *Les Mosquées du Caire.* 2 vols. Paris: E. Leroux, 1932.

al-Hawwari, Hasan Muhammad. "Une maison de l'époque toulonide." *Bulletin de l'Institut d'Égypte* XV (1932-33): 79-87.

Hay, Robert. *Illustrations of Cairo.* London: Tilt and Bogue, 1804.

den Heijer, J. "Une inscription fatimide de la mosquée d'Ibn Tulun au Caire. Essai d'interprétation paléographique, philologique et historique." *Comptes-rendus des séances de l'Académie des Inscriptions et Belles-Lettres*, 155e année, Fascicule 2 (April-June 2011): 951-73.

Herz Pasha, Max. *Catalogue Raisonné des Monuments Exposés dans le Musée National de l'Art Arabe.* Cairo: IFAO, 1906.

Hillenbrand, Robert. "Egypt." In *The Islamic Architecture of North Africa*, edited by D. Hill and L. Golvin, 19-39. London: Faber and Faber, 1976.

Hoag, John. *Islamic Architecture.* New York: Harry N. Abrams, 1977.

Holt, P.M. Ann, K.S. Lambton, and Bernard Lewis. *The Cambridge History of Islam.* 2 vols. Cambridge: University Press, 1970.

Ibrahim, Laila Ali. "Four Cairene Mihrabs and their Dating." *Kunst des Orients* VII/1 (1970-71): 30-39.

——. "The Transition Zones of Domes in Cairene Architecture." *Kunst Des Orients* X. (1975): 5-23.

Ibrahim, Laila Ali and Adil Yasin. "A Tulunid Hammam in Old Cairo." *Islamic Archaeological Studies* III (1988): 33-78.

Al-Ibrashy, May. "The Sabil of Sultan al-Nasir Muhammad and His Sons." In *A Future for the Past, Restorations in Islamic Cairo 1973-2004*, edited by Wolfgang Mayer and Philipp Speiser, with contributions by Nairy Hampikian, Sylvie Denoix, Nelly Hanna, May Al-Ibrashy, and Giorgio Nogara, 129-41. Mainz: Verlag Philipp Von Zabern, 2007.

Index to Mohammedan Monuments in Cairo. Egypt: Maslahat al-Misaha, Cairo: S.N., 1951.

'Isa, Ahmad. *Tarikh al-bimaristanat fi-l-Islam.* Beirut: Dar al-Ra'id al-'Arabi, 1981.

Jomard, E.F. "Description de la ville du Kaire." In *Description de l'Égypte.* 2nd ed. Vol. XVIII, *État Moderne*, 307-308. Paris: Panckoucke, 1820.

——. "Description abrégée de la ville et de la citadelle du Kaire." In *Description de l'Égypte.* 2nd ed. Vol. II, *Planches, État Moderne*, 579-778. Paris: Panckoucke, 1822.

——. "Environs de Babylone, Le Kaire." In *Description de l'Égypte.* 2nd ed. Vol. V, *Planches, Antiquités*, plate 25. Paris: Panckoucke, 1822.

Jum'a, Ibrahim. *Dirasa fi tatawwur al-kitabat al-kufiya 'ala al-ahjar fi Misr fi-l-qurun al-khamsa al-ulla li-l-hijra.* Cairo: Dar al-Fikr al-'Arabi, 1969.

——. "The Development of Kufic Inscriptions on Stone in Egypt During the First Five Centuries of Hijra." Typed manuscript, The Rare Books and Special Collections Library (formerly known as the Creswell Library). The American University in Cairo, 1943.

Karnouk, Gloria Sergine Ohan. "Cairene Bahari Mamluk Minbars, with a Provincial Typology and Catalogue." Master's thesis, The American University in Cairo, 1977.

Kashif, Sayyida Isma'il. *Ahmad Ibn Tulun*. Cairo: al-Dar al-Misriya li-l-Ta'lif wa-l-Tarjama, n.d.

Kashif, Sayyida Isma'il, and Hasan Ahmad Mahmud. *Misr fi 'asr al-tuluniyin wa-l-ikhshidiyin*. Cairo: Maktabat al-Anjalu al-Misriya, 1960.

Khusraw. *Safarnama*. Translated and edited by Yahiya Khashshab. Cairo: Matba'at Lajnat al-Ta'lif wa-l-Tarjama wa-l-Nashr, 1945.

King, David. *Islamic Astronomical Instruments*. London: Variorum, Aldershot, 1982.

King, David, and L. Janin. "Le cadran solaire de la mosquée d'Ibn Tulun au Caire." *Journal for the History of Arabic Science* 2 (1978): 331–51.

Lane, Edward. *Cairo Fifty Years Ago*. London: J. Murray, 1896.

Lane-Poole, Stanley. *The Art of the Saracens in Egypt*. London: Chapman and Hall, 1886.

———. *Cairo: Sketches of Its History, Monuments, and Social Life*. London: J.S. Virtue, 1895.

———. *A History of Egypt in the Middle Ages*. London: Frank Cass and Co. Ltd, 1968.

———. *The Story of Cairo*. London: J.M. Dent and Co., 1906.

Lewis, Bernard. "Egypt and Syria." *The Cambridge History of Islam*, edited by P. M. Holt, Ann K. S. Lambton, and Bernard Lewis, 175–230. Cambridge: Cambridge University Press, 1970.

MacDonald, Fiona and Joan Ullathome. *Ibn Tulun: The Story of a Mosque*. Amideast, 1995.

El-Masry, Kamal. *Die Tulunidische Oranmentik der Moschee des Ahmad Ibn Tulun*. Mainz: Johannes Gutenberg Universität, 1964.

Marcais, George. *L'Architecture Musulmane d'Occident*. Paris: Arts et métiers graphiques, 1954.

Marcel, Jean Joseph. "Inscriptions, Monnaies et Médailles." In *Description de l'Égypte*. 2nd ed. Vol. II, *Planches, État Moderne*, plates C, D, E, F. Paris: Panckoucke, 1817.

———. "Mémoire sur la Mosquée de Touloun et les Inscriptions qu'elle Renferme, Comprenant un précis de la Dynastie des Toulounides." In *Description de l'Égypte*. 2nd ed. Vol. XVIII/3, *État Moderne*, 1–34. Paris: Panckoucke, 1830.

———. "Mémoire sur les inscriptions koufiques recueillies en Égypte et sur les autres caractères employés dans les monuments des Arabes." In *Description de l'Égypte*. 2nd ed. Vol. XV, *État Moderne*, 525–44. Paris: Pankoucke, 1826.

———. "Mémoire sur le Meqyas de L'Ile de Roudah, et sur les Inscriptions que Renferme ce Monument." In *Description de l'Égypte*. 2nd ed. Vol. II, *État Moderne*, 29–90. Paris: Impr. de C.L.F. Panckoucke, 1821–29.

———. *Égypte, depuis la conquête des Arabes jusqu'à la domination française*. Paris: Firmin Didot, Freres, 1848.

Mayer, L.A. *Islamic Astrolabists and their Works*. Geneva: A. Kundig, 1956.

Mayer, Wolfgang, "The History of Preserving Historic Islamic Monuments 1976–2006." In *A Future for the Past: Restorations in Islamic Cairo 1973–2004*, edited by Wolfgang Mayer and Philipp Speiser, with contributions by Nairy Hampikian, Sylvie Denoix, Nelly Hanna, May Al-Ibrashy, and Giorgio Nogara, 42–53. Mainz: Verlag Philipp Von Zabern, 2007.

McPherson, J.W. *The Moulids of Egypt (Egyptian Saints Days)*. Cairo: N.M. Press, 1941.

Mehren, A.F. *Câhirah og Kerafât, historiske studier under et ophold i Aegypten*. 2 vols in 1. Copenhagen: J.H. Schultz, 1869–70.

Michell, George, ed. *Architecture of the Islamic World*. London: Thames and Hudson, 1978.

Migeon, Gaston. *Le Caire, le Nil et Memphis*. Paris: H. Laurens, 1909.

Ministry of Awqaf. *The Mosques of Egypt*. 2 vols. Giza: Survey of Egypt, 1949.

Ministry of Culture. *Historic Cairo*. Cairo: The Supreme Council of Antiquities, February 2002.

Mubarak, 'Ali Basha. *al-Khitat al-jadida al-tawfiqiya li-Misr wa-l-Qahira*. New edition. Vol. II. Cairo: al-Hay'a al-'Amma li-l-Kitab, 1982.

———. *al-Khitat al-tawfiqiya al-jadida li-Misr wa-l-Qahira*. 20 vols. Cairo: al-Matbạ`ah al-Kubrá al-Amīrīya, 1888.

Muhammad, Ghazi Rajab. "The Minaret of Ibn Tulun: Its Construction and Description." *Summer* XXIII/1 and 2 (1967): 83–96.

Muqarnas 8. "Creswell and His Legacy," edited by Oleg Grabar (1991).

Nafi', Abd al-Hamid. *Dhayl khitat al-Maqrizi*. Edited by Khalid Azab and Muhammad al-Sayyed Hamdi al-Mitwalli. Cairo: Maktabat al-Dar al-'Arabiyah lil-Kitab, 2006.

Necipoglu, Gulru. "An Outline of Shifting Paradigms in the Palatial Architecture of the Pre-Modern Islamic World." *Ars Orientalis* XXIII (1993): 3-24.

Northedge, Alistair. "An Interpretation of the Palace of the Caliph at Samarra (Dar al-Khilafa of Jawsaq al-Khaqani)." *Ars Orientalis* XXIII (1993): 143-70.

——. "The Race-courses at Samarra." *Bulletin of the School of Oriental and African Studies* 53 (1990): 31-56.

O'Kane, Bernard. *The Illustrated Guide to the Museum of Islamic Art in Cairo*. Cairo: The American University in Cairo Press, 2012.

Ormos, Istvan. *Max Herz Pasha 1856-1919: His Life and Career*. Études Urbaines 6/1. Cairo: IFAO, 2009.

Pardieu, Charles Comte de. *Excursion en Orient, le Mont Sinai, l'Arabie, la Palestine, le Syrie, le Liban*. Paris: Garnier, 1851.

Paton, A.A. *History of the Egyptian Revolution*. 2 vols. London: Trubner, 1870.

Patterson, James Laird, *Journal of a Tour in Egypt, Palestine, Syria and Greece*. London: C. Dolman, 1852.

Pauty, Edmond. *La Mosquée d'Ibn Toulun et ses alentours*. Promenade Archéologique. Cairo: n.p., 1936.

Pellat, Charles. "Ibn Said al-Maghribi." In *Encyclopedia of Islam*, 926. 2nd ed. Leiden: E.J. Brill, 1960.

Prisse d'Avennes, Émile. *L'Art arabe d'après les monuments du Kaire depuis le VIIe siècle jusqu'à la fin du XVIIIe*. 4 vols. Paris: A. Morel, 1869-77.

——. *Arab Art As Seen through the Monuments of Cairo from the 7th Century to the 18th*. Translated by J.I. Erythraspis. London and Paris: Le Sycomore, 1983.

Protain, Jean-Constantin. "Le Kaire." In *Description de l'Égypte*. 2nd ed. Vol. I, *Planches, État Moderne*, plates 29, 30, 31. Paris: Pancoucke, 1822.

al-Qahira al-Tarikhiya. *Jami' Ahmad Ibn Tulun*. Cairo, 2004.

Raymond, André. *Cairo*. English translation by Willard Wood. Cambridge, MA: Harvard University Press, 2000.

Rhoné, Arthur. *L'Égypte à petites journées: Le Caire d'autrefois*. Paris: Société Générale d'Édition, 1910.

——. *Coup d'œil sur l'état du Caire ancien et moderne*. Paris: A. Quantin, 1882.

Rogers, John Michael. "al-Ḳāhira." In *Encyclopedia of Islam*, 424-41. 2nd ed. Leiden: E.J. Brill, 1960.

Roorda, Taco. *Vita Abul Abbasi Amedis Tulonidarum Primi Vita et Res Gestae*. Leiden: Lugdani Batavorum, S. and J. Luchtmans, 1825.

Russel, Dorothea. *Medieval Cairo and the Monasteries of Wadi Natrun: A Historical Guide*. London: Weidenfeld and Nicolson, 1962.

Salmon, George. *Études sur la topographie du Caire, la Kal'at al-Kabsh et la Birkat al-Fil*. Cairo: IFAO, 1902.

Sebah, Pascal. *Egypt*. Rome: L. Olivieri, n.d.

Sedky, Ahmed. *Living with Heritage in Cairo: Area Conservation in the Arab City*. Cairo: The American University in Cairo Press, 2009.

Serageldin, Ismail and James Steele, eds. *Architecture of the Contemporary Mosque*. Great Britain: Academy Group Ltd, 1996.

Shaer, May. *Restoration of Ahmad Ibn Tulun Mosque, Cairo, Egypt*. 2010 On Site Review. Cairo: The Aga Khan Award Publications, 2010. http://archnet.org/system/publications/contents/1575/original/FLS1819.pdf?1384750740.

Shafi'i, Farid. "An Early Fatimid Mihrab in the Mosque of Ibn Tulun." *Bulletin of the Faculty of Arts, University of Cairo* XV/1 (1953): 67-81.

——. *al-'Imara al-'arabiya fi Misr al-islamiya*. 2 vols. Cairo: al-Hay'a al-'Amma li-l-Ta'lif wa-l-Nashr, 1970.

——. "Ma'dhanat masjid Ibn Tulun: ra'i fi takwinaha al-mi'mari." *Majallat kulliyat al-adab* IV (952): 167-84.

Shayyal, G.E. "al-Balawi." In *The Encyclopedia of Islam*, 990. 2nd ed. Leiden: E.J. Brill, 1960.

Shawkat, Yahia. "Destruction Alert: Ibn Tulun's Aqueduct in Basatin," *Cairo Observer*, January 30, 2012, http://cairobserver.com/post/16766637427/destruction-alert-ibn-tulun-aqueduct-in-basateen.

Slane, William MacGuckin baron de, trans. *Wafayāt al-a'yān: Ibn Khallikan's biographical dictionary*. Paris: printed for the Oriental Translation Fund of Great Britain and Ireland, 1843-71.

Speiser, Philipp. "The Egyptian-German Restoration of the Darb al-Qirmiz, Cairo. In *The Restoration and Conservation of the Islamic Monuments in Egypt*, edited by Jere Bacharach, 22-45. (Cairo: The American University in Cairo Press, 1995).

———."The Palace of the Amir Bashtak." In *A Future for the Past: Restorations in Islamic Cairo 1973-2004*, edited by Wolfgang Mayer and Philipp Speiser, with contributions by Nairy Hampikian, Sylvie Denoix, Nelly Hanna, May Al-Ibrashy, and Giorgio Nogara, 78-85. Mainz: Verlag Philipp Von Zabern, 2007.

———. "The History of Preserving Historic Islamic Monuments 1881-1975." In *A Future for the Past: Restorations in Islamic Cairo 1973-2004*, edited by Wolfgang Mayer and Philipp Speiser, with contributions by Nairy Hampikian, Sylvie Denoix, Nelly Hanna, May Al-Ibrashy, and Giorgio Nogara, 37-41. Mainz: Verlag Philipp Von Zabern, 2007.

Swelim, Tarek. "Antinopolis." In *An Encyclopedia of Roman Archaeology*, edited by Catherine Bard, 139-41. London and New York: Routledge, 1999.

———. "The Complex of Sultan al-Mu'ayyad Shaykh at Bab Zuwayla." Master's thesis, The American University in Cairo, 1986.

———. "The Lost City of al-Fustat." In *The History and Religious Heritage of Old Cairo: Its Fortress, Churches, Synagogue, and Mosque*, edited by Carolyn Ludwig and Moris Jackson, 270-79. Cairo: The American University in Cairo Press, 2012.

———. "The Minaret of Ibn Tulun Reconsidered." In *The Cairo Heritage: Essays in Honor of Laila Ali Ibrahim*, edited by Doris Behrens-Abouseif, 77-91. Cairo and New York: The American University in Cairo Press, 2000.

———. "The Mosque of 'Amr Ibn al-'As." In *The History and Religious Heritage of Old Cairo: Its Fortress, Churches, Synagogue, and Mosque*, edited by Carolyn Ludwig and Moris Jackson, 280-317. Cairo: The American University in Cairo Press, 2012.

———. "The Mosque of Ibn Tulun: A New Perspective." PhD diss., Harvard University, 1994

Thompson, Jason. *A History of Egypt*. Cairo: The American University in Cairo Press, 2008.

Vollers, K. *Fragmente aus dem Mughrib des Ibn Sa'îd*. Berlin: Emil Felber, 1894.

Waqfiya (endowment deed) of Sultan Lajin, *Hujat waqf al-Sultan Husam al-Din Lajin*, Dar al-Watha'iq wa-l-Mahfudhat, documents no. 17/3 and 18/3.

Warner, Nicolas. *The Monuments of Historic Cairo: A Map and Descriptive Catalogue*. An American Research Center in Egypt Edition. The American University in Cairo Press: Cairo, 2005.

Wiet, Gaston. *Matériaux pour un Corpus Inscriptionum Arabicarum*. 2nd part. Cairo, Paris: IFAO, 1929-30.

———. *Répertoire Chronologique d'Epigraphie Arabe*. 16 vols. Cairo: IFAO, 1931.

———. *Mémoires Publiés par les Membres de l'Institut Français d'Archéologie Orientale du Caire sous la Direction de M. Pierre Jouguet* 52. Cairo: IFAO, 1930.

William, Nassau Senior, *Conversations and Journals in Egypt and Malta*. London: S. Low, Marston, Searle & Rivington, 1882.

Williams, Caroline. *Islamic Monuments in Cairo: The Practical Guide*. Cairo: The American University in Cairo Press, 2002.

———. "Transforming the Old: Cairo's New Medieval City." *Middle East Journal* 56 (Summer 2002): 457-75.

Williams, Robert. "The Kibla or praying niche in the Mosque of Ahmad Ibn Touloun, Cairo." *The Architect and Contract Reporter* XCII (July 3, 1914): 6-7.

———. "The Mosque of Ibn Tulun." *The Muslim World* VIII/3 (July 1981): 221-35.

Yeomans, Richard. *The Art and Architecture of Islamic Cairo*. Reading, UK: Garnet Publishing, 2006.

———. *The Story of Islamic Architecture*. New York: New York University Press, 2000.

Zaki, 'Abd al-Rahman. *al-Qahira*. Cairo: Dar al-Mustaqbal, 1943.

Notes

Chapter 1

1 K.A.C. Creswell, *Early Muslim Architecture*, vol. I (Oxford: The Clarendon Press, 1932), preface page.

2 It is important to note that the decoration of the mosque of Ibn Tulun is not part of this book, as it is thoroughly reviewed in Kamal el-Masry, "Die Tulunidische Ornamentik der Moschee des Ahmad Ibn Tulun in Kairo," unpublished thesis (Mainz, 1964), which I did not use. Two recent publications by Matthew Gordon, which I was unable to consult as I had access to them in a very short time before this book went to the press, are his: "Ibn Tulun, al-Qata'i' and the Legacy of Samarra," in *Hundert Jahre Grabungen in Samarra (Beitrage zur Islamischen Kunst und Archaologie, Bd. 4)*, edited by Julia Gonnella, Rania Abdellatif, and Simone Struth, fur das Museum fur Islamische Kunst, Berlin, Wiesbaden 2014: Dr. Ludwig Reichert Verlag, 63-77; and "Ahmad ibn Tulun and the Politics of Defence," in *Islamic Cultures, Islamic Contexts, Essays in Honor of Professor Patricia Crone*, edited by Behnam Sadeghi, Asad Q. Ahmed, Adam Silverstein, and Robert Hoyland (Leiden/Boston: Brill, 2015), 229-56. I would like to thank Matthew Gordon for sending me copies of his articles.

Chapter 2

1 Zaki Muhammad Hasan, *Les Tulunides, études de l'Égypte musulmane à la fin du IXe siècle, 868-905* (Paris: Etablissement Busson, 1933), 11-16; Sayyida Ismail Kashif, *Ahmad Ibn Tulun* (Cairo: al-Dar al-Misriya li-l-Ta'lif wa-l-Tarjama, n.d.), 7-14.

2 Ahmad ibn Abi Ya'qub al-Ya'qubi, *Kitab al-buldan* (Najaf: al-Matba'a al-Haydariya, 1957); *Tarikh al-Ya'qubi*, 2 vols (Beirut: Dar Sadir, 1960).

3 Abu Ja'far Ahmad Ibn Yusuf al-Katib Ibn al-Daya, *Kitab al-mukafa'a*, ed. Amin 'Abd al-'Aziz (Cairo: al-Maktaba al-Adabiya, 1914); Ibn Sa'id al-Maghrabi, *al-Mughrib fi hula al-Maghrib*, text and German translation K. Vollers, Semitistische Studien I (Berlin: Emil Felber, 1894), which contains a separate chapter on the history of Ibn Tulun, entitled *Kitab al-durr al-maknun fi hula dawlat Bani Tulun*. Another edition is by K. Vollers, *Fragmente aus dem Mughrib* (Berlin: Emil Felber, 1894), the Egypt section is edited by Zaki Muhammad Hasan, Shawqi Dayf, and Sayyida Kashif (Cairo, 1953). For this see Charles Pellat, "Ibn Said al-Maghribi," in *Encyclopedia of Islam*, 926, 2nd ed.; Hasan, *Les Tulunides* (Paris: Etablissement Busson, 1933), 12; Kashif, *Ahmad Ibn Tulun* (Cairo: al-Dar al-Misriya li-l-Ta'lif wa-l-Tarjama, n.d), 9.

4 Ibn al-Daya, *Kitab al-mukafa'a*.

5 Abu Muhammad 'Abd Allah Ibn Muhammad al-Madini al-Balawi, *Sirat Ahmad Ibn Tulun*, ed. by Muhammad Kurd 'Ali (Dimashq: al-Maktaba al-'Arabiya fi Dimashq, 1939).

6 Muhammad ibn Ahmad Muqaddasi, *Ahsan al-taqasim fi ma'rifat al-aqalim*, ed. De Goeje (Leiden: Brill, 1967).

7 Nasiri Khusraw, *Safarnama*, trans. and ed. Yahiya Khashshab (Cairo: Matba'at Lajnat al-Talif wa-l-Tarjama wa-l-Nashr, 1945).

8 Ibn Jubayr, *The Travels of Ibn Jubayr*, trans. and ed. R.J.C. Broadhurst (London: J. Cape, 1952).

9 *Hujat waqf al-Sultan Husam al-Din Lajin*, Dar al-Watha'iq wa-l-Mahfudhat.

10 Sarim al-Din Ibrahim Ibn Muhammad Ibn Aydumur al-'Ala'i al-Misri Ibn Duqmaq, *Kitab al-intisar li-wasitat 'aqd al-amsar*, ed. K. Vollers (Beirut: Markaz al-Mawsu'at al-'Alamiya, 1893); Taqi al-Din Abu al-Mahasin 'Abbas Ahmad Ibn 'Ali al-Maqrizi, *al-Mawa'iz wa-l-i'tibar bi-dhikr al-khitat wa-l-athar*, ed. Ayman Fu'ad Sayyid (London: Mu'assasat al-Furqan li-l-Turath al-Islami, 2002); Taqi al-Din Ahmad al-Maqrizi, *Kitab al-suluk fi*

ma'rifat duwwal al-Muluk I/II, ed. Mustafa Ziyada (Cairo, 1956).

11 He should not be confused with the Mamluk historian with the same name, who is actually the historian Ibn 'Abd al-Hakam, *Kitab futuh Misr wa akhbaruha*. See Maqrizi, *Khitat* II, 265, 267.

12 Muhammad Ibn 'Abd al-Rahman al-Sakhawi, *Tuhfat al-ahbab was baghaiyat al-tullab fi-l-khitat wa-l-mazarat wa-l-tarajum wa-l-buqa wa-l-mubarakat*, edited by Ahmad Nash'at, Mahmud Rabi', and Hasan Qasim (Cairo: Matba'at al-'Ulum wa-l-Adab, 1937).

13 Al-Nawawi, *Tahdhib al-asma'* (Boettingen, 1842-47); Shihab al-Din Ahmad al-Nuwayri, *Nihayat al-arb fi funun al-'adab*, ed. Ahmad Zaki Pasha (Cairo: Dar al-Kutub al-Misriya, 1923-60); 'Abd al-Rahman Ibn Khaldun, *Tarikh Ibn Khaldun* (Beirut: Mu'assasat al-'Alami, 1971); Abu al-'Abbas Ahmad Ibn 'Ali al-Qalqashandi, *Subh al-'asha fi sina'at al-insha'*, vol. III (Cairo: al-Matbi'at al-Amiriya, 1913-17); Badr al-Din al-'Ayni, *'Iqd al-juman fi tarikh ahl al-zaman*, 762-855 ah / 1360-1451 ad, 23 vols. Cairo: Dar al-Kutub al-Misriya, Tarikh no. 1584; Jamal al-Din Abu al-Mahasin Yusuf Ibn Taghribirdi al-Atabki (813-874 ah / 1410-1469 ad), *al-Nujum al-zahira fi muluk Misr wa-l-Qahira* (Cairo: Dar al-Kutub, 1929); Ibn Hajar al-'Asqalani, *Inba' al-ghumr bi-anba' al-'umr* (Cairo, 1973); and Jalal al-Din 'Abd al-Rahman al-Suyuti, *Husn al-muhadara fi tarikh Misr wa-l-Qahira*, 2 vols, ed. Muhammad Abu al-Fadl Ibrahim (Cairo: Dar Ihiya' al-Kutub al-'Arabiya, 1968).

14 Evliya Çelebi, *Siyahatnamesi*, 10 vols, ed. S.A. Kahrama, Y. Dagli, R. Dankoff (Istanbul, 2007).

15 'Abd al-Rahman al-Jabarti, *'Aja'ib al-athar fi-l-tarajim wa-l-akhbar* I (Beirut: Dar al-Gil, n.d.).

16 Taco Roorda, *Vita Abul Abbasi Amedis Tulonidarum Primi Vita et Res Gestae* (Leiden: Lugdani Batavorum, S. and J. Luchtmans, 1825).

17 Jean Joseph Marcel, "Inscription, Monoies et Medailles," in *Description de l'Égypte*, 2nd ed., vol. II, *Planches, État Moderne* (Paris: Panckoucke, 1817), plates E and F.

18 It is worth noting that later Marcel republished his study of the inscriptions in the second edition of the *Description*. See Jean Joseph Marcel, "Mémoire sur la mosquée de toulon et les inscriptions qu'elle renferme, comprenant un précis de la dynastie des toulonides," in *Description de l'Égypte*, 2nd ed, vol. XVIII, *État Moderne* (Paris: Panckoucke, 1830), 1-34; Marcel, "Mémoire sur les inscriptions koufiques recueillies en Égypte et sur les autres caractères employés dans les monuments des Arabes," in *Description de l'Égypte*, 2nd ed, vol. XV, *État Moderne* (Paris: Panckoucke, 1826), 525-44.

19 Edme François Jomard also adds an engraving of a granite sarcophagus from the ancient Egyptian period that was said to have been found in the mosque of Ibn Tulun. See E.F. Jomard, "Environs de Babylone, Le Kaire," in *Description de l'Égypte*, 2nd ed, vol. V, *Planches, Antiquités* (Paris: Panckoucke, 1822), plate 25.

20 Protain, "Le Kaire," in *Description de l'Égypte*, 2nd ed, vol. V, *Planches, Antiquités* (Paris: Panckoucke 1822).

21 Pascal Coste, *Architecture arabe ou monuments du Kaire* (Paris: Firmin Didot Frere, 1839); Robert Hay, *Illustrations of Cairo* (London: Tilt and Bogue, 1840); Prisse d'Avennes, *L'Art arabe d'après les monuments du Kaire depuis le VIIe siècle jusqu'à la fin du XVIIIe* I (Paris: A. Morel, 1869-77).

22 'Ali Basha Mubarak, *al-Khitat al-jadida al-Tawfiqiya li-Misr wa-l-Qahira* II, new edition (Cairo: al-Hay'a al-Misriya al-'Ammah li-l-Kitab, 1982).

23 Edward Lane, *Cairo Fifty Years Ago* (London: J. Murray, 1896), 9-14, 103-109; Stanley Lane-Poole, *The Art of the Saracens in Egypt* (London: Chapman and Hall, 1886), 54-59; *Cairo: Sketches of Its History, Monuments, and Social Life* (London: J.S. Virtue, 1895), 20-24; *A History of Egypt in the Middle Ages* (London: Chapman and Hall, 1968), 60-77; *The Story of Cairo* (London: J.M. Dent and Co., 1902), 72-90.

24 Eustace K. Corbet, "The Life and Works of Ahmad Ibn Tulun," *Journal of the Royal Asiatic Society* XXIII/4 (October 1891).

25 Robert Williams, "The Mosque of Ibn Tulun," *The Muslim World* VIII/3 (July 1918): 221-35.

26 Hasan, *Les Tulunides*.

27 Gaston Migeon, *Le Caire, le Nile et Memphis* (Paris: H. Laurens, 1909).

28 Yusuf Effendi Ahmad, *Jami' Ahmad Ibn Tulun* (Cairo: Matba'at al-Taraqi, 1917).

29 Mahmud 'Akkush, *Tarikh wa wasf al-jami' al-tuluni* (Cairo: Dar al-Kutub al-Misriya, 1927).

30 Hasan 'Abd al-Wahhab, *Tarikh al-masajid al-athariya allati sulla fiha faridat al-jum'a al-salih Faruq alawwal*, 2 vols. (Cairo: Matba'at Dar al-Kutub al-Misriya, 1946); Hautecœur and Wiet, *Les mosquées du Caire* (Paris: Librairie Ernest Leroux, 1932).

31 Ministry of Awqaf, *The Mosques of Egypt I* (Cairo, 1949), figures 12–15, plates 2–9; *Comité de Conservation des Monuments de l'Art Arabe: Procès Verbaux des Séances*, 41 vols. (Cairo, 1882–1956).

32 Mahmud Ahmad, "al-Jami' al-Tuluni," *al-Handasa* XII (Cairo, 1932), 402–11; Hasan al-Basha, *al-Qahira: Tarikhuha, fununuha wa atharuha* (Cairo: Dar al-Kitab al-Jadid, 1970); Ahmad Fikri, *Masajid al-Qahira wa madarisuha* (Cairo: Dar al-Ma'arif, 1961); Farid Shafi'i, "Ma'dhanat masjid Ibn Tulun: Ra'i fi takwiniha al-mi'mari," *Majallat kulliyat al-adab* IV (1952).

33 Max Van Berchem, *Materiaux pour un Corpus Inscriptionum Arabicarum*, Premiere Partie, Égypte (Cairo: IFAO, 1894–1903); Gaston Wiet, *Mémoires publiés par les membres de l'Institut Français d'Archéologie Orientale du Caire sous la direction de M. Pierre Jouguet 52* (Cairo: IFAO, 1930).

34 Jean David-Weill, *Les bois à épigraphes jusqu'à l'époque Mamlouke*, vols. I–II, Catalogue général du Musée Arabe du Caire (Cairo: IFAO, 1931).

35 Ibrahim Jum'a, *Dirasa fi tatawwur al-kitabat al-kufiya 'ala al-ahjar fi Misr fi-l-Qur'an al-khamsa al-ulla li-l-hijra* (Cairo: Dar al-Fikr al-'Arabi, 1969). Also see *The Development of Kufic Inscriptions on Stone in Egypt During the First Five Centuries of Hijra*, typed manuscript located at The Rare Books and Special Collections Library (formerly known as the Creswell Library), The American University in Cairo, 1943.

36 Samuel Flury, "Le décor épigraphique des monuments fatimides du Caire," *Syria* XVII (1912): 365–76; "Samarra und die Ornamentik der Moschee des Ibn Tulun," *Der Islam* IV (1913): 421–32; *Die Ornamente der Hakim-und Azhar-Moschee* (Heidelberg: C. Winter, 1912).

37 George Salmon, *Études sur la topographie du Caire, la Kal'at al-Kabch et la Birkat al-Fil* (Cairo: IFAO, 1902).

38 Marcel Clerget, *Le Caire: étude de géographie urbaine et historie économique*, 2 vols (Cairo: Imprimerie E. and R. Schindler, 1934).

39 James Aldridge, *Cairo* (London: Macmillan, 1970).

40 'Abd al-Rahman Zaki, *al-Qahira*, 2 vols (Cairo: Dar al-Mustaqbal, c. 933–35); Becker, "Cairo," in *Encyclopedia of Islam*, 1st ed., 815–26; Becker, "Egypt," in *The Encyclopedia of Islam*, 1st ed., 4–23; John Michael Rogers, "al-Kaira," in *The Encyclopedia of Islam*, 2nd ed. (Leiden, 1978), 424–41; Zaki Muhammad Hasan, "Ahmad B. Tulun," in *The Encyclopedia of Islam*, 2nd ed., 278–79.

41 André Raymond, *Cairo* (Cambridge, MA: Harvard University Press, 2000)

42 Hasan Muhammad al-Hawwari, "Une Maison de l'Epoque Toulounide" *Bulletin de l'Institut d'Égypte XV* (1932–33), 79–87; Laila Ali Ibrahim and Adil Yasin, "A Tulunid Hammam in Old Cairo," *Islamic Archaeological Studies* III (1988), 33–78.

43 Oleg Grabar, *The Coinage of the Tulunids* (New York: American Numismatic Society, 1957)

44 J.W. McPherson, *The Moulids of Egypt (Egyptian Saints Days)* (Cairo: N.M. Press, 1941); R.G. John Gayer-Anderson Pasha, *The Legends of Bait al-Kretliya "Asatir Bayt al-Kritliya"* (Ipswich: East Anglian Daily Times Co. Ltd., 1951).

45 Doris Behrens-Abouseif, *Minarets of Cairo* (Cairo: The American University in Cairo Press, 2011); Jonathan Bloom, *Minaret: Symbol of Islam* (Oxford: Oxford University Press, 1989).

46 Tarek Swelim, "The Minaret of Ibn Tulun Reconsidered," in *The Cairo Heritage: Essays in Honor of Laila Ali Ibrahim*, edited by Doris Behrens-Abouseif (Cairo and New York: The American University in Cairo Press, 2000). However, there are aspects in this article that I no longer agree with.

47 Farid Shafi'i, "Ma'dhanat masjid Ibn Tulun: Ra'i fi takwiniha al-mi'mari," *Majallat kulliyat al-adab* IV (1952); Ghazi Rajib Muhammad, "The Minaret of Ibn Tulun: Its Construction and Description," *Summer* 23 I/1 and 2 (1967), 83–96.

48 Caroline Williams, *Islamic Monuments in Cairo: The Practical Guide* (Cairo: The American University in Cairo Press, 2002).

49 Henriett Caroline Devonshire, *Rambles in Cairo* (Cairo: E. and Schindler, 1931); Dorothea Russel, *Medieval Cairo and the Monasteries of Wadi Natrun: A Historical Guide* (London: Weidenfeld and Nicolson, 1962).

50 Richard Ettinghausen and Oleg Grabar. *The Art and Architecture of Islam 650-1250* (London: Penguin Books Harmondsworth, 1987).

51 Robert Hillenbrand, *Islamic Architecture: Form, Function and Meaning* (Edinburgh University Press, 1994), p. 75, fig. 2.93. It presents a beautiful hand-drawn prespective of the mosque of Ibn Tulun, viewed from the unusual south corner of the mosque looking north, which incorrectly shows the *ziyada* wall surrounding the walls of the mosque proper on four sides, rather than on three sides only.

52 Istvan Ormos, *Max Herz Pasha 1856-1919: His Life and Career* I (Cairo: IFAO, Études Urbaines 6/1-2009).

53 I would like to thank the staff of the Rare Books and Special Collections Library of the American University in Cairo for allowing me to have digitized images of this invaluable source. I would like to thank Ola Seif for her dedication and interest in my study. This unique collection is that of K.A.C. Creswell himself. The original negatives and photographs are at the Ashmolean Musuem, while a copy is located at the American University in Cairo.

54 K.A.C. Creswell, *Early Muslim Architecture* (New York: Hacker Art Books, 1969); *Muslim Architecture of Egypt* (New York: Hacker Art Books, 1978).

55 Creswell later acknowledges Balawi in his *A Short Account of Early Muslim Architecture* (Beirut: Librairie du Liban, 1968), 302; see also the new edition by James W. Allen (Aldershot: Scolar Press, 1989), 392.

56 Doris Behrens-Abouseif, *Islamic Architecture in Cairo: An Introduction* (Cairo: The American University in Cairo Press, 1989); George Michell, ed., *Architecture of the Islamic World* (London: Thames and Hudson, 1978); John Hoag, *Islamic Architecture* (New York: Harry N. Abrams, Inc. Publishers, 1977); Robert Hillenbrand, "Egypt" in *The Islamic Architecture of North Africa*, eds. D. Hill and L. Golvin (London: Faber and Faber, 1976); Markus Hattstein and Peter Delius, eds., *Islam: Art and Architecture* (Cologne: Könemann, 2004).

57 Richard Yeomans, *The Story of Islamic Architecture* (New York: New York University Press, 2000); *The Art and Architecture of Islamic* Cairo (Reading, UK: Garnet Publishing, 2006).

58 Nicolas Warner, *The Monuments of Historic Cairo: A Map and Descriptive Catalogue*, (Cairo: American Research Center and the American University in Cairo Press, 2005).

59 Fiona MacDonald and Joan Ullathome, *Ibn Tulun: The Story of a Mosque* (Amideast, 1995).

Chapter 3

1 Abu Muhammad 'Abd Allah Ibn Muhammad al-Madini al-Balawi, *Sirat Ahmad Ibn Tulun*, ed. Muhammad Kurd 'Ali (Cairo: Maktabat al-Thaqafa al-Diniya, circa. 1939), 33. He adds that later she bore his brother Musa, and sisters Habisa and Summana. Also copied by Taqi al-Din Ahmad al-Maqrizi, *al-Maw'iz wa-l-i'tibar fi dhikr al-khitat wa-l-athar al-ma'ruf bi-l-khitat al-Maqriziya*, vol. II (London: Mu'assasat al-Furqan lil-Turath al-Islami), 81.

2 Balawi, *Sirat Ahmad Ibn Tulun*, 33; copied by Maqrizi, *Khitat* II, 81; according to Ibn Khallikan, Nuh Ibn Asad was the governor of Bukhara. See *Wafayat al-a'yan: Ibn Khalikan's Biographical Dictionary*, trans. William MacGuckin Baron de Slane, vol. I (Paris: printed for the Oriental Translation Fund of Great Britain and Ireland, 1843-71), 154; and in Creswell, *Early Muslim Architecture*, vol. III (New York: Hacker Art Books, 1969), 327.

3 Balawi, *Sirat Ahmad Ibn Tulun*, 33; copied by Maqrizi, *Khitat* II, 81.

4 Balawi, *Sirat Ahmad Ibn Tulun*, 34.

5 Balawi, *Sirat Ahmad Ibn Tulun*, 34; Maqrizi, *Khitat* II, 80.

6 Bernard Lewis, "Egypt and Syria," in *The Cambridge History of Islam*, eds. P.M. Holt, Ann K.S. Lambton, and Bernard Lewis, vol. 1 (Cambridge: University Press, 1970), 178.

7 Balawi, *Sirat Ahmad Ibn Tulun*, 34; Maqrizi, *Khitat* II, 81.

8 Balawi, *Sirat Ahmad Ibn Tulun*, 35; Maqrizi, *Khitat* II, 81.

9 Balawi, *Sirat Ahmad Ibn Tulun*, 35; Maqrizi, *Khitat* II, 81. The latter gives the name Majur, while Balawi does not.

10 Balawi, *Sirat Ahmad Ibn Tulun*, 39; Maqrizi, *Khitat* II, 82.

11 Balawi, *Sirat Ahmad Ibn Tulun*, 39-40; Maqrizi, *Khitat* II, 82.

12 Balawi, *Sirat Ahmad Ibn Tulun*, 39; Maqrizi, *Khitat* II, 82.

13 Balawi, *Sirat Ahmad Ibn Tulun*, 39-40; Maqrizi, *Khitat* II, 82.

14 Balawi, *Sirat Ahmad Ibn Tulun*, 40.

15 Balawi, *Sirat Ahmad Ibn Tulun*, 42; Maqrizi, *Khitat* II, 82.

16 Balawi, *Sirat Ahmad Ibn Tulun*, 42; Maqrizi, *Khitat* II, 82.

17 Balawi, *Sirat Ahmad Ibn Tulun*, 42; Maqrizi, *Khitat* II, 83.

18 Balawi, *Sirat Ahmad Ibn Tulun*, 41-43; Maqrizi, *Khitat* II, 83.

19 Balawi, *Sirat Ahmad Ibn Tulun*, 178.

20 Lewis, "Egypt and Syria," 178.

21 Lewis, "Egypt and Syria," 178.

22 Balawi, *Sirat Ahmad Ibn Tulun*, 81-85; Lewis, "Egypt and Syria," 179; Zaki Muhammad Hasan, "Ahmad B. Tulun," in *The Encyclopedia of Islam*, 2nd ed. (Leiden: E.J. Brill, 1960), 278.

23 Balawi, *Sirat Ahmad Ibn Tulun*, 82-83; Lewis, "Egypt and Syria,"179; Hasan, "Ahmad B. Tulun," 278.

24 Balawi, *Sirat Ahmad Ibn Tulun*, 52;

25 Balawi, *Sirat Ahmad Ibn Tulun*, 51-52.

26 Balawi, *Sirat Ahmad Ibn Tulun*, 51-52 Lewis, "Egypt and Syria," 179.

27 Balawi, *Sirat Ahmad Ibn Tulun*, 52.

28 Balawi, *Sirat Ahmad Ibn Tulun*, 91.

29 Balawi, *Sirat Ahmad Ibn Tulun*, 92-93, 96-70; Lewis, "Egypt and Syria," 179

30 Balawi, *Sirat Ahmad Ibn Tulun*, 109. One would expect that such a treaty was signed, although Balawi only gives the reasons why such a treaty was needed, without mentioning whether an agreement was made.

31 Hasan, "Ahmad B. Tulun," 279; for this see Oleg Grabar, *The Coinage of the Tulunids* (New York: The American Numismatic Society, 1958).

32 Balawi, *Sirat Ahmad Ibn Tulun*, 343-347; Maqrizi, *Khitat* II, 100; Lewis, "Egypt and Syria," 180.

33 Balawi, *Sirat Ahmad Ibn Tulun*, 111-12.

34 Balawi, *Sirat Ahmad Ibn Tulun*, 115-17.

35 Balawi, *Sirat Ahmad Ibn Tulun*, 118-22.

36 Balawi, *Sirat Ahmad Ibn Tulun*, 122.

37 Balawi, *Sirat Ahmad Ibn Tulun*, 123.

38 Balawi, *Sirat Ahmad Ibn Tulun*, 124.

39 Balawi, *Sirat Ahmad Ibn Tulun*, 125-26.

40 Balawi, *Sirat Ahmad Ibn Tulun*, 126-27.

41 Balawi, *Sirat Ahmad Ibn Tulun*, 321-23

42 Balawi, *Sirat Ahmad Ibn Tulun*, 325-27

43 Balawi, *Sirat Ahmad Ibn Tulun*, 328-29

44 Balawi, *Sirat Ahmad Ibn Tulun*, 330-31

45 Balawi, *Sirat Ahmad Ibn Tulun*, 336

46 Balawi, *Sirat Ahmad Ibn Tulun*, 338

47 Balawi, *Sirat Ahmad Ibn Tulun*, 339

48 Balawi, *Sirat Ahmad Ibn Tulun*, 339-40

49 Balawi, *Sirat Ahmad Ibn Tulun*, 341-42

50 Balawi, *Sirat Ahmad Ibn Tulun*, 340-41

51 Balawi, *Sirat Ahmad Ibn Tulun*, 349

52 Balawi, *Sirat Ahmad Ibn Tulun*, 349

53 Hasan, "Ahmad B. Tulun," 279.

54 Maqrizi, *Khitat* II, 102.

55 Maqrizi, *Khitat* II, 103-104.

56 Maqrizi, *Khitat* II, 95.

Chapter 4

1 Date is provided by Sarim al-Din Ibrahim Ibn Muhammad Ibn Aydumur al-'Ala'i al-Misri Ibn Duqmaq, *Kitab al-intisar li-wasitat 'aqd al-amsar*, ed. K. Vollers (Beirut: Markaz al-Mawsu'at al-'Alamiya, 1893), 121.

2 Abu Muhammad 'Abd Allah Ibn Muhammad al-Madini al-Balawi, *Sirat Ahmad Ibn Tulun*, ed. Muhammad Kurd 'Ali (Cairo: Maktabat al-Thaqafa al-Diniya, circa. 1939), 54; quoted by Taqi al-Din Ahmad al-Maqrizi, *al-Maw'iz wa-l-i'tibar fi dhikr al-khitat wa-l-athar al-ma'ruf bi-l-khitat al-Maqriziya*, vol II (Beirut: Dar Sadir, n.d), 85; George Salmon, *Études sur la topographie du Caire, la Kal'at al-Kabch et la Birkat al-Fil* (Cairo: IFAO, 1902), 6, provides an incomplete study of these markets.

3 Balawi, *Sirat Ahmad Ibn Tulun*, 53.

4 Balawi, *Sirat Ahmad Ibn Tulun*, 53; Ibn Duqmaq, *Kitab al-intisar,* 121; Maqrizi, *Khitat* II, 85. Neither of the latter two historians gives credit to Balawi, who was their original source.

5 Ahmad ibn Abi Ya'qubi, *Kitab al-buldan* (Najaf: al-Matba'a al-Haydariya, 1957), 26-27; K.A.C Creswell, *Early Muslim Architecture* II (New York: Hacker Art Books, 1969), 227-45.

6 Balawi, *Sirat Ahmad Ibn Tulun*, 54.

7 Balawi, *Sirat Ahmad Ibn Tulun*, 54; quoted by Maqrizi*, Khitat* II, 85; Salmon, *Études sur la*

topographie du Caire, 6, provides an incomplete study of these markets.

8 Ya'qubi, *Kitab al-buldan*, 26-27.

9 Ibn Duqmaq, *Kitab al-intisar,* 121; Maqrizi, *Khitat* I, 313.

10 Maqrizi called it "Mashhad al-Ras"–"Memorial of the Head" (*Khitat* II, 80).

11 Creswell, *Early Muslim Architecture* II, 328.

12 Creswell, *Early Muslim Architecture* II, 328.

13 I tend to prefer translating Shari' al-A'zam to be "Greatest Street," as if it were just "Great Street," the name would have been al-Shari' al-'Azim instead. The difference is therefore clear.

14 Balawi, *Sirat Ahmad Ibn Tulun*, 55.

15 Balawi, *Sirat Ahmad Ibn Tulun*, 55. He does not refer to a marker, but to a side corner, which must have had a specific mark or sign.

16 Balawi, *Sirat Ahmad Ibn Tulun*, 55.

17 The only triumphal/honorific arch in Egypt that had survived during the period of Ibn Tulun was in the city of Antinopolis (at the village of Sheikh Abada in Upper Egypt today), built by the Roman Emperor Hadrian in 130 ad. Could Ahmad Ibn Tulun have visited that site and saw it, and therefore, greatly been impressed by it? We do not know of another triumphal arch to have been built anywhere else in Egypt. If not, then he might have seen others in similar Roman cities like Palmyra and Bosra in Syria and Gerash in Jordan.

18 Ya'qubi, *Kitab al-buldan*, 25.

19 A thorough historical and architectural study of the Aqueduct of Basatin is found in Creswell, *Early Muslim Architecture* II, 329-32.

20 Quoted as Abi Ibn Khalid, but it was preceded by the letter "*b*" in Arabic, which is a *harf garr* therefore, it is written as Abi, whereas without the "*b*" the name should be Abu Ibn Khalid, see: Balawi, *Sirat Ahmad Ibn Tulun*, 56, 76, 180; Maqrizi (quoting the historian al-Quda'i) says that it was located at the site of al-Maghafir, instead of al-Ma'afir–he must have wrongly copied the name where the aqueduct was located, or it was misprinted (*Khitat* IV/2, 893).

21 Maqrizi, *Khitat* IV/2, 894. For more details of this event, see: Tarek Swelim, "The Mosque of Ibn Tulun: New Perspectives," unpublished PhD diss. (Harvard University, 1994), 74, note 80.

22 Balawi, *Sirat Ahmad Ibn Tulun*, 180; Maqrizi, *Khitat* IV/2, 894.

23 Balawi, *Sirat Ahmad Ibn Tulun*, 182; Maqrizi, *Khitat* IV/2, 894.

24 Balawi, *Sirat Ahmad Ibn Tulun*, 56, 76.

25 Balawi, *Sirat Ahmad Ibn Tulun*, 181-82.

26 Balawi, *Sirat Ahmad Ibn Tulun*, 181-82.

27 Balawi, *Sirat Ahmad Ibn Tulun*, 181-82. It is worth noting that the actual name of the architect is not known, although he has been referred to by the Medieval historians as *al-Nasrani*, meaning 'the Christian.' Most scholars are inclined to believe he was an Egyptian Copt, but Gaston Wiet has pointed out that if he were a Copt then the word used would have been *Kibti*, and therefore suggests that al-Nasrani was a Christian from Mesopotamia whom Ibn Tulun brought with him. See Creswell, *Early Muslim Architecture* II, 332, note 12.

28 For this see, Roland-Pierre Gayraud, et al., "Istabl 'Antar (Fostat) 1987-89: Rapport de fouilles," *Annales Islamologiques* XXV (Cairo: IFAO, 1991), 57-87.

29 Balawi, *Sirat Ahmad Ibn Tulun*, 182; quoted by Maqrizi, *Khitat* IV/2, 894.

30 For the study of the Great Aqueduct along the Salah Salem Road, see Creswell, *The Muslim Architecture of Egypt*, vol. II (New York: Haker Art Books, 1978), 255-60.

31 For a ground plan of the water-intake tower of the Basatin Aqueduct, see Creswell, *Early Muslim Architecture* II, 331, fig. 244.

32 For the recent state of the Aqueduct, see, Yahia Shawkat, "Destruction Alert: Ibn Tulun's Aqueduct in Basatin," *Cairo Observer*, January 30, 2012, http://cairobserver.com/post/16766637427/destruction-alert-ibn-tulun-aqueduct-in-basateen.

33 Balawi, *Sirat Ahmad Ibn Tulun*, 76; Maqrizi, *Khitat* IV/1, 70.

34 Ibn Jubayr, *Rihlat Ibn Jubayr* (Beirut: Dār Ṣadir lil-Ṭibā'ah wa-al-Nashr, 1959), 52.

35 Maqrizi, *Khitat* IV/2, 691.

36 Maqrizi, *Khitat* IV/2, 691; Ibn Duqmaq, *Kitab al-intisar,* 99.

37 Maqrizi, *Khitat* IV/2, 691; Ibn Duqmaq, *Kitab al-intisar,* 99. The *Dar al-Diwan, al-Asakifa*, and unnamed *qaisariya* are only mentioned by Maqrizi.

38 Maqrizi, *Khitat* IV/2, 691-2.

39 Balawi, *Sirat Ahmad Ibn Tulun*, 76.
40 Maqrizi, *Khitat* IV/2, 691.
41 Maqrizi, *Khitat* IV/2, 691.
42 Maqrizi, *Khitat* IV/2, 691, al-Ma'afir is briefly mentioned; Ibn Duqmaq, 99; also listed by Ahmad 'Isa, *Tarikh al-bimaristanat fi-l-Islam* (Beirut, Dar al-Ra'id al-'Arabi, 1981), 66.
43 'Isa, *Tarikh al-bimaristanat*, 76.
44 This *bimaristan* is still operating as an eye hospital until today.
45 Maqrizi, *Khitat* IV/2, 691.
46 Maqrizi, *Khitat* II, 56.
47 Salmon, *Études sur la topographie du Caire*, 3–11; Creswell, *Early Muslim Architecture* II, 329.
48 Balawi, *Sirat Ahmad Ibn Tulun*, 52–53.
49 Maqrizi, *Khitat* II, 269; *al-Khitat wa-l-athar* I, 313.
50 Balawi, *Sirat Ahmad Ibn Tulun*, 183.
51 Balawi, *Sirat Ahmad Ibn Tulun*, 183.
52 Maqrizi, *Khitat* IV/1, 80.
53 Balawi, *Sirat Ahmad Ibn Tulun*, 183.
54 Jere L. Bacharach, "Administrative Complexes, Palaces, and Citadels: Changes in the loci of Medieval Muslim Rule," in *The Ottoman City and Its Parts, Urban Structure and Social Order*, edited by Irene Bierman, Rifa'at Abou-El-Haj, and Donald Presziosi (New Rochelle, NY: A.D. Caratzas, 1991), 111–28.
55 A description of this building is in K.A.C. Creswell and James Allen, *A Short Account on Early Muslim Architecture* (Cairo: The American University in Cairo Press, 1989), 370–72; the same building is referred to by Gulru Necioglu, "An Outline of Shifting Paradigms in the Palatial Architecture of Pre-Modern Islamic World," *Ars Orientalis* XXIII (1993): 10, note 38.
56 One can also assume that the cistern of the *sabil* of the Gayer-Anderson House/Museum, was not yet dug. While discussing this issue with Dr. Khaled Azab, he speculated that the source of water was from a *siqaya* located in the area of Qala'at al-Kabsh where ground level is much higher than at the mosque. He added that the water could have run through underground canals to a cistern that was probably below the *sabil* of Qaitbay (or Lajin), which was not yet built. From that cistern the water could have been branched through two canals, one to the Tulunid *fawara* and another to the Dar al-Imara. This interesting speculation could only be proved after some serious excavations that would take place in that area.
57 Ibn Duqmaq, *Kitab al-intisar,* 123.
58 Ibn Duqmaq, *Kitab al-intisar,* 123.
59 Ibn Duqmaq, *Kitab al-intisar,* 124.
60 This is the double house of Amna bint Salem al-Gazzar (index no. 559), built in 947 ah / 1540 ad and that of 'Abd al-Qadir al-Haddad (index no. 321), built in 1041 ah / 1631 ad, also known as Bayt al-Kiritliya, which was later bought by Major Gayer-Anderson in 1935–42 from the Egyptian authorities. Today, this is known as the Gayer-Anderson House/Museum and is open to the public.
61 Also see, J.W. McPherson, *The Moulids of Egypt (Egyptian Saints Days)* (Cairo: N.M. Press, 1941), 206–207, and a photograph opposite page 26.
62 As told by Sheikh Sulayman al-Kretli, the guardian of this tomb who was born and lived in that house his whole life.
63 According to R.G. John Gayer-Anderson, *Legends of the Bait al-Kretliya* (Ipswich, UK: East Anglican Daily Times Co. Ltd, 1952), 90–98; also mentioned by Caroline Williams, *Islamic Monuments in Cairo: The Practical Guide* (Cairo: The American University in Cairo, 2002), 68. In addition, McPherson was proud to record that the *mulid* or *mawalid* (birthday celebrations) of Sidi Harun had been revived and re-established by Gayer-Anderson, who bought those houses and lived in them in 1935. He adds that the *mulid* took place during the month of Sha'ban each year and describes its social atmosphere. He says that it was Gayer-Anderson who had put the tomb in order, illuminated it, and adorned it.
64 Ibn Duqmaq, *Kitab al-intisar,* 121; Maqrizi, *Khitat* II, 85. The latter says that it started in the month of Sha'ban of that year.
65 Balawi, *Sirat Ahmad Ibn Tulun*, 54; repeated by Maqrizi, *Khitat* II, 86.
66 Balawi, *Sirat Ahmad Ibn Tulun*, 54; repeated by Maqrizi, *Khitat* II, 86.
67 The word 'hippodrome' is used in the following sources: Ya'qubi, *Les Pays,* trans. Gaston Wiet (Cairo: IFAO, 1937); Jean-Joseph Marcel, "Mémoire sur la mosquée de Toulon et les Inscriptions qu'elle renferme, comprenant un précis de la dynastie des

Toulonides," in *Description de l'Égypte*, 2nd ed., vol. XVII, *État Moderne* (Paris: Pancoucke, 1830), 1-34; *Égypte, depuis la conquête des Arabes jusqu'à la domination française* (Paris: Firmin Didot, Freres, 1877), 71-75; Eustace Corbet, "The Life and Works of Ahmad Ibn Tulun," *Journal of the Royal Asiatic Society* (1891): 527-62; Paul Casanova, trans., *Livre des admonitions et de l'observation pour l'histoire des quartiers et des monuments ou descriptions historique et topographique de l'Égypte* (Cairo: IFAO, 1906), 204-48; Edward Lane, *Cairo Fifty Years Ago* (London: J. Murray, 1986), 9-14, 103-109; Stanely Lane-Poole, *The Art of the Saracens in Egypt* (London: Chapman and Hall, 1886), 54-59; *A History of Egypt in the Middle Ages* (London: Chapman and Hall, 1968), 60-77; *The Story of Cairo* (London: J.M. Dent and Co., 1906) 72-90; Creswell, *Early Muslim Architecture* II, 328. However, the *maydans* at Samarra are referred to as "race-courses" by Alistair Northedge, "The Race-courses at Samarra," *Bulletin of the School of Oriental and African Studies* 53 (1990): 31-56.

68 Ibn Duqmaq, *Kitab al-intisar*, 121; Maqrizi, *Khitat* II, 80.

69 Maqrizi, *Khitat* II, 80.

70 Balawi, *Sirat Ahmad Ibn Tulun*, 53-54; also recorded by Maqrizi, *Khitat* II, 86.

71 Balawi, *Sirat Ahmad Ibn Tulun*, 55.

72 Maqrizi, *Khitat* II, 86.

73 Maqrizi, *Khitat* II, 86.

74 Maqrizi, *Khitat* II, 91; the Dar al-Haram is not mentioned by Balawi.

75 Balawi, *Sirat Ahmad Ibn Tulun*, 55; Ibn Duqmaq, *Kitab al-intisar*, 121; Maqrizi, *Khitat* I, 315.

76 Balawi, *Sirat Ahmad Ibn Tulun*, 55.

77 Balawi, *Sirat Ahmad Ibn Tulun*, 55.

78 Maqrizi, *Khitat* II, 86.

79 The term 'honorific arch' is preferred over 'triumphal arch," according to William MacDonald in his wonderful course on the legacy of Roman architecture, during my years at Harvard.

80 Balawi, *Sirat Ahmad Ibn Tulun*, 55. However, this interior connection is not mentioned by Balawi.

81 The excavations at Samarra show that there was a *majlis* above the Bab al-'Amma, which was reached by a ramp on its south side, overlooking the Tigris and the flood plain. For this see Alistaire Northedge, "An Interpretation of the Palace of the Caliph at Samarra (Dar al-Khalifa or Jawsaq al-Khaqani), *Ars Orientalis* XXIII (1993): 146. The link between the Bab al-Salah or Bab al-Siba' and that in Samarra is also referred to by Gulru Necipoglu, "Shifting Paradigms in the Palatial Architecture of the Pre-Modern Islamic World," *Ars Orientalis* XXIII (1993): 9-10.

82 Balawi, *Sirat Ahmad Ibn Tulun*, 55. He also says that it was located at the beginning of the animal market *(souq al-dawwab)* in his time and was known by the name of *thalathat abwab* (triple gates).

83 Balawi, *Sirat Ahmad Ibn Tulun*, 56; Maqrizi, *Khitat* II, 87. The latter calls it Bab Madinat al-Fustat (Gate of the city of Fustat); Casanova, *Livre des admonitions*, 213. The historians do not tell us where this gate is located.

84 Maqrizi, *Khitat* II, 94.

85 Maqrizi, *Khitat* II, 93.

86 Shams al-Din Abu 'Abd Allah Muhammad Ibn Nasir al-Din al-Ansari al-Ma'ruf bi Ibn al-Zayyat, *al-Kawakib al-sayyara fi-l-tarikh al-ziyara* (Baghdad: Maktabat al-Mythanna, 1968), 278; the same information is only repeated by Muhammad Ibn 'Abd al-Rahman al-Sakhawi, *Tuhfat al-ahbab wa baghaiyat al-tullab fi-l-khitat wa-l-mazarat wa-l-tarajum wa-l-buqa wa-l-mubarakat*, ed. Ahmad Nash'at, Mahmud Rabi', and Hasan Qasim (Cairo: Matba'at al-'Ulum wa-l-Adab, 1937), 369-70.

87 *Index to Mohammedan Monuments in Cairo* (Egypt: Maslahat al-Misaha, Cairo: S.N.), 1951.

88 An inscription on one of the tombstones gives the name of Husayn Bey al-Jamashuji, 1276 ah / 1859 ad. I would like to say that it was the wonderful late Laila Ali Ibrahim who drew my attention to these two buildings.

89 The only exception is Mamluk Sultan Sha'ban, who built a superb *madrasa*-mosque in the area of Darb al-Ahmar in Cairo, where he chose to have his mother buried in the large domed mausoleum and a smaller one for himself in the same complex. It was therefore named after the sultan's mother as the *madrasa* of Umm (mother of) al-Sultan Sha'ban.

90 I would like to thank Jaraslow Dobrovolski for pointing out this idea to me.

91 The reason I say foliated rather than floriated is due to the closest ones being the marble inscriptions that date back to the later Ikhshidid period, that are reused in the mausoleum of the Mamluk Sultan al-Mu'ayyad Sheikh in Cairo.

92 Ibn Duqmaq (*Kitab al-intisar*, 121) describes Ibn Tulun's action as "*hadam*," while Maqrizi (*Khitat*, 315) uses the verb "*amara bi-harth*"–ordered them to be ploughed.

93 For this, see Tarek Swelim, "Antinopolis," in *An Encyclopedia of Roman Archaeology*, edited by Catherine Bard (London and New York: Routledge, 1999), 139–41.

94 The Caliph al-Ma'mun was the son of the Caliph Harun al-Rashid. He was a lover of arts, literature, and philosophy. In Egypt, he is remembered for tunneling in the outer façade of the Great Pyramid of Khufu in Giza, and reaching the corridor that leads to the burial chambers. Until his period, the pyramid of Khufu was still covered entirely by the white outer facing of Tura Limestone. Ever since, it was constantly being ripped off.

95 Maqrizi, *Khitat* II, 313.

96 Maqrizi, *Khitat* II, 202.

97 The following pages are based on the account by James Aldrige, *Cairo* (London: Macmillan, 1970), 55–58.

98 Maqrizi, *Khitat* II, 88; accounted for by Aldridge, *Cairo*, 56.

99 Maqrizi, *Khitat* II, 88; Aldridge, *Cairo*, 56.

100 Maqrizi, *Khitat* II, 88–9; Aldridge, *Cairo*, 56.

101 Maqrizi, *Khitat* II, 89; Aldridge, *Cairo*, 56.

102 Maqrizi, *Khitat* II, 89 and 316; Aldridge, *Cairo*, 56.

103 Maqrizi, *Khitat* II, 89; accounted for by Aldridge, *Cairo*, 56.

104 Aldridge, *Cairo*, 56.

105 Ibn Duqmaq, *Kitab al-intisar*, 122; Maqrizi, *Khitat* II, 89; Aldridge, *Cairo*, 57, calculates it as thirteen hundred feet square.

106 Maqrizi, *Khitat* II, 89; Aldridge, *Cairo*, 57.

107 Maqrizi, *Khitat* II, 89.

108 Maqrizi, *Khitat* II, 90; accounted for by Aldridge, *Cairo*, 56.

109 Maqrizi, *Khitat* II, 90–91; accounted for by Aldridge, *Cairo*, 56.

110 Maqrizi, *Khitat* II, 91; accounted for by Aldridge, *Cairo*, 57.

111 Maqrizi, *Khitat* II, 92; accounted for by Aldridge, *Cairo*, 56.

112 The concept of a zoo was only repeated during the reign of the Khedive Isma'il in the 1860s, as part of his Europeanization program. The zoo was created in Giza by the Frenchman Barillet des Champs to be the largest zoological garden in the world when it was built.

113 Maqrizi, *Khitat* II, 103–104.

114 Maqrizi, *Khitat* II, 104.

Part Two

1 Sarim al-Din Ibrahim Ibn Muhammad Ibn Aydumur al-'Ala'i al-Misri Ibn Duqmaq, *Kitab al-intisar li-wasitat 'aqd al-amsar*, ed. K. Vollers (Beirut: Markaz al-Mawsu'at al-'Alamiya, 1893), 122; Taqi al-Din Ahmad al-Maqrizi, *l-Mawa'iz w-al-'itibar fi dhikr al-khitat w-al-athar* IV/1, ed. Ayman Fu'ad Sayyid (London: Mu'assasat al-Furqan lil-Turath al-Islami, 2002), 64.

2 The earliest surviving Islamic monument in Egypt is the Nilometer of Roda (247 ah / 861 ad).

Chapter 5

1 The word *riwaq* has no direct translation in the English language. However, it is usually incorrectly interpreted as hypostyle–a series of columns with capitals that support lintels supporting a ceiling. However a *riwaq* is a series of columns (or piers) supporting arches, which in turn support a ceiling. The term *riwaq* will therefore be used in this study. George Scanlon taught me this when I was his student during the early 1980s.

2 These are not the original stucco decorations, but they have been restored.

3 I would like to thank Dr. Gawdat Gabra for the accurate description of these capitals.

4 K.A.C. Creswell, *Early Muslim Architecture* II (New York: Hacker Art Books, 1979), 350

Chapter 6

1 Sarim al-Din Ibrahim Ibn Muhammad Ibn Aydumur al-'Ala'i al-Misri Ibn Duqmaq, *Kitab al-intisar li-wasitat 'aqd al-amsar*, ed. K. Vollers (Beirut: Markaz al-Mawsu'at al-'Alamiya, 1893),

123; Taqi al-Din Ahmad al-Maqrizi, *al-Mawa'iz w-al-'itibar fi dhikr al-khitat w-al-athar* IV/1, ed. Ayman Fu'ad Sayyid (London: Mu'assasat al-Furqan lil-Turath al-Islami, 2002), 64.

2 Abu Muhammad 'Abd Allah Ibn Muhammad al-Madini al-Balawi, *Sirat Ahmad Ibn Tulun*, ed. Muhammad Kurd 'Ali (Damascus: al-Maktaba al-'Arabiya fi Dimashq, 1939), 56.

3 Balawi, *Sirat Ahmad Ibn Tulun*, 56.

4 Ibn Duqmaq, *Kitab al-intisar*, 122; Maqrizi, *Khitat* IV/1, 64.

5 Maqrizi, *Khitat*, IV/1: 61; Balawi, *Sirat Ahmad Ibn Tulun*, 182.

6 Maqrizi, *Khitat* IV/1, 64.

7 Maqrizi, *Khitat* IV/1, 61.

8 Balawi, *Sirat Ahmad Ibn Tulun*, 182; Ibn Duqmaq, *Kitab al-intisar*, 123; Maqrizi, *Khitat* IV/1: 61.

9 Ibn Duqmaq, *Kitab al-intisar*, 123, Maqrizi, *Khitat* IV/1, 72. No evidence of such a feature has been found, and no other source mentions this story. Thus, it might have become an exaggerated legend spread by word of mouth and just became part of the folk traditions related to the mosque.

10 Ibn Duqmaq, *Kitab al-intisar*, 123.

11 Balawi, *Sirat Ahmad Ibn Tulun*, 183; Maqrizi, *Khitat* IV/1: 61.

12 Ibn Duqmaq, *Kitab al-intisar*, 123.

13 Ibn Duqmaq, *Kitab al-intisar*, 123.

14 Ibn Duqmaq, *Kitab al-intisar*, 123. He refers to the *jabal al-thalith* (third hill); however, by comparing Ibn Duqmaq's statement with that of Maqrizi's, we are led to understand that the former means the Muqattam Hills.

15 Ibn Duqmaq, *Kitab al-intisar*, 123.

16 Ibn Duqmaq, *Kitab al-intisar*, 123.

17 Balawi, *Sirat Ahmad Ibn Tulun*, 56, 76. Also translated as "Pharaoh's Furnace" in Doris Behrens-Abouseif, *The Minarets of Cairo* (Cairo: The American University in Cairo Press, 1985), 103.

18 Maqrizi, *Khitat* IV/1, 70.

19 Balawi, *Sirat Ahmad Ibn Tulun*, 76; Maqrizi, *Khitat* IV/1, 70.

20 Jamal al-Din Abu al-Mahasin Yusuf Ibn Taghribirdi (813–874 ah / 1410–1469 ad), *al-Nujum al-zahira fi muluk Misr wa-l-Qahira* III (Cairo: Dar al-Kutub, 1929), 10.

21 Balawi, *Sirat Ahmad Ibn Tulun*, 76; Maqrizi, *Khitat* IV/1, 70.

22 Balawi, *Sirat Ahmad Ibn Tulun*, 76; Maqrizi, *Khitat* IV/1, 70.

23 Balawi, *Sirat Ahmad Ibn Tulun*, 182. However, the main *mihrab* is currently flanked by four columns rather than two. Could we then assume that the original plan of the mosque was later on modified?

24 Balawi, *Sirat Ahmad Ibn Tulun*, 182. The issue of the architect, al-Nasrani, will be discussed in the chapter on the lost city of al-Qata'i'.

25 Ibn Duqmaq, *Kitab al-intisar*, 122; Maqrizi, *Khitat* IV/1, 59.

26 Ibn Duqmaq, *Kitab al-intisar*, 123.

27 Ibn Duqmaq, *Kitab al-intisar*, 124; Maqrizi, *Khitat* IV/1, 59. However, according to religious belief, God spoke to the prophet Moses on top of Mount Sinai, where he received the Ten Commandments. At the same time, the remnants of the Burning Bush are believed to be on the premises of the Monastery of Saint Catherine in Sinai.

28 Caroline Williams, *Islamic Monuments in Cairo: The Practical Guide* (Cairo: The American University in Cairo Press, 2002), 46. However, I could not find another source to support this piece of information.

29 Maqrizi, *Khitat* II, 85.

30 Ibn Duqmaq, *Kitab al-intisar*, 124; Maqrizi, *Khitat* IV/1, 59.

31 Ibn Duqmaq *Kitab al-intisar*, 123. This information was only believed in folk legends of the time, but it is true that there was a tomb (or memorial) of the Prophet Harun in Sinai, close to the monastery of Saint Catherine, and another tomb atop Gabal Harun in the mountains of Petra in the Hashemite Kingdom of Jordan.

32 Ibn Duqmaq, *Kitab al-intisar*, 123.

33 Eustace K. Corbet, "The Life and Works of Ahmad Ibn Tulun," *Journal of the Royal Asiatic Society* XXIII/4 (October 1891): 539; Robert Williams, "The Mosque of Ibn Tulun," *The Moslem World* VIII/3 (July 1918): 223; Mahmud 'Akkush, *Tarikh wa wasf al-jami' al-tuluni* (Cairo: Matba'at Dar al-Kutub al-Misriya, 1927), 41; K.A.C. Creswell, *Early Muslim Architecture* II (New York: Hacker Art Books, 1969), 338.

34 R.G. John Gayer-Anderson, *The Legends of Bait al-Kretliya "Asatir Bayt al-Kritliya,"* (Ipswich, UK: East Anglian Daily Times Co. Ltd., 1951), 47.

35 This was pointed out in George Scanlon's seminar on the architecture of Cairo, in 1983.

36 I am grateful to George Scanlon for pointing out this observation to me.

37 In 1992, it was indeed tested during the terrible earthquake that hit Egypt. Only the spiral-shaped stone minaret of the mosque of Ibn Tulun shook and became unstable, while the rest of the mosque was not affected and did not suffer any damage. In spite of the city of Fustat being totally destroyed, the excavations made by George Scanlon and others have shown this in the foundation of buildings.

38 Ibn Duqmaq, *Kitab al-intisar*, 123.

39 Maqrizi, *Khitat* IV/1, 70. Another version of the story concerning the main *mihrab* was that a man complained to Ibn Tulun that the *mihrab* of the mosque was actually too small. In any case, Ibn Tulun responded that he had a dream in which he had seen the Prophet Muhammad, who had in fact designed that *mihrab* for him (meaning Ibn Tulun) in that fashion. He added that after he woke up, he went to the mosque and surprisingly found that the designated area where the *mihrab* should have been was actually swarming with ants. This story, however, does not involve anything about an incorrectly oriented *mihrab*.

40 According to Jaroslaw Dobrowolski who calculated it for me, for which I would like to thank him.

41 By comparison with other mosques in Cairo, we find the orientations are as follows: the original Fatimid mosque of al-Azhar—129.5 degrees (deviation -7 degrees); the mosque of al-Hakim—132 degrees (deviation -4.5 degrees); al-Salih al-Tala'i'—131.5 degrees (deviation -5 degrees); al-Salih Nagm al-Din Ayyub—126 degrees (deviation -10.5 degrees); the mosque of al-Nasir Muhammad (Citadel)—128 degrees (deviation -8.5 degrees); that of al-Ashraf Barsbay (Muski)—128 degrees (deviation -8.5 degrees); Sultan Barquq (Bayn al-Qasrayn)—119 degrees (deviation -17.5 degrees); al-Mu'ayyad Sheikh—120 degrees (deviation -16.5 degrees)' Malika Safiya—127.5 degrees (deviation -9 degrees); and the mosque of Muhammad 'Ali Pasha (Citadel)—132.5 degrees (deviation -4 degrees). I am grateful to Jaroslaw Dobrowolski for calculating this for me.

42 Balawi, *Sirat Ahmad Ibn Tulun*, 182; Maqrizi, *Khitat* IV/1, 60.

43 Balawi, *Sirat Ahmad Ibn Tulun*, 182; Maqrizi, *Khitat* IV/1, 60.

44 Two things need to be pointed out here: 1) The second mosque in Egypt—the mosque of al-'Askar—no longer exists as it was destroyed, and therefore the kind of columns used in it are not known; 2) There were no *riwaq*-style mosques built in the Ayyubid period.

45 Ibn Duqmaq, *Kitab al-intisar*, 123.

46 Maqrizi, *Khitat* IV/1, 70.

47 Maqrizi, *Khitat* IV/1, 64.

48 Maqrizi, *Khtiat* IV/1, 64.

49 Creswell, *Early Muslim Architecture* II, 343.

50 Robert Williams, *The Moslem World* VIII/3 (July 1918), 229.

51 James Aldridge, *Cairo*, (London: Macmillan, 1970), 55.

52 Hautecoeur and Wiet, *Les mosquées du Caire* (Paris: Librairie Ernest Leroux, 1932), 207; mentioned by Creswell, *Early Muslim Architecture* II, 343, note 2.

53 Unfortunately, the mosque of al-Hakim was heavily restored to such an extent that it is impossible to distinguish the old from the new. Old photographs of the mosque of al-Hakim do not show exactly how the arches looked because of its poor condition before the restorations undertaken by the Bohras in the 1980s. However, when one examines the modern arches properly, it is evident that they do not show the slight return as in those of Ibn Tulun. Whether this was original or simply an error made by the restorers cannot be determined. In spite of not being sure of the style of the arches in the mosque of Tabataba, we may assume that they were pointed as in the mosque of Ibn Tulun, since this was probably the norm of that period. However, we cannot be sure of that either.

54 An idea inspired by Ahmad Fikri, *Masajid al-Qahira wa madarisuha* (Cairo: Dar al-Ma'arif, 1961), 113-14. Tarek Swelim, *The Mosque of Ibn Tulun: New Perspectives*, PhD diss., Harvard University, 1994, 188-89.

55 Creswell, *Early Muslim Architecture* II, 341.

56 Ibn Duqmaq, *Kitab al-intisar*, 123.

57 See the different enlargements of the Mosque of 'Amr, in Tarek Swelim, "The Mosque of 'Amr Ibn al-'As," in *The History and Religious Heritage of Old Cairo: Its Fortress, Churches, Synagogue, and Mosque*, ed. Carolyn Ludwig and Moris Jackson (Cairo: The American University in Cairo Press, 2012), 281.

58 Swelim, "The Mosque of 'Amr Ibn al-'As," 293.

59 Maqrizi, *Khitat* IV/1, 70.

60 Maqrizi, *Khitat* IV/1, 72.

61 Maqrizi, *Khitat* IV/1, 64; Ibn Duqmaq *Kitab al-intisar*, 123.

62 Maqrizi, *Khitat* IV/I, 64; Ibn Duqmaq *Kitab al-intisar*, 123.

63 Ya'qubi, Ahmad ibn Abi Ya'qub, *Kitab al-buldan* (Najaf: al-Matba'a al-Haydariya, 1957), 124; Ya'qubi, *Les Pays*, trans. Gaston Wiet (Cairo: Imprimerie de l'Institut Français, 1937), 243.

64 Ya'qubi, *Les Pays*, 243; *Kitab al-buldan*, 124. See also Tarek Swelim, "The Minaret of Ibn Tulun Reconsidered," in *The Cairo Heritage: Essays in Honor of Laila Ali Ibrahim*, ed. Doris Behrens-Abouseif (Cairo and New York: The American University in Cairo Press, 2000), 77–91.

65 Ghazi Rajib Muhammad, "The Minaret of Ibn Tulun: Its Construction and Description," *Summer* 23 I/1 and 2 (1967): 84.

66 Muhammad Ibn Ahmad al-Muqaddasi, *Ahsan al-taqasim fi ma'rifat al-aqalim*, ed. M.J. De Goeje (Leiden: Brill, 1967), 199. For more on the minaret, see Tarek Swelim, "The Minaret of Ibn Tulun Reconsidered," 77–91.

67 Maqrizi, *Khitat* IV/1, 64.

68 Maqrizi, *Khitat* IV/1, 72; Ibn Duqmaq, *Kitab al-intisar*, 124.

69 Maqrizi, *Khtiat* IV/1, 61, Ibn Duqmaq, *Kitab al-intisar*, 123.

70 Referred to in Behrens-Abouseif, *Minarets of Cairo*, 104.

71 Maqrizi, *Khitat* IV/1, 72.

72 Evliya Çelebi, *Siyahatnamesi*, ed. S.A. Kahrama, Y. Dagli, and R. Dankoff, 10 vols. (Istanbul, 2007), 207; referred to in Behrens-Abouseif, *The Minarets of Cairo*, 103.

73 In Egyptian and Middle Eastern cultures, sometimes this expression is said in a joking way, rather than an accusation of being negative.

74 Balawi, *Sirat Ahmad Ibn Tulun*, 183; also related by Maqrizi, *Khitat* IV/1, 62.

75 Creswell, *EMA* II, 337.

76 Protain, "Le Kaire," in *Description de l'Égypte*, 2nd ed., vol. 1, *Planches*, État Moderne (Paris: Panckoucke, 1822), plate 29.

77 The elegant pointed arches with their slight returns appear more like gothic arhes in Protain's engraving (1798–1801), *Description de l'Égypte* I, plate 31.

78 E.F. Jomard, "Description de la ville du Kaire," in *Description de l'Égypte*, 2nd ed., vol. XVIII/2, *État Moderne* (Paris: Panckoucke, 1820), 579–778. Also translated in Creswell, *Early Muslim Architecture* II, 351.

79 Pascal Coste, *Architecture Arabe Au Monuments du Kaire* (Paris: Firmin Didot Frere, 1839), plate IV/1.

80 Robert Hay, *Illustrations of Cairo* (London: Tilt and Bogue, 1840), plate V.

81 Antoine Jean Gors, *Bonaparte visiting the plague victims in Jaffa*, oil on canvas, Musée du Louvre, Paris (1804).

82 Prisse d'Avennes, *L'Art arabe d'après les monuments du Kaire depuis le VIIe siècle jusqu'à la fin du XVIIIe* I (Paris: A. Morel, 1869–1877), plate II.

83 For more on this, see Behrens-Abouseif, *Minarets of Cairo*, 56, 102.

84 'Abd al-Rahman al-Jabarti, *'Aja'ib al-athar fi-l-tarajim wa-l-akhbar* I (Beirut: Dar al-Gil, n.d.), 45, gives the date of its fall as Ramadan 12, 1105 / May 8, 1693.

85 Creswell, *Early Muslim Architecture* II, 351–52.

86 Photographs and illustrations are found before 1892 in Gaston Migeon, *Le Caire, Le Nil et Memphis* (Paris: H. Laurens, 1909), 42; Julius Franz Pasha, *Kairo von Franz Pascha* (Leipzig: E.A. Seemann, 1903), figure 2; (ca. 1870–1892) Pascal Sebah, *Égypte* (Roma: L. Olivieri, n.d.), no. 15; (between 1862–84) interior view by A. Beato, in the Creswell Photo Collection A8, plate 52; (before 1882) Ebers, *Egypt: Descriptive, Historical and Picturesque* I, translated from German by Clara Bell (London: Cassell, Petter and Galpur, 1881–82), 217; (between 1887–92) Lekegian and Co. in the Creswell Photo Collection A8, plate 49 A.

87 'Akkush, *Tarikh wa wasf*, 103.

88 It is discussed later, in chapter 8, that the present minaret had to be asymmetrical due the fact that when it was being built, the remains of the old

Tulunid one were still there and therefore there was no space to build on top of it, especially since it was built of stone.

89 Contrary to the view of Behrens-Abouseif (*Minarets of Cairo*, 106), who believes that the placement of the current minaret of Ibn Tulun (being asymmetrical to the main axis of the mosque) was due to its symmetry with the multiple entrances into the building. She adds that the original plan with symmetrical entrances in the walls of the mosque were corresponding to those of the *ziyada*, which allowed an axial entrance through both of the two walls opposite the *mihrab* and if the minaret was placed axially, it would have blocked the axial entrance of the *ziyada* and the mosque. One needs to be reminded that the discussion is on the present minaret and not on the original Tulunid one.

90 Muqaddasi, *Ahsan al-taqasim*, 199.

91 Muqaddasi, *Ahsan al-taqasim*, 199. The Well of Zamzam is located in the haram area of the Ka'ba in Mecca, where Muslims go to purify themselves during their pilgrimage.

92 Ibn Duqmaq, *Kitab al-intisar*, 123; Maqrizi, *Khitat* IV/1, 74.

93 Ibn Duqmaq, *Kitab al-intisar*, 123; Maqrizi, *Khitat* IV/1, 74. It is worth noting that teak wood is precious, as it is imported from Burma, India, and Malaysia, as well as from China and Latin America. It seems rather strange that it was imported from such faraway countries. The fact may be that it was not from those countries, but rather that it was a very precious kind of wood that was used in this *fawwara*, hence giving it more importance.

94 Maqrizi, *Khitat* IV/1, 62.

95 Corbet ("Life and Works," 543), regarded by Creswell as an ingenious idea (*Early Muslim Architecture* II, 333). Corbet further imagines the *fawwara* to have once been ornamented by signs of the zodiac. This is curious as Maqrizi does not refer to any signs of a zodiac. However, it seems that Corbet was confused by Maqrizi's description and concluded that it was decorated by zodiac rather than simply "decorated."

96 Maqrizi, *Khitat* IV/1, 62.

97 Maqrizi (*Khitat* IV/1, 74) mentions that portable *mihrab*s were added to the mosque of 'Amr Ibn al-'As in that year.

98 One needs to remember that there are three wonderful masterpieces of portable wooden *mihrab*s in the Museum of Islamic Art in Cairo, namely those of al-Amir in the mosque of al-Azhar (1126), that of Sayyida Nafisa (1138–46), and that of Sayyida Ruqayya (1154–60).

99 Maqrizi, *Khitat* II, 267–68

100 See Swelim, "The Minaret of Ibn Tulun Reconsidered," 81.

101 Maqrizi, *Khitat* IV/1, 62.

102 Maqrizi, *Khitat* IV/1, 62.

103 Maqrizi, *Khitat* IV/1, 62.

104 'Ali Basha Mubarak, *al-Khitat al-jadida al-tawfiqiya li-Misr wa-l-Qahira* II, new edition (Cairo: al-Hay'a al-Misriya al-'Amma li-l-Kitab, 1982), 309.

105 Mubarak, *al-Khitat al-jadida* II, 309.

106 Creswell (*Early Muslim Architecture* II, 335 note 14; 357) mentions that this drawing is in Sir Gardiner Wilkinson's Album of drawings preserved in Harrow School Library, sheet 6, figure F4. I was not able to see these drawings.

107 Karl Baedeker, *Handbook to Lower Egypt* (German edition, 1877), 286; quoted by Corbet, "Life and Works," 539.

108 Corbet makes an interesting calculation. He says: "Taking the first eight lines of the inscription, which are entirely Koranic, and in which we can therefore restore the missing words to a letter, we find that the surviving portion contains two hundred letters, while that to be supplied contains 160, thus giving the proportions between the surviving and the missing of five to four exactly." "Life and Works," 557, note 1.

109 Corbet ("Life and Works," 558, note 1) notes that it is the oldest of any extent and of certain date. M. Marcel, in the elaborate essay on the Nilometer in the *Expedition de l'Égypte* (vol. XV, 392 ff.), supposes parts of the surviving inscriptions of that monument to belong to al-Ma'mun 199 ah / 814 ad, and to the two restorations under al-Mutawakkil in 233 / 847 and 247 / 861 respectively. Of these, the last belongs to the reign of Ahmad Ibn Tulun himself. In any case, they consist of very few words. I know of no other

inscriptions of so early a date. There are early Fatimid inscriptions on the minarets of al-Hakim (inside the buttresses of Baybars al-Gashankir), and late Fatimid ones on Bab al-Nasr (480 / 1087) and on the Guyushi Mosque (498 / 1104).

110 Corbet, "Life and Works," 558–62. He says that his work is quite decipherable with the aid of a good glass. He provides a transcription and a translation of the inscription.

111 Jean Joseph Marcel, "Inscriptions, monnaies et médailles," in *Description de l'Égypte*, 2nd ed., vol. II, *Planches, État Moderne* (Paris: Imprimerie Impériale, 1817), plates f, g. One tablet has thirty-one lines, while the other has thirty-four. Max Van Berchem (*Materiaux pour un Corpus Inscriptionum Arabicarum,* Premiere Partie, Égypte (Cairo: IFAO, 1894–1903), 27–29), points out that Marcel has drawn the two halves to a slightly different scale, which makes them appear to be parts of two different tablets. See also Creswell, *Early Muslim Architecture* II, 335, note 15.

112 Jean Joseph Marcel, *Égypte depuis la conquête des Arabes jusqu'à la domination française* (Paris: Firmin Didot Frères, 1878), 71–75, plates 2, 20.

113 Marcel, *Égypte depuis la conquête*, 74, note 1

114 Van Berchem, *Materiaux*, 29.

115 Maqrizi, *Khitat* II, 80; IV/1, 62. Balawi does not mention this story.

116 See Oleg Grabar, *The Coinage of the Tulunids* (New York: American Numismatic Society, 1957), 39, note 5. Grabar argues that it could be open to doubt whether the formula when used after the names of governors and financial administrators throughout the Ummayad and Abbasid periods on stamps and weights meant much more than a personal relationship to the caliph. Grabar believes that during that time most titles were not yet formalized and that one should consider the formula as the expression of a personal relationship between the caliph and his subordinate, perhaps a delegation of authority but certainly not a sharing of it, since the formula was used too often after the name of comparatively minor officials. Grabar adds that the same problem applied to the title *amir*, which refers either to a function or to a title. He says that there seems to be a distinction between the third and ninth centuries between the titles given and the titles that were assumed. Either Ahmad Ibn Tulun liked to be known as a military leader, or we are dealing here with the first steps in a formalization of titles that would be achieved completely in the following centuries.

117 Grabar, *Coinage,* 41.

118 Gaston Wiet, *Mémoires publiés par les membres de l'Institut Français d'Archéologie Orientale du Caire sous la direction de M. Pierre Jouguet* 52. (Cairo: IFAO, 1930), 80.

119 Wiet, *Mémoires*, 80.

120 Tarek Swelim, "The Mosque of Ibn Tulun," PhD diss., Harvard University, 1994, 199.

121 Marcel, *Description de l'Égypte* II, *État Moderne, Planches*, plates C and E. (Please note that plate D is not included.)

122 I would like to thank Bernard O'Kane for pointing this idea out to me.

123 Contemporary historians do not provide any information regarding this. However, Creswell shows that some stucco inscriptions and foundation inscriptions had traces of a blue background (*Early Muslim Architecture* II, 346). Grohmann also proves that the inscriptions of the Nilometer at Roda had letters in white marble on a blue background at one time. He also adds that there was a preference for blue and gold in old Qur'anic manuscripts, an idea that is no longer accepted because the only gold on blue manuscripts is a Fatimid creation in Tunis. See Sir Thomas W. Arnold and Adolf Grohmann, *The Islamic Book: a contribution to its art and history from the VII–XVIII century* (Paris: The Pegasus Press; New York: Harcourt, Brace and Company, 1929), 21; Creswell, *Early Muslim Architecture* II, 304; Jonathan Bloom, "Al-Ma'mun's blue Koran?" *Revue des Études Islamiques* LIV (1986): 64.

124 I used to believe it was the work of Sultan Lajin because of the substantial work carried out by him in the Mosque of Ibn Tulun. See Swelim, "The Mosque of Ibn Tulun," 131. However, after so many years of research and visits to the mosque, I am doubtful about this idea.

125 The best explanation of its function can be seen in a beautiful and popular nineteenth century illustration by David Roberts, which shows the *muballigh* (deliverer) or *muqri'* (reader) sitting on

the *dikka* of the mosque of al-Mu'ayyad Sheikh at Bab Zuwayla.

126 The windows have been studied and surveyed by Creswell in *Early Muslim Architecture* II, 345–47.

127 Creswell, *Early Muslim Architecture* II, 346.

128 The main *mihrab*, which does not have a window above, has a diagonal approach that is also visually centered (figs. 157–58). Creswell has pointed out that the doors in the walls are not made to correspond to the arches. In some cases, they lie directly below the windows; while in other cases they are located below but between the windows. See Creswell, *Early Muslim Architecture* II, 346.

129 Balawi, *Sirat Ahmad Ibn Tulun*, 183; Maqrizi, *al-Khitat wa-l-athar* II, 80; IV/1, 80.

130 Balawi, *Sirat Ahmad Ibn Tulun*, 183; Maqrizi, *al-Khitat wa-l-athar* II, 80; IV/1, 80.

131 Coste, *Architecture Arabe*, plate III; D'Avennes, *L'Art Arabe*, plate VI (opposite page 94).

132 Swelim, "The Mosque of Ibn Tulun," 227.

133 Robert Hillenbrand, "Egypt," in *Islamic Architecture of North Africa*, edited by D. Hill and L. Golvin (London: Faber and Faber, 1976), 74. However, Jarek Dobrowolski calculated the human space required during prayers relative to the size of the mosque and found that the mosque in Samarra could accommodate around 96,000 worshipers. Therefore, Hillenbrand is almost exactly correct. I thank Jarek Dobrowolski for provding me with this piece of information.

134 I thank Jarek Dobrowolski for making this interesting comparison and calculation.

135 K.A.C. Creswell, *Muslim Architecture of Egypt* (New York: Hacker Art Books, 1978), 355.

136 Creswell, *Muslim Architecture of Egypt*, 355.

137 See Swelim, "The Mosque of 'Amr Ibn al-'As," 292.

Chapter 7

1 The following passages are from Tarek Swelim, "The Mosque of 'Amr Ibn al-'As," *The History and Religious Heritage of Old Cairo: Its Fortress, Churches, Synagogue, and Mosque*, ed. Carolyn Ludwig and Moris Jackson (Cairo: The American University in Cairo Press, 2012), 284.

2 Jonathan Bloom, *Arts of the City Victorious: Islamic Art and Architecture in Fatimid North Africa and Egypt* (Cairo: The American University in Cairo Press, 2008), 59.

3 Swelim, "The Mosque of 'Amr Ibn al-'As," 284.

4 A list of these shrines built in the Fatimid period are as follows: al-Lu'lu'a (tenth century), al-Guyushi (1030), Ikhwat Yusuf (twelfth century), Sayyida Atiqa and Ga'fari (1120–25), Umm Kalthum (1122), Sayyida Ruqayya (1133), Yahya al-Shabihi (1150), and Sayyidna al-Husayn (1154). As for the shrines of Sayyida Zaynab, Sayyida 'Aisha and Sayyida Sukayna, these were reconstructed and enlarged in the early twentieth century.

5 Swelim, "The Mosque of 'Amr Ibn al-'As," 284.

6 The shrines that lie in the neighborhood of the mosque of Ibn Tulun include that of Sayyida 'Aisha, Sayyida Nafisa, Sayyida 'Atiqa and Ga'fari, Sayyida Ruqqaya, Sayyida Sukayna, and the most famous of all being that of Sayyida Zaynab.

7 One may also add the mosque of Fakahani, but it was completely restored during the Ottoman period (1735). However, its doors are definitely Fatimid and date to 1148.

8 Taqi al-Din Ahmad al-Maqrizi, *al-Mawa'iz w-al-'itibar fi dhikr al-khitat w-al-athar* IV/1, ed. Ayman Fu'ad Sayyid (London: Mu'assasat al-Furqan lil-Turath al-Islami, 2002), 81.

9 Max Van Berchem (*Materiaux pour un Corpus Inscriptionum Arabicarum*, Premiere Partie, Égypte (Cairo: IFAO, 1894–1903), 35–36; Gaston Wiet, *Répertoire chronologique d'épigraphie arabe* XIII (Cairo: IFAO, 1931), 175–76; Creswell, *Early Muslim Architecture* II (New York: Hacker Art Books, 1979), 336.

10 Jean Joseph Marcel, "Inscriptions, monnaies et médailles," *Description de l'Égypte*, 2nd ed., vol. II, *Planches, État Moderne*, (Paris: Panckoucke, 1817), plate e (6).

11 Marcel, "Inscriptions, monnaies et médailles," plate e (6).

12 Similarly, the tomb of Sidi Harun al-Husayni, who was believed to have supernatural powers, may be confused with that of the Prophet Harun (Aaron), the brother of Moses, as shall be discussed later (compare with Ibn Duqmaq, *Kitab al-intisar*, 124).

13 Sarim al-Din Ibrahim Ibn Muhammad Ibn Aydumur al-'Ala'i al-Misri Ibn Duqmaq, *Kitab al-*

intisar li-wasitat ʿaqd al-amsar, ed. K. Vollers (Beirut: Markaz al-Mawsuʿat al-ʿAlamiya, 1893), 123.

14 Ibn Duqmaq, *Kitab al-intisar*, 123. Finally, he states that it was said that it was the mother of the Caliph al-ʿAziz who ordered the *fawwara* to be rebuilt, under the supervision of Rashid al-Khafifi, who must have been an architect. Maqrizi, however, refers to the architect as Rashid al-Hanafi instead, who must have been the same person. He adds that the work was also supervised by Ibn al-Rumiya and Ibn al-Banna'. See Maqrizi, *Khitat* IV/1, 74.

15 Maqrizi, *Khitat* IV/1, 74.

16 Ibn Duqmaq, *Kitab al-Intisar*, 123; Maqrizi, *al-Khitat wa-l-athar* IV/1, 74. This information is confirmed by K.A.C. Creswell, *Early Muslim Architecture* II (New York: Hacker Art Books, 1979), 334, note 1. However, Creswell mistakenly copies Ibn Duqmaq's date of Jumada 10, 269 ah / 882 ad, instead of Jumada 10, 279 / 892.

17 Maqrizi, *al-Khitat wa-l-athar* IV/1, 15, 17; Swelim, "The Mosque of ʿAmr Ibn al-ʿAs," 285.

18 Nasiri Khusraw, *Safarnama*, trans. and ed. Yahiya Khashshab (Cairo: Matbaʿat Lajnat al-T'alif wa-l-Tarjama wa-l-Nashr 1945), 58.

19 Nasiri Khusraw, *Safarnama*, 58.

20 Nasiri Khusraw, *Safarnama*, 58. Creswell misinterprets the ending of this story by saying that al-Hakim made the descendants of Ibn Tulun repurchase the minaret for 5,000 dinars. This misinterpretation was due to following a mistake made in the translation of Schefer's *Safer nameh* (Paris: E. Leroux, 1881). See Doris Behrens-Abouseif, *The Minarets of Cairo* (Cairo: The American Univeristy in Cairo Press, 1985), 52; Jonathan Bloom, *Minaret: Symbol of Islam* (Oxford: Oxford University Press, 1989), 128, note 12.

21 The story is referred to as "Juha and the Nail" by Jonathan Bloom (*Arts of the City Victorious: Islamic Art and Architecture in Fatimid North Africa and Egypt* (Cairo: The American University in Cairo Press, 2008), 137, while it is referred to as "*mismar Juha*" by Behrens-Abouseif (*The Minarets of Cairo*, 105). Juha, after selling his house, would return everyday to see about all sorts of things that were hanging from a certain nail, in a particular place in that house. When the new owners protested, he told them that they had agreed to sell the house but not the nail.

22 Maqrizi, *Khitat* IV/1, 21; Nasiri Khusraw, *Safer nameh*, trans. Charles Schefer, 148; also in Creswell, *Early Muslim Architecture* II, 172; Swelim, "The Mosque of ʿAmr Ibn al-ʿAs," 288.

23 Tarek Swelim, "The Mosque of Ibn Tulun: New Perspectives," PhD diss. (Harvard University, 1994), 110.

24 Swelim, "The Mosque of ʿAmr Ibn al-ʿAs," 288.

25 Creswell, *Early Muslim Architecture* II, 336; Tarek Swelim, "The Minaret of Ibn Tulun Reconsidered," in *The Cairo Heritage: Essays in Honor of Laila Ali Ibrahim*, edited by Doris Behrens-Abouseif (Cairo and New York: The American University in Cairo, 2000), 81.

26 Maqrizi, *Khitat* II, 556; Ghazi Rajib Muhammad, "The Minaret of Ibn Tulun: Its Construction and Description," *Summer* 23 I/1 and 2 (1967): 87; Bloom, *Minaret*, 129; Swelim, "Minaret of Ibn Tulun," 80.

27 Ghazi Muhammad, "Minaret," 87; Swelim, "Minaret of Ibn Tulun," 81.

28 Jason Thompson, *A History of Egypt* (Cairo: The American University in Cairo Press, 2008), 179.

29 Maqrizi, *Khitat* IV/1, 74.

30 Van Berchem, *Materiaux*, 31.

31 Van Berchem, *Materiaux*, 31; Creswell, *Early Muslim Architecture* II: 336.

32 Maqrizi, *Khitat* IV/1, 74.

33 Swelim, "The Mosque of Ibn Tulun," 112.

34 Swelim, "The Mosque of Ibn Tulun," 112.

35 Van Berchem, *Materiaux*, 31; Swelim, "The Mosque of Ibn Tulun," 112.

36 For further study on the inscription of Badr al-Gammali, see J. den Heijer, "Une inscription fatimide de la mosquée d'Ibn Tulun au Caire. Essai d'interprétation paléographique, philologique et historique," *Comptes-rendus des séances de l'Académie des Inscriptions et Belles-Lettres*, 155e année, Fascicule 2 (April–June 2011): 951–73.

37 According to Van Berchem, *Materiaux*, 32; and referred to in Creswell, *Early Muslim Architecture* II, 336. See also, Swelim, "The Mosque of Ibn Tulun," 112.

38 Swelim, "The Mosque of Ibn Tulun," 113.

39 Van Berchem, *Materiaux*, 33; Wiet, *Répertoire* VIII, 4-5; Swelim, "The Mosque of Ibn Tulun," 113.

40 Van Berchem, *Materiaux*, 33-34. His dating is based on the fact that al-Afdal succeeded his father in the first half of 487 ah / 1094 ad, and that the Caliph al-Mustansir died in Dhu'l-Hijja of the same year. For this *mihrab*, also see Wiet, *Répertoire* VIII, 4-5; Creswell, *Early Muslim Architecture* II, 349. Creswell also gives a thorough description and says that the *mihrab* of al-Afdal is one of the very few that bears an inscription, and that of Sultan Lajin on its opposite side, also bears the same one, see his *Muslim Architecture of Egypt* II, 220-22.

41 For this *mihrab*, see Creswell, *Early Muslim Architecture* II, 346; idem, *Muslim Architecture of Egypt* II, 226; Van Berchem, *Matériaux*, 88; Wiet, *Répertoire* XIII, 154-55; Samuel Flury, *Die Ornamente der Hakim-und Azhar-Moschee* (Heidelberg: C. Winter, 1912), 15-16, Taf. XVI/1.

42 Bloom, *Arts of the City Victorious*, 137

43 Bloom, *Arts of the City Victorious*, 137

44 Bloom, *Arts of the City Victorious*, 139

45 Bernard O'Kane, *The Illustrated Guide to the Museum of Islamic Art in Cairo* (Cairo: The American University in Cairo Press, 2012), inv. no. 3099 (opposite page 83).

46 Stanley Lane-Poole, *A History of Egypt in the Middle Ages* (London: Frank Cass and Co. Ltd, 1968), 164-65.
Bloom, *Arts of the City Victorious*, 137.

Chapter 8

1 Tarek Swelim, "The Mosque of 'Amr Ibn al-'As," *The History and Religious Heritage of Old Cairo: Its Fortress, Churches, Synagogue, and Mosque*, edited by Carolyn Ludwig and Moris Jackson (Cairo: The American University in Cairo Press, 2012), 288.

2 Jason Thompson, *A History of Egypt* (Cairo: The American University in Cairo Press, 2008), 183.

3 Swelim, "The Mosque of Ibn Tulun: A New Perspective," PhD diss., Harvard University, 1994, 118.

4 Ibn Jubayr, *The Travels of Ibn Jubayr*, trans. and ed. by R.J.C. Broadhurst (London: J. Cape, 1952), 44.

5 Tarek Swelim, "The Minaret of Ibn Tulun Reconsidered," in *The Cairo Heritage: Essays in Honor of Laila Ali Ibrahim*, ed. Doris Behrens-Abouseif (Cairo and New York: The American University in Cairo, 2000), 80.

6 Taqi al-Din Ahmad al-Maqrizi, *al-Mawa'iz w-al-'itibar fi dhikr al-khitat wa-l-athar* IV/1, ed. Ayman Fu'ad Sayyid (London: Mu'assasat al-Furqan lil-Turath al-Islami, 2002), 74. One must not understand the text of Maqrizi to mean that the Maghribis were using the mosque during the Fatimid period, even if the text seems to say so. It is known that sometimes Maqrizi's text is confusing and disorganized.

7 This usage is discussed by Swelim, "The Mosque of Ibn Tulun," 115-18.

8 Ibn Jubayr, *Travels*, 44.

9 Ibn Jubayr, *Travels*, 199; Ibn Jubayr, *Rihlat Ibn Jubayr* (Beirut: Dār Ṣadir lil-Ṭibā'ah wa-al-Nashr, 1959), 26-27.

10 Swelim, "The Mosque of Ibn Tulun," 116-18.

11 Swelim, "The Minaret of Ibn Tulun," 85.

12 Swelim, "The Minaret of Ibn Tulun," 85.

13 Swelim, "The Minaret of Ibn Tulun," 87.

14 Farid Shafi'i, "Ma'dhanat masjid Ibn Tulun: ra'i fi takwiniha al-mi'mari," *Majallat kulliyat al-adab* IV (1952): 177; Ghazi Rajib Muhammad, "The Minaret of Ibn Tulun: Its Construction and Description," *Summer* 23 I/1 and 2 (1967): 88. This feature is found in the mosque of Cordova, 346 ah / 958 ad, and because of that it is considered that the Ummayads used them in al-Andalus. But owing to the continuous wars and troubles, it seems that these elements were carried elsewhere to other Spanish cities and to Morocco. See also George Marcais, *L'Architecture Musulmane d'Occident* (Paris: Arts et métiers graphiques, 1954), 165. Such an element was also used at St. Milan at Segovi in 1057; Swelim, "The Minaret of Ibn Tulun," 83.

15 Maqrizi, *Khitat* IV/1, 72; also mentioned in Swelim, "The Minaret of Ibn Tulun," 80.

16 Swelim, "The Minaret of Ibn Tulun," 85.

Chapter 9

1 Sultan Baybars also built the Madrasa al-Zahiriya in Damascus, which incorporated his mausoleum where he was buried, close to the Great Ummayad Mosque, as well as the tomb of Salah al-Din.

2 This *madrasa* only has a wall remaining, as the entire building was demolished in the nineteenth century to build the street of Bayt al-Qadi.

3 Taqi al-Din Ahmad al-Maqrizi, *Kitab al-suluk fi ma'rifat duwwal al-muluk* I/II, ed. Mustafa Ziyada (Cairo: Matba'at Lajnat al-Ta'lif, 1956), 58; cited by K.A.C. Creswell, *Early Muslim Architecture* II (New York: Hacker Art Books, 1979), 337.

4 Maqrizi, *Kitab al-suluk* I, 1/3: 827; translated by Eustace Corbet in "The Life and Works of Ahmad Ibn Tulun," *Journal of the Royal Asiatic Society* (1891): 251; repeated by Creswell, *Muslim Architecture of Egypt* II (New York: Hacker Art Books, 1978), 223.

5 Maqrizi, *Kitab al-suluk* I, 1/3, 827.

6 Sarim al-Din Ibrahim Ibn Muhammad Ibn Aydumur al-'Ala'i al-Misri Ibn Duqmaq, *Kitab al-intisar li-wasitat 'aqd al-Amsar*, ed. K. Vollers (Beirut: Markaz al-Mawsu'at al-'Alamiya, 1893), 124.

7 Maqrizi, *Kitab al-suluk* I, 1/3: 827; and omitted in his *Khitat* IV/1, 77

8 Maqrizi, *Kitab al-suluk* I, 508.

9 Ibn Duqmaq, *Kitab al-intisar*, 124.

10 Ibn Duqmaq, *Kitab al-intisar*, 124; Maqrizi, *Kitab al-suluk* I, 1/3, 827.

11 Maqrizi, *Kitab al-suluk* I, 1/3:827, while omitted in his *Khitat* IV/1, 78

12 The roosters are only mentioned by Ibn Duqmaq, *Kitab al-intisar*, 124, and not by Maqrizi; they are omitted by Creswell. Moreover, it is not recorded in the *waqfiya* of Sultan Lajin.

13 Ibn Duqmaq, *Kitab al-intisar*, 124.

14 Maqrizi, *Khitat* IV/1, 78.

15 Maqrizi, *Khitat* IV/1, 76.

16 Maqrizi, *Khitat* IV/1, 78.

17 Maqrizi, *Khitat* IV/1, 78.

18 Maqrizi does not specifically mention Dar al-Imara, but that there were ruined buildings in the area behind the mosque, see *Khitat* IV/1, 78

19 Maqrizi, *Khitat* IV/1, 78.

20 Maqrizi, *Khitat* IV/1, 78.

21 Creswell, *Early Muslim Architecture* II, 346.

22 Creswell, *Early Muslim Architecture* II, 346.

23 Abu Muhammad 'Abd Allah Ibn Muhammad al-Madini al-Balawi, *Sirat Ahmad Ibn Tulun*, ed. Muhammad Kurd 'Ali (Damascus: al-Maktaba al-'Arabiya fi Dimashq, 1939), 183; reported by Maqrizi (*Khitat* I, 313), where he actually confirms that the door was part of the mosque, which would lead one to deduce that he meant the *qibla* wall. Also see, Maqrizi, *Khitat* IV/1, 80.

24 'Ali Basha Mubarak, *al-Khitat al-jadida al-tawfiqiya li-Misr wa-l-Qahira* II, new edition (Cairo: al-Hay'a al-Misriya al-'Amma li-l-Kitab, 1982), 100; also A.F. Mehren, *Câhirah og Kerafât, historiske studier under et ophold i Aegypten* (Copenhagen: J.H. Schultz, 1869–70), 50.

25 Creswell, *Muslim Architecture of Egypt* II, 227.

26 This is according to Bernard O'Kane, who kindly offered this piece of information. See B. Brentjes, "Zu Einigen Samanischen und Nachsamanidischen Holzbildwerken des Seravscantales im Western Tadshikistans," *Central Asiatic Journal* 15 (1971): 295–97, plates 5, 7, and 8.

27 *Hujat Waqf al-Sultan Husam al-Din Lajin*, Dar al-Watha'iq wa-l-Mahfudhat (no. 18), 18: 6 and 7.

28 The *waqfiya* of Sultan Lajin, 25: 7 and 8.

29 Another edition of the *waqfiya* of Sultan Lajin (no. 17), 2: 13 and 16.

30 An example of this is at the Mosque of Sultan al-Mu'ayyad Sheikh (818–23 ah / 1415–20 ad) (index no. 190). For this, see Tarek Swelim, "The Complex of Sultan al-Mu'ayyad Sheikh at Bab Zuwayla," Master's thesis, The American University in Cairo, 1986, 129–30.

31 As stated above, see note *124 of chapter 6; Swelim, "The Mosque of Ibn Tulun," 131.

32 Van Berchem, *Matériaux*, 37; Wiet, *Répertoire* XIII, 156 (no. 5022); Mahmud 'Akkush, *Tarikh wa wasf al-jami' al-tuluni* (Cairo: Dar al-Kutub al-Misriya, 1927), 86; translated by Creswell, *Muslim Architecture of Egypt* II, 225. It is worth mentioning that Yusuf Ahmad does not provide the correct Arabic text of this inscription; consequently, Creswell refers to him by mistake (*cf.* Yusuf Ahmad, *al-Khatt al-kufi*, (Cairo: Matba'at Hijazi, 1939), 33, and Creswell, *Muslim Architecture of Egypt* II, 225, note 3). In addition, before this inscription was properly read, the builder of this edifice was not known. Creswell argued that the edifice must have the work of Sultan Lajin on the grounds that the original *fawwara* of the mosque was burnt and then replaced during the Fatimid period in 385 ah / 995 ad. Creswell has no doubt

that it had fallen into ruins by 696 ah / 1296 ad, when Lajin was living in the mosque, and that he must have erected this one instead. His argument is based on the fact that this edifice bears Naskhi inscriptions, and that this type of script did not appear in Egypt before Salah al-Din. Moreover, since the earlier work in the mosque had taken place during the Fatimid period, the surviving building must have been built during the time of Sultan Lajin (*Muslim Architecture of Egypt* II, 333–34, 350). However, Van Berchem could not read this much-worn inscription because of its height (Van Berchem, *Matériaux*, 37; Corbet, "Life and Works," 544), but according to Creswell (*Muslim Architecture of Egypt* II, 225), he mentions that the inscription is published by Yusuf Ahmad. However, Ahmad only describes the edifice and does not offer this inscription. He was able to read it as saying "has ordered the restoration of this mosque our lord the Sultan al-Malik al-Mansur Husam al-Duniya wa-l-Din Lajin" (*al-Khatt*, 33).

33 Described by Creswell, *Muslim Architecture of Egypt* II, 224–25.

34 Jean Joseph Marcel, "Inscriptions, monnaies et médailles," in *Description de l'Égypte*, 2nd ed., vol. II, *Planches, État Moderne* (Paris: Panckoucke, 1817), plate C (2). The sundial is also studied by David King and L. Janin, "Le Cadran Solaire de la Mosquee d'Ibn Tulun au Caire," *Journal for the History of Arabic Science* 2 (1978): 331–51; and David King, *Islamic Astronomical Instruments* (London: Variorum, Aldershot, 1982), XVI. No information is provided in L.A. Mayer, *Islamic Astrolabists and their Works* (Geneva: A. Kundig, 1956).

35 The study by King (*Islamic Astronomical Instruments*) deals with the technical and scientific aspects of the sundial, but does not deal with its relation to the building or the mosque of Ibn Tulun.

36 *Hujat Waqf al-Sultan Husan al-Din Lajin, Dar al-Watha'iq wa-l-Mahfudhat*, documents no. 17/3 and 18/3, according to Muhammad Amin, *Fihrist watha'iq al-Qahira hatta nihayat 'asr al-salatin al-Mamalik*, Catalogue des documents d'archives du Caire (Cairo: Institut Français d'Archéologie Orientale du Caire, 1981), 7.

37 Francis Bedford, *Cities, Sights, and Citadels of the Near East: Francis Bedford's Nineteenth-Century Photographs of Egypt, the Levant, and Constantinople* (Cairo: The American University in Cairo Press, published by arrangement with the RCT, 2014).

38 Protain, "Le Kaire," *Description de l'Égypte*, 2nd ed., vol. I, *Planches, État Moderne* (Paris: Panchoucke, 1822), plate 30/6; Pascal Coste, *Architecture arabe ou monuments du Kaire* (Paris: Firmin Didot Freres, 1839) plate IV/1; 'Akkush, *Tarikh wa wasf*, plate 3; Ministry of Awqaf, *The Mosques of Egypt*, vol. 1, (Giza: Survey of Egypt, 1949), plate 15; and Creswell, *Early Muslim Architecture* II, 342, figs. 246 and 347.

39 Creswell states that the lower inscription is of *sura* V/6, but the latter is inscribed in the other inscription at the top of the dome. However, he indicates the latter as of *sura* IV, but does not identify the *aya*.

40 For a good photo of the squinches of Salar and Sangar, see Doris Behrens-Abouseif, *Cairo of the Mamluks: A History of the Architecture and its Culture* (Cairo: The American University in Cairo Press, 2007), 159, fig. 104.

41 In that respect, the elevations of Protain (*Description de l'Égypte*, plate 30/6) depict water springing out of the fountain. However, it is unlikely that this fountain was functioning during the time of his visit between 1798 and 1801.

42 According to Creswell (*Muslim Architecture of Egypt* II, 226), Herz argues that the building was used for banquets like those found in the mosque of al-Mu'ayyad and Sultan Barquq. He says there is express mention of a *mayda'a* and a fountain in the middle of the *sahn* and that later, with the advent of the Turks, it became a habit for mosques to have both a *mayad'a* and a fountain. But Creswell does not agree with this, he notes instead the existence of the verse from the Qur'an of *Ayat al-Wudu'* (verse of the ablutions), carved in stucco in the dome of the building and also in the center at the apex of the dome, giving instructions for ablutions. He concludes by stating that, "It is difficult to believe, in spite of Herz's thesis, that the building we have described was not originally intended for ablution." Creswell's study was made before the endowment deed (*waqfiya*) of Sultan Lajin was

investigated. The *waqfiya* states that the *fisqiya* under the dome *(qubba)*, in the middle of the *sahn*, was intended for ablutions *(al-wudu')*.

43 Creswell, *Muslim Architecture of Egypt* II, 226: on the basis that the *shahada* formula given in the Naskhi inscriptions of glass mosaics cannot be earlier than the time of Salah al-Din, who introduced this calligraphic style to Egypt. If it were earlier (that is, Fatimid), then it would have ended by saying: "Ali Wali Allah," but it does not. Also, the marble paneling on the lower part cannot be earlier than 1250, since it first appeared in Egypt in the mausoleum of Salih Nagm al-Din Ayyub (641-48 ah / 1243-50 ad).

44 The other mosaic *mihrab*s are the mausoleum of Queen Shagaret al-Durr (648 ah / 1250 ad); the *madrasa*-mosque of Sultan Qalawun (683-84 ah / 1284-85 ad); the *madrasa* Taibarsiya/al-Azhar Mosque (709 ah / 1309-1310 ad) and the *madrasa* Aqbughawiya (740 ah / 1340 ad).

45 In 1888, Lane-Poole recognized that this wooden dome and the squinches were later than the mosque. Creswell attributes the dome to Sultan Lajin, see *Early Muslim Architecture* II, 348; *Muslim Architecture of Egypt* II, 226-27.

46 Such domes are found in the mosques of al-Zahir Baybars (665-667 ah / 1266-1269 ad), al-Nasir Muhammad at the Citadel (735 ah / 1335 ad), Maridani (739-40 ah / 1339-40 ad), and the mosque of Aqsunqur. We later find it in the *khanqa* of Farag Ibn Barquq, but on a much smaller scale.

47 For this *mihrab*, see Creswell, *Early Muslim Architecture* II, 346; *Muslim Architecture of Egypt* II, 226; Van Berchem, *Matériaux Pour un Corpus Inscriptionum Arabicarum*, Égypte, 88; Gaston Wiet *Répertoire Chrnologique d'Epigraphie Arabe* XIII, (Cairo: IFAO, 1931), 154-55; Samuel Flury, *Die Ornamente der Hakim-und Azhar-Moschee* (Heidelberg: C. Winter, 1903), 15-16, Taf. XVI/1.

48 Creswell, *Early Muslim Architecture* II, 350. Corbet believes that it is either the work of Sultan al-Nasir Muhammad or Sultan Lajin. See Corbet, "Life and Works," 552-53; Swelim, "The Mosque of Ibn Tulun," 124.

49 For the *minbar*, see A.F. Mehren, *Câhirah og Kerafât,* 49; Mubarak, *al-Khitat al-jadida* IV, 48; Van Berchem, *Matériaux*, première partie, 36.

50 Creswell, *Early Muslim Architecture* II, 337.

51 Yusuf Effendi Ahmad, *Jami' Ahmad Ibn Tulun* (Cairo: Matba'at al-Taraqi, 1917), 21

52 Gloria Sergine Ohan Karnouk, "Cairene Bahari Mamluk Minbars, with a Provincial Typology and Catalogue," Master's thesis, The American University in Cairo, May 1977, 47-61.

53 Karnouk, "Cairene Bahari Mamluk Minbars," 47-57.

54 It was logical for Patricolo to conduct his test on the southwestern side of the minaret and not on the opposite (northernwestern) side, as the workers would have been able to climb on top of the building added in the Ottoman period known as the *zawiya* and tomb of Sheikh al-Madini (or Sheikh al-Bushi). See Tarek Swelim, "The Minaret of Ibn Tulun," 83, note 20.

55 Behrens-Abouseif, *The Minarets of Cairo*, 104; Swelim, "The Minaret of Ibn Tulun," 83.

56 For a good photo of the minaret of Sunqur Sa'di, see Behrens-Abouseif, *Cairo of the Mamluks*, 167, fig. 111.

57 Maqrizi, *Khitat* IV/1, 79

58 Mubarak, *al-Khitat al-jadida*, 101.

59 For Pascal Coste's elevation of the mosque showing the minaret of Qadi Karim al-Din, see plate IV/1 of *Architecture*. However, it is not indicated in his plan of the mosque, see plate III of *Architecture*. Similarly, these minarets are not indicated in the plans of Protain in *Description de l'Égypte* I, Plate 30, nor in that of Prisse d'Avennes, *L'Art arabe d'après les monuments du Kaire depuis le VIIe siècle jusqu'à a la fin du XVIIIe*, (Paris: A. Morel, 1869-77), plate IV, opposite p. 94.

60 The ground plan of Herz Bey locates the minaret on the eastern corner of the *ziyada* of the mosque, where it was actually located in the eastern corner of the mosque proper and *qibla* wall, as indicated in figure 106. See Comité *de Conservation des Monuments de l'Art Arabe, Exercices* (1890), plate 1.

61 References to the old photos of the minaret of Qadi Karim al-Din are as follows: figure 80 (Creswell Collection A8, plate 48B); figure 81 (Creswell Photo Collection A9, plate 40D); figure 82 (Creswell Photo Collection A8, plate 47B); figure 83 (Creswell Photo Collection A9, plate 1). Another good photo is seen in Doris Behrens-Abouseif, *The*

Minarets of Cairo (Cairo: The American University in Cairo Press, 2007), p. 105, fig. 162.

62 Comité, *Exercices 1933-35* (1940), 47 and 111.

63 Stanley Lane-Poole, *The Art of the Saracens in Egypt* (London: Chapman and Hall, 1886), 55.

64 Pascal Sebah, *Egypt* (Rome: L. Olivieri, n.d.).

65 An early illustration by George Moritz Ebers (*Egypt: Descriptive, Historical and Picturesque,* vol. 1, trans. Clara Bell (London: Cassell, Petter and Galpur, 1881-82), 213, shows the state of the *qibla riwaq* without a ceiling before 1881, but does not show the southern minaret. It is illustrated by Lane-Poole, *The Art of the Saracens*, 55. Note that my previous dating on those illustrations are incorrect, see Tarek Swelim, "The Mosque of Ibn Tulun," PhD thesis, Harvard University, 1994, figures 86 and 87.

66 Maqrizi (*Khitat* II, 269) also provides a brief biography of this man and says that he died on Saturday, Safar 14, 793 ah / 1391 ad; Creswell, *Early Muslim Architecture* II, 337.

67 Robert Williams, "The Mosque of Ibn Tulun," *The Muslim World* VIII/3 (July 1981): 234.

68 Yusuf Ahmad, *al-Khatt al-kufi*, 45 and figure 10; 'Akkush, *Tarikh wa wasf*, 99 and figure II.

69 Swelim, "The Mosque of Ibn Tulun," 137-38.

70 Maqrizi, *Suluk* I, 827; his *Khitat* II, 268.

71 Shams al-Din al-Sakhawi, *al-Daw' al-lami' li-ahl al-qarn al-tasi'* III (Cairo: Manshurat Dar Maktabat al-Hayat, 1966), 231.

72 Corbet, "Life and Works," 552.

73 Corbet, "Life and Works," 552, note 1.

Chapter 10

1 Mubarak. *al-Khitat al-jadida al-tawfiqiya li-Misr wa-l-Qahira*, new edition, vol. II (Cairo: al-Hay'a al-Misriya al-'Amma li-l-Kitab, 1982), 309.

2 Yusuf Effendi Ahmad, *Jami' Ahmad Ibn Tulun* (Cairo: Matba'at al-Taraqi, 1917), 45.

3 Yusuf Effendi Ahmad, *Jami' Ahmad Ibn Tulun*, 45; this inscription is published by Van Berchem, *Matériaux pour un Corpus Inscriptionum Arabicarum* (Cairo: IFAO, 1894-1903) 37-38, and is mentioned by Mahmud 'Akkush, *Tarikh wa wasf al-jami' al-tuluni* (Cairo: Matba'at Dar al-Kutub al-Misriya, 1927), 100.

4 Robert Williams, "The Mosque of Ibn Tulun," *The Muslim World* VIII/3 (July 1981): 232

5 Jean-Constantin Protain, "Le Kaire," in *Description de l'Égypte*, 2nd ed., vol. I, *Planches, État Moderne* (Paris: Pancoucke, 1822), plate 29. It is strange that it is not shown on his ground plan, plate 30 (a); Robert Hay, *Illustrations of Cairo* (London: Tilt and Bogue, 1804), plate 5.

6 Williams, "The Mosque of Ibn Tulun," 232.

7 This is also confirmed in Dorothea Russel (*Medieval Cairo and the Monasteries of Wadi Nutrun: A Historical Guide* (London: Weidenfeld and Nicolson, 1962), 123), who found in the wooden roofing of the tomb about a dozen planks of that inscription, some of them used upside down.

8 Williams, "The Mosque of Ibn Tulun," 232.

9 'Akkush, *Tarikh wa wasf*, 28-29, figure 2; Yusuf Effendi Ahmad, *Jami' Ahmad Ibn Tulun*, plate 10, shows a plan of the mosque before the mosque's restoration. It is strange that Creswell ignores the above-mentioned studies and does not cite the study of Robert Williams in his long bibliography (see Creswell, *Early Muslim Architecture* II, 356-59). Consequently, this building is not included in his section on the "Later History of the Mosque," 336-37.

10 Figure 88 (Creswell Photo Collection A 9, plate 41 B); figure 89 (Creswell Photo Collection A 9, plate 41 B); figure 90 (Creswell Photo Collection A 9, plate 41 D).

11 Hasan 'Abd al-Wahhab, *Tarikh al-masajid al-athariya allati sulla fiha faridat al-jum'a al-aalih Faruq al-awwal* I (Cairo: Matba'at Dar al-Kutub al-Misriya, 1946), 45.

12 Mubarak, *al-Khitat al-jadida*, 309.

13 'Abd al-Rahman al-Jabarti, *'Aja'ib al-athar fi-l-tarajim wa-l-akhbar* I (Beirut: Dar al-Gil, n.d.), 408-85.

Chapter 11

1 'Abd al-Rahman al-Jabarti, *'Aja'ib al-athar fi-l-tarajim wa-l-akhbar* I (Beirut: Dar al-Gil, n.d.), 211; Eustace Corbet ("The Life And Works of Ahmad Ibn Tulun," *Journal of the Royal Asiatic Society* (1891): 539 dates this earthquake to Sunday, June 8, 1814.

2 al-Jabarti, *Aja'ib al-athar* I, 211.

3 Karl Baedeker, *Handbook to Lower Egypt*, German edition (Leipsic: Karl Baedeker Publisher, 1877), 286; also quoted by Corbet "The Life and Works," 539; and K.A.C. Creswell, *Muslim Architecture of Egypt* II (New York: Hacker Art Books, 1978), 338.

4 Confirmed by A.A. Paton, *A History of The Egyptian Revolution* II (London: Trubner, 1870), 322–23; also quoted by Corbet, "Life and Works," 554; and K.A.C. Creswell, *Early Muslim Architecture* II (New York: Hacker Art Books, 1979, 338.

5 Confirmed by Paton, *The Egyptian Revolution* II, 322–23; also quoted by Corbet, "Life and Works," 554; and Creswell, *Early Muslim Architecture* II, 338.

6 Arthur Rhoné, *L'Égypte à petites journées: Le Caire d'autrefois* (Paris: Société Générale d'Edition, 1910), 444; after Istvan Ormos, *Max Herz Pasha 1856–1919: His Life and Career* I, Études Urbaines 6/1 (Cairo: IFAO, 2009), 200.

7 Abd al-Hamid Nafi', *Dhayl khitat al-Maqrizi*, ed. Khalid Azab and Muhammad al-Sayyed Hamdi al-Mitwalli (Cairo: Maktabat al-Dar al-Arabiyah lil-Kitab, 2006), 73, mentions a "*fabrica li-l-haddadin*" (factory for ironsmiths); after Ormos, *Max Herz Pasha*, 200.

8 Prisse d'Avennes, *L'Art arabe d'après les monuments du Caire depuis le VIIe siècle jusqu'à la fin du XVIIIe I* (Paris: A. Morel, 1869–1877), 96–98; also confirmed by Corbet, "Life and Works," 554. In addition, Creswell believes that decision to add the walls must have been taken around 1842 (*Early Muslim Architecture* II, 338). He believes that the work did not begin immediately, as the traveler Ampere said nothing about it when he had visited the mosque in 1841. Creswell adds that in 1849, Spencer visited the mosque and says that the colonnades had been converted into houses of two sides by order of the government. Creswell adds that during the same year (1849), Pardieu wrote: "Cette mosquée abandonée est toute delabrée et sert de magazins. Ou meme mure une partie des arcades, pour former les galleries" (Pardieu, *Excursion en Orient, le Mont Sinai, l'Arabie, la Palestine, le Syrie, le Liban* (Paris: Garnier, 1851), 47; Creswell therefore concludes that the walling up of the arcades must have begun sometime between 1846 and 1849. The walling-up of the arcades is best indicated in a plan by Yusuf Effendi Ahmad, *Jami' Ahmad Ibn Tulun* (Cairo: Matba'at al-Taraqi, 1917), 56, Plate 10, and another by A. Gayet, *L'Art Arabe* (Paris: Libraries-Imprimeris Reunies, 1893), 49, figure 11. It is worth noting that the latter is more of a sketch than a plan of the mosque, as it does not have a scale.

9 Confirmed by Paton, *The Egyptian Revolution* II, 322–23; also quoted by Corbet, "Life and Works," 554; and Creswell, *Early Muslim Architecture* II, 338.

10 D'Avennes, *L'Art arabe*, 98.

11 Corbet, "Life and Works," 554. He adds that the western part of the northwestern *riwaq*, suffered to the point that this area had to be supported by filling up the arches, sometime during the reign of Muhammad 'Ali Pasha (1220–65 ah / 1805–48 ad). Corbet, "Life and Works," 539.

12 For this interesting perspective see: Mine Ener, *Managing Egypt's Poor and the Politics of Benevolence, 1800–1952*, (Princeton: Priceton University Press, 2003), 50. Thanks to Dr. Khaled Fahmy who drew my attention to this source.

13 For the Egyptian heritage and how the various governments of Egypt perceived it, I would like to thank Hind Mostafa Nabil for her valuable discussions and hours spent on the subject.

14 Supreme Council of Antiquities official website, www.sca-egypt.org.

15 By the mid-nineteenth century, the Ezbekiya collection was so small that it could be housed in a single room at the Citadel (Supreme Council of Antiquities website, www.sca-egypt.org).

16 James Laird Patterson, *Journal in a Tour in Egypt, Palestine, Syria and Greece* (London: C. Dolman, 1852), 170; quoted by Creswell, *Early Muslim Architecture* II, 338.

17 According to the official website of the Supreme Council of Antiquities (www.sca-egypt.org), 'Abbas Hilmi I offered this gift in the year 1855, when it could not have happened during that year as 'Abbas Hilmi I died in 1854. One may assume that either the date is incorrect, or that 'Abbas Hilmi never offered that gift, but rather his successor did.

18 William Nassau Senior, *Conservations and Journals in Egypt and Malta, Sampson Low, 1882* II (London: S. Low, Marston, Searle & Rivington, 1882), 135; quoted by Creswell, *Early Muslim Architecture* II, 338.

19 An old sycamore tree, but no palm trees can be seen in a photograph by Francis Bedford,

Cities, Sights, and Citadels of the Near East: Francis Bedford's Nineteenth-Century Photographs of Egypt, the Levant, and Constantinople (The American University in Cairo Press, published by arrangement with the RCT, 2014); Nassau Senior saw them and wrote about them in his letter dated February 24, 1856 (Nassau Senior, *Conservations and Journals*, 135); also quoted by Corbet, "Life and Works," 554, note. 4. The palm trees can be seen in Protain's illustration in *Description de l'Égypte, Volume I: Planches, État Moderne*, plate 30, which the Comité had removed later on.

20 Francis Bedford, *Cities, Sights, and Citadels of the Near East: Francis Bedford's Nineteenth-Century Photographs of Egypt, the Levant, and Constantinople*, Cairo: The American University in Cairo Press, 2014). Photograph taken on March, 24, 1862. (photograph courtesy of Royal Collection Trust© Her Majesty Queen Elizabeth II, 2014).

21 Recorded by Erner, *Managing Egypt's Poor*, 51.

22 Erner, *Managing Egypt's Poor*, 51.

23 Erner, *Managing Egypt's Poor*, 51.

24 D'Avennes, *L'Art arabe* I, plate II.

25 Baedker, *Handbook to Lower Egypt*, 286; quoted by Corbet, "Life and Works," 539, and Creswell, *Early Muslim Architecture* II, 338 and shown in his plan.

26 Islamic Art Network website, www.islamic-art.org.

27 Islamic Art Network website, www.islamic-art.org.

28 According to Creswell, *Early Muslim Architecture* II, 338.

29 Arthur Rhoné, *Coup d'œil sur l'état du Caire ancien et moderne* II (Paris: A. Quantin, 1882), 67; after Ormos, *Max Herz Pasha*, 200.

30 Stanley Lane-Poole, *Cairo: Sketches of Its History, Monuments and Social Life* (London: J.S. Virtue, 1895), 22–24; after Ormos, *Max Herz Pasha*, 200.

31 *Mubarak, *al-Khitat wa-l-athar* II, 309; IV, 101; translated after Ormos, *Max Herz Pasha*, 200.

32 Comité, *Exercices 1890* (1890), 40. The report then lists an evaluation of the restoration expenses and shows that the work required in order to revive it to its original state was estimated at a cost of LE 2,000. The work included the following elements: 1) the removal of the buildings around the mosque and cleaning, clearing the *sahn*, and the rubble; 2) the repair of the dome above the area of the *mihrab* and *minbar*; 3) consolidating the original structure of the mosque; 4) the addition of a new ceiling and preserving parts of the old one; 5) repainting the building; 6) consolidating the crenellations; 7) the restoration of the spiral-shaped minaret and its stairs; 8) the repair of the stucco grilles; 9) the restoration of the *minbar* by the School of Arts and Crafts of Bulaq; 42–43.

33 Ormos, *Max Herz Pasha*, 200.

34 Comité, *Exercices 1890*, 83; also reported by 'Akkush, *Tarikh wa wasf*, 102.

35 Comité, *Exercices 1891* (1891), 27, 64–65.

36 Louis Hautecœur and Gaston Wiet, *Les Mosquee du Caire* I (Paris: E. Leroux, 1932), 216; Edmond Pauty, *La Mosquée d'Ibn Toulun et ses alentours*, Promenade Archaeologique (Cairo: n.p., 1936), 54–55; also mentioned by Ormos, *Max Herz Pasha*, 200.

37 Ormos, *Max Herz Pasha*, 200.

38 Corbet, "Life and Works," 555.

39 Comité, *Exercices* 1892 (1892), 98. The *fisqiya* is actually referred to as the *fawwara* in the report. However, I prefer to use its original name *fisqiya* instead, following its title in the accompanying inscription.

40 Ormos, *Max Herz Pasha*, 201. The map is also signed by Barois and Grand Bey (Ormos, *Max Herz Pasha*, note 372)

41 Comité, *Exercices 1894* (1908), 36, 41, 67. The report also mentions that the ground plan of Herz Bey was checked and examined by the Diwan al-Awqaf to see its accuracy regarding property and land ownership for the area around the mosque. See also 'Akkush, *Tarikh wa wasf*, 103.

42 Comité, *Exercices* (1909), 35. Another report says that the same year, an explosion in store rooms of the citadel caused some of the stucco windows which were being prepared there to fall off (see Comité, *Exercices*, 1902), also mentioned by 'Akkush (*Tarikh wa wasf*, 104). The explosion occurred on November 18, 1909 and the damage cost of those windowpanes was 14 Egyptian pounds and 282 milliemes. These were intended for the windows above the main *mihrab*, all of which was paid for by the authorities and repairs were undertaken in due course. See also Ormos, *Max Herz Pasha*, 201, note 372.

43 Comité, *Exercices 1907* (1908), 120-21. This minaret is wrongly placed in Herz Pasha's ground plan.

44 For this see Ormos, *Max Herz Pasha*, 201. He gives the specific day when that investigation took place being March 4, 1900. However, the latter only refers to the archives of the Supreme Council of Antiquities, but does not refer to a specific publication.

45 Comité, *Exercices* 1908 (1909), 29 and 35; the wooden shelter—but not the copy of the Fatimid *mihrab*—is mentioned by 'Akkush, *Tarikh wa wasf*, 105.

46 Hautecœur and Wiet, *Les Mosquée du Caire* I, 216; Pauty, *La Mosquée d'Ibn Toulon*, 54-55; also mentioned by Ormos, *Max Herz Pasha*, 200.

47 Comité, *Exercices 1909* (1910), 22-25.

48 Comité, *Exercices 1914* (1916), 77-78 and 130.

49 Comité, *Comptes Rendus des Exercices 1915-19* (1922), 36. As a result of his examination, Robert Williams published two articles: "The Kibla or Prayer Niche in the Mosque of Ahmad Ibn Touloun, Cairo," *The Architect and Contract Reporter* (July 3, 1914): 7-9; "The Mosque of Ibn Tulun," *The Moslem World* VIII/3 (July 1918): 221-35. (The latter does not record the inscriptions.)

50 Comité, *Comptes Rendus des Exercices 1915-19* (1922), 389, 643.

51 Comité, *Comptes Rendus des Exercices 1915-19* (1922), 638.

52 'Akkush, *Tarikh wa wasf*, 107-108.

53 Comité, *Comptes Rendus des Exercices 1915-19* (1922), 624, 638

54 Comité, *Exercices 1920-24*, (1928), 16.

55 Comité, *Exercices 1920-24* (1928), 55.

56 Comité, *Exercices 1920-24* (1928), 344-45. It is worth noting that the same sad condition still existed in the mosque of Ibn Tulun in the early 1990s. See Swelim, "The Mosque of Ibn Tulun: A New Perspective," PhD. diss., Harvard University, 1994, 161-62.

57 'Akkush, *Tarikh wa wasf*, 107-108.

58 Comité, *Exercices 1927-29* (1934), 104-105. Strangely, it was decided that the tiles made in Marseille (France) were much better than those made in the Egyptian town of Ma'sara. See Swelim, "The Mosque of Ibn Tulun," 166.

59 Comité, *Exercices 1927-29* (1934), 3-4.

60 Comité, *Exercices 1927-29* (1934), 195-96. For the missing arcade facing the *sahn*, see the ground plan of Creswell.

61 Comité, *Exercices 1930-32* (1936), 75. The intention was to publish these six pieces in the museum Catalogue of new acquisitions, but were not, and instead they were published by Jean David-Weill, in *Les bois à épigraphes jusqu'à l'époque Mamlouke*, Catalogue général du Musée Arabe du Caire (Cairo: IFAO, 1931), 2021, no. 622, 623, 624, 625, 627, and plate III.

62 I am using this description as an homage to the late Dr. George T. Scanlon, who always described the mosque of Maridani as such.

63 Comité, *Exercices 1933-35* (1940), 47, 96-97.

64 It was being removed in March 1934, see Comité, *Exercices 1933-35* (1940), 47, 111.

65 Islamic Art Network website, www.islamic-art.org.

66 Comité, *Exercices 1936-40* (1944), 146-47; *Exercices 1946-1953* (1961), 40-41.

67 Comité, *Exercices 1946-1953* (1961), 40-41; *Exercices 1941-45* (1951), 64. The trees are indicated in the plan of the Ministry of Awqaf, *The Mosques of Cairo* I (Giza: Survey of Egypt, 1947), 15; a published photo is in Ahmad Fikri, *Masajid al-Qahira wa madarisuha* (Cairo: Dar al-Ma'arif), plate 55.

68 Comité, *Exercices 1941-45* (1951), 64, 209, 279.

69 Comité, *Exercices 1941-45* (1951), 208-209, 244.

70 Comité, *Exercices 1941-45* (1951), 250.

71 These blocked windows could still be seen in 1993, before the resotrations of 2000. A good photograph is in Swelim, "The Mosque of Ibn Tulun," fig. 128.

72 Comité, *Exercices 1946-53* (1961), 126.

73 Hasan 'Abd al-Wahhab, *Tarikh al-masajid al-athariya allati sulla fiha faridat al-jum'a al-salih Faruq al-awwal*, 2 vols. (Cairo: Matba'at Dar al-Kutub al-Misriya, 1946).

74 Comité, *Exercices 1946-53* (1961), 192.

75 Pascal Coste, *Architecture arabe ou monuments du Kaire* (Paris: Firmin Didot Freres, 1839), plate III.

76 Comité, *Exercices 1946-53* (1961), 196

77 Comité, *Exercices 1946-53* (1961), 280.

CHAPTER 12

1 Comité, *Exercices 1946-53* (1961), 327.

2 Islamic Art Network website, www.islamic-art.org. However, the Comité existed from 1882 until 1953. See Philipp Speiser, "The History of Preserving Historic Islamic Monuments 1881-1975," in *A Future for the Past: Restorations in Islamic Cairo 1973-2004*, ed. Wolfgang Mayer and Philipp Speiser, with contributions by Nairy Hampikian, Sylvie Denoix, Nelly Hanna, May Al-Ibrashy, and Giorgio Nogara (Mainz: Verlag Philipp Von Zabern, 2007), 38.

3 Verbal communication with Dr. Khaled Azab, 2014.

4 Wolfgang Mayer, "The History of Preserving Historic Islamic Monuments 1976-2006," in *A Future for the Past: Restorations in Islamic Cairo 1973-2004*, edited by Wolfgang Mayer et al. (Mainz: Verlag Philipp Von Zabern, 2007), 42-43.

5 For the restoration of the complex of Amir Qurqumas, see Jaroslav Dobrolowski, "A Polish-Egyptian Restoration Project at the Eastern Cemetery in Cairo," in *The Restoration and Conservation of Islamic Monuments in Egypt*, ed.ited by Jere Bacharach (Cairo: The American University Press, 1995), 76-79.

6 For the restoration projects by the German Archaeological Institute in Cairo, see *A Future for the Past: Restorations in Islamic Cairo 1973-2004*, ed.ited by Wolfgang Mayer et al. (Mainz: Verlag Philipp Von Zabern, 2007); also see Philipp Speiser, "The Egyptian-German Restoration of the Darb al-Qirmiz, Cairo," in *The Restoration and Conservation of Islamic Monuments in Egypt*, ed.ited by Jere Bacharach (Cairo: The American University Press, 1995), 22-45; Nairy Hampikian, "The Restoration of the Mausoleum of al-Salih Najm al-Din Ayyub," in *The Restoration and Conservation of Islamic Monuments in Egypt*, ed.ited by Jere Bacharach (Cairo: The American University Press, 1995), 46-58; Nairy Hampikian, "The Mausoleum of Sultan al-Salih Najm al-Din," *A Future for the Past*, edited by Wolfgang Mayer et al. (Mainz: Verlag Philipp Von Zabern, 2007), 121-28; "The Minaet of the Salihiya Madrasa," *A Future for the Past*, ed.ited by Wolfgang Mayer et al. (Mainz: Verlag Philipp Von Zabern, 2007), 129-38; May Al-Ibrashy, "The Sabil of Sultan al-Nasir Muhammad and His Sons," *A Future for the Past*, ed.ited by Wolfgang Mayer et al. (Mainz: Verlag Philipp Von Zabern, 2007), 139-41.

7 About the restoration of this building, see Philipp Speiser, "The Palace of the Amir Bashtak," *A Future for the Past*, ed.ited by Wolfgang Mayer et al. (Mainz: Verlag Philipp Von Zabern, 2007), 78-85.

8 Wolfgang Mayer, "The History of Preserving Historic Islamic Monuments 1976-2006," *A Future for the Past*, ed.ited by Wolfgang Mayer et al. (Mainz: Verlag Philipp Von Zabern, 2007), 43; Guiseppe Fanfoni, "The Italian-Egyptian Restoration Center's Work in the Mevlevi Complex in Cairo," in *The Restoration and Conservation of Islamic Monuments in Egypt*, ed.ited by Jere Bacharach (Cairo: The American University Press, 1995), 59-75.

9 Mayer, "The History of Preserving Historic Islamic Monuments," 43.

10 Mayer, "The History of Preserving Historic Islamic Monuments," 42.

11 Mayer, "The History of Preserving Historic Islamic Monuments," 42.

12 Caroline Williams, "Transforming the Old: Cairo's New Medieval City," *Middle East Journal* 56 (Summer 2002), 459.

13 Mayer, "The History of Preserving Historic Islamic Monuments," 43.

14 This information was given to me by Dr. Fahmy Abd al-Alim in 1993, who was then the director of Islamic Monuments at the Supreme Council of Antiquities.

15 Jere Bacharach, "Conserving Historic Cairo's Splendid Legacy," in *Preserving Egypt's Cultural Heritage*, ed.ited by Randi Danforth (Cairo: American Research Center in Egypt, 2010), 163. For further reading on the subject, see *The Restoration and Conservation of Islamic Monuments in Egypt*, ed.ited by Jere Bacharach (Cairo: The American University in Cairo Press, 1995); Mayer, "The History of Preserving Historic Islamic Monuments," 42-48; Williams, "Transforming the Old," 457-73.

16 Williams, "Transforming the Old," 471-72.

17 For this see, Dina Ishak Bakhoum, "The Madrasa of Umm al-Sultan Sha'ban before and after Creswell," in *Creswell Photographs Re-examined:*

New Perspectives on Islamic Architecture, edited by Bernard O'Kane (Cairo: The American University in Cairo Press, 2009), 99-120.

18 Caroline Williams considered it to have been downgraded to the status of one of the Ministry of Culture's steering committees to become the SCA. See Williams, "Transforming the Old," 459.

19 Mayer, "The History of Preserving Historic Islamic Monuments," 45.

20 Williams, "Transforming the Old," 471. The project is criticized, though sometimes on a false basis, in Ahmed Sedky, *Living with Heritage in Cairo: Area Conservation in the Arab City* (Cairo: The American University in Cairo Press, 2009), 182-191, which requires a future response.

21 I thank Iman Abdulfattah for her constructive criticism and discussions about that issue.

22 See my description of this area in 1993-94, in Swelim, "The Mosque of Ibn Tulun: A New Perspective," 4.

23 For more on the project, see Williams, "Transforming the Old," 458-68.

24 See Agnieszka Dobrowolska and Jaroslaw Dobrowolski, *The Sultan's Fountain: An Imperial Story of Cairo, Istanbul, and Amsterdam,* (Cairo: The American University in Cairo Press, 2005).

25 Ministry of Culture, *Historic Cairo* (Cairo: Supreme Council of Antiquities, February 2002), 250-62.

26 Ministry of Culture, *Historic Cairo*, 250-62.

27 Ministry of Culture, *Historic Cairo*, 250-62.

28 al-Qahira al-Tarikhiya, *Jami' Ahmad Ibn Tulun* (Cairo, 2004).

29 May Shaer, *Restoration of Ahmad Ibn Tulun Mosque, Cairo, Egypt,* 2010 On Site Review (Cairo: the Aga Khan Award Publications, 2010). Appendix 1 gives a thorough, detailed technical report of the mosque's restoration. An earlier report was also presented by Mohammad al-Asad, *Restoration of Ahmad Ibn Tulun Mosque, Cairo, Egypt*, 2007 On Site Review (Cairo: the Aga Khan Award Publications, 2007), http://archnet.org/sites/1522/publications/1575.

30 Good photographs of the mosque lit at night can be seen in al-Qahira al-Tarikhiya, *Jami' Ahmad Ibn Tulun*.

31 Williams, "Transforming the Old," 462.

32 Williams, "Transforming the Old," 462.

33 Megawra website, http://megawra.com.

34 I would like to thank May Al-Abrashy for her valuable discussions on the subject.

CHAPTER 13

1 Jean Joseph Marcel, *Égypte, depuis la conquête des Arabes jusqu'à la domination française* (Paris: Firmin Didot, Freres, 1848), plate 20.

2 D.S. Margoliouth, *Cairo, Jerusalem and Damascus, three chief cities of Egyptian sultans* (New York: Dodd Mead & Co, 1907).

3 Several modern buildings erected outside of Egypt were inspired by the mosque of Ibn Tulun: In the Holy City of Medina, in Saudi Arabia, is the mosque of al-Miqat, which was rebuilt sometime after 1986 by famous Egyptian architect Abdel-Wahid El Wakil, and was directly inspired by the shape of the minaret and the facades of the mosque–see, *Architecture of the Contemporary Mosque*, edited by Ismail Serageldin and James Steele (Great Britain: Academy Group Ltd, 1996), 68-71. In Doha, in Qatar, there are two buildings that are directly inspired by the spiral-shaped minaret of Ibn Tulun. One is a short tower in the upscale area of the Pearl area, and another is a landmark tower known as the FANAR, which serves as the Qatar Islamic Cultural Center. At a distance, opposite the FANAR, is the wonderful cubical building of the Museum of Islamic Art (MIA), designed by world-renowned architect I.M. Pei. It is inspired by the domical *fisqiya* in the middle of the open court of the mosque of Ibn Tulun, and not its spiral-shaped minaret.

INDEX

Numbers in italic indicate pages with illustrations.